LIARS, BRUTES, AND GLUTTONS

EMORY STUDIES IN EARLY CHRISTIANITY

Vernon K. Robbins, General Editor
Roy R. Jeal, General Editor
Robert H. von Thaden Jr., Associate Editor
David B. Gowler, Associate Editor
Meghan Henning
Susan E. Hylen
Donghyun Jeong
Mikeal C. Parsons
Russell B. Sisson
Shively T. J. Smith

Number 29

LIARS, BRUTES, AND GLUTTONS

A Relevance-Theory Solution for Titus 1:12

Isaiah Allen

 PRESS

Atlanta

Copyright © 2025 by Isaiah Allen

Publication of this volume was made possible by the generous support of the Pierce Program in Religion of Oxford College of Emory University.

All rights reserved. No part of this work may be reproduced or transmitted in any form or by any means, electronic or mechanical, including photocopying and recording, or by means of any information storage or retrieval system, except as may be expressly permitted by the 1976 Copyright Act or in writing from the publisher. Requests for permission should be addressed in writing to the Rights and Permissions Office, SBL Press, 825 Houston Mill Road, Atlanta, GA 30329 USA.

Library of Congress Control Number: 2025930104

Cover design is an adaptation by Bernard Madden of Rick A. Robbins, Mixed Media (19" x 24" pen and ink on paper, 1981).

Dedicated to

Gilbert and Irma Allen,

loving parents, with gratitude

Contents

Acknowledgments	ix
Abbreviations	xi
Introduction: Unresolved Issues in Titus 1:12	1
A Plausible Alternative Interpretation	2
Miso-Cretan Reading Assumptions	3
Why Titus 1:12?	7
Why Relevance Theory?	9
Summary	14
1. Prevailing Interpretations of Titus 1:12	15
Authorship	15
Composition	17
Miso-Cretan Interpretations	30
2. Relevance Theory: Insights for Biblical Interpretation	69
Disambiguating Schools of Pragmatics	70
General Description	70
Three Key Insights	88
3. Basic Pragmatic Processes	113
Referential and Deictic Speech	116
Procedural and Logical Connectives and Particles	132
Lexical Pragmatics	138
4. Higher-Level Explicatures	147
The Speaker's Attitude toward a Sentence	148
Use versus Mention	153
In-Group and Out-Group Insult Language	156
Paul's Reversal of Religious Designations	166

5.	The Role of the Hearer in Communication	177
	Mismatched Contextual Assumptions	178
	Mismatched Salience	236
6.	The Nonpropositional Dimensions of Communication	249
	The Relevance of Speech-Act Theory	250
	What Speakers Do with Language	253
	The Economy of Cognitive Effects	254
	Social and Behavioral Outcomes	265
	Ethics and Redemption as Sound Doctrine	271

Conclusions and Implications	281
A Relevance-Guided Biblical Hermeneutic	284
Titus and Pastoral Epistles Scholarship	285
Modern-Day Appropriation of Titus's Message	287
Implications for Canonical Esteem	290
Bibliography	295
Ancient Sources Index	315
Modern Authors Index	322
Subject Index	326

Acknowledgments

I wish I could adequately thank all those who have supported me in completing this book. I identify some of them here as a token of how I valued their influence.

I appreciate the clarity, professionalism, and support of SBL Press. I am grateful to Vernon Robbins for considering my research for publication in Emory Studies in Early Christianity and to Roy Jeal for editing the volume. I thank the anonymous reviewers for their critical comments and advice. I studied under Roy at Booth University College years ago, and he has challenged and encouraged me in various ways since. I am thankful for the improvements he recommended and for his friendship.

I began this research during my two-year postgraduate fellowship in biblical languages at Asbury Theological Seminary. Fredrick Long advised me to examine the application of cognitive linguistics to biblical interpretation. I am thankful for his responsive and generous critique and encouragement. Asbury's expert resources, faculty, and staff helped and influenced me while faithful friends and fellow scholars welcomed me into a vital community. They inspired me to aim at more than an increase in knowledge but also at love and justice.

Friends at my Salvation Army church home encouraged me in the otherwise isolating work of research and writing. Colonel Janet Munn, faculty and staff at the College for Officer Training, and particularly Robin Rader and the Brengle Library team gave vital intellectual, moral, and practical support. James Read reviewed my manuscript closely and provided excellent advice. I am honored by their interest in my research.

Faculty at London School of Theology critiqued and encouraged me during my PhD candidacy. Society of Biblical Literature members and conference attendees offered early critique as I tried out ideas. Tangible and moral support from Booth University College and my fine colleagues here has helped me to complete this project within my first couple of years on faculty.

My scholarship grows from the passion for Scripture my mother, Irma, ignited in me. My wife, Ellen, has supported me in countless ways. During my research, we went through major family relocations, bereavements, the pandemic, and more. She did not let me quit, and I could not have accomplished it without her.

With gratitude and love,
Isaiah Allen
Fall 2023
Winnipeg, Manitoba

Abbreviations

1739	minuscule, Great Lavra monastery, Athos, Greece
AB	Anchor Bible
ABD	Freedman, David Noel, ed. *Anchor Bible Dictionary*. 6 vols. New York: Doubleday, 1992.
ACCS	Ancient Christian Commentary on Scripture
Aem.	Plutarch, *Aemilius Paullus*
AEQ	*Anthropology and Education Quarterly*
ALH	*Acta Linguistica Hungarica*
An.	Tertullian, *De anima*
Ant.	Josephus, *Jewish Antiquities*
Ant. rom.	Dionysius of Halicarnassus, *Antiquitates romanae*
ANTC	Abingdon New Testament Commentaries
ASHUJS	*Annals of Spiru Haret University, Journalism Studies*
ASTHLS	Amsterdam Studies in the Theory and History of Linguistic Science IV—Current Issues in Linguistic Theory
Ath. pol.	Aristotle, *Athēnaīn politeia*
BBC	Blackwell Bible Commentaries
BBR	*Bulletin of Biblical Research*
BBRSup	Bulletin for Biblical Research Supplement
BDAG	Danker, Frederick W., Walter Bauer, William F. Arndt, and F. Wilbur Gingrich, eds. *Greek-English Lexicon of the New Testament and Other Early Christian Literature*. 3rd ed. Chicago: University of Chicago Press, 2000.
BHGNT	Baylor Handbook on the Greek New Testament
BibInt	*Biblical Interpretation*
BJRL	*Bulletin of the John Rylands University Library of Manchester*
BP	The Bible and Postcolonialism
BT	*The Bible Translator*
BTB	*Biblical Theology Bulletin*

BTCB	Belief: A Theological Commentary on the Bible
BrazosTCB	Brazos Theological Commentary on the Bible
BZNW	Beihefte zur Zeitschrift für die neutestamentliche Wissenschaft
CBQ	*Catholic Biblical Quarterly*
CC	*Cross Currents*
CCSS	Catholic Commentary on Sacred Scripture
Cels.	Origen, *Contra Celsum*
Cho.	Aeschylus, *Choephori*
CILT	Current Issues in Linguistic Theory
CJAL	*Canadian Journal of Applied Linguistics*
Strom.	Clement of Alexandria, *Stromateis*
Comm. Gal.	Jerome, *Commentariorum in Epistulam ad Galatas libri III*
Comm. Tit.	Jerome, *Commentariorum in Epistulam ad Titum liber*
CornBC	Cornerstone Biblical Commentary
CSL	Cambridge Studies in Linguistics
CTL	Cambridge Textbooks in Linguistics
CTR	*Criswell Theological Review*
CTSR	*Chicago Theological Seminary Register*
D	Codex Claromontanus. National Library, Paris
Div.	Cicero, *De divinatione*
DNTB	Evans, Craig A., and Stanley E. Porter, eds. *Dictionary of New Testament Background*. Downers Grove, IL: InterVarsity, 2000.
Doctr. chr.	Augustine, *De doctrina christiana*
EBib	*Études bibliques*
EC	*Early Christianity*
ECL	Early Christianity and Its Literature
EFTE	Éditions de al Faculté de Théologie Évangélique
ESEC	Emory Studies in Early Christianity
ESV	English Standard Version
F	Codex Augiensis. Trinity College, Cambridge
FC	Fathers of the Church
G	Codex Boernerianus. Saxon State and University Library Dresden, Dresden
Geogr.	Strabo, *Geographica*
Haer.	Irenaeus, *Adversus haereses* (*Elenchos*)
HBT	*Horizons in Biblical Theology*
HCS	Hellenistic Culture and Society

HeyJ	*Heythrop Journal*
Hist.	Thucydides, *Historiae*; Polybius, *Historiae*
Hist. eccl.	Socrates of Constantinople, *Historia ecclesiastica*
HPH	Handbook of Pragmatic Highlights
HThKNT	Herders Theologischer Kommentar zum Neuen Testament
HUT	Hermeneutische Untersuchungen zur Theologie
Hymn.	Callimachus, *Hymni*
I	Codex Freerianus. Smithsonian Institution, Washington, DC
ICC	International Critical Commentary
IJST	*International Journal of Systematic Theology*
Inim. util.	Plutarch, *De capienda ex inimicis utilitate*
IRP	*International Review of Pragmatics*
IVPNTC	IVP New Testament Commentary
JBL	*Journal of Biblical Literature*
JETS	*Journal of the Evangelical Theological Society*
JFSR	*Journal of Feminist Studies in Religion*
JGL	*Journal of Greek Linguistics*
JPrag	*Journal of Pragmatics*
JSNTSup	Journal for the Study of the New Testament Supplement Series
JTI	*Journal for Theological Interpretation*
JTS	*Journal of Theological Studies*
J.W.	Josephus, *Jewish War*
LangSci.	*Language Sciences*
LB	Linguistica Biblica
LBRS	Lexham Bible Reference Series
LBS	Linguistic Biblical Studies
LCL	Loeb Classical Library
LEC	Library of Early Christianity
Leg.	Plato, *Leges*; Athenagoras, *Legatio pro Christianis*
Legat.	Philo, *Legatio ad Gaium*
Life	Josephus, *The Life*
LL	*Language & Literature*
L&N	Louw, Johannes P., and Eugene A. Nida, eds. *Greek-English Lexicon of the New Testament: Based on Semantic Domains.* 2nd ed. New York: United Bible Societies, 1989.
LPS	Library of Pauline Studies
LXX	Septuagint
M&L	*Mind & Language*

MM	Moulton, James H., and George Milligan. *The Vocabulary of the Greek Testament.* London, 1930. Reprint, Peabody, MA: Hendrickson, 1997.
NA[28]	*Novum Testamentum Graece.* Nestle-Aland, 28th ed.
NAC	New American Commentary
Nat.	Pliny the Elder, *Naturalis historia*
NCB	New Century Bible
NCBNT	New Clarendon Bible: New Testament
NCCS	New Covenant Commentary Series
NEB	New English Bible
NICNT	New International Commentary on the New Testament
NIGTC	New International Greek Testament Commentary
NIV	New International Version
NLT	New Living Translation
NovT	*Novum Testamentum*
NRSV	New Revised Standard Version
NTC	The New Testament in Context
NTG	New Testament Guides
NTS	*New Testament Studies*
NTT	New Testament Theology
OCD	Hornblower, Simon, and Antony Spawforth, eds. *Oxford Classical Dictionary.* 3rd ed. Oxford: Oxford University Press, 2003.
OHO	Oxford Handbooks Online
Or. Graec.	Tatian, *Oratio ad Graecos* (*Pros Hellēnas*)
P&B	Pragmatics & Beyond
PB	*Psychological Bulletin*
PCC	Paul in Critical Contexts
Philops.	Lucian, *Philopseudes*
Pol.	Aristotle, *Politica*
Post.	Quintus Smyrnaeus, *Posthomerica*
PP	*Philosophical Psychology*
Protr.	Clement of Alexandria, *Protrepticus*
R&T	*Religion and Theology*
RBL	*Review of Biblical Literature*
Rep.	Cicero, *De republica*
RevExp	*Review and Expositor*
Rhet.	Aristotle, *Rhetorica*
RNT	Regensburger Neues Testament

RRRMC	Routledge Research in Religion, Media and Culture
SemeiaSt	Semeia Studies
SFSL	Studies in Functional and Structural Linguistics
SHBC	Smyth & Helwys Bible Commentary
SNTSMS	Society for New Testament Studies Monograph Series
Sol.	Plutarch, *Solon*
SP	Sacra Pagina
Spec.	Philo, *De specialibus legibus*
SRA	Studies of Religion in Africa
SS	Syntax and Semantics
StBibLit	Studies in Biblical Literature
STI	Studies in Theological Interpretation
STP	*Social Theory & Practice*
STR	*Southeastern Theological Review*
STR	Studies in Theology and Religion
Theog.	Hesiod, *Theogonia*
THNTC	Two Horizons New Testament Commentary
ThTo	*Theology Today*
Tim.	Lucian, *Timon*
TIPS	*Translational Issues in Psychological Science*
TLL	Topics in Language and Linguistics
TLZ	*Theologische Literaturzeitung*
TNTC	Tyndale New Testament Commentary
TynBul	*Tyndale Bulletin*
UBS⁵	Aland, Barbara, Kurt Aland, Johannes Karavidopoulos, Carlo M. Martini, and Bruce M. Metzger, eds. *The Greek New Testament*. 5th ed. Stuttgart: Deutsche Bibelgellschaft; United Bible Societies, 2014.
UBSHS	UBS Handbook Series
UBSMS	UBS Monograph Series
UCLWPL	*UCL Working Papers in Linguistics*
Urb. cond.	Livy, *Ab urbe condita*
Virt.	Philo, *De virtutibus*
Vit. phil.	Diogenes Laertius, *Vitae philosophorum*
WBC	Word Biblical Commentary
WGRW	Writings from the Greco-Roman World
WisC	Wisdom Commentary
WJL	The William James Lectures
WTJ	*Westminster Theological Journal*

WUNT	Wissenschaftliche Untersuchungen zum Neuen Testament
ZNW	*Zeitschrift für die neutestamentliche Wissenschaft und die Kunde der älteren Kirche*
Ψ	Codex Athous Laurae. Great Lavra monastery, Athos, Greece

Introduction: Unresolved Issues in Titus 1:12

"Cretans are always liars, evil brutes, lazy gluttons" (Titus 1:12b). The writer's point is obvious: Cretans qua Cretans are ne'er-do-wells. It is one of the New Testament's well-known quotations. *Cretan* has come to label someone as idle, wicked, untrustworthy, morally inferior, or reprobate.[1] This understanding of Titus 1:12 is almost irresistible.

Scholars recognize that the pejorative essence of the Cretan quotation contradicts the canonical image of Paul. The Paul we know from Romans, Galatians, and even Acts would never have written such a disparaging statement about a tender, predominantly gentile congregation. He more likely would have opposed anyone who advanced such a notion. Such uncharacteristic behavior is one of the reasons why scholars are justified to conclude that the historical Paul did not write Titus. The apostle could marshal scathing language to defend or to shame, but Paul's missionary strategy did not seem to involve sweeping insults of an intrinsic nature.[2] The conclusion that the apostle Paul did not write Titus is as obvious as the

---

1. William D. Mounce, for instance, explains, "This verse ... has given rise to the colloquial use of 'Cretan' to describe a reprobate person." See Mounce, *Pastoral Epistles*, WBC 46 (Nashville: Nelson, 2000), 398. OED cites several sources in English literature where *Cretan* is used not based on its geo-ethnic reference but as an insult. See "Cretan, adj. and n.," OED Online. *Cretan* is commonly confused with *cretin*, an English word traditionally labeling a person afflicted with hypothyroidism due to iodine deficiency. See "cretin, n.," OED Online. The disparaging use of this word is grounded in ableism rather than ethnic bigotry.

2. Paul defends his congregations from opponents that he refers to as "the circumcision": "I wish those who unsettle you would castrate themselves!" (Gal 5:12); "Beware of the dogs, beware of the evil workers, beware of those who mutilate the flesh" (Phil 3:2). He also defends them from greedy, presumptuous leaders: "For such boasters are false apostles, deceitful workers ... his [Satan's] ministers" (2 Cor 11:13–15). Paul directly addresses a congregation: "You foolish Galatians! Who has bewitched you?" (Gal 3:1). Paul expresses each of these colorful rants to target a group for its problematic behaviors but not to berate his missionary congregations or to

interpretation of this passage. But unexamined assumptions underlie this prevalent interpretation of Titus 1:12.

A Plausible Alternative Interpretation

As this study progresses, it exposes and explains some of the problems with prevalent interpretations of Titus 1:12 on sociohistorical, exegetical, and linguistic grounds and proposes a simpler and more likely interpretation, one that coincides with the impulses of some earlier interpreters (e.g., Jerome, Theodore) but that was dismissed through the history of interpretation based on flawed assumptions.

This plausible alternative interpretation is as follows: In Titus 1:10–12, Paul described troublemakers in the Cretan church, identifying most of them as Jewish members (μάλιστα οἱ ἐκ τῆς περιτομῆς, 1:10).[3] From Paul's perspective, divisive people (αἱρετικόν ἄνθρωπον, 3:10) disrupted church households or congregations (ὅλους οἴκους ἀνατρέπουσιν, 1:11) by teaching that Cretans, as gentiles, were morally and religiously inferior. The troublemakers' interest in "genealogies," "quarrels over Torah" (γενεαλογίας, μάχας νομικάς, 3:9), "Jewish myths" (Ἰουδαϊκοῖς μύθοις, 1:14), and other features of Jewish religious culture reinforced an attitude of superiority over any who did not exhibit status symbols or cultural aptitudes that were valid in their system, namely, gentile Cretans. When Paul framed the famous quotation (1:12), he was completing his general description of the troublemakers with a specific and characteristic example of their teaching. The speaker who concerns Paul comes from the group of troublemakers. In their eyes, not in Paul's, this bigot was a prophet (ἐξ αὐτῶν ἴδιος αὐτῶν προφήτης, 1:12a).

The quotation may or may not have come to Paul as a fragment of ancient Cretan literature. For the troublemakers, it justified their doctrine of ethno-religious inferiorization. Although a Cretan origin of the saying cannot be confirmed, if it did originate in Crete, then anyone who used the slur could have pointed back with a shrug and said, "Even they speak this way about their own kind!" For Paul, the quotation contradicted the transformative power of the gospel (3:3–7), but he was certain (ἡ μαρτυρία

---

assert that they possess intractable faults. All the quotations in this footnote follow the NRSV. Unless otherwise indicated, other Scripture translations are mine.

3. Throughout this study, I use *Paul* as shorthand to refer to the writer without committing to any particular meaning for that name other than "the author of Titus," which I avoid because it is clumsy.

αὕτη ἐστὶν ἀληθής, 1:13a) that someone among the troublemakers (τις ἐξ αὐτῶν, 1:12a) was propagating it. Whoever was doing so and the community that harbored them needed to be stopped and corrected (οὓς δεῖ ἐπιστομίζειν, 1:11a; ἔλεγχε αὐτοὺς ἀποτόμως, 1:13b).

Although it is quite common for readers of Titus 1:12 to assume that Paul was participating in bigotry, he seems to have been exposing and rebuking it. This study offers reasons for considering this reading and calls into question key assumptions of other interpretations.

The prevalent interpretations of the passage contradict the broad thrust of the New Testament, the personality of the purported writer, and the message of the letter in which it appears. The history of its interpretation is contentious and riddled with contradictory proposals, making it a problem passage. Interpreters need consistent hermeneutical strategies to illuminate alternative possibilities.[4] Perhaps a strategy that recommends itself to constituencies who approach the text from diverse starting points could help to ameliorate contention.[5] To develop such a strategy, I explain three key insights from a well-developed theory of utterance interpretation—relevance theory—and demonstrate their practical application on Titus 1:12 and representative interpretations. The theory provides sound rationale for questioning some conclusions in preference to others and offers a hermeneutical foundation for reexamining the issues this passage presents. Before saying more about relevance theory, I offer a critique of prevailing interpretations of this passage in Titus.

Miso-Cretan Reading Assumptions

Many interpretations of Titus 1:12 are on offer. No single reading prevails, but most feature several basic assumptions that are described briefly

---

4. Quoting Paul Kiparsky, Anne Furlong argues that literary interpretation too often depends on different interpreters accounting for a "different set of facts." See Furlong, "Relevance Theory and Literary Interpretation" (PhD diss., University College London, 1995), 36–37. Hence the need for a consistent hermeneutic. This concern applies to biblical interpretation, especially of problem passages.

5. Tim Meadowcroft argues that relevance theory promises a "mediating category" by which to resolve some of the tensions between the critical environment of his scholarship as an Anglican and his evangelical institutional setting. He aimed to "discover a hermeneutic that makes sense of the polarities and holds them together in some way." See Meadowcroft, "Relevance as a Mediating Category in the Reading of Biblical Texts: Venturing beyond the Hermeneutical Circle," *JETS* 45 (2002): 613.

below and evaluated in chapter 1. To the extent that an interpretation adheres to this set of assumptions, I refer to it as a miso-Cretan reading. Although scholars in recent decades have approached this text with sensitivity and sophistication, most seem unable to escape the gravitational pull of the assumption that Paul tacitly sympathizes with the quotation's crude description of Cretans. Over the course of this study, I call this assumption into question. According to a miso-Cretan interpretation, the quotation, irrespective of other factors, was also the substance of Paul's opinion of the Cretans; furthermore, he advanced the quotation's assessment of Cretans as the view Titus should have going forward in his ministry. Titus must not think too highly of his gentile missionary congregation.[6] Paul asserted the intractable and thorough reprobation of the Cretan people.

Whatever merits this letter might otherwise have, surely the presence of a truly bigoted remark would be a blemish on it, perhaps even an affront to the canonical Paul, the "apostle to the nations" (Rom 11:13) who would "become all things to all people in order to save some" (1 Cor 9:22). Furthermore, Titus would have the tough luck of leading a community of incorrigible reprobates. Jerome Quinn is representative of this reading:

---

6. I use the term *missionary* as shorthand for a basic reality that obtained in the first-century church: a Christian community, only a few generations old, planted by geographic and ethnic nonnatives, and still largely influenced by these founders. For an examination of mission in the Pastoral Epistles, see Chiao Ek Ho, "Mission in the Pastoral Epistles," in *Entrusted with the Gospel: Paul's Theology in the Pastoral Epistles*, edited by Andreas J. Köstenberger and Terry L. Wilder (Nashville: B&H Academic, 2010), 241–67. See also Ho's dissertation on the same subject, "Do the Work of an Evangelist: The Missionary Outlook of the Pastoral Epistles" (PhD diss., University of Aberdeen, 2000); and Andreas J. Köstenberger, "An Investigation of the Mission Motif in the Letters to Timothy and Titus with Implications for the Pauline Authorship of the Pastoral Epistles," *BBR* 29 (2019): 49–64. T. Christopher Hoklotubbe's argument that the author aimed to make his Christian communities seem more winsome and honorable to their Roman neighbors and less prone to ostracism and persecution yields a kind of missionary outlook for the Pastoral Epistles though from a different perspective. See Hoklotubbe, *Civilized Piety: The Rhetoric of Pietas in the Pastoral Epistles and the Roman Empire* (Waco, TX: Baylor University Press, 2017). *Pace* Jouette M. Bassler, who argues that missionary implications are less relevant: "Since the letter is pseudonymous and the Cretan setting is probably artificial, one does not need to speculate on the impact of such an attitude on Titus's missionary activity in Crete." See Bassler, *1 Timothy, 2 Timothy, Titus*, ANTC (Nashville: Abingdon, 1996), 190.

Introduction: Unresolved Issues in Titus 1:12

With deadly seriousness the author of Titus has Paul vouch for the truth of the cruel ancient jibe, thus solemnly joining the witness of an apostle to the oracle of the prophet-poet. The latter [Epimenides] is cited as "a prophet" not only because the Hellenistic world so conceived him but also with an irony pointed at the Jewish-Christian troublemakers.[7]

Later I provide several reasons why Paul's metonym for the speaker, *prophet*, does not reflect the assessment of "the Hellenistic world" but rather Paul's sarcastic assessment of the speaker's standing among the troublemakers. Quinn links his interpretation to a specific attribution despite the evidence he presents that the quotation could not be reliably traced to Epimenides or any other Cretan writer and that it was a narrow group of troublemakers who deserved rebuke, not the Cretan populace.[8]

Given the influence of miso-Cretan readings, it is not surprising that Annette Bourland Huizenga fiercely critiques the consequences of that conventional interpretation and charts a reading strategy *against* the text. She explains the problem incisively: "What I ... find especially troubling is that the negative assessments of Jews, Jewish traditions, and the ethnic Cretans seem to have influenced several modern commentators to adopt a similar prejudice, which then leads to a tendency to read the rest of the letter as if it were written to a culturally and morally backward community."[9]

The five features that characterize what I am calling a miso-Cretan interpretation are: (1) Paul's authorial sympathy with the quotation's propositional claims, (2) ancient literary or archaeological corroboration of the veracity of the quotation, (3) contextual discontinuity between the thrust of the quotation and the surrounding material, (4) conflation of the troublemakers and the general Cretan church populace, and (5) dubious attribution of the quotation to Epimenides of Crete. Interpretations align with this miso-Cretan categorization to the extent that they depend on or emphasize some or all of these points. I will now briefly describe each of the five assumptions that pertain to miso-Cretan readings. In subsequent

---

7. Jerome D. Quinn, *The Letter to Titus: A New Translation and Commentary and an Introduction to Titus, I and II Timothy, the Pastoral Epistles*, AB 35 (New York: Doubleday, 1990), 109.

8. Quinn, *Letter to Titus*, 109.

9. Annette Bourland Huizenga, *1–2 Timothy, Titus*, WisC 53 (Collegeville, MN: Liturgical Press, 2016), 141.

chapters, I offer a more substantial critique in dialogue with scholars who maintain such readings.

1. Authorial Sympathy

First, miso-Cretan interpretations commonly assume the author's sympathetic attitude toward the contents of the statement as linguistically encoded. The question of authorial attitude is pivotal. According to many, Paul approved of and endorsed the statement, "Cretans are always liars, evil brutes, lazy gluttons" (Titus 1:12). Relevance theory illuminates the need and process for interpreters to assess when an author is writing *descriptively* or *interpretively*—when their words represent their own opinions or those of others.[10]

2. Ancient Corroboration

Second, many scholarly adherents to a miso-Cretan reading assume that ancient literary or archaeological evidence objectively and unambiguously demonstrates that the Cretan people actually were or were purported to be just as the quotation describes. Several commentators search, find, and present evidence that appears to corroborate the disparaging claims of the quotation. In this case, Paul joined a host of critics and echoed the verdict of history: Cretans are innately delinquent.

3. Contextual Discontinuity

Third, the miso-Cretan reading requires an abrupt change in topic within the paragraph (1:10–16). Rather than the quotation functioning within a continuous argument against troublemakers in the Cretan church, Paul supposedly begins railing against ethnic Cretans mid-paragraph and returns to address insolent leaders after this brief, non sequitur interruption. Whether or not commentators discuss the discontinuity between addressing inappropriate leadership and insulting the Cretan populace, this maneuver is assumed in most interpretations.

4. Target Conflation

Fourth, several prominent interpreters conflate all targets of the letter's critical rhetoric so that their interpretations do not maintain the categori-

---

10. As I explain later, relevance theory adds technical precision to these concepts.

zations established in the discourse itself.[11] They tend to read the negative judgments surrounding the Cretan quotation as leveled against all of these groups and do not distinguish between concerns with troublemakers versus ordinary church members. In other words, Paul was a bigot in general rather than taking issue with particular groups for specific reasons. Tracking the corrective logic of Titus requires more careful attention to exactly who is targeted.

5. Dubious Attribution

Fifth, most commentators who discuss attribution assume that a fifth- or sixth-century (BCE) Cretan poet, Epimenides, originated the quotation, but this is far from certain. The quotation has no reliable attribution. Modern writers invoke his name overconfidently, but ancient authors painted a vague and contradictory picture of his era, occupation, and characteristics. They hardly provide the kind of evidence to support strong assertions that Paul borrowed authority from a well-known Cretan to lend credibility to an insult he wished to level against Cretans.

The five tendencies described above constitute the quintessential array of assumptions that lead to miso-Cretan readings. Most interpretations of Titus 1:12 rely on some or all of them. Each assumption is carefully detailed and critiqued in chapter 1.

Why Titus 1:12?

Like many Christians, I encountered Titus first as the Scripture of the church, part of the Christian canon, the sacred library of a community of faith. Outside such ecclesial connections, this literature interests readers historically, aesthetically, spiritually, and so forth, but the coherence of interpreting any part of the collection in light of the others or of ascribing more authority to it than to other literature primarily holds within the scope of Christian hermeneutics. As Walter Moberly asserts, "The

---

11. The block quotation from Huizenga at the beginning of this section exemplifies this tendency. According to Huizenga, Paul vocalizes animus toward several categories of people and practices at once. Overlapping targets include reference to features of Jewish religious culture ("circumcision," 1:10; "commandments," 1:14, "genealogies," 3:9), troublemakers in the church (1:10–11), and—through the quotation—native Cretans (see Huizenga, *1–2 Timothy, Titus*, 141).

authority of the [Pastoral] letters is secured not by their authorship as such, but by their canonical status, historic reception and historic fruitfulness.... Literary theory makes it possible to take the first-person voice of the letters with full imaginative seriousness."[12]

Yet like many Christians, I rarely heard Titus read during the liturgy.[13] Modern lectionary plans do not typically set out to cover the entire canon, but a fundamental question of canon for the patristic church was which texts to read aloud in the gathered community.[14] For a text to be so neglected seems to diminish long-held canonical status. This neglect may derive from a general queasiness modern liturgists have about reading authoritatively from a book that their validity criteria tell them to hold in suspicion. Although they may not have examined the particular issues rigorously themselves, pastors sense the shadow cast over the trustworthiness of Titus's self-presentation as a letter from the apostle Paul.

The reasons are several and serious, and Moberly expresses well the dilemma pastors are in as tradents in canonical Scripture for particular Christian communities.[15] Normally, modern readers encounter Titus 1, which never appears in the *Revised Common Lectionary*, in contexts such as individual devotional reading, scholarship, or small group study. It is not possible to track interpretations from such diverse and private occasions, but undoubtedly miso-Cretan readings are represented among them. I was never personally satisfied with the coherence of a miso-Cretan reading, and the alternative I summarized above seems natural to me. I want to understand how readers could come to such different interpreta-

---

12. R. Walter L. Moberly, "Biblical Hermeneutics and *Ecclesial* Responsibility," in *The Future of Biblical Interpretation: Responsible Plurality in Biblical Hermeneutics*, ed. Stanley E. Porter and Matthew R. Malcolm (Downers Grove, IL: IVP Academic, 2013), 156.

13. Portions of Titus are only listed in the *Revised Common Lectionary* as readings for Christmas Eve and Christmas Day (Titus 2:11–14, 3:4–7). See *The Revised Common Lectionary: Consultation on Common Texts; Includes Complete List of Lections for Years A, B and C* (Nashville: Abingdon, 1992). Congregations I was part of did not always follow the lectionary or hold Christmas Eve and Christmas Day worship services.

14. Consider, e.g., the Muratorian Fragment, which distinguishes between books for reading in the gathered community and for reading in private. See Daniel J. Theron, "Muratorian Fragment," in *Evidence of Tradition*, ed. and trans. Theron (Grand Rapids: Baker, 1980), 112–13.

15. Moberly, "Biblical Hermeneutics," esp. 133–34.

tions. I lacked a theoretical explanation for why I sensed intuitively that miso-Cretan readings were mistaken.

Insofar as the bigotry of Paul in the letter to Titus and suspicion about the authenticity of Jew-gentile relations in Titus's Cretan church are reasons to doubt Pauline authorship, exposing flawed assumptions may allow criticism of Titus to proceed on sounder footing. I perceive deep and nuanced theological teaching in Titus and even an understanding of the logic of the gospel attributable to Paul. So, I come to Titus 1:12 from deep personal interest in what I see as a *crux interpretum*.

I perceive that Titus 1:12 calls for an extended treatment due to the extent of the issues that interpretations of this verse have precipitated and due to the promise of relevance theory for helping interpreters be more conscious of the ways language works. Therefore, I devote much to explaining details of relevance theory and its implications for understanding language and the literature of the Bible, and I work with the text of Titus at a detailed level.

Why Relevance Theory?

Escaping the gravitational pull of a miso-Cretan reading requires a strategy that can disentangle texts qua utterances from the assumptions imposed on them by their history of interpretation—a strategy illuminated by but not tethered to historic, traditional, or conventional readings. So, as David Bauer and Robert Traina argue concerning biblical hermeneutics in general, the strategy must be inductive, evidence based, and radically open to the results of inquiry.[16] While being radically open, the strategy cannot be amorphous or incoherent; it must aid interpreters in the careful process of reconstructing meaning faithful to the original context. The strategy needs to appreciate the kind of object Titus is: a written specimen of *ostensive inferential communication* from which readers seek to discern an authorial aim.[17]

The miso-Cretan assumptions summarized above are problems with *reading* Titus, so I sought an approach for critiquing readings—in other

---

16. David R. Bauer and Robert A. Traina, *Inductive Bible Study: A Comprehensive Guide to the Practice of Hermeneutics* (Grand Rapids: Baker Academic, 2011), 23–25.

17. The meaning of "ostensive inferential communication" is explained below. For more detail, see Billy Clark, *Relevance Theory*, CTL (Cambridge: Cambridge University Press, 2013), 112–19.

words, a way of discerning how readers inferred meaning and discerning how those processes succeeded or failed in understanding the text according to its author's communicative intent. What makes relevance theory so appropriate to my inquiry is that it pursues an understanding of language by asking how hearers reach conclusions and not by asking what semantic forms (words, syntax, etc.) mean in themselves. It may be original to put it this way, but relevance theory reverse-engineers language to discern how audiences arrive at their interpretations from semantically underdeterminative inputs.

Relevance theory begins with the success of human language as a premise and asks philosophically and empirically how hearers are able to comprehend speakers when it is clear that natural language is inherently underdeterminative. According to relevance theory, speech triggers a customary response in hearers that sets them on a quest for the relevance of the spoken input to concerns in their mind. This is a quest for *cognitive effects*. In order to achieve these cognitive effects, the hearer must infer the speaker's intention to his satisfaction.[18] This inferential process is rapid and intuitive, even though it involves encyclopedic recall, dialectic weighing of possible meanings, and enrichment of vague inputs. Relevance theory aims to explain the processes of ostensive inferential communication with the understanding that communication is successful when hearers are successful, and therefore it primarily examines the hearer's role in communication. In this sense, relevance theory is a promising solution to the problem of sorting out competing readings because it helps us discern *how* humans come to their interpretations.

The assumptions of relevance theory include (1) that speakers ostensibly intend outcomes by their utterances—hearers ascribe meaning to them because utterances themselves trigger this assumption; (2) that communication is an *inferential* process from incomplete semantic input—that is, it is not simply a matter of decoding the meaning of a speaker's words; (3) that hearers will combine speaker input with encyclopedic and environmental information as well as fundamental reasoning to arrive at their inferences; and (4) that hearers will reject meanings that violate their assumptions or conflict with their reasoning but that they will stop processing and accept a conclusion once they are (subconsciously) satisfied

---

18. The convention in almost all relevance-theoretical literature is to refer to a generic speaker using feminine pronouns and a generic hearer using masculine pronouns for simple differentiation.

that it meets the criterion of relevance and results in adequate cognitive effects. On this very spare account of relevance theory, one can already see that distance (cultural, linguistic, temporal, etc.) between original audiences and modern audiences can complicate the processes that modern readers intuitively go through and yield divergent interpretations.

So, is relevance theory an appropriate theory to apply to texts such as Titus? In short, relevance theory is about communication, and written speech is a species of communication. Specific issues that raise the question of appropriateness include the fact that texts are heard or read asynchronously, that the environmental factors of live speech (e.g., tone, gesture, relationship, location) are not available through text, and that the Bible in particular is an ancient text, far removed from its modern readers. I address each of these concerns later but summarize here. First, relevance theory assumes that all communication involves underdeterminacy; therefore, the impact of missing environmental or other inputs is merely quantitative rather than qualitative. It does not preclude the ability of readers from another time and place to understand texts that supply sufficient other data to fund reasonable inferences. Second, texts allow some contextual benefits that the environments of live speech do not. For instance, the speaker and the hearer can slow the process down, be more deliberate, explicit, or precise. Third, asynchronicity does not present a problem, because relevance theory has been fruitfully applied to many literary studies and to the Bible.[19] The insights of relevance theory are particularly

---

19. Among the best examples of such are Kevin G. Smith, "Bible Translation and Relevance Theory: The Translation of Titus" (DLitt diss., University of Stellenbosch, 2000); Stephen W. Pattemore, *Souls under the Altar: Relevance Theory and the Discourse Structure of Revelation*, UBSMS 9 (New York: United Bible Societies, 2003); Pattemore, *The People of God in the Apocalypse: Discourse, Structure, and Exegesis*, SNTSMS 128 (Cambridge: Cambridge University Press, 2004); Philip W. Goodwin, *Translating the English Bible: From Relevance to Deconstruction* (Cambridge: Clarke, 2013); and Sarah H. Casson, *Textual Signposts in the Argument of Romans: A Relevance-Theory Approach*, ECL 25 (Atlanta: SBL Press, 2019). Although every work has its shortcomings, several pieces written at this juncture of disciplines—relevance theory and biblical studies—are particularly weak, confused, or misleading. Gene L. Green provides probably the most accurate general presentation of relevance theory for biblical-studies audiences. See, e.g., Green, "Lexical Pragmatics and the Lexicon," *BBR* 22 (2012): 315–33; Green, "Relevance Theory and Biblical Interpretation," in *Oxford Encyclopedia of Biblical Interpretation*, ed. Steven L. McKenzie (London: Oxford University Press, 2013), 2:266–73.

helpful for interpreting utterances for which the intuitive, organic, rapid, and complex processes that original audiences employed to discern meaning are no longer available, as is the case for Bible readers.

Relevance theory is grounded in decades of philosophical reasoning and detailed observation of human cognition. Although relevance theory is not a method of interpretation per se, it can enhance the critique of previous interpretations by adding precision and by grounding such critique in a sound theory of communication. On the basis of relevance theory, critics can discern the problems in previous interpreters' inferential processes and how they may be ameliorated. Over the past generation, theorists have developed and refined the discipline of relevance theory so that it is increasingly informed by empirical evidence and rigorous critical dialogue.[20] At this stage, the theory is mature enough to illuminate the development of a biblical reading strategy. I take Titus 1:12 as a test case for such a strategy built on and sensitive to the insights of relevance theory. By developing and demonstrating this strategy, I not only offer an alternative perspective on the Cretan quotation but also introduce an interpretive strategy that may be amenable to scholars who recognize the need for more attention to linguistic theory—not simply to discrete issues of language such as lexicon and grammar—in biblical hermeneutics.

While practicing biblical hermeneutics, few commentators articulate a philosophy of language; yet clarity, transparency, and consistency regarding language are appropriate for the Bible as written communication. In any paragraph, a commentator may assume that a lexeme is paramount; in another, it is the syntax. Elsewhere, the same interpreter will emphasize the nuance of fluid and nonliteral use and then decode meaning on the grounds of monumental history, inscriptions, a cultural artifact or practice. Another interpreter may cycle through a completely different set of considerations without a transparent or consistent guideline for weighing evidence and evaluating among possible interpretations. Few discuss in advance how they see language functioning in general, yet interpretive problems often have linguistic explanations. Concluding an article on lexical pragmatics, Gene Green notes, "Very few students of biblical

---

20. Theorists have developed relevance theory from a philosophical to a cognitive discipline with increasing consonance with neurology, psychology, sociology, and other sciences. Although these later developments are interesting, they are not as pertinent to our inquiry as the theory's central principles.

studies have engaged the field of linguistics, and those who do have often not taken advantage of texts, courses, and programs based on pragmatics. This field of linguistics, and especially RT [relevance theory], is a domain ripe for rich new research and teaching."[21] Working from a single principle (relevance) that is appropriate to the kind of material under examination helps expose flaws with some interpretations and draw attention to neglected evidence for understanding a passage.

Three key insights from relevance theory govern the structure of this study. I do not describe the theory in full detail, but I provide sufficient explanation for readers to grasp how the specifics that I address fit into the theory, appreciate its impact on interpretations of Titus 1:12, and discern the value of a relevance-guided biblical hermeneutic for interpreting Scripture generally.[22] Chapter 1 describes problems with prevailing interpretations of Titus 1:12 in more detail. Chapter 2 describes relevance theory with reference to key theorists and explains the rationale for a reading strategy. There I introduce the three key insights on which chapters 3–6 focus. Chapters 3–4 address the inferential nature of all communication. Chapter 5 explains the hearer's role in communication. Chapter 6 discusses the nonpropositional dimensions of communication. The conclusion presents the implications of this study.

Relevance theory is suitable for four reasons. The first is *appropriateness*: Scripture is written communication and expression, subsisting in (or inhabiting) language; no discipline is more fitting for the nature of the subject. The second is *timing*: relevance theory, over the past generation, has matured as a discipline and become prominent within cognitive linguistics, although its exposure in biblical scholarship is limited. The third is *material*: Titus and its particular issues have received few thoroughgoing treatments from a relevance-theoretical viewpoint. The fourth is *promise*: after considering other methods (e.g., sociohistorical criticism, cultural hermeneutics), relevance theory seems to offer the most potential for delivering what is needed in the case of Titus 1:12, that is, a fresh look.

---

21. Green, "Lexical Pragmatics and Lexicon," 333.

22. For fuller descriptions of relevance theory and its general application to biblical interpretation, see esp. Pattemore, *Souls under the Altar*, 16–45; Green, "Relevance Theory and Biblical Interpretation"; Gene L. Green, "Relevance Theory and Biblical Interpretation," in *The Linguist as Pedagogue: Trends in the Teaching and Linguistic Analysis of the Greek New Testament*, ed. Stanley E. Porter and Matthew Brook O'Donnell (Sheffield: Sheffield Phoenix, 2009), 217–40.

Relevance theory is worthy of effort and confidence, particularly because it incorporates the most eclectic sources of evidence and evaluates them by a single, economic scale—*relevance*.

Summary

In due course, I propose an interpretation of Titus 1:12 that coincides with the evidence, namely, that Paul was rebuking bigotry in the Cretan church, not participating in it. In other words, this Paul was not himself shaming, describing, or comparing the Cretans but rather addressing those who did so as troublemakers.

It should become increasingly evident that prevalent readings of Titus 1:12 and its famous Cretan quotation are unsustainable on linguistic, literary, and historical grounds. Applying key insights from relevance theory to evaluate previous interpretations and to discern a historically and linguistically responsible reading, I will establish the plausibility of the alternative interpretation proposed above. This study demonstrates the promise of a relevance-guided biblical hermeneutic. If relevance theory can help interpreters read this problematic passage with greater clarity, it can potentially illuminate interpretive problems in other texts.

1
Prevailing Interpretations of Titus 1:12

This chapter details several of the critical issues with common interpretations of Titus 1:12 indicated earlier. But, to understand the context of those particulars better, I begin by discussing the whole—specifically, how views of provenance affect reading. Assumptions about provenance influence meaning even when interpreters give no explicit comment, extended attention, or intensive study to the issue. For Titus, the two crucial issues are authorship (who wrote it?) and composition history (what is it?).[1] Although my argument is substantially unaffected by and therefore ambivalent about provenance, assumptions about these matters influence interpretation enough to require comment.

Authorship

The church has received the book of Titus as a letter by the apostle Paul to his junior colleague, Titus, providing instructions for church leadership and laity grounded in moral and theological teaching. It has normally appeared with 1 and 2 Timothy, forming a trio that has been commonly designated the Pastoral Epistles, a de facto collection within the Pauline corpus of the New Testament canon.[2]

Although other issues, such as views toward women and church organization, interest scholars of the Pastoral Epistles, Raymond Collins

---

1. See Raymond F. Collins's succinct introduction to his entry in "Pastorals—Biblical Studies," Oxford Bibliographies Online, https://tinyurl.com/SBLPress4832a1.

2. These three books have been known as the Pastoral Epistles for as long as can be remembered. A similar designation goes back at least to Thomas Aquinas as per C. K. Barrett. In the first instance, this label did not imply their compositional unity but their topical commonality. See Barrett, *The Pastoral Epistles in the New English Bible*, NCBNT (Oxford: Clarendon, 1963), 1.

explains that "the issue of the authorship of the Pastorals has dominated scholarly investigation of these texts ... and the concomitant issues of interpretation that the views on authorship entail."[3] Modern scholars are dubious of the traditional provenance of Titus and the other Pastoral Epistles, largely due to the linguistic peculiarities they perceive between the Pastoral Epistles and the undisputed Pauline corpus.[4] This uncertainty calls for a measure of tentativeness. As Stanley Porter explains, "The methods used to determine authorship are almost as varied as the scholars doing the calculations, with very little control on what criteria are being used and what would count as an adequate test of the method."[5] Nevertheless, regardless of who the author might have been, several factors, including certain principles of relevance theory that I explain in chapter 2, encourage optimism about discerning authorial intentions by careful analysis.

---

3. Collins, "Pastorals—Biblical Studies."

4. See esp. Jermo Van Nes, *Pauline Language and the Pastoral Epistles: A Study of Linguistic Variation in the Corpus Paulinum*, LBS 16 (Leiden: Brill, 2018), 8, 36, and passim. The first modern scholar to doubt the authenticity of Titus in particular seems to have been Edward Evanson in 1792 (Van Nes, *Pauline Language*, 8–10). See also Van Nes, "On the Origin of the Pastorals' Authenticity Criticism: A 'New' Perspective*," *NTS* 62 (2016): 315–20. Statistical analysis of corpus language was a factor that, especially in the 1980s and 1990s through computer-aided research, swayed many to regard the Pastoral Epistles as un-Pauline (see, e.g., Van Nes, *Pauline Language*, 67–68, 120–21). A. Dean Forbes writes, "Most distressingly, we have repeatedly seen investigations embarked upon with sweeping claims of assent-demanding objectivity only to witness their ultimate invalidation through special pleading and selective attention to results. One need not be a statistician to detect when an outcome has hinged on a researcher/*thaumaturge* [wonderworker] and audience blinking at critical moments." See Forbes, "Statistical Research on the Bible," *ABD* 6:204. Mounce, although generally ambivalent about authorship, nevertheless provides one of the most thorough critiques of linguistic style-based arguments against the authenticity of the Pastoral Epistles (*Pastoral Epistles*, xcix–cxviii). Problems reconciling known history with representations in the Pastoral Epistles also influenced many to doubt their authenticity. But, concerning the correspondence between historical realities and even *authentic* literary reconstructions of them, James W. Aageson writes, "It would be a methodological fallacy to assume congruence between the two when there may in fact be little or none." See Aageson, *Paul, the Pastoral Epistles, and the Early Church*, LPS (Peabody, MA: Hendrickson, 2008), 10. In other words, the question of accuracy does not answer the question of authenticity.

5. Stanley E. Porter, *The Apostle Paul: His Life, Thought, and Letters* (Grand Rapids: Eerdmans, 2016), 413–14.

Even while taking the Pastoral Epistles to be pseudonymous, Huizenga says, "Modern readers may still presume that he [the author of Titus] has painted a realistic picture of the structure and dynamics of at least some Christian communities of his own place and time. As a result, he formulates a representation that would be historically plausible to the earliest readers."[6] For this reason, modern readers should not dismiss the potential of these letters to illumine real historical issues. Philip Towner makes a similar point: "The PE [Pastoral Epistles] are recognized as presenting a coherent theological and ethical argument to a real church or churches somewhere in time."[7]

Since assumptions about authorship affect interpretation and vice versa, it is equally as valid to form conclusions about authorship beginning with a close study of the text as to form conclusions about meaning from the standpoint of an assumed compositional history. The same stands for those who accept one of the numerous proposals for pseudonymity and also for those who view the letters as authentically Pauline.[8] One may legitimately approach the question from either orientation—that is, authorship's implications for interpretation or interpretation's implications for authorship. I do not aggressively address this otherwise important issue because the main contentions of my proposal stand whether the book is authentically Pauline or pseudonymous. Like James Aageson, I begin "by assuming neither the authenticity nor pseudonymity of" Titus.[9] Rather, I seek to discern the meaning of a passage on the basis of the available evidence. My research nevertheless bears implications for the question of authorship.

Composition

The commonalities of the Pastoral Epistles prompt interpreters to consider how each letter addresses the themes they share. We do not, however, know the nature of their relationship or the direction of influence or dependence. The average reader may not realize how numerous and complex the propos-

---

6. Huizenga, *1–2 Timothy, Titus*, xlviii.

7. Philip H. Towner, "Pauline Theology or Pauline Tradition in the Pastoral Epistles: The Question of Method," *TynBul* 46 (1995): 288.

8. For a detailed taxonomy of authorship proposals, see Van Nes, *Pauline Language*, 76–110.

9. Aageson, *Paul, the Pastoral Epistles*, 11. He refers to all three Pastorals.

als are of how these books relate to one another. Some hold that they were individual letters that the church collected and passed down as it had done with Philippians or Galatians.[10] Others suggest that portions of actual Pauline correspondence were incorporated into the documents.[11] David Cook attacks this last theory—the fragmentary hypothesis—on the grounds that the purported fragments were in the same style as the rest of the compositions.[12] I. Howard Marshall rebuts that an author incorporating fragments might cast them in his own style; therefore the style is not a decisive argument against the presence of fragmentary material.[13] Nevertheless, scholars do not agree on which portions constitute authentic fragments and therefore cannot distinguish them from the rest of the material with confidence. The common view that these letters were written as a single composition possibly intended to simulate a private letter collection has influenced interpretation most profoundly and requires additional comment.

Titus and the Single-Document Hypothesis

The most common modern assumption about the origins of the Pastoral Epistles is that they were initially written as a single composition to imitate

---

10. E.g., Donald Guthrie, *The Pastoral Epistles: An Introduction and Commentary*, 2nd rev. ed., TNTC 14 (Downers Grove, IL: InterVarsity, 1990); Philip H. Towner, *The Letters to Timothy and Titus*, NICNT (Grand Rapids: Eerdmans, 2006); Luke Timothy Johnson, *The First and Second Letters to Timothy: A New Translation with Introduction and Commentary*, AB 35A (New York: Doubleday, 2001). Claiming Pauline authorship does not make the history of composition, collection, and distribution simple, as can be seen in David Trobisch, *Paul's Letter Collection: Tracing the Origins* (Minneapolis: Fortress, 1994).

11. For example James D. Miller, *The Pastoral Letters as Composite Documents*, SNTSMS 93 (Cambridge: Cambridge University Press, 1997); Burton Scott Easton, *The Pastoral Epistles: Introduction, Translation, Commentary and Word Studies* (New York: Scribner's, 1947); Robert Alexander Falconer, *The Pastoral Epistles: Introduction, Translation, and Notes* (Oxford: Oxford University Press, 1937); P. N. Harrison, *The Problem of the Pastoral Epistles* (London: Oxford University Press, 1921). Why the fewest number of such fragments should appear in the longest of the letters (1 Timothy) is a common question, suggesting that this hypothesis is unsatisfactory as an explanation of origins.

12. David Cook, "The Pastoral Fragments Reconsidered," *JTS* 35 (1984): 120–31.

13. I. Howard Marshall, *A Critical and Exegetical Commentary on the Pastoral Epistles*, ICC (Edinburgh: T&T Clark, 1999), 72–73. For an early and multifaceted analysis of problems with the fragmentary hypothesis, see C. F. D. Moule, "The Problem of the Pastoral Epistles: A Reappraisal," *BJRL* 47 (1965): 430–52.

1. Prevailing Interpretations of Titus 1:12

a personal letter collection. Luke Timothy Johnson describes this prevalent theory:

> The letters to Timothy and Titus are, therefore, not real letters in the sense that they were sent to actual individuals with the names Timothy and Titus, or even that they were composed separately and sent to anyone. Rather, the three "letters" actually form a *single literary production* in which each "composition" plays a distinct role. The "Pastoral Letters" are, in this understanding, not real correspondence, but the fictional rendering of a correspondence. Thus they are not to be read with reference to Paul's letters (written some generations earlier), but only with reference to one another and, possibly, to other literature considered contemporaneous to their production.[14]

Even when commentators do not explicate their starting assumptions, this hypothesis has influenced most modern scholarly interpretations of these books.[15] As Johnson opines, numerous readers believe the Pastoral Epis-

---

14. Johnson, *First and Second Letters*, 79. Here and throughout this book all emphases are original unless noted otherwise.

15. Treatments of provenance are often concerned with the implications of pseudonymity for *canon*, whereas my concern here is its implications for *interpretation*. These treatments are customary in the literature, and it is not necessary for me to revisit all of the issues here. The following scholars represent various angles: Terry L. Wilder argues that, because early Christians rejected pseudonymity when detected, the only reasonable (though problematic) explanation for pseudonymity is that they were fooled. See Wilder, *Pseudonymity, the New Testament, and Deception: An Inquiry into Intention and Reception* (Lanham, MD: University Press of America, 2004). David G. Meade considers kinds of pseudonymity and conditions for accepting it within Jewish and early Christian milieux. See Meade, *Pseudonymity and Canon: An Investigation into the Relationship of Authorship and Authority in Jewish and Earliest Christian Tradition*, WUNT 39 (Tübingen: Mohr Siebeck, 1986). Armin Daniel Baum, examining several ancient critiques of irregular authorship claims (including in the Pastoral Epistles), explains that apostolic authorship was not a sufficient criterion for canonicity but that it was nevertheless a necessary one. See Baum, "Literarische Echtheit als Kanonkriterium in der alten Kirche," *ZNW* 88 (1997): 97–110. Baum addresses the issue of stylistics, which is perhaps the most common angle of argument for or against Pastoral Epistles authenticity in "Semantic Variation within the Corpus Paulinum: Linguistic Considerations concerning the Richer Vocabulary of the Pastoral Epistles," *TynBul* 59 (2008): 271–92. Baum offers his original assessment of the stylistic argument against Pauline authorship more fully in *Pseudepigraphie und literarische Fälschung im frühen Christentum: Mit ausgewählten Quellentexten samt deutscher Übersetzung*, WUNT 2/138 (Tübingen: Mohr Siebeck, 2001). According to

tles to be a forged letter collection because they were told so in college, not because they have personally examined them. He writes:

> Little real discussion of the issue of authenticity still occurs. But I remind the reader that this consensus resulted as much from social dynamics as from the independent assessment of the evidence by each individual scholar. For many contemporary scholars, indeed, the inauthenticity of the Pastorals is one of those scholarly dogmas first learned in college and in no need of further examination.[16]

Adopting the single-document hypothesis profoundly influences how one interprets the Pastoral Epistles, but the reasons for doing so are contested.[17] Towner argues that uncritical acceptance of this theory has biased interpretation, that reading the letters solely as a corpus skews their individual meaning and reinforces the assumption that they are inauthentic and inferior without regard to their actual substance.[18] Therefore, in order to examine Titus afresh, I begin transparently with its literary self-presentation as an individual letter. The reasons for this choice will become clear.

Several scholars in recent years have argued, based on distinctions between the Pastoral Epistles, that they were individual letters addressing specific local situations.[19] Although not everyone gives the question extended critical energy, assumptions regarding provenance nevertheless

---

Marshall, differing convictions about provenance do not utterly negate a solid evidence-based interpretation. He writes, "I do not think that at any significant point my exegesis is incompatible with a more conservative hypothesis regarding authorship." See I. Howard Marshall, "The Pastoral Epistles in Recent Study," in Köstenberger and Wilder, *Entrusted with the Gospel*, 274–75.

16. Johnson, *First and Second Letters*, 55.

17. Johnson later adds, "The grounds for declaring them inauthentic are so flawed as to seriously diminish the validity of the scholarly 'majority opinion'" (*First and Second Letters*, 91).

18. Towner, *Letters to Timothy and Titus*, 27–28. Trobisch advances a proposal that Paul engaged in the conventional authorial practice of curating and publishing his own letter collection (*Paul's Letter Collection*). Ancient letter collections typically contained letters that, although redacted, represented actual correspondence. The single-document hypothesis requires that the Pastoral Epistles did not circulate separately at all; their appearance as letters was a ruse.

19. Rüdiger Fuchs, *Unerwartete Unterschiede: Müssen wir unsere Ansichten über die "Pastoralbriefe" revidieren?* (Wuppertal: Brockhaus, 2003); Jens Herzer, "Zwischen Mythos und Wahrheit: Neue Perspektiven auf die sogenannten Pastoralbriefe," *NTS*

underlie their readings. Interpreting passages from the Pastoral Epistles without at least tacitly subscribing to some conclusion (often furnished by another, trusted scholar) about their compositional history is almost impossible. Concluding a survey on Pastoral Epistles scholarship from 2000 to 2010, Marshall's first point is that in recent years, "a number of writers are emphasizing the individuality of the Pastorals as three separate compositions."[20] He then summarizes their various reasons and positions. Marshall's overview includes scholars such as Aageson, Rüdiger Fuchs, Jens Herzer, Michael Prior, and Towner.[21] Marshall shows that scholars representing several cross-sections of opinion on authorship and authenticity nevertheless argue for the individuality of the Pastoral Epistles. In harmony with the general movement in Pastoral Epistles scholarship toward seeing these letters as distinct compositions, this study treats Titus as an individual letter. This choice does not materially affect the linguistic aspects of this study, but it keeps my focus narrow, my parameters firm, and my approach transparent.

I now explain and demonstrate how assuming the single-document hypothesis unduly biases interpretations of Titus. The two issues stemming from this assumption that most profoundly affect interpretation are the tendency to treat the concerns of all three Pastoral Epistles as an undifferentiated amalgam and the tendency to assume a lack of coherence in their structure and message. These tendencies have a self-confirming and self-reinforcing effect, but recent research questions them.

---

63 (2017): 428–50; Aageson, *Paul, the Pastoral Epistles*. Marshall identifies others who argue the individuality of the letters ("Pastoral Epistles," 304–8).

20. Marshall, "Pastoral Epistles," 308. T. Christopher Hoklotubbe briefly discusses trends to distinguish Titus from the other Pastoral Epistles. See Hoklotubbe, "Civilized Christ-Followers among Barbaric Cretans and Superstitious Judeans: Negotiating Ethnic Hierarchies in Titus 1:10–14," *JBL* 140 (2021): 375 n. 21.

21. See, e.g., Aageson, *Paul, the Pastoral Epistles*; Fuchs, *Unerwartete Unterschiede*; Michael Prior, *Paul the Letter-Writer and the Second Letter to Timothy*, JSNTSup 23 (Sheffield: Sheffield Academic, 1989); Towner, *Letters to Timothy and Titus*. The names identified here are representative. This trend has not diminished since Marshall's writing. Jens Herzer has advanced the argument in "Was ist falsch an der 'fälschlich so genannten Gnosis'? Zur Paulusrezeption des Ersten Timotheusbriefes im Kontext seiner Gegnerpolemik," *EC* 5 (2014): 68–96. His ideas on the letters' individuality have been incorporated into his "Zwischen Mythos und Wahrheit." See also Herzer, "Abschied vom Konsens? Die Pseudepigraphie der Pastoralbriefe als Herausforderung an die neutestamentliche Wissenschaft," *TLZ* 129 (2004): 1267–82.

The Amalgamation of the Pastorals

Assuming that the Pastoral Epistles constitute a single literary composition has led to the amalgamation of their particular messages and personalities, conflicts and remedies. C. K. Barrett demonstrates the constraints of this conventional wisdom when he presumes to discuss "the false doctrine the author had in mind" as "difficult to ascertain"[22] because he feels obliged to read the three books as a single work. Examples of homogenizing tendencies skewing interpretation are numerous, but one of the more unfortunate is when the theology of Titus is regarded as a static and lifeless "deposit" (παραθήκη, 1 Tim 6:20; 2 Tim 1:12, 14), a word or idea that arguably does not represent Paul's perception of the gospel in the Epistle to Titus, if even in the letters to Timothy.[23]

Another error takes the argument from one of the Pastoral Epistles to interpret the other Pastoral Epistles strictly despite intracontextual evidence. For example, Barrett says that, as far as the Pastoral Epistles are concerned, "women have no place" in the ministry "from theological grounds."[24] He cites Titus 2:4, which does not contribute to the argument as Barrett frames it, but ignores 2:3, which instructs older women to be "good-teachers" (καλοδιδασκάλους), that is, teachers of what is good. In Titus, teaching is a leadership role.

Viewing these letters as a single composition and amalgamating their distinctives leads Huizenga to claim, "Indeed, the Pastorals assert that the organization of the whole cosmos is based on God's οἰκονομία, 'household management' (1 Tim 1:4)," even though that Greek lemma appears only in 1 Cor 9:17; Eph 1:10; 3:2, 9; Col 1:25; and 1 Tim 1:4 among all the New Testament epistles—a surprising distribution for a concept considered both un-Pauline and pivotal to Titus.[25] Paul compares the "elders" (πρεσβύτερος, 1:5) whom Titus is supposed to appoint with a metaphori-

---

22. Barrett, *Pastoral Epistles*, 12. Furthermore, Barrett makes the odd connection that "Timothy must cease to abstain from wine" (1 Tim 5:23), *because* "to the pure all things are pure" (Titus 1:15), *rather than* by Paul's own logic: "for the sake of your stomach and frequent ailments" (*Pastoral Epistles*, 21).

23. For a representative example of this particular error, see Barrett, *Pastoral Epistles*, 31.

24. Barrett, *Pastoral Epistles*, 32.

25. Huizenga, *1–2 Timothy, Titus*, xlii. The lemma also appears in Isa 22:19, 21 (LXX); Luke 16:2–4.

cal "household manager" (οἰκονόμος, 1:7), but this analogy of leadership role may not strongly reflect a programmatic theology across the Pastoral Epistles. Furthermore, οἰκονόμος also has a telling distribution in the New Testament: Luke 12:42; 16:1, 3, 8; Rom 16:23; 1 Cor 4:1–2; Gal 4:2; Titus 1:7; 1 Pet 4:10. It is difficult to see this pattern as both distinctive to the Pastoral Epistles and un-Pauline. Whereas Marshall and Towner argue that topical redundancy across the Pastoral Epistles is a reason to doubt their original unity, Huizenga claims that the author repeated material among the Pastorals "to add authoritative weight to his opinions."[26] That significant concerns are *not* shared by some Pastorals casts doubt on this explanation of the redundancies, which assumes that the Pastorals are more univocal about topics between component letters than Paul's undisputed works. Furthermore, Huizenga's claim that Paul articulates the nature of conflict in his undisputed letters but not in the Pastorals is not sustainable upon closer examination.[27] I explain below how the author of Titus is more specific than typically appreciated in identifying what he sees to be the cause of upheaval in Crete.

The single-document hypothesis obscures the context of Titus, amalgamates its themes and concerns with the other Pastoral Epistles, and stifles its unique voice. Marshall exposes an example of these problems when he discusses the relation of ἐγκράτεια ("discipline," Acts 24:25, Gal 5:23, 2 Pet 1:6; and cognates ἐγκρατεύομαι, 1 Cor 7:9, 9:25, and ἐγκρατῆς, Titus 1:8) and σωφροσύνη ("discipline" and cognates in Titus 1:8; 2:2, 4–6, 12; 1 Tim 2:9, 15; 3:2; 2 Tim 1:7). They are part of a cluster of virtues that, commentators repeat the claim, are both characteristic and distinctive of the Pastoral Epistles. Marshall points out, however, that they do not have the same prominence or sense in 2 Timothy that they have elsewhere.[28] He explains that ἐγκράτεια was common in Greek virtue lists but that it had less importance for Paul's concerns in the Pastorals as contrasted with his prolific use of σωφροσύνη and cognates in Titus and 1 Timothy but not in 2 Timothy.[29]

---

26. E.g., Marshall, *Critical and Exegetical Commentary*, 1–2; Huizenga, *1–2 Timothy, Titus*, 133.

27. Huizenga, *1–2 Timothy, Titus*, xliv.

28. See Marshall, *Critical and Exegetical Commentary*, 182–83.

29. Marshall, *Critical and Exegetical Commentary*, 185. Van Nes argues that his research "underlines the importance of respecting the Pastorals as individual letter compositions" (*Pauline Language*, 224). Further, according to his analysis, "Titus

Some scholars disallow the undisputed Paulines from illuminating issues in Titus, even though these books share many themes and ideas.[30] As Donald Guthrie writes, "These three Epistles ... have always been treated as a single group."[31] Commentators commonly refer to the features of the Pastoral Epistles as a whole, even when those features do not obtain in particular books. For example, T. Christopher Hoklotubbe makes assertions about the Pastoral Epistles on the basis of a fine examination of the presence and development of the language of "piety" (e.g., εὐσέβεια) as it appears in 1 Timothy. He makes minimal reference to its development or presence in Titus or 2 Timothy and shows less appreciation for this word group elsewhere (e.g., Rom 1:18, 25; 4:5; 5:6; 11:26; 2 Thess 2:4).[32] *The Pastoral Epistles* in the subtitle of Hoklotubbe's volume could therefore mislead uncritical readers. Impressed by his thorough inquiry into 1 Timothy and notions of piety in the ancient world, they might think that the same considerations obtain evenly across Titus and 2 Timothy. However, the actual distribution of εὐσέβεια does not unambiguously support this claim. There are two instances in Titus (1:1, 2:12) and eight in 2 Peter (1:3, 6, 7; 2:5, 6, 9; 3:7, 11). Although Hoklotubbe's argument that this word group was of special interest under Trajan and Hadrian is probably correct as far as coinage, inscriptions, and monumental history are concerned, its distribution across the New Testament canon seems more ambiguous. Compare five instances of its cognate ἀσέβεια and none of εὐσέβεια in Jude (4, 15, 18) with the pattern in Romans: four instances of ἀσέβεια (1:18, 4:5, 5:6, 11:26) and one nonprefix cognate (σεβάζομαι, 1:25). A key text from Titus where the cognates ἀσέβεια and εὐσεβῶς are used virtually as antonyms (2:12) casts doubt on the counterargument that the presence of a common root does not entail a close relation of ideas in this instance.[33]

---

never proves to differ significantly from the undisputed Paulines" with respect to the five significant areas of linguistic peculiarities he measured: *hapax legomena*, lexical richness, missing indeclinables, interclausal relations, or syntactic irregularities (223).

30. See Johnson, *First and Second Letters*, 79.

31. See Guthrie, *Pastoral Epistles*, 19. He is correct as long as by *always*, he means "in the modern era."

32. Hoklotubbe, *Civilized Piety*. Note also Baum's more general corpus analysis in "Semantic Variation," 271–92.

33. In fact, every explanation for the peculiarities of the Pastoral Epistles seems to have its counterexplanation. For a systematic summary, see, e.g., Van Nes, *Pauline Language*, 76–110.

The dual tendency to amalgamate the issues presented in Titus with those of the other Pastorals and to distinguish them carefully from the undisputed Paulines is methodologically unsound. This common practice leads to the assumption that these books have never had an independent life of their own but have always shared an identical historical and literary context. Nevertheless, as noted above, a growing number of scholars propose that these books were written and circulated separately, even that they may have had distinct provenances in terms of place, time, authorship, and so forth.[34]

The practice of harmonizing all Pastoral Epistles polemic to present one vague, monolithic opponent to the Pastoral Epistles community does not yield lucid interpretations. Careful observation reveals that the offending parties in Crete were distinct. Towner exposes the tacit treatment of the Pastoral Epistles as a single, inseparable composition and shows that the amalgamation of opposition presented in each locale with that of the others is a problematic consequence of this tendency.[35] For an example of this amalgamating tendency, although neither *Satan* nor *devil*, nor "false teaching" as such, appears in Titus, Derek Brown argues that the Pastoral Epistles represent a marked development in the Pauline tradition toward attributing contrary doctrine to evil, nonhuman agents.[36] As I explain, Titus's opponents in Crete had specific characteristics and arguments.

One's ability to discern the exact nature of opposition in Titus is admittedly limited. On the surface, Paul does not articulate the troublemakers' teaching directly; rather, he derogates it with epithets such as "stupid," "worthless," and "empty" (3:9); and he instructs his delegates, Titus and the elders he appoints (1:5–9), to rebuke its practitioners (1:9, 13; 2:15; 3:9–10). As Barrett explains, "He was more concerned to combat the evil moral effect of his adversaries' teaching … than to analyze their beliefs."[37] Certain limitations may prevent us from reconstructing the troublemakers' teaching and practices in satisfying detail, but we must be cautious not to mingle Titus's

---

34. E.g., William A. Richards, *Difference and Distance in Post-Pauline Christianity: An Epistolary Analysis of the Pastorals*, StBibLit 44 (New York: Lang, 2002); Herzer, "Zwischen Mythos und Wahrheit."

35. See Towner, *Letters to Timothy and Titus*, 27–36.

36. See Derek Brown, "Satan: The Author of False Teaching in the Pastoral Epistles" (paper presented at the Annual Meeting of the Society of Biblical Literature, Atlanta, 30 November 2015).

37. Barrett, *Pastoral Epistles*, 12.

distinct portrayals with those of the other Pastoral Epistles. Now, let us consider one other implication that stems from accepting the single-document hypothesis.

Incoherence of the Pastorals

Assuming that the Pastoral Epistles are a literary unit, one rightly wonders whether they have a coherent, cohesive message. The question might not arise apart from the single-document hypothesis.[38] If the Pastoral Epistles are a patchwork of Pauline fragments arranged arbitrarily or were simply composed with little attention to argument, then readers are under no obligation to discern a coherent structure or message. Barrett refers to a number of passages that P. N. Harrison considered to be authentic Pauline fragments within the Pastoral Epistles as "artless—and in some ways pointless."[39] Some commentators are fashionably unimpressed with the "artless" Pastorals and view them as logically incoherent, impersonal, theologically and rhetorically impoverished.[40] Several level the criticism that

---

38. If the Pastoral Epistles constitute a single composition, a second question arises: In what order should they appear? The canonical ordering may not be original. Some speculate the original ordering of the Pastoral Epistles to have been Titus, 1 Timothy, 2 Timothy, as Quinn, Marshall, and others suggest, pointing to some manuscript evidence, the Muratorian Fragment, Titus's longer introductory greeting, and 2 Timothy's extended epistolary conclusion. Their order affects interpretation of the presumed whole but, based on how interpreters see the Pastoral Epistles illuminating one another, they can decide this question at the stage of "establishing the text." See Gordon D. Fee, *New Testament Exegesis: A Handbook for Students and Pastors*, 3rd ed. (Louisville: Westminster John Knox, 2002), 81–91. For the present concern, the canonical presentation suffices (see, Quinn, *Letter to Titus*, 2–3; Marshall, *Critical and Exegetical Commentary*, 1–2). Both Quinn and Marshall deliberately order their works to comment on Titus first, out of the canonical order, because they argue that their approach may follow the appropriate historical and literary order more closely. For both, however, the more pressing concern is pulling Titus out of 1 Timothy's shadow.

39. Barrett, *Pastoral Epistles*, 11. He interacts with Harrison, *Problem of Pastoral Epistles*.

40. E.g., Cook, "Pastoral Fragments," 122. He argues against the Pauline nature of the Pastorals and attempts to foreclose the suggestion that any portion came from the hand of Paul. Moule generally agrees that they are "artless" (Barrett's term), but he attributes the artlessness to the hand of an amanuensis—Luke. I cannot agree that the hypothetical effect of Luke's involvement in writing "at Paul's behest" would have

the Pastorals present an arbitrary and incoherent collection of material.⁴¹ Anthony Tyrrell Hanson writes, "The Pastorals are made up of a miscellaneous collection of material. They have no unifying theme; there is no development of thought."⁴² Frances Young describes the general "scholarly estimate of the theology of the Pastorals" as "a fairly arbitrary, inconsistent, unthought-out amalgam with little coherence."⁴³ Even advocates of Pauline authorship level such criticisms. Guthrie writes of the Pastoral Epistles, "There is a lack of studied order, some subjects being treated more than once in the same letter without apparent premeditation."⁴⁴ So, the books appear to lack the typical Pauline touch.⁴⁵

Some scholars critique these views. Commentators' general agreement about the logical outline of Titus, in particular, has shown its straightforward organization. Ray Van Neste extensively argues that the Pastoral Epistles have a telling structure and logical coherence.⁴⁶ Although Lewis Donelson does not believe them to be Pauline, he recognizes that "the Pastorals appear to present carefully structured arguments which follow the paraenetic canons of their day."⁴⁷ Scholars consistently observe, especially in Titus, a simple logical structure.

---

downgraded their quality (see Moule, "Problem of the Pastoral Epistles," 433–34; also Van Nes, *Pauline Language*, 94–97).

41. See references in Andreas J. Köstenberger, "Hermeneutical and Exegetical Challenges in Interpreting the Pastoral Epistles," in Köstenberger and Wilder, *Entrusted with the Gospel*, 1–27. See also Miller, *Pastoral Letters*, 61, 100, 139, and passim.

42. Anthony Tyrrell Hanson, *The Pastoral Epistles*, NCB (Grand Rapids: Eerdmans, 1982), 42.

43. Frances Young, *The Theology of the Pastoral Letters*, NTT (Cambridge: Cambridge University Press, 1994), 47.

44. Guthrie, *Pastoral Epistles*, 20.

45. In the words of Robert J. Karris, "These three small epistles [the Pastoral Epistles], which bear the name of Paul, are often neglected because of their confusing reasoning, and are frequently maligned for their inferior theological achievements." Karris, review of *Pseudepigraphy and Ethical Argument in the Pastoral Epistles*, by Lewis R. Donelson, *JBL* 107 (1988): 560.

46. Ray Van Neste, *Cohesion and Structure in the Pastoral Epistles*, JSNTSup 280 (New York: T&T Clark International, 2004); Van Neste, "Cohesion and Structure in the Pastoral Epistles," in Köstenberger and Wilder, *Entrusted with the Gospel*, 84–104.

47. Lewis R. Donelson, *Pseudepigraphy and Ethical Argument in the Pastoral Epistles*, HUT 22 (Tübingen: Mohr Siebeck, 1986), 69.

A generation ago, after a flurry of renewed critical interest in the formerly drab Pastoral Epistles, Donelson observed, "a change in mood on the Pastoral Epistles. No longer do scholars simply assume, as they did for several generations, that these letters are awkward combinations of diverse literary forms."[48] In a review of James Miller's published dissertation, Towner points out that Miller acknowledges "the current trend in Pastorals research which maintains that the author of the Pastorals … succeeds in communicating a dynamic message replete with coherent theological and ethical substance."[49] Scholars increasingly appreciate the coherence of the Pastorals regardless of their stance on whether they are Pauline. Andreas Köstenberger quotes Marshall's assessment that "there is a growing body of evidence that the Pastoral Epistles are not a conglomerate of miscellaneous ideas roughly thrown together with no clear plan, purpose or structure. On the contrary, they demonstrate signs of a coherent structure and of theological competence."[50] The critical move toward viewing the Pastoral Epistles as separate compositions probably aids this perception.

Even if critics see the Pastoral Epistles as artless compositions, attending to matters of theme and structure supports interpretation more than presuming their rhetorical poverty. Donelson presumes the need to "pretend to find another theological genius lurking in these rather pedestrian letters" as compared with what "we detect in [the undisputed] Paul"; yet he acknowledges that they display a perceivable logic, albeit counter to Donelson's reading of the authentic Paul.[51]

---

48. Lewis R. Donelson, "The Structure of Ethical Argument in the Pastorals," *BTB* 18 (1988): 108–13; also cited in Van Neste, "Cohesion and Structure," 87.

49. Philip H. Towner, review of *The Pastoral Letters as Composite Documents*, by James D. Miller, *JBL* 118 (1999): 372–74. Miller otherwise uses the assumed incoherence of the Pastoral Epistles as a starting point for his inquiries (see *Pastoral Letters*). I suspect, however, that interpreters may claim that a text is incoherent when they object to or have not grasped its message. Conflicting opinions cause one to question whether the artlessness ascribed to the letters is a matter of their composition or reception.

50. Köstenberger, "Hermeneutical and Exegetical Challenges," 12. He quotes from I. Howard Marshall, "The Christology of Luke-Acts and the Pastoral Epistles," in *Crossing the Boundaries: Essays in Biblical Interpretation in Honour of Michael D. Goulder*, ed. Stanley E. Porter, Paul Joyce, and David E. Orton (Leiden: Brill, 1994), 167–82.

51. See Donelson, *Pseudepigraphy and Ethical Argument*, 1.

1. Prevailing Interpretations of Titus 1:12

The expectation of encountering a coherent message comports with the approach of reading each letter on its own terms practiced and advocated by Aageson.[52] Describing his own approach to the Pastoral Epistles, Aageson says that he "takes seriously the literary and conceptual world of each of the individual letters as discrete documents that have integrity in their own right." He goes on to say, "This is not the case in much scholarship on the Pastorals. They are often treated as a Pastoral corpus, which disguises the substantive differences between them."[53] Based on its form of presentation, he hears Titus as an individual letter prior to investigating peculiarities that may lead him toward some other theory of compositional origins.[54] Similarly, Titus is treated here as a standalone composition with its own author, audience, and setting (both real and implied). I do not argue that it must be read only in this fashion, but I think that lucid interpretations depend on first hearing the book in its own epistolary context without undue influence from other texts, even the Pastorals.[55]

The present form of Titus appears to have been composed at least to look like and implicitly be treated as a single epistolary composition, complete with a meaningful but ordinary (by New Testament standards) opening and closing. So, all else being equal, I take the literary context of the letter itself to be the weightiest evidence in interpretation—before the cotext of the Pastoral Epistles, the Pauline Corpus, the New Testament, or other early Christian literature.[56] With these descriptions of broad issues that influence interpretations of Titus, I turn now to examining common interpretations of the Cretan quotation.

---

52. Aageson, *Paul, the Pastoral Epistles*, 11, 18.
53. Aageson, *Paul, the Pastoral Epistles*, 16.
54. The tendency to amalgamate the Pastoral Epistles places a burden on readers of the secondary literature to sift through comments and assertions to discern their relevance or accuracy for individual letters. So, throughout this study, I present scholars' comments on the Pastorals as comments on Titus to the extent that they apply without further qualification.
55. Johnson also argues for this approach in *First and Second Letters*, xi, 14, 357, 369, and passim.
56. I acknowledge that external evidence can profoundly affect interpretation; this qualification simply asserts that we should not construe the book to mean something contrary to the intracontextual evidence, that is, its "inner texture." See Vernon K. Robbins, *Exploring the Texture of Texts: A Guide to Socio-rhetorical Interpretation* (Valley Forge, PA: Trinity Press International, 1996), 3–4, 7–37.

Miso-Cretan Interpretations

A cluster of what I call miso-Cretan assumptions has been an invisible accomplice in many unsustainable interpretations of Titus 1:12. Most treatments of the passage require or assume some level of adherence to these assumptions. The secondary literature on Titus exhibits diverse hermeneutical approaches, so I have selected several representative interpreters with whom to engage regarding the critical issues. They practice sociohistorical, confessional, feminist, critical, and canonical approaches. I demonstrate that available evidence challenges interpretations that rely on miso-Cretan reading assumptions. In subsequent chapters, I detail how these assumptions are also questionable when examined in light of relevance theory.

1. Authorial Sympathy

The Cretan quotation invites easy categorizations of the *other*. Huizenga asserts that Paul "has simply adopted the common perceptions about Cretans that designate them as the 'other.'" Accordingly, Paul's "rhetoric serves to set them apart from 'good' Greeks and 'good' Romans and now excludes them from the category of 'good' Pauline Christians."[57] Having heard the quotation, one no longer needs to wonder about the character of Cretans.[58] One has no reason to doubt the assessment until such people are encountered. Titus, however, was supposed to encounter ethnic Cretans daily, so how was this quotation supposed to serve his mission?

Despite Paul's often recognized inclusivity and accommodating approach to ministry, according to William Mounce, Paul abandoned his signature missionary strategy when it came to the Cretan church. Why? Mounce says that it was because "the Cretan social standards were evidently so low that there was, in essence, nothing to which Paul could accommodate." Paul himself was, after all, "a person who says that Crete is full of liars, evil beasts, and gluttons."[59] Mounce clearly holds some assumptions of the miso-Cretan reading. He writes, "The problems in Crete are those

---

57. Huizenga, *1–2 Timothy, Titus*, 141–42.
58. Compare the concept of scapegoating discussed in Monica R. Miller, *Religion and Hip Hop*, RRRMC (New York: Routledge, 2013), 29. According to Cathy J. Cohen, quoted by Miller, scapegoating does "not need irrefutable evidence to be effective."
59. Both quotations from Mounce, *Pastoral Epistles*, 418.

expected of a young church in a pagan environment. Paul wants their salvation from lives of sin (Titus 1:12–13...)."[60] This diagnosis obscures the ethno-religious character of the problems to which Paul alludes (1:10–16, 3:9–10). Although Paul points to Jewish believers (1:10–12), Mounce agrees with the quotation's assessment that the problem with the church in Crete was its pagan converts (i.e., Cretans) and their inherent degradation.

Quinn provides an example of the social problems with miso-Cretan readings. The quotation appears to have come from a poetic source: its first strophe is a Greek hexameter sentence that appears extant in a hymn by Cyrenian poet and scholar Callimachus (310–240 BCE; *Hymn.* 1.8–9). Quinn therefore notes its poetic features and attempts to convey its aesthetic nature in a more conventional English form:

> Liars ever, men of Crete,
> Nasty brutes that live to eat.[61]

Repoeticizing the quotation may help English readers appreciate its aesthetic qualities, but it has dubious value for interpretation. First, the quotation had already been excised from its poetic context to function as a crude slur. Second, recapturing the poetic effect does not solve the problem of why Paul mentioned the quotation in a context addressing leadership malpractice (Titus 1:5–16).

Conclusions that follow from accepting the miso-Cretan interpretation are alarmingly prejudicial. Marshall characterizes the Cretan church as one "struggling to break free from depraved patterns of behavior, such as were widely associated with Crete."[62] Even though Greg Couser acknowledges that Paul's main conflict in Crete had "a Jewish, law-based flavor," he assumes that Paul used the quotation to judge Cretan culture: "What stridency we find arises from the potential threat and, maybe more so, the challenge posed by the Cretans' cultural heritage (or lack thereof, 1:12)."[63] Couser thus demeans ancient Cretan culture. Johnson writes,

---

60. Mounce, *Pastoral Epistles*, lxi.
61. Quinn, *Letter to Titus*, 97.
62. Marshall, *Critical and Exegetical Commentary*, 165. Replace *Crete* with any contemporary social label (e.g., gender, race, religion, ethnicity), and Marshall's words become offensive, yet scholars accept such statements when they refer to Cretans.
63. Greg A. Couser, "The Sovereign Savior of 1 and 2 Timothy and Titus," in Köstenberger and Wilder, *Entrusted with the Gospel*, 105–36. Huizenga criticizes com-

"The unsavory character of the local population that was already suggested ... becomes explicit: even a native Cretan prophet testified truly to their coarse and evil ways."[64] Tacitly sympathetic to the quotation's negative view of Cretans, Johnson asks of instructions for young women in Titus 2, "Is this a sign of the savageness and incivility of the native population, that responses ordinarily thought to be 'natural' should require teaching?"[65] These comments are merely representative. Dozens more could be listed. Doubtless, reading the text in this way has affected people's opinions about ancient Cretans. Some take it even further, however, and attempt to prove the validity of a miso-Cretan reading.

2. Ancient Corroboration

The efforts of scholars to bolster miso-Cretan reading assumptions are socially and historically as well as linguistically problematic. Several interpretive problems in Titus 1:12 came to light when Anthony Thiselton, in a scathing 1994 article, vehemently criticized commentators' dubious practice of garnering evidence for the historical accuracy of the attitude expressed in the Cretan quotation.[66] Many scholars essentially try to corroborate the miso-Cretan reading through evidence in ancient literature and archaeology.[67] Thiselton objects to the modern quest to demonstrate that the quotation's assessment of Cretans is historically justified. First, the quest fails on historical grounds, because the evidence is weak. Second, the quest fails on literary grounds, because it asks the wrong question. Huizenga also critiques this quest:

> The value judgments of Cretan culture as untruthful and gluttonous (and thus, rudimentary, corrupt, savage, uncivil, etc.) do not arise from any

---

mentators who are influenced by the prejudicial view that she sees Paul exhibit in Titus (*1–2 Timothy, Titus*, 149).

64. Luke Timothy Johnson, *Letters to Paul's Delegates: 1 Timothy, 2 Timothy, Titus*, NTC (Valley Forge, PA: Trinity Press International, 1996), 228.

65. Johnson, *Letters to Paul's Delegates*, 234.

66. Anthony C. Thiselton, "The Logical Role of the Liar Paradox in Titus 1:12, 13: A Dissent from the Commentaries in the Light of Philosophical and Logical Analysis," *BibInt* 2 (1994): 207–23.

67. E.g., Stephen M. Baugh, "Titus," in *Zondervan Illustrated Bible Backgrounds Commentary*, ed. Clinton E. Arnold (Grand Rapids: Zondervan, 2009), 3:499–511; Mounce, *Pastoral Epistles*, 397–99.

"sociological" studies of the population but rather from the simple proverbial sayings and ancient reports. It is impossible for later readers to tease out the facts about life on Crete during the Roman Empire, and we cannot know the cultural realities for various people and groups when they are framed in such polemical and stereotypical ways.[68]

Significant methodological problems accompany the scramble to find corroborating evidence for the miso-Cretan interpretation. It represents a misuse of sociohistorical-critical methods.

Commentators attempt to gather historical evidence that implicates Cretans in any wrongdoing that can be found—regardless of the kind of wrongdoing or its chronological distance from the era of Titus. Some ancient literary reports of Cretan malfeasance show that some Cretans at some time in history were accused of some kind of wrongdoing or an inclination toward it. But commentators are often not careful either to correlate the nature of the reported wrongdoing with the moral concerns of the quotation and of the book of Titus or to correlate the era of the reported wrongdoing with the era of the book of Titus. It suffices merely to find ancient evidence that harmonizes with negative stereotypes toward Cretans, even when the broader context of the evidence does not suggest that Cretan wrongdoings were of special concern to the ancient writer. Anna Strataridaki argues, in agreement with early twentieth-century classical historian and archaeologist Henri Van Effenterre, that "no good reason exists for these people to have had a bad name either in their early history or in later times."[69] Furthermore, commentators typically fail to demonstrate that the Cretans were *more* despised or *more* accused than people of other ethnicities or that the same amount of disparaging material could not also be found against other groups in ancient ethnographies.

Mounce assumes that Paul shared the view of Cicero (106–43 BCE), who wrote in Latin more than one hundred years earlier than Titus that "Moral principles are so divergent that the Cretans ... consider highway robbery honorable" (*Rep.* 3.9.15).[70] Titus 1:12, however, does not mention any kind of theft or assault. Patrick Gray infers that Odysseus's impersonation of a Cretan man in the second half of Homer's *Odyssey* (14.41–199)

---

68. Huizenga, *1–2 Timothy, Titus*, 141.
69. Anna Strataridaki, "Epimenides of Crete: Some Notes on His Life, Works and the Verse 'Κρῆτες Ἀεὶ Ψεῦσται,'" *Fortunatae* 2 (1991): 220.
70. Trans. Mounce, *Pastoral Epistles*, 418.

reflects the prevalence of Cretans' unfavorable reputation, but such a conclusion is not necessarily suggested by the context. The explicit impersonation begins at line 199, but the story is favorable or ambivalent to Cretan moral character. Its main purpose is to build up the drama of Odysseus and what he went through to survive the Trojan War and to protect his identity. Gray, however, overplays his assumption: "So pervasive is this view of Crete that it finds its way into the pages of the New Testament. The author of the Letter to Titus describes the local population as 'always liars, evil beasts, lazy gluttons.'"[71] The framing of the quotation in Titus does not require it to be a straightforward description. Therefore, it is uncertain that an ancient prejudice about Titus's missionary outpost, as reflected in classical Greek myth, aids interpretation here. Commentators nevertheless accumulate evidence to support the notion that Cretans historically were vicious or were at least considered to be so by an ancient writer. Stephen Baugh gathers evidence of Cretan malfeasance (e.g., piracy, treason), but his examples do not correspond to the specific moral concerns of the quotation or come from a close historical period or geographic location.[72]

Interpreters often must distinguish between a writer mentioning someone else's opinion and expressing her own. Exodus 5:7–9 provides an analogy. Pharaoh considered the Hebrews to be lazy liars, but scholars have generally known better than to seek historical justification for that opinion. They understand that it was expressed within a context that reveals it as an unreliable claim, revealing more about the Pharaoh's attitude toward the Hebrews than about the Hebrews themselves. Seeking corroborating evidence for the veracity of Pharaoh's opinion from ancient writing and archaeology would rightly be critiqued as anti-Semitic; and, to Huizenga's point above, could any truly relevant, representative, or useful data really be found from such a quest?

Chiao Ek Ho presents an incriminating list of offensive Cretan actions: "known for its warring cities, piracy, wild pagan worship, and immoral practices. Lying was apparently regarded as acceptable in Cretan culture; thus the coining of the term κρητίζω (from the island's name, Crete [Κρήτη]), which means 'to play the Cretan,' that is, 'to lie.'"[73] Ho derives most of these behaviors from archaeological and literary depictions that

---

71. Patrick Gray, "The Liar Paradox and the Letter to Titus," *CBQ* 69 (2007): 302–14.

72. Baugh, "Titus," 499–511.

73. Ho, "Mission in Pastoral Epistles," 243.

are geographically and chronologically removed from first- or second-century CE Crete, and he includes some behaviors that do not coincide with the quotation. He may establish that certain people at some point considered Cretans to be wicked people, and historical evidence may show that some Cretans did bad things. Does Paul rightly disparage them, then? According to Ho, Paul uses the quotation for straightforward description. He seems to be neglecting the more relevant question: What is Paul doing with this quotation? Ho's only comment on its rhetorical thrust is that Paul contrasts Cretan "liars" (ψεῦσται, 1:12) with the "unlying God" (ἀψευδὴς θεός, 1:2). Although Ho argues in his doctoral thesis that Paul was always controlled by a "missionary outlook" in the Pastorals, this miso-Cretan interpretation complicates this view.[74]

Aside from its unsavory ring, two additional counterpoints deflate attempts to prove historically the moral reprobation of Cretans. First, the biblical portrayal of Cretans, although not prolific, is generally not negative (see, e.g., 1 Macc 10:67; Acts 2:7–11; 27:7–13, 21). Second, one may scour written history with a selective brush to locate unflattering commentary about any selected ethnicity (e.g., see comments below on Cicero, *Rep.* 3.9.15).[75] Anyone with a search engine can muster a collection of disparaging judgments against a given ethnicity from its detractors and its internal critics and thus rally literature and archaeology to censure an ancient or modern category of people—just enter the term.

Such pursuits constitute confirmation bias more than truly discovery-oriented sociohistorical research. Although Thiselton does not speak in terms of confirmation bias, he argues that commentators have been

---

74. Ho, "Do the Work."

75. Tertullian (ca. 160–ca. 230) presented pluriform influences that beget virtues and vices in people from a long list of various nations, exclaiming, "Even St. Paul brands all Cretans as 'liars'" (*An.* 20). He essentially attributes moral difference to nurture rather than nature. Most of his premodern conjectures are scientifically unsound. He does not explicitly attribute the label for Cretans, "liars," to anyone but Paul. See Tertullian, *On the Soul*, in *Tertullian: Apologetical Works and Minucius Felix: Octavius*, trans. Edwin A. Quain, FC 10 (Washington, DC: Catholic University of America Press, 2008), 226–27. See also Jerome, *Comm. Gal.* 3:1a, where he lists (partly dependent on Tertullian) the associated virtues and vices of various ethnicities (including Cretan) and complicates the notion that the apostle Paul was simply rebuking the Galatians for their ethnic idiosyncrasies. See Jerome, *Commentaries on Galatians, Titus, and Philemon*, trans. Thomas P. Scheck (Notre Dame, IN: University of Notre Dame Press, 2010), 117–19.

grasping for "further empirical grounds" to validate the content of Paul's supposed assertion.[76] They want to verify it historically, but doing so requires a speculative reconstruction of Paul's, Titus's, and the Cretans' cultural exposure to the writings and histories of writers widely dispersed in time, space, and discipline (e.g., drama, ethnography, geography, history, philosophy, poetry). Beside this limitation, the approach also ignores ancient literature that provides either a positive or neutral but certainly a more holistic impression of the Cretans (e.g., Polybius, *Hist.* 6.43–45; Quintus Smyrnaeus, *Post.* 345–351; Strabo, *Geogr.* 5.2.4; 6.1.8; 10.3.11–13, 19; 10.4.9, 16, 20–22; Thucydides, *Hist.* 6.43).[77]

The moral teaching in Titus may amount to a lifestyle apologia, as Reggie Kidd argues.[78] In the context of the letter, however, this aspect of ethics is predicated on Paul's operating assumption that Cretan society *is* morally discerning and *is* concerned with reputation. Although Kidd highlights what he sees as a chiasm between 1:12 and 2:12 encompassing all of the moral material of Titus, I contend that the moral concerns of the quotation do not align with Paul's moral instruction elsewhere in the letter. The possible presence or validity of Kidd's chiasm does not aid or harm his main argument. The miso-Cretan reading and its corollary assumptions, however, retain much of their influence. Kidd takes the quotation as descriptive of moral faults that concern Paul and that the Cretans need to amend by attaining to associated virtues. Kidd argues that the triad of Hellenistic moral virtues in 2:12 is a corrective against the triad of Cretan vices in 1:12. The correlation he posits is plausible; yet when

---

76. Thiselton, "Logical Role," 211.

77. Strabo (63 BCE–23 CE) focuses on Crete in a multifaceted description of its geography, history, and law (*Geogr.* 10.4.1–22). He has many positive things to say about the society, customs, and values, yet he does indicate at several points that Roman impositions caused the society to decline both morally and socioeconomically. Strabo's descriptions are valuable because they include his firsthand accounts and are more contemporary with Titus than most other ancient literature scholars bring to bear. Yet because his is not an unambiguously negative portrayal, he is often overlooked by readers with miso-Cretan assumptions. George Wieland argues for the relevance of understanding first-century Cretans as the recipient community of Titus in "Roman Crete and the Letter to Titus," *NTS* 55 (2009): 338–54. Even Clement of Alexandria indicates that Cretans "enjoyed the best laws" in the same passage where he attributes the quotation to Epimenedes (*Strom.* 1.14).

78. Reggie M. Kidd, "Titus as Apologia: Grace for Liars, Beasts, and Bellies," *HBT* 21 (1999): 185–209.

he assumes that the quotation is simply descriptive of Paul's assessment of Cretan morality, as others do, he pairs disparate evidence and relies on some of the literature I reassess below (e.g., Pliny, *Nat.* 8.83; Plutarch, *Inim. util.* 1 [86c]).[79]

Those who assert that Cretans were historically notorious often do not match their evidence with the moral issues that the quotation raises, diminishing the applicability of their claims. Greek historian Polybius (200–116 BCE) specifically criticized Crete's lucrative land ownership and private property laws from a time in Crete hundreds of years removed from the New Testament era, yet Mounce considers Polybius's following comments pertinent: "Greed and avarice are so native to the soil in Crete, that they are the only people in the world among whom no stigma attaches to any sort of gain whatever" (*Hist.* 6.46).[80] Polybius was not critiquing Cretan character but the laws that made it possible for citizens to amass unusual wealth. His comments are pertinent not to Titus 1:12 itself but to sustaining a miso-Cretan interpretation of it and only when removed from their literary and historical context. Mounce also cites negative attitudes toward Cretans in Greek writer Plutarch (46–120 CE), but the context of the story that Mounce cites, while including a stereotypical disparagement of Cretans, pivots to show that the story's villain is actually cheating a band of mercenary Cretans—an act referred to as "Cretanizing the Cretans" (κρητίζων πρὸς Κρῆτας, *Aem.* 23).[81] In other words, the story does not unambiguously paint Cretans themselves as evil.

---

79. Kidd, "Titus as Apologia," 186, 190, and passim. Kidd's section boundaries, as I show in chapter 5 under the heading "Literary Context," do not cohere with the basic logical structure of Titus, though they may reflect a rhetorical-aesthetic structure. According to Arthur M. Eckstein, Polybius considered the center of Cretan sin to be "uncontrolled avarice and lust for gain" (αἰσχροκερδία καὶ πλεονεξία). See Eckstein, *Moral Vision in the Histories of Polybius*, HCS (Berkeley: University of California Press, 1995), 72. Πλεονεξία does not appear in Titus, but these concepts correspond to specific undesired traits that Paul identified in Titus 1:7, 11 and perhaps 2:10; nevertheless, these traits do not overlap semantically with the characteristics in the quotation (see, e.g., L&N 33.251–255 and other domains from the quotation), *pace* Kidd, "Titus as Apologia," 191. In Titus 1, Paul focuses mainly on church leadership, not the general population.

80. Translation quoted in Mounce, *Pastoral Epistles*, 397. Ancient authors often had clear ethnic biases. Eckstein notes that Polybius, for instance, is seen to be "persistently hostile toward Crete" (*Moral Vision*, 72 n. 58).

81. The phrase seems to have been rarely used. I have only found two instances of

Mounce also cites a narrative by Livy (ca. 64 BCE–ca. 12 CE) in which, first, he tells of Perseus's talented and trusted Cretan Lieutenant Evander being unable to finish a rallying speech because the Macedonian crowd saw their king's grief, and then he tells of a mishap in which underpaid Cretan mercenaries accidentally sank a ship they were trying to board (*Urb. cond.* 44.45).[82] The narrative mentions Cretans but is not about Cretan character in general. Various ancient writers may have stereotyped the Cretans and other ethnic groups as vicious, but such does not prove their actual reprobation or get Paul off the hook for bigotry simply because others shared his supposed opinion.

Commentators cite Cicero's *Republic* (3.9.15) to corroborate the view that ancient people had little esteem for Cretans.[83] Within the same literary context where Cicero refers to Cretan acceptance of "piracy and brigandage," however, he also devotes a similar amount of space to listing the supposed moral faults and concessions of Egyptians, Gauls, Athenians, Lacedemonians, Carthaginians, and others. Scholars typically cite the portion that is unfavorable toward Cretans; in the larger section, Cicero is highlighting differences of opinion among nations of the world rather than accusing any single nation of having an intrinsically and objectively corrupt character. No ethnicity is exempt from accusation or bigotry. Aside from the fact that these were hearsay accusations and historically removed, sometimes by hundreds of years, from Titus, they also do not coincide with the kinds of moral degradation mentioned in the Cretan quotation. The applicability of this evidence to the task of interpretation is therefore highly questionable.

To emphasize how common human corruption and intrigue was in *every* nation, Plutarch mentions a rumor that Crete alone did not have any haunts for wild animals. The rumor is also found in a naturalistic context by Pliny the Elder (23–79 CE), who says, quite without any negative connotations toward the people of Crete, that the island seems to have "no baneful animal," except a certain spider (*Nat.* 8.83). Plutarch's original point is that depraved humans are so much more common than depraved animals *the world over* that there is even a nation that is rumored not to

---

it (though cf. Polybius, *Hist.* 8.16, where the stereotype is present without the phrase). See Plutarch, *Aemilius Paullus*, in *Plutarchi Vitae Parallelae*, 2nd ed., ed. Konrat Ziegler (Leipzig: Teubner, 1964), 2.1:184–222.

82. See Mounce, *Pastoral Epistles*, 397.
83. E.g., Marshall, *Pastoral Epistles*, 198; Mounce, *Pastoral Epistles*, 418.

have the latter—although it certainly has the former, as any nation did. Plutarch continues, "A government which has not had to bear with envy or jealous rivalry or contention—emotions most productive of enmity—has not hitherto existed" (*Inim. util.* 1 [86c] [Babbitt]); that is, *every* nation exhibits these negative features. Quinn embellishes Plutarch's meaning concerning Crete not having wild beasts as evidence that Cretans, above other nationalities, are vicious people. Quinn writes, "The poet asserts that the human beings there give the lie to that belief. They are beasts of prey, not working for their food but idly prowling about for something to satisfy their hunger."[84] Following Quinn, Mounce writes, "While most countries had to deal with wild beasts, in Crete the same problem was posed by people who, in the absence of wild animals, assumed the role themselves."[85] These connections emerge not from a careful reading of Titus or of other ancient literature but from the assumptions that pertain to a miso-Cretan interpretation. They are nevertheless representative of mainstream scholarship on the topic. Grasping for historical narratives that sketch a generally negative portrait of the Cretans has led even the most respectable scholars toward biased and irrelevant sources that do not really help to understand what Paul was doing with the quotation.

More contemporary with Titus, Philo of Alexandria (*Spec.* 3.43–45), lamenting the depravity of various nations (especially with sensitivity to Jewish religious and moral scruples), relates the myth of the Cretan minotaur, which came into being from the lustful sexual union of Pasiphaë, the wife of King Minos of Crete, with a wild bull. Philo explicitly, along with his contemporaries presumably, rejects the reality of the myth but uses it as an example of the extent to which humans might inordinately associate with beasts. Although this legend may have given rise to the prejudices expressed in the second hemistich of the Cretan quotation, the problems with attributing these prejudices to Paul remain. It is as likely that Paul objected to such prejudices, based as they may have been in Greek mythological pornography.[86]

---

84. Quinn, *Letter to Titus*, 108; Quinn and others take more ancient references out of context to support the miso-Cretan reading than I have room to deal with.

85. Mounce, *Pastoral Epistles*, 398.

86. Numerous examples could be provided of ancient authors saying negative things about the Cretans (e.g., Aeschylus, *Cho.* 613–620; Plutarch, *Aem.* 23; Polybius, *Hist.* 24.4; Thucydides, *Hist.* 2.85–86, 7.57). Often the era or type of misdemeanor is unrelated to Titus 1:12. Aside from that, the existence of enduring prejudices against

The scramble to find corroborating evidence does not reckon with material from the ancient world that was complimentary toward Crete and Cretans.[87] Commentators attempt to marshal real-world facts to justify a prejudicial statement, but the utterance likely had a pragmatic effect independent of its truth-conditional value. The quest to reinforce highly selective knowledge of ancient Cretans with additional facts even when those facts are in most other ways irrelevant can be misguided and embarrassing.

3. Contextual Discontinuity

Scholars generally recognize that the pejorative essence of the Cretan quotation contradicts the canonical image of Paul. What is less commonly acknowledged is that it also conflicts with its immediate passage and book context in Titus. The miso-Cretan reading presents problems at four levels of context: (1) immediate grammatical context, (2) discursive paragraph context, (3) compositional book context, and (4) broad literary-canonical context. Whereas Kidd contends that the quotation is programmatic of Paul's moral instructions throughout Titus and tries to ameliorate the apparent topical breach without undermining the conventional reading,[88] I argue that the contextual features I describe below and the foundational assumptions of the miso-Cretan reading cannot both be sustained. I introduce, describe, and provide examples of each of these four contextual problems below and revisit them throughout the study from a relevance theory–informed perspective.

Overlooking the Grammar of the Immediate Context

First, accepting the miso-Cretan interpretation risks causing readers to overlook the grammar of the passage and assign unsuitable values to

---

Cretans does not necessitate that Paul held them. In fact, he may have been trying to confront them.

87. E.g., Polybius commends the Cretan constitution (*Hist.* 6.43), and Strabo relates the virtue of Cretan law (*Geogr.* 10.4.9).

88. Kidd, "Titus as Apologia," 185–209. Kidd perceives a chiastic triplet in Titus 1:12 and 2:12, but I judge that it requires seeing both verses outside their contexts. The obligations to self, others, and God in 2:12 do not correspond transparently to 1:12. For Kidd, the quotation is aspirational of a better life. He allows a broad range of ancient literary data to inform the meaning of the quotation more than Titus's literary context ("Titus as Apologia," 191).

words. Miso-Cretan readings often overlook some aspects of grammar in the immediate context. George Knight, for example, without explaining the unusual maneuver, assigns Cretans as the referent of "their" (αὐτῶν) in 1:12.[89] Because Huizenga aims to locate and expose aspects of the Pastorals that may be construed as negative toward the disenfranchised, she takes special interest in the quotation.[90] Even though Paul attributes the quotation to someone else, Huizenga pins it directly on him: "One of his most offensive tactics is to put into writing an ethnic insult."[91] If Paul intended to insult the Cretans, then his attribution of the quotation to someone else would serve an ambiguous function. What *kind* of distance did he intend—a distance of deference, or a distance of rejection, or something else?

The relative pronoun in Paul's statement "whom [someone] must silence" (οὓς δεῖ ἐπιστομίζειν, 1:11)[92] clearly refers to the troublemakers introduced in the previous verse and not to Cretans in general. Nevertheless, some scholars conflate these groups. In a single paragraph, Jouette Bassler writes, "Through it [the Cretan quotation] the opponents are dehumanized (Gk. *kaka thēria*; NRSV: 'vicious brutes'), and the accompanying instructions are to muzzle or gag them (Gk. *epistomizein*; NRSV: 'silence'). Moreover, all Cretans are included in this brutal condemnation."[93] What Bassler refers to as "accompanying instructions" appear four clauses earlier, so she confuses the object of Paul's criticism with the referents of the quotation. Bassler asserts that Paul was condemning both the troublemakers in Crete whom Paul identifies as a particular group (1:10–11) and the entire Cretan populace. If all Cretans are included, then the instruction to gag them is absurd, especially as a missionary strategy.[94] Titus would need many gags indeed! This reading also renders Paul's description of the troublemakers extraneous and misleading (1:10–11).

---

89. George W. Knight, *The Pastoral Epistles: A Commentary on the Greek Text*, NIGTC (Grand Rapids: Eerdmans, 1992), 298–99.
90. Huizenga is transparent about the purpose of her commentary and the Wisdom series (*1–2 Timothy, Titus*, xli–lii).
91. Huizenga, *1–2 Timothy, Titus*, 139.
92. Or "whom it is necessary to silence."
93. Bassler, *1 Timothy*, 190.
94. Noted also by Manuel Vogel, "Die Kreterpolemik des Titusbriefes und die antike Ethnographie," *ZNW* 101 (2010): 252–66. He cites Norbert Brox, recognizing the absurdity of disparaging the Cretans as a missional or pastoral tactic at 253.

An often ignored or tacitly misassigned pronoun within the context provides another example of the grammatical contextual problems with the miso-Cretan reading: Paul instructs Titus to rebuke certain people severely, using the personal pronoun "them" (αὐτοὺς, 1:13). This usage prompts the question, Whom is Titus expected to rebuke? Interpreters usually assume that the pronoun refers either to Cretans or to presumptuous (i.e., self-appointed) leaders in the Cretan church, with whom Paul seems to be concerned (1:9b–12a). Is Paul instructing Titus to rebuke sternly the entire native ethnic group on the basis that they are hereditarily vicious? This seems offensive, ridiculous, and implausible. On the other hand, if Paul is instructing Titus to rebuke the troublemakers of 1:10–11, then why assign them as the referent to the personal pronoun in 1:13 but not in 1:12? Most commentators do not adequately address this dilemma.

Wolfgang Stegemann, following the first option (i.e., that Titus is to rebuke Cretans), says that Paul "assumes that all members of the ethnic group of the Cretans have negative characteristics, which disqualify them morally and in the end place them outside the human race."[95] Mounce implicitly adopts both options by recognizing that the rebuke of Titus 1:13 is aimed at the troublemakers of 1:10–11 but then paraphrasing the verse exactly as follows: "'rebuke them [the Cretans] sharply' (Titus 1:13)."[96] He equates the referent of this pronoun ("them," αὐτοὺς, 1:13) with the target of the derogatory quotation (1:12b). Mounce recognizes the comparisons and contrasts between the Cretan population and troublemakers within the church (whom I contend held distorted views of Cretans as per the Cretan quotation), but he conflates the troublemakers in specific with the Cretans in general. For Mounce, the object of rebuke includes the very people disparaged by the Cretan quotation, but he does not address Paul's concern with those who were disparaging them.[97] Thomas Aquinas considers the troublemakers of 1:10–11 worthy of rebuke, but he justifies it based on 2 Tim 2:14 rather than Titus 1:13 nearby. He also typifies the miso-Cretan reading by assuming a shift in topic between 1:11 and 1:12 and by missing the continuity between Paul's concerns with ethno-religious bullies and his rebuke throughout 1:10–16.[98] Let me now address such contextual shifts.

---

95. Quoted in Huizenga, *1–2 Timothy, Titus*, 140.
96. Mounce, *Pastoral Epistles*, 392.
97. See Mounce, *Pastoral Epistles*, 408, 438.
98. Thomas Aquinas, *Commentaries on St. Paul's Epistles to Timothy, Titus, and*

Assuming a Topical Diversion within the Paragraph Context

Second, miso-Cretan readings assume that the writer diverts from his topic, thus muddying one of the most vivid and incisive passages in Titus. After the epistolary introduction, the first chapter of Titus focuses on leadership—good (1:5-9) and bad (1:10-16). Mounce explains that "for" (γάρ, 1:10) connects the paragraph under examination (1:10-16) with the preceding (1:5-9).[99] The macro relationship between the paragraphs is one of hortatory substantiation—instructions followed by rationale.[100] Paul instructs Titus to appoint elders of noble character in each town (1:5-9) *because of* the presence of presumptuous leaders (1:10-16). Titus 1:10-16 primarily concerns these troublemakers, their moral character and behavior, what Titus is expected to do about it and why.

The argumentative structure of Titus is otherwise so straightforward that it is surprising more interpreters do not question the break in thought assumed by the miso-Cretan reading. Jerome (347-420 CE; *Comm. Tit.* 1.12-14), however, agonizes over the presumed break in Titus 1:10-16. He cannot see why such an insult would appear in the midst of Paul's otherwise continuous concern with belligerent leaders. In the end, he conflates the troublemakers of Crete (Titus 1:10-11) with the Cretans in general in deference to Clement of Alexandria (150-215 CE; *Strom.* 1.14) before him.[101]

Writers can move from topic to topic freely and without warning, but they customarily relate one sentence to another in sensible and transparent

---

Philemon, trans. Chrysostom Baer (South Bend, IN: St. Augustine's, 2007), 164-65 (comments on Titus 1:10-16). I have not seen a commentator correlate the disqualification of "bullies" (πλήκτης, Titus 1:7) with the behaviors of the troublemakers in Crete—e.g., "upsetting entire households" (ὅλους οἴκους ἀνατρέπουσιν, 1:11). Paul's instructions concerning moral character and behavior do not form in a vacuum; they correlate to Titus's actual context.

99. Mounce, *Pastoral Epistles*, 395-96.

100. For descriptions of such logical relationships, see Bauer and Traina, *Inductive Bible Study*, 107-8.

101. See Jerome's full dialogue in *Comm. Tit.* 1.10-16. See telling excerpts in Peter Gorday and Thomas C. Oden, eds., *Colossians, 1-2 Thessalonians, 1-2 Timothy, Titus, Philemon*, ACCS (Downers Grove, IL: IVP Academic, 2000), 291. Jerome takes the attribution to Epimenedes for granted when he discusses the apostle Paul's use of "secular literature" (Scheck's translation) in his comments on Gal 4:24a (*Commentaries on Galatians*, 186-87).

ways or mark off diversions with caveats and resumptive words or phrases.[102] Miso-Cretan readings allow for scant contextual relations between the contents of the quotation and the surrounding sentences. Commentators do not seem to question their assumptions when they affirm that Paul jumps from one topic to another in Titus 1:12 with almost no sense of continuity.[103] Paul, however, seems to have thought that his presentation of the quotation had a clear logical relation to the material both before and after, using resumptive logical connectives and cross-contextual referentials such as the personal and relative pronouns of 1:12–13, which are discussed in chapter 3 under "Basic Pragmatic Processes."

One premodern and one modern example will suffice. Theodoret of Cyrus (ca. 393–ca. 460) notes that, according to his reading, Paul shifts from speaking in verses 10–11 about false teachers to speaking in verse 12 about those deceived by the troublemakers. He reasons that Paul must have drawn the metered quotation from Callimachus, who was a gentile, whereas the false teachers were Jewish.[104] Like many other commentators, he does not consider whether Paul might have been quoting his opponents.[105]

Barrett admits, "The introduction of *Cretans* [in 1:12] is not easy to understand after the reference in v. 10 to Jewish converts."[106] He recognizes the contextual disjunction that obtains under the influence of the miso-Cretan interpretation, but it is only problematic for him because of his assumption that Paul's *speaker* was not Jewish but an ethnic Cretan. The English translation that Barrett uses (NEB) reinforces this assumption by inserting "Cretan" into the quotative frame of Titus 1:12a.[107] Context,

---

102. E.g., the resumptive discourse functions of οὐκ οἶδα, ὁ θεὸς οἶδεν in 2 Cor 12:2, 3 or καί in Eph 2:6.

103. Vogel asks why the author of Titus would make such a detour. He ultimately explains that "Paul" attributed heresy as much to despised Cretans as to Jews so that the real-life audience would distance themselves from both. See full argument in Vogel, "Die Kreterpolemik," question at 256.

104. Theodoret, *Commentary on the Letters of St. Paul*, trans. Robert Charles Hill, 2 vols. (Brookline, MA: Holy Cross Orthodox Press, 2001), 2:253–54.

105. I discuss the pragmatic effects of Paul quoting his opponents in ch. 6.

106. Barrett, *Pastoral Epistles*, 131. He continues, "Either the author has not fully thought through his material … or the Jews are to be thought of as in great measure assimilated to Cretan life." Commentators sometimes pin faults, such as dullness, vice, or incoherence, on a writer rather than a reader.

107. "Cretan" does not appear in any manuscript of Titus 1:12a, the quotative

however, may suggest that the speaker was one of the (predominantly Jewish) troublemakers.

In contrast to the dense structure of 1 Timothy, which presents diverse topics with complex logical and thematic progression, Titus's structure is simple and transparent. Its organization and argument are relatively easy to grasp, except when readers tacitly assume a topical diversion between 1:12 and its surrounding verses. Huizenga recognizes that "Jewish opponents [are] mentioned in 1:10 and 1:14," but she takes the verse between them (1:12) as Paul's statement against gentiles.[108] In chapter 5 under "Mismatched Salience," I propose one reason readers see a diversion here.

Rather than seeing a topical diversion, Mounce conflates the subjects of Paul's complaint about the troublemakers in 1:10–11 with the subjects of the Cretan quotation in 1:12b.[109] He is correct that the vices of children that disqualified their parents from becoming elders (1:7) paralleled the troublemakers' traits (1:10–11), but he does not adequately distinguish between the specific designation Paul gives of the troublemakers—"especially those from the circumcision" (μάλιστα οἱ ἐκ τῆς περιτομῆς, 1:10)—and the generic subject of the quotation—"Cretans" (Κρῆτες, 1:12).

Distorting the Moral and Theological Instruction in the Book Context

Third, this miso-Cretan assumption leads readers to distort the epistle's moral and theological instruction in order to comport with a degraded view of the Cretan congregations. We have already seen some examples. Paul does not transparently develop a concern with gluttony, laziness, or even lying as such later in Titus.[110] He does, however, consistently evoke relations between Jews and gentiles and between Christians and the society

---

frame. Smith indicates, according to relevance theory–informed translation principles, that adding such ethnic information is justified in an indirect translation when it is known that the original audience would have supplied it—an uncertain proposition ("Bible Translation and Relevance Theory," 140–41).

108. Huizenga, *1–2 Timothy, Titus*, 173.

109. Mounce, *Pastoral Epistles*, 390, 392 (comments under Titus 1:7b, 1:9b).

110. *Pace* Kidd, "Titus as Apologia," 185–209; Riemer A. Faber, "'Evil Beasts, Lazy Gluttons': A Neglected Theme in the Epistle to Titus," *WTJ* 67 (2005): 135–45. Faber addresses two problems: (1) how the quotation fits into Titus and (2) the question of authenticity. He demonstrates the conceptual allusions between the end of 1:12 and 1:15–16. Yet I highlight that these are local, not global, contextual developments.

around them. The troublemakers impressed ethnic Cretans with a sense of religious and moral inferiority. The power brokers of the religious community questioned Cretan legitimacy. When Paul mentions Jewish religious and cultural interests, he addresses the contention that gentiles could not be full members of the Christian community without attending to the traditions of Jewish religious culture—circumcision (1:10) chief among them.[111] Rather than seeing Paul develop the ethical instruction of Titus in this palpable social context, many commentators take their cue from miso-Cretan interpretations and assume that Paul's subsequent admonitions are remedial and defensive.[112] Some treatments of Titus suggest that its ethic is primarily informed by concerns for legitimacy in the broader world rather than Paul's gospel.[113] Yet it would be reductionistic to argue that the ethics of Titus is about Christian public relations and damage control.

Discounting the Literary-Canonical Context of Titus

Fourth, and finally, adhering to that surface reading discounts the weight of the literary-canonical context of Titus—that is, the conceptualization of persons, places, and situations inherited by its writer and readers. Many scholars believe that the audience of Titus did not have direct personal knowledge of Paul and Titus and knew them primarily as literary and historical figures. Therefore, appreciating the contribution that Titus makes to the New Testament canon involves understanding how it presumes the audience's familiarity with inherited notions of Paul and Titus. Robert Wall explains that the author of Titus, in an attempt to carry on the "Pauline Apostolate" for new generations of Christians with relevant adjustments for his contemporary church, relied on the audience's knowledge of Paul from other canonical Scriptures.[114] Therefore, we rightly ask, What feature

---

According to him, "liars" is a minor point in the quotation because of the dubious connection to Callimachus.

111. See ch. 5 under the heading "Contextual Assumptions." There was no dilemma for the false teachers, contrary to Hanson, because they were not primarily ethnic Cretans (*Pastoral Epistles*, 111).

112. Beyond the scope of this study, the paraenesis of Titus is far more nuanced than generally appreciated, and its transformational soteriology is profound.

113. E.g., Kidd, "Titus as Apologia"; Hoklotubbe, *Civilized Piety*. I discuss this more in ch. 6 under the heading "Ethics and Redemption as Sound Doctrine."

114. Robert W. Wall and Richard B. Steele, *1 and 2 Timothy and Titus*, THNTC (Grand Rapids: Eerdmans, 2012), 332 and passim.

of Paul's literary persona in the New Testament is more prominent than that he was the "apostle to the gentiles" (Rom 11:13); the one who memorably said, "I have become all things to all people" (1 Cor 9:20–22) and "[God] worked in me [to be an apostle] to the gentiles" (Gal 2:8)?

Although they may articulate it in different terms, most scholars judge that the literary-canonical context of early Christian writings is more relevant to the interpretation of Titus than the sociohistorical context of the apostle Paul's actual relationship with Titus during his lifetime. If they are right, then it is reasonable to suspect that the author of Titus intended to evoke Paul's subversions and objections to ethno-religious stratification as seen in his undisputed writings (as in Rom 2:1–29; Gal 3:28; 4:17; 5:3–4, 12; Phil 3:2–7). Furthermore, it is reasonable to consider how the author might have portrayed Paul as subverting, not endorsing, the bigotry evident in the Cretan quotation. A miso-Cretan reading overlooks this literary-canonical aspect of Titus.

Suppose the pseudonym aimed to evoke the authentic Paul to the extent he could. He may have bumbled Paul's style or contradicted Paul's theology in subtle ways, but interpreters hardly noticed for hundreds of years—the deception was so convincing. If not personally, then the pseudonym knew Paul through his letters and perhaps through Acts.[115] Based on these, no biographical attribute seems more prominent than Paul's radically inclusive mission to the gentiles. Some commentators have even gone so far as to consider specific undisputed Pauline texts anti-Semitic (e.g., Gal 2:21, 3:10, 5:12, Phil 3:2).[116] Likewise, based on the treatment of Jewish religious culture in Titus (e.g., 1:10, 14; 3:9), several scholars label the author anti-Semitic.[117] It therefore seems unreflective to claim that the author was using the Cretan quotation to disparage the island's primary (gentile) ethnic group.

---

115. Mounce finds it curious: "In light of the frequent scholarly distrust of the reliability of Acts, it is interesting that here its reliability becomes the standard against which the PE are judged" (*Pastoral Epistles*, lxxxv).

116. Pamela M. Eisenbaum provides focused discussion in "Is Paul the Father of Misogyny and Antisemitism?," *CC* 50 (2001): 506–24. She acknowledges ambiguity in several passages but ultimately argues that Paul was not anti-Semitic.

117. Wolfgang Stegemann, "Anti-Semitic and Racist Prejudices in Titus 1:10-16," in *Ethnicity and the Bible*, ed. Mark G. Brett, trans. David E. Orton (Leiden: Brill, 1996), 271–94; Huizenga, *1–2 Timothy, Titus*, 141; Jay Twomey, *The Pastoral Epistles through the Centuries*, BBC (Chichester: Wiley-Blackwell, 2009), 192.

Martin Dibelius and Hans Conzelmann explain that the Cretan quotation serves "to add local flavor" to the pseudonymous epistle by peppering it with concrete ethnic references and a famous slur, thus reinforcing the ruse of Pauline authorship.[118] But does the pseudonym do so by having Paul assert something that everyone knows is out of character for the apostle? Whose reconstruction of the apostle Paul would disparage his missionary population in this way? A writer capable of the literary accomplishment, ethical argument, and theological coherence of Titus could have portrayed a more passable Paul. Yet this problem only exists for a miso-Cretan reading.

4. Target Conflation

Target conflation means reticence to distinguish between the group that the quotation disparaged and the group with which Paul was primarily concerned. Because this issue overlaps significantly with contextual issues, I have already addressed some instances of target conflation. At one level, as I explain later, Paul ironically echoes some of the themes of the quotation in his rebuke of the troublemakers in Crete (Titus 1:13–16), turning the tables on their ridicule.[119] In this sense, as several commentators recognize, Paul is using the quotation that disparages Cretans against the troublemakers, but one or more of three aspects of conflation remain. First, the troublemakers are assumed to fit unambiguously into the ethnic category of Cretans. Second, the veracity of the quotation's hereditary assessment of the Cretans is assumed to be the basis of the behavioral rebuke (vv. 13–14). Third, the incongruence between the moral concerns of the quotation (v. 12b) and the presumptuous leadership behaviors of the troublemakers (vv. 10–11 or 10–12a, 14–16) is largely ignored. Such conflation glosses over unanswered questions.

---

118. Martin Dibelius and Hans Conzelmann, *The Pastoral Epistles: A Commentary*, ed. Helmut Koester, trans. Philip Buttolph and Adela Yarbro, Hermeneia (Philadelphia: Fortress, 1972), 135. Jerome D. Quinn critiques their treatment of the *Sitz im Leben* of the Pastoral Epistles as follows: "The tortuous argumentation of D.-C. about the historical situation of 1–2 Tim and Tit ... can scarcely escape charges of obscurity or inconsistency." See Quinn, "Review of *The Pastoral Epistles* (Hermeneia) by Martin Dibelius and Hans Conzelmann, Trans. by Philip Buttolph and Adela Yarbro," *CBQ* 36 (1974): 583.

119. See ch. 5 under "Table Turning."

1. Prevailing Interpretations of Titus 1:12

Stegemann acknowledges the Jewish religious interests of Paul's opponents. But, instead of concluding that they would have favorable attitudes toward Jews and disfavorable attitudes toward Cretans, he considers all ethnic references to contribute to a singular, generalized bigotry. He blends Paul's correctives, writing of Titus 1:10–16, "The rejected group is connected with *implicit* prejudices about Judaism and *explicit* prejudices about the Cretans."[120] Huizenga assumes Paul's sympathy toward the substance of the Cretan quotation when she refers to "the author's prejudices about Jews and Cretans."[121] Manuel Vogel claims that, although Paul identifies the opponents as Jews, he insults them as Cretans. In his interpretation, the author blames poor Cretan character (1:12) for all of the offenses attributed to the troublemakers (1:10–11).[122] Huizenga pits Paul against the entire local population, without differentiating Paul's argument as for or against specific constituencies, when she writes, "He assumes that his audience will agree with his depiction of his opposition ('those of the circumcision,' Cretans, and others) as belonging to the broad category of 'corrupt and unbelieving ... detestable, disobedient, unfit for any good work.'"[123] These writers conflate the purveyors of bigotry with its targets.

The influence of target conflation prevents us from considering the life that this quotation had outside the letter and how Paul arrived at it. Paul becomes a blunt instrument of bigotry doling out ethnic insults without regard to their suitability to the issues that he named. Although he was concerned with leadership actions presumptuously taken by a circumcision faction (vv. 10–11), he supposedly found the general insult adequate to his purposes. We should not fail to recognize the qualitative difference between holding leaders accountable and expressing ethnic slurs, between correction and scorn. Target conflation flattens Paul, Titus, and what might have really been going on in the Cretan church. I have already noted above a few interpreters who conflate the targets of Paul's rebuke with the targets of the insult, so I now examine one last critical assumption in greater detail—the historical attribution of the Cretan quotation.

---

120. Stegemann, "Anti-Semitic and Racist Prejudices," 284; see also 273, 280–91.
121. Huizenga, *1–2 Timothy, Titus*, 145.
122. See Vogel, "Die Kreterpolemik," 264: "Sie werden zwar als Juden identifiziert, jedoch als Kreter beschimpft. Alles Fehlverhalten und alle Fehlhaltungen, die der Verfasser den Gegnern ab V. 10 anlastet, entspringen dem kretischen Volkscharakter, nicht dem jüdischen."
123. Huizenga, *1–2 Timothy, Titus*, 142.

5. Dubious Attribution

The overconfident assumption that Paul's Cretan quotation comes from Epimenides, a Cretan poet of the fifth or sixth century BCE, is not an assured fact. Even ancient writers confuse exactly who Epimenides was, and none of Epimenides's writings remain extant, so it is not possible to confidently verify the claim.[124] Several ancient commentators attribute at least a portion of the quotation to another figure, and some modern scholars advance other ancient writers as the originators of the sentence.[125] The quotation has no reliable attribution.

Clement of Alexandria was the first to attribute the quotation to Epimenides of Crete (*Strom.* 1.14).[126] Following him, Jerome and Socrates of Constantinople (380–439 CE) also said that it was excerpted from the works of Epimenides. In fact, every writer who attributes the quotation to Epimenides seems to be indebted to this one source. If this attribution is correct, then it suggests that the original context was poetic, perhaps ironic, caustic, or humorous, but unlikely merely descriptive.[127] J. Albert

---

124. Plato includes what he makes out to be a quotation from Epimenides—a prosaic, oral military prediction in favor of Athenians against Persians delivered on the occasion of Epimenides's cultic sacrifices (*Leg.* 1.642d–e). Plato may have reconstructed the statement.

125. E.g., G. M. Lee, "Epimenides in the Epistle to Titus (1:12)," *NovT* 22 (1980): 96; George Leonard Huxley, *Greek Epic Poetry from Eumelos to Panyassis* (Cambridge: Harvard University Press, 1969), 81–82.

126. It is clear from Clement of Alexandria, in a context unconcerned with the New Testament book of Titus, that Clement knows the first hemistich of the quotation to be from Callimachus, whom he mistakenly refers to as a Cretan, revealing his ability to make mistakes with respect to this attribution (*Protr.* 2.32; cf. 4.42, where Clement names two supposedly Cretan sculptors yet admits that his ethnic attribution is dubious). See Clement of Alexandria, *Exhortation to the Greeks, The Rich Man's Salvation, To the Newly Baptized*, ed. Jeffrey Henderson, trans. George W. Butterworth, LCL (Cambridge: Harvard University Press, 1919), 78–81, 106–7.

127. Although we cannot recover it completely, the quotation was likely not a general statement about Cretans in its original context. It arose in the context of pious pagan poetry, drama, or philosophy, and the broad accusation emerged from one offense. The most famous lie seems to have been that Zeus—who, according to legend (e.g., Hesiod, *Theog.* 474–479), was born on Crete—had a tomb on Crete and was thereby claimed to have died. The idea that the Cretans built a tomb for Zeus may emerge from Callimachus (*Hymn.* 1.8–9). Cretans, despite the occasional and ambiguous use of Κρητίζω, were not considered in general to be liars. Katja Kujan-

Harrill, however, suggests that Clement originally made this attribution casually and that it is not reliable. Harrill writes, "This identification of Epimenides as the original author of the text comes to Clement as obvious, showing no signs that Clement is aware of any debate over the attribution."[128] Jerome seems to depend on Clement but to consider the precise attribution unimportant (*Comm. Tit.* 1.12-14). In the discourse, "On the Emperor's Prohibiting Christians Being Instructed in Greek Literature, [etc.]," Socrates may also be dependent on Clement's claim when he refers to "the oracles of Epimenides" (*Hist. eccl.* 3.16). After describing Jerome's process of elimination,[129] Harrill explains that Jerome reasoned that Epimenides of Crete was "that island's most famous poet."[130] Harrill suggests that Clement did what people do countless times—misattribute quotations to the most convenient or esteemed character they can think of, someone whose name will lend credibility. Clement came to this attribution apart from any emphasis on Paul's part.

Succeeding generations of commentators followed this well-established lead in spite of its dubious nature until it became the majority opinion. Jerome explicitly resists Clement's attribution on account of the grammatical context of the passage but accepts it on Clement's authority (*Comm. Tit.* 1.12-14). Quinn acknowledges that Jerome's attribution to Epimenides was tentative, based on a second-hand report (*dicitur*).[131] Towner writes, "But in fact the attribution of the saying to [Epimenides] is

---

pää delineates two major linguistic theories on quotation and applies them to Paul's usage in Romans. She explains that when speakers take quotations from one context and place them in another, a change in meaning inevitably occurs. See Kujanpää, "From Eloquence to Evading Responsibility: The Rhetorical Functions of Quotations in Paul's Argumentation," *JBL* 136 (2017): 186, 192, 200.

128. See J. Albert Harrill, "'Without Lies or Deception': Oracular Claims to Truth in the Epistle to Titus," *NTS* 63 (2017): 453.

129. Jerome also cites but does not follow Origen of Alexandria (184-253 CE), whose commentary on Titus is no longer extant but who apparently attributed the quotation to Callimachus, not to Epimenides (Jerome, *Comm. Tit.* 1.12-14).

130. Harrill, "'Without Lies of Deception,'" 458.

131. Quinn, *Letter to Titus*, 107. Witherington also recognizes the citations of Clement and Jerome but not Jerome's ambivalence about the attribution (*Socio-rhetorical Commentary*, 122-24). Marshall suggests that Irenaeus might have considered Paul to be quoting from a known Greek author if the similarity between Irenaeus's Homeric quotative framing (*Haer.* 4.33.3) and that of Titus 1:12a were deliberate, but we cannot verify whether this was the case (Marshall, *Critical and Exegetical Commentary*, 199 n. 129).

somewhat uncertain."[132] Some premodern authors represent early countervailance to the now-conventional attribution to Epimenides. Theodore of Mopsuestia (350–428 CE) is one of several who identifies Callimachus, not Epimenides, as the originator of the quotation.[133] In his commentary on Titus, he writes,

> Those who have written against Christian doctrines have said that here the blessed Paul accepts the poet's voice and testifies to him that he rightly said these things on behalf of Zeus about the Cretans, paying no attention to the manner of the apostle's usage or to his statement, *this testimony is true*. For he does not accept the poem or the poet's voice but uses the poet's voice as a proverb, since the people at that time used the voice just as many other sayings current among the ancients came to be used as proverbs by people later on.[134]

Commentators who seek historical or literary justification for the offensive saying have difficulty explaining why it appears in its present context.[135] Mounce writes, "It is somewhat surprising to find such a strong condemnation in the letter, offensive as it would have been to the Cretans."[136] Thiselton's criticism is incisive: in sum, the writer is not using the quotation descriptively of the Cretans at all; and a search for real-world evidence or "*further empirical grounds*" that Cretans, as distinct from any other ethnic group, should be portrayed in such vicious terms is misguided.[137] Marshall is one of a few commentators who briefly discusses the cloistered debate regarding attribution, but in the end (and after unsatisfying argument) he pronounces, "We are left with some uncertainty.... But the probability is that the author

---

132. Towner, *Letters to Timothy and Titus*, 700.

133. Theodore of Mopsuestia, *Commentary on the Minor Pauline Epistles*, vol. 2, *1 Thessalonians–Philemon, Appendices, Indices*, ed. Henry Barclay Swete (Cambridge: Cambridge University Press, 1882), 243; also in English translation: Theodore of Mopsuestia, *Commentary on the Minor Pauline Epistles*, trans. Rowan A. Greer, WGRW 26 (Atlanta: Society of Biblical Literature, 2010).

134. See Theodore, *Commentary on the Minor Pauline Epistles*, 2:753. Theodoret of Cyrus (ca. 393–ca. 460) also knew the first hemistich of the quotation only from Callimachus (*Commentary on the Letters*, 2:253–54; cf. 259 n. 7).

135. Vogel acknowledges this difficulty in "Die Kreterpolemik," 253.

136. Mounce, *Pastoral Epistles*, 399. Vogel emphasizes how strong the Cretan quotation is against Cretans in comparison to Paul's words about other groups (see "Die Kreterpolemik," esp. 253). My interpretation offers a plausible reason for this difference.

137. Thiselton, "Logical Role," 211.

thought that he was citing Epimenides."[138] Lorenz Oberlinner indicates that there are two problems regarding attribution: who originated the quotation and what was meant in its original context. The second may have no importance for Paul, but Oberlinner, like Harrill, suggests that the traditional attribution to Epimenides may have simply been convenient.[139] Clement, the earliest writer to attribute the quotation to anyone beside Paul's contemporaries (*Strom.* 1.14), may have grasped for Epimenides as the most famous or the only Cretan poet he knew.[140] What harm could it cause?

Who Is Epimenides?

Supposedly, a Cretan poet named Epimenides was speaking about people of his own ethnicity. Whether it was in lament, humor, irony, or something else cannot be ascertained. Numerous commentators on Titus rely on or mention the typically unexamined attribution to Epimenides, but we cannot say with confidence exactly who he was. Multiple Cretan Epimenideses are known from antiquity—a philosopher, a diviner, and possibly a poet as well, although ancient writers confuse them with each other (compare Plato, *Leg.* 1.642d-e; Aristotle, *Ath. pol.* 1-2; *Rhet.* 3.17.10). Plutarch describes a certain Epimenides as a seventh-century BCE Cretan priest whose cultic genius was in demand in ancient Greece, Athens in particular (*Sol.* 12). Scouring Greek literature for appearances of this figure reveals that none of his works is extant and that there was a general confusion about his identity: Was he a poet, a politician, a soothsayer, or a scholar? The few ancient sources that mention an Epimenides do not agree on when he lived or what he did.[141] The seemingly assured attribution of this quotation to Epimenides has given scholars more confidence to make assertions about its meaning than is merited by our limited historical knowledge or by its use in the context of Titus.

Plato does not refer to the ancient Cretan soothsayer named Epimenides as prophet (*Leg.* 1.642; cf. Titus 1:12).[142] Diogenes Laertius (third

---

138. Marshall, *Critical and Exegetical Commentary*, 200-201.
139. Lorenz Oberlinner, *Kommentar zum Titusbrief*, HThKNT 3 (Freiburg im Breisgau: Herder, 1996), 38-39.
140. As argued by Harrill in "'Without Lies or Deception,'" 453-58.
141. See Alan H. Griffiths, "Epimenides," *OCD*, 546.
142. In fact, *pace* Guthrie, after an extensive search, I have found no ancient Greek writers who label Epimenides προφήτης ("prophet"), let alone "many" (see Guthrie, *Pastoral Epistles*, 209). The term seems to come entirely from Paul's usage context.

century CE) claims that Epimenides could predict the future (*Vit. phil.* 1.114 Epimenides), but that claim would not necessarily qualify him as a prophet in prominent Judeo-Christian conceptions of the role, and neither does it lend the kind of authority to the quotation that the miso-Cretan reading expects.[143] Lucian (third century CE) calls Epimenides a "soothsayer" (χρησμολόγος, *Tim.* 6) and associates him with the initial portion of the Cretan quotation, but he is probably just following Clement in this attribution.[144] Cicero lists Epimenides of Crete alongside other ancient soothsayers who artlessly attempted to predict the future in a "prophetic frenzy" (*vaticinantibus per furorem*; *Div.* 1.34), but his sketch of Epimenides diverges still from others mentioned above. Cicero attributes "prophetic" characteristics to Epimenides, but early Christians might not have recognized Cicero's description of him as a prophet. In spite of the coincidental English cognate *prophet* used in the English translation of Cicero's words, Cicero's behavioral description and Paul's literary label do not coincide. No single ancient figure fits the description of Epimenides the Cretan poet.

Marshall identifies some of the difficulties in determining who this Epimenides might have been: no extant works remain, and ancient writers refer to their Epimenides in various eras and in descriptions that do not fit what little context Paul provides.[145] George Leonard Huxley claims that Plato errs in his description (*Leg.* 1.642d–e), but he also acknowledges a general confusion about who Epimenides was, which would seem to have been less of a problem had there been a repository of his works at hand.[146] Although modern writers invoke his name with confidence, ancient authors were far less clear. Existing evidence does not strongly support

---

143. Diogenes Laertius, *Vitae Philosophorum*, ed. Herbert S. Long (Oxford: Clarendon, 1964), 1:1.114. In the cited text, he writes regarding Epimenides, λέγουσι δέ τινες ὅτι Κρῆτες αὐτῷ θύουσιν ὡς θεῷ· φασὶ γὰρ καὶ [προ]γνωστικώτατον γεγονέναι. Robert D. Hicks translates: "Some writers say that the Cretans sacrifice to him as a god; for they say that he had superhuman foresight." See *Lives of Eminent Philosophers, Books 1–5*, trans. Robert D. Hicks, LCL (Cambridge: Harvard University Press, 1925), 114.

144. Lucian writes, ὁ Ἐπιμενίδης Κρὴς ἦν χρησμολόγος, οὗ καὶ τὸ "Κρῆτες ἀεὶ ψεῦσται" λόγιον ("Epimenides of Crete was an oracle utterer, of whom also [came] the saying 'Cretans [are] always liars'"). See Lucian, *Scholia in Lucianum*, ed. Hugo Rabe (Leipzig: Teubner, 1906), 110.

145. Marshall, *Critical and Exegetical Commentary*, 199–201.

146. Huxley, *Greek Epic Poetry*, 83.

assertions that Paul borrowed authority from a known Cretan to vouch for the veracity of an insult he wished to level against Cretans.

Overconfidence that this quotation came from a Cretan poet has resulted in misleading translations and interpretations that would not have been likely without a commitment to this attribution. The NEB translates εἶπεν τις ἐξ αὐτῶν ἴδιος αὐτῶν προφήτης (Titus 1:12a) very loosely as "It was a Cretan prophet, one of their own countrymen, who said." Several interpretive choices in this translation are indebted to assumptions of the miso-Cretan interpretation and have introduced misleading semantic ideas into the English text of this verse, for example, ethnicity ("Cretan") and nationality ("countrymen").[147] These ideas are not native to the context. Kevin Smith assumes the attribution to Epimenides and argues that adding the extra detail pointing to a Cretan originator rather than a false teacher is justified on a relevance-theoretical basis. He writes, "This is a clear case where pragmatic concerns override grammar,"[148] yet he does not point to pragmatic concerns as his basis for this choice. Rather, he points to the assumed attribution, thus begging the question.[149] Instead, the context seems to point at the troublemakers as an improvised group not defined strictly by ethnicity or nationality but more so by attitude and behavior.[150]

Assuming the attribution to Epimenides as well as the appropriateness of the label *prophet*, the more recent ESV renders the portion, "One of the

---

147. Goodwin quotes Eugene Nida and Charles Taber: "One is not free to make in the text any and all kinds of explanatory additions and/or expansions.... One may not simply add interesting cultural information which is not actually present in the meanings of the terms used in the passage." Nida and Taber, *The Theory and Practice of Translation* (Leiden: UBS, 1969), 111, quoted in Goodwin, *Translating the English Bible*, 122 n. 1. Green discusses the challenge translators face of whether to supply information in "Relevance Theory and Biblical Interpretation" (2013), 270.

148. Smith, "Bible Translation and Relevance Theory," 140.

149. See Smith, "Bible Translation and Relevance Theory," 139–42. Smith's indirect translation provides added details that insist on this uncertain attribution, making his explanation of the "testimony" and "rebuke" (Titus 1:13) practically contradict his claim that the false teachers were not in view in 1:12a. He succumbs to miso-Cretan reading assumptions, something conceptually akin to what Goodwin repeatedly refers to as the "Holy Marriage" between traditional interpretation and the original language text (*Translating the English Bible*, passim).

150. See ch. 3 under "Referentials" and ch. 5 under "Literary Context"; see also Barrett, *Pastoral Epistles*, 131.

Cretans, a prophet of their own, said." The NRSV translates ἡ μαρτυρία αὕτη ("this testimony," Titus 1:13a) as "that testimony," an interpretive choice that takes the proximal discourse deictic as a distal temporal deictic.[151] These translational choices can be traced to the assumption that the quotation originated with a certain Cretan Epimenides, a point Paul may not have been interested in making.[152] Taking the quotation out of its grammatical context, which does not suggest that a Cretan said it, Felix Jacoby inserts a clarification into his collection of ancient references to Epimenides: "εἶπέν τις ἐξ αὐτῶν (scil. τῶν Κρητῶν), ἴδιος αὐτῶν προφήτης."[153] If Jacoby had not assumed the traditional but uncertain attribution, he would have no reason to include the biblical verse in his list, let alone his supposed clarification.

Commentators frequently claim that Epimenides originated the entire hexameter quotation, but none of Epimenides's writing survives. Most modern scholars accept this attribution without question.[154] Barrett, for instance, writes that it was "almost certainly Epimenides of Crete (6th–5th century B.C.)."[155] The attribution is not necessarily incorrect, but attention to the quotation's origin obscures an appreciation of Paul's use of it in its context. Titus is the full quotation's earliest extant witness, and Paul never precisely identifies its originator. One may too readily assume that his audience recognized the quotation and its author. Nothing clearly suggests that ancient origins were either important or even known to Paul. He refers elliptically to the *speaker* of this quotation, without a clear indication that its original historical and literary contexts had any bearing on his choice to present it to Titus.[156] Not only is the attribution to Epimenides

---

151. See ch. 3 under "Deixis."

152. While generally following a miso-Cretan reading, Laansma recognizes, "There is nothing in such a citation to suggest general knowledge of a literary source in any event." See Jon C. Laansma, "2 Timothy, Titus," in *1 Timothy, 2 Timothy, Titus, and Hebrews*, ed. Philip W. Comfort, CornBC 17 (Carol Stream, IL: Tyndale House, 2009), 243.

153. Felix Jacoby, ed., "Epimenides von Kreta (457), Fragmenta," in *Die Fragmente der griechischen Historiker* (Leiden: Brill, 1955), 3B:390–94.

154. See, e.g., Larry J. Perkins, *The Pastoral Letters: A Handbook on the Greek Text*, BHGNT (Waco, TX: Baylor University Press, 2017), 254, note on αὕτη in 1:13.

155. Barrett, *Pastoral Epistles*, 131.

156. Tatian (ca. 120–ca. 180 CE) is disinterested in attribution when he ridicules credulous pagans by accentuating the contradiction between the celebrated tomb of Olympic Zeus in Crete with the pagan line that Cretans are liars (*Or. Graec.* 27.1):

far from certain, but scholars from the modern and premodern eras have advanced others as the original source of the quotation.

Who Else Could Have Written It?

The earliest commentators on Titus were not certain about the origins of the quotation. Outside Titus, the only extant portion appears in the works of Callimachus (*Hymn.* 1.8–9).[157] He may have borrowed the phrase from an earlier poem by Epimenides and incorporated it into his own work as an ironic jab against the misconstrued atheism of the Cretans, but such a speculation is unnecessary. The line seems to echo a misunderstanding, not an actual offense. In this poem's initial phrase, "Cretans [are] always liars" (Κρῆτες ἀεὶ ψεῦσται), Callimachus calls Cretans superlative liars because he supposes that they claim to possess the tomb of the immortal Zeus—a lie, of course, because "you [Zeus] did not die, because you are forever" (σὺ δ' οὐ θάνες, ἐσσὶ γὰρ αἰεί, *Hymn.* 1.9). Callimachus's first *Ode to Zeus* ridicules their seeming audacity. The tomb for Zeus in question does not reference the Greek god but a Cretan hero. So, Callimachus is not attributing lying in general to the Cretans but piously castigating them for claiming to have buried Zeus, who cannot die. He confuses *which* and *what kind of* Zeus the Cretans claimed to have buried.[158] John Calvin, citing previous interpreters and some patristic writers, explains that Callimachus's original claim about Cretan lying was based on this historical misconstrual. Calvin nevertheless takes the quotation at face value as Paul's opinion of the Cretans and asserts, "Paul accepts the truth that he has spoken, for there is no doubt that the Cretans … were very wicked men. The apostle … would not have spoken so harshly of the Cretans without the best of reasons."[159]

τάφος τοῦ Ὀλυμπίου Διὸς καθ' ὑμᾶς δείκνυται κἂν ψεύδεσθαί τις τοὺς Κρῆτας λέγῃ ("the burial of the Olympic God is shown to you, even though someone might say Cretans to be lying"). Harrill suggests that Tatian deliberately obscures Paul's mention of this claim because he wants to distance Christianity from Greek philosophy ("'Without Lies or Deception,'" 454).

157. Callimachus, *Hymns and Epigrams*, ed. George P. Goold, trans. Alexander W. Mair, LCL (Cambridge: Harvard University Press, 1921), 36–37.

158. For a more prosaic version of this tradition, see also Lucian, *Philops.* 3.

159. John Calvin, *Commentaries on the Second Epistle of Paul the Apostle to the Corinthians, and the Epistles to Timothy, Titus, and Philemon*, ed. David W. Torrance

Quinn recognizes that the quotation cannot be attributed with confidence and cites early Christian attempts to identify the "someone" (τις, Titus 1:12) who was saying these things. He writes that, as early as Theodore, people suspected that, "the citation was a popular proverb rather than a quotation of an ancient poem as such."[160] Such roots suggest that the quotation's ancient purveyors may have been either ignorant of, or ambivalent about, its supposed Cretan origins and cast doubt on interpretations that depend on an attribution to Epimenides, first-person speech, or a liar paradox.[161] In addition to Theodore of Mopsuestia, Origen of Alexandria (184–253 CE) attributes the quotation to Callimachus, showing full knowledge of the statement and its context from Callimachus but not from Epimenides (*Cels.* 3.43.1–35). Origen also seems to think that only the portion of the quotation found in the Callimachus hymn was of ancient origin. Among other early writers, Athenagoras (ca. 133–ca. 190 CE) knows the quotation from Callimachus and probably Titus but does not mention Epimenides (*Leg.* 30.3–5). Athenagoras is not, however, making explicit claims about the relationship between the Epistle to Titus and the Callimachus hymn.[162]

Huxley devotes a chapter to Epimenides in his 1969 *Greek Epic Poetry*, and Mounce refers to Huxley's argument as "either unknown or not followed."[163] Huxley points to three main factors that, for him, make Epimenides unlikely to be the author of the quotation. First, he judges the brief sentence to be written in the Doric Greek dialect—what Huxley refers to as "Hesiodic language."[164] Second, the only fragment purported

---

and Thomas Forsyth Torrance, trans. John W. Fraser (Grand Rapids: Eerdmans, 1960), 249–50 (comments on Titus 1:13).

160. Quinn, *Letter to Titus*, 107.

161. See Wolfgang Künne, "On Liars, 'Liars' and Harmless Self-Reference," in *Mind, Values and Metaphysics: Philosophical Essays in Honor of Kevin Mulligan*, ed. Anne Reboul (New York: Springer, 2014), 355–429, for a careful argument that the liar paradox is misapplied to Titus and to Epimenedes, esp. at 376–86. He notes that "are liars" and "always lie" are not equivalent statements and explains that no paradox exists for the Greek statement as is.

162. Tatian (ca. 120–ca. 180 CE) possibly knew the shorter version from Callimachus and likely knew Titus, too, but his citation is corrupted (*Or. Graec.* 27.1). See Tatian, *Die ältesten Apologeten: Texte mit kurzen Einleitungen*, ed. Edgar J. Goodspeed (Göttingen: Vandenhoeck & Ruprecht, 1915), 268–305.

163. Mounce, *Pastoral Epistles*, 398.

164. Huxley, *Greek Epic Poetry*, 81.

to be original to Epimenides appears to regard the voyage of the *Argo*.[165] Huxley conjectures that Epimenides may have invented a Cretan stop on that voyage to add prestige to his island, which may have led a Delphic, non-Cretan poet to retaliate by insulting the Cretans.[166] Third, Huxley considers the attribution to Epimenides the "Apostle's mistake;" because, as he observes, saying that "Cretans are always liars" would be a logical contradiction if spoken by a Cretan. Huxley ignores two important possibilities: first, that Paul is not in fact attributing the quotation to a Cretan; and second, that Paul could have deliberately exploited it as a logical contradiction, as Thiselton, Gray, and others argue. Weaknesses in Huxley's argument aside, he raises doubts about the quotation's conventional attribution.

Christof Zimmer recognizes that the attribution to Epimenides is conjectural, based, even from the earliest sources, "only on indirect references."[167] Zimmer makes an often-neglected argument that the quotation should actually be attributed to Eubulides of Miletus and not a Cretan at all. A great portion of Zimmer's argument has to do with the historical development of the liar paradox in Greek philosophy, and it deserves consideration. He builds up to the following assertion: "it is therefore obvious that a connection between the liar paradox and Epimenides could at best have an illustrative character but by no means any historical one."[168] It must be understood that Zimmer is not referring to the assignment of the paradox to Epimenides in general but to the quite specific attribution of this supposed instance of it in Titus to Epimenides. The plausibility of this quotation not originating with a Cretan undermines interpretations based on the presence of a liar paradox. Zimmer cross-examines proposals for the origin of the quotation and suggests that Clement's attribution to Epimenides—followed unquestioningly by numerous scholars thereafter—was a matter of convenience and conjecture. Epimenides was simply the

---

165. Epimenides, "Die 'Kleinen' griechischen Historiker heute," in *Lustrum*, trans. Hans Joachim Mette (Göttingen: Vandenhoeck & Ruprecht, 1978), 21:29.

166. Huxley, *Greek Epic Poetry*, 81.

167. In Zimmer's words: "lediglich auf indirekte Verweisungen." See Christoph Zimmer, "Die Lügner-Antinomie in Titus 1,12," *LB* 59 (1987): 79.

168. In Zimmer's words: "Es ist deshalb offenbar, dass ein Zusammenhang zwischen der Lügner-Antinomie und Epimenides höchstens illustrativen Charakter haben könnte, keineswegs aber einen irgendwie gearteten historischen" ("Die Lügner-Antinomie," 91).

most famous Cretan that came to Clement's mind.[169] With the attribution to Epimenides so assured in the minds of many, few have interacted with Zimmer's claims. I see only one integral weakness in Zimmer's argument: He makes a very simple but critical oversight—he assumes that the pronouns Paul uses to frame the quotation expect an ethnic Cretan as their referent, which is why Zimmer and many others categorize the quotation as a liar paradox. In chapter 3, under "Basic Pragmatic Processes," I argue that even this assumption is due to the prevalence of miso-Cretan assumptions. Clement of Alexandria's possibly mistaken but benignly intentioned attribution may have hampered unbiased interpretation.[170]

From dubious attributions to embarrassing attempts at historical proof, the history of interpreting this passage exhibits attempts to excuse, condemn, or validate Paul's bigotry. These efforts are especially misdirected if he was not even asserting the substance of the quotation in the first place. The linguistically encoded content of the quotation nevertheless represents a slur on the Cretan people. Careful scholars from the earliest period to the present day do not accept some of the assumptions commensurate with a miso-Cretan reading. Given that the apostle Paul is the purported author of this letter, this interpretive history causes us to ask, Why does Paul appear to be such a bigot here? Does this passage merely serve to disparage Cretans and give readers a negative impression of their innate characteristics and candidacy for redemption, or are we misreading it?

Whether we wish to condemn or excuse Paul, relevance theory now helps us to explain what makes the miso-Cretan interpretation so difficult to resist. As with other passages, the accidents of interpretive history have influenced prevailing interpretations of Titus 1:12 more than the text itself. In other words, Paul appears to be such a bigot in Titus as a result

---

169. Zimmer, "Die Lügner-Antinomie," 81. For additional proposals, see Dibelius and Conzelmann, *Pastoral Epistles*, 136.

170. Marshall explains that some scholars have resisted the temptation to follow Clement in attributing this quotation directly to a Cretan. On account of the grammar and context, they insist that Paul is referring to ne'er-do-wells in the Christian community (with the spare ethno-religious attribute, μάλιστα οἱ ἐκ τῆς περιτομῆς; Titus 1:10), who are causing trouble for the Cretans. Marshall identifies the main problem with this hypothesis as the question of why such an attack on the Cretans would come from a Christian (i.e., Paul), but my proposal rejects the assumption that Paul's use of the quotation is descriptive at all. It serves, rather, an argumentative function (see Marshall, *Critical and Exegetical Commentary*, 198–99).

of our interpretations and not as a result of the epistle's language. I have described several unresolved problems within the history of interpretation of Titus 1:12. Having detailed specific issues that hamper interpretation of this passage, the following summarizes how various interpreters defy some but not all of the assumptions of a miso-Cretan reading.

Inadequate Solutions

Interpreters tend to accommodate their readings to miso-Cretan assumptions largely without questioning them. Bruce Malina and John Pilch, for instance, attempt to illuminate Titus with sensitivity to "an array of social sciences such as anthropology, social psychology, sociolinguistics, and the like,"[171] but they reiterate dubious assumptions that are foreign to the text, attributing the Cretan quotation to Epimenides, advancing already ancient and—they admit—oblique legends of Cretan malfeasance, and accepting the author's sympathy with the quotation's linguistically encoded propositions. "The Pastor concurs!" they exclaim.[172] Their readers do not derive new insights regarding the Cretan quotation, because their social-scientific approach leans on the accretions of interpretive history.

Vogel insists that the concrete details of the Pastoral Epistles, even those unique to the Pastoral Epistles, merely echo the apostle Paul's undisputed works and Acts—mimicking an authentic letter in order to convey a message to an unknown audience. This assumption allows Vogel to present an interpretation of the Cretan quotation in which the author uses the audience's prejudices against both Jews (who presumably no longer had any real influence in the church) and Cretans (an ethnicity they would have liked to distance themselves from) to effect moral reform and theological compliance. According to Vogel, the theology of Titus, especially the nature of the heretical teaching, is vague.[173] He argues that the author placed the heresy in ethnic categories (i.e., Jews and Cretans) from which the audience already wished to distance themselves. The actual audience's distance from the circumstances described in the pseudepigraphic letter facilitated their decision to behave in accordance with the author's instructions.

---

171. Bruce J. Malina and John J. Pilch, *Social-Science Commentary on the Deutero-Pauline Letters* (Minneapolis: Fortress, 2013), xi.
172. Malina and Pilch, *Social-Science Commentary*, 78.
173. Vogel, "Die Kreterpolemik," 255–56.

Vogel offers valuable insights on how ancient ethnography functioned, but in order to sustain his interpretation, he has to ignore critical details in Titus and insist that the message functions only if the entire setting of the letter is fictional.[174] Further, his interpretation requires that the author, as might have been commonplace in the mid-second century, leveraged the ethnocentrism of his audience rather than questioning it. But we should not take for granted that all ancient people, and certainly not the apostle Paul, uncomplicatedly embraced conventional ethnocentric attitudes. Radical questioning of ethnocentric assumptions was not a fringe but a central aspect of the apostle's gospel. Assuming that Titus was written to evoke the apostle Paul and his gospel, nothing would have seemed more out of the ordinary than such an ethnocentric jibe taken at face value.

Several scholars recognize that the contents of the quotation seem to correlate to Paul's concerns with the troublemakers, but they still generally assume that Paul tacitly and uncritically holds a negative view of the Cretans. Towner, for instance, concludes that Paul employs the quotation to highlight a comparison between the proposition of the quotation and the behavior of the presumptuous leaders (1:10–16) as well as a contrast with a good leader's character (1:5–9). Towner is correct about this logical structure and function, but he betrays the power of the miso-Cretan reading to influence interpretation when he goes on to assume that Paul was *also* providing a description of the Cretan population. Towner suggests that households were being disrupted by "dangerous teaching that was tinged with Cretan permissiveness (and other elements more Jewish perhaps)."[175] "Cretan permissiveness" may be implicit in the context of the text on which he is commenting (1:11) but is brought into focus by assuming Paul's sympathy with the quotation. The silent accomplice of miso-Cretan reading also emerges when Towner says that instructions to older women

---

174. See, e.g., Vogel, "Die Kreterpolemik," 257. There Vogel questions the validity of accepting any historical details in Titus, such as the Jewish origin of the opponents' polemic, given the assumption that any such detail must be fictitious (e.g., "Unter dieser Voraussetzung dient die Etikettierung der Häretiker und ihrer Lehre als 'jüdisch' lediglich dazu, den Wirkungsgrad der Polemik noch zu steigern, womit der historischen Aussagekraft auch dieser Details enge Grenzen gesetzt wären"). Vogel perceives, in harmony with the letter's surface portrayal, that the community behind Titus must have afforded social prestige to Jewish-Christian concerns (265).

175. Towner, *Letters to Timothy and Titus*, 697.

(Titus 2:3–5) are "to show themselves as older wives who had successfully emerged from the Cretan way of life."[176] In an earlier commentary, Towner explained that the Cretan quotation was part of Paul's sustained concern with the troublemakers and that the semantics of the quotation correlated to other parts of the rebuke.[177]

Ben Witherington proposes that the jab was directed only against leaders who were ethnically Cretan.[178] Yet the quotation and its frame does not clearly specify such a specific group, and Paul does not portray the troublemakers of Titus 1:10–11 as primarily of Cretan ethnicity. In the end, most scholars concede a reading that requires Paul either to agree with or advance an extremely negative and essentially bigoted view of the Cretan ethnicity.

Most readers readily acknowledge a disjunction between the attitude of the Cretan quotation and the reputation of the apostle Paul. The broader ethical, theological, and anthropological teachings of Titus, especially as represented in the gospel summaries of 2:11–14 and 3:3–7, understand God's activity in history and in individual lives to be redemptive and transformative. The miso-Cretan reading and its accompanying assumptions do not countenance such change.

The text of Titus exhibits more subtlety than the miso-Cretan reading allows, but scholars continue to hold some of its doubtful assumptions. Thiselton, for instance, proposes that Paul presented a classic logical paradox, a deliberate contradiction to expose the severe limitations of language to define people truthfully. Thiselton explains that, in order to reset the controversy in Crete, Paul demonstrates the absurdity and futility of labeling selves and others on account of the asymmetry between third- and first-person speech.[179] Paul indicates that the quotation was spoken in the third person. On the lips of a Cretan, however, it could be taken ironically, humorously, as a self-defeating "liar paradox"—a device well-known and enjoyed in antiquity. Thiselton rightly insists that identifying the group to which Paul's speaker belonged is essential to interpretation. Thiselton

---

176. Towner, *Letters to Timothy and Titus*, 724.

177. Philip Towner, *1–2 Timothy and Titus*, IVPNTC 14 (Downers Grove, IL: InterVarsity, 1994), 229–32, esp. 231.

178. See Ben Witherington III, *A Socio-rhetorical Commentary on Titus, 1–2 Timothy and 1–3 John*, vol. 1 of *Letters and Homilies for Hellenized Christians* (Downers Grove, IL: IVP Academic, 2006), 122–24.

179. Thiselton, "Logical Role," 221.

explains that the grammatical distinction between first- and third-person speech leads to a logical conundrum that uncovers Paul's real point—the Cretans had been mislabeled as irredeemably vicious, which would be a problem for the gospel in Crete. According to Thiselton, Paul wants his audience to see that first-person self-contradictions are unreliable means of labeling persons. But Paul seems to be more disturbed by the troublemakers (1:10–11) than Thiselton's explanation suggests. Paul does not ask for a cordial apology; rather, he orders a stern rebuke (1:13). Thiselton's proposal also depends on assuring the attribution of this quotation, which is uncertain.[180]

Three fundamental assumptions of Thiselton's proposal are problematic. First, his interpretation assumes that Paul draws the quotation from a Cretan, specifically Epimenides. This attribution is uncertain but necessary for his reading. The self-contradictory logic of the liar paradox disintegrates in the mouth of a third-person speaker.[181] It is not certain that Paul pointed to the speaker of this statement as someone other than a contemporary troublemaker; the possible ancient origins of the quotation do not appear to concern Paul. Thus, Thiselton acquiesces to one of the premises of the miso-Cretan reading. Second, his interpretation requires that several of the pronouns in the context have an unusual usage (e.g., cataphoric, rather than anaphoric; resumptive, rather than continuative) or difficult-to-process referent (e.g., null or distal). Third, his view requires multiple steps of reasoning and considerably specific background knowledge to process properly, making it less plausible if a more straightforward interpretation is available.

I have shown how scholars assume that Paul's use of the quotation simply aligned with general negative attitudes toward Cretans. To Mounce,

---

180. Thiselton, "Logical Role," 219–21. Hanson also sees the quotation as an example of the liar paradox but assumes that the dilemma is between either admitting the moral viciousness of Cretans or denouncing Epimenedes as untrustworthy. Although he begins his comments on the phrase "one of themselves" (1:12), "This should mean one of the heretics," he ignores this fitting intuition under the influence of miso-Cretan reading assumptions (see Hanson, *Pastoral Epistles*, 176–77).

181. The earliest attribution of the quotation to Epimenides (Clement of Alexandria, *Strom.* 1.14) does not mention a liar paradox. Jerome's reading, explicitly following Clement, negates a liar paradox (*Comm. Tit.* 1:12), because he takes the quotation at face value as an insult Paul leveled. Hoklotubbe points out that interpretations that depend on the rhetorical thrust of the liar paradox may not "do justice to the" entire saying ("Civilized Christ-Followers," 374).

for instance, the quotation stands on its own as Paul's indictment against them, "in agreement with the worldwide reputation of the Cretans."[182] This claim, however, does not comport with Mounce's structural observation that Paul contrasts ideal leaders in 1:5–9 "with the characteristics of the opponents" in 1:10–16.[183] The troublemakers' *behavior* is just as much in view as their character. The reference to genealogies in 3:9 further suggests a hereditary-ethnic dimension to the problem. Mounce recognizes that Paul objects to those "who taught Jewish myths and human commandments (1:10–16)," but does not consider how the act of degrading the Cretan populace might have expressed the ethno-religious superiority myth that Paul opposed.[184]

To make the Cretan quotation of Titus more intelligible within its cultural context, Hoklotubbe contextualizes it alongside a carefully examined collection of near-contemporary and other ancient ethnographic literature illumined by postcolonial theory. His sociological approach places Titus in the context of early Christian identity formation within a hierarchy including imperial Romans, cultural Greeks, Cretans (with their own claims to Greek prestige foiled by the quotation), and Christians (of all, potentially the most despised as "barbaric and superstitious").[185] According to Hoklotubbe, the anonymous author of Titus was trying to help readers envision and embody a more dignified identity on this hierarchy by demeaning (in harmony with imperial Roman culture) both Jews and inferior Cretans. Hoklotubbe does not claim that this aim was primary for the author but that it does explain some of the derogatory dynamic toward both Jews and Cretans that he perceives in the letter.

Hoklotubbe's examination of competitive imperial and ancient ethnography in reconstructing the cultural context of Titus offers a valuable sociological background to how the quotation might fit into the discourse, yet I do not think that his conclusions are assured. We examine the text from different angles (his sociological, mine linguistic), but I challenge several assumptions that seem both necessary for his argument and yet uncertain: (1) the attribution of the quotation to Epimenides; (2) the dating of Titus to the mid-second century; (3) that respectability was a chief concern for the author; (4) the importance within Titus of key con-

---

182. Mounce, *Pastoral Epistles*, 404.
183. Mounce, *Pastoral Epistles*, 406.
184. Mounce, *Pastoral Epistles*, 408 (see also 413, 416).
185. Hoklotubbe, "Civilized Christ-Followers," 370, 375, 387.

cepts in Hoklotubbe's argument (e.g., achieving esteem through παιδεία); (5) that the relations between the social identities in play were known and stable enough to accomplish the triangulation he proposes; (6) that, for the sake of "the colonial gaze," the author sets the audience as a "third and superior entity" over against the author's "inscribed opponents," who fit the description of "barbaric Cretans and superstitious Judeans," rather than as an entity that overlaps in reality with both groups and that must learn to honor its members.[186] It seems that Paul calls out the presumptions of the circumcision group (Titus 1:10) because he objects to their inferiorizing program, not because he is trying to place Christians more favorably on a preestablished imperial hierarchy.[187]

Several of the claims that the above-referenced scholars make about the Cretan quotation are sound and helpful for interpretation. First, some demonstrate that the substance of the quotation compares with the behavior of the troublemakers of Titus 1:10–16.[188] Second, some contend that Paul employed subtle uses of logic and rhetoric to subvert the surface meaning of the quotation.[189] Third, many recognize the thrust of the quotation as inherently disparaging, although they pursue different solutions—for example, harmonizing it with Paul's other concerns for the church or highlighting prejudicial attitudes elsewhere in the book.[190] These helpful intermediate conclusions may ameliorate

---

186. Hoklotubbe, "Civilized Christ-Followers," 385, 370, and passim. On the importance within Titus of key concepts in Hoklotubbe's argument (e.g., achieving esteem through παιδεία, see esp. 378–84. The subject of the verb παιδεύω is God's grace, not classical Greek culture. Even though I grant that the list of vices to eschew and virtues to adopt corresponds to a "flexible set of cardinal virtues" (385), Paul is not accepting the usage in any uncomplicated way. In fact, he seems to subvert it.

187. According to Hoklotubbe, the author of Titus intended to "elevate followers of Christ along an ethnic hierarchy and to construct a 'civilized,' Christ-following subject, distinguished from barbaric 'Cretans' and superstitious 'Judeans'" ("Civilized Christ-Followers," 375). "One strategy available to the author of Titus to persuade Romans of the relative 'civility' of Christ-followers was to highlight the deficiencies of other competing ethnic groups, while simultaneously emphasizing the superior virtues of his own group in order to elevate their status along an ethnic hierarchy" (384).

188. E.g., Johnson, *Letters to Paul's Delegates*, 225–29; Towner, *Letters to Timothy and Titus*, 74–76, 699–700.

189. E.g., Thiselton, "Logical Role"; Gray, "Liar Paradox"; Thomas G. Long, *1 and 2 Timothy and Titus*, BTCB (Louisville: Westminster John Knox, 2016), 263–67.

190. E.g., Kidd, "Titus as Apologia"; Faber, "'Evil Beasts, Lazy Gluttons'"; Stege-

some of the worst and most offensive appropriations of the passage, but they do not lead to an entirely satisfying understanding of Paul's use of the quotation. One thing that gets in the way, as I have shown, is that each interpreter succumbs to one or all of the questionable assumptions of the miso-Cretan reading.

Communication Theory as a Way Forward

Some approaches to Titus do not set out to ascertain its meaning within its context as a distinct literary production with communicative intent. Among them are those who assume the fragmentary nature of the Pastorals or their artless assembly. "In modern scholarship," Jay Twomey writes, "They have compared the innovation of Paul to the traditionalism of the Pastor, and they have found the Pastor wanting."[191] Attempts to contextualize Paul's use of the quotation, under such views, are misguided and futile. Extracted units of meaning that would otherwise be the building blocks of an argument only serve to answer anachronistic questions.[192]

Paul's use of the Cretan quotation is mainly a question for those who are interested in Titus at the level of *ostensive communication*—uses of words that have communicative intent, as opposed to various forms of word salad, event logs, or other forms of writing not intended to convey a cohesive and coherent message but simply to keep information on record. The fuller phrase "ostensive inferential communication" used in relevance theory is implicit because of the inferential nature of all communication.[193] If Titus is communication, then a communication theory is in order.

Harrison's view that the Pastorals are a patchwork of Pauline fragments and/or late first- and early second-century traditions crudely cobbled

---

mann, "Anti-Semitic and Racist Prejudices"; Huizenga, *1–2 Timothy, Titus*.

191. Twomey, *Pastoral Epistles*, 4; see also Miller, *Pastoral Letters*. For a thorough argument against the Pastoral Epistles containing even a remnant of authentic Pauline material, see Hanson, *Pastoral Epistles*; also Cook, "Pastoral Fragments Reconsidered."

192. E.g., the detailed but fragmented approach toward the quotation by Dibelius and Conzelmann, *Pastoral Epistles*, 135–37.

193. Italicized above for its technical significance, referring to the stock and trade of relevance theory. See, e.g., Clark, *Relevance Theory*, 112–19; Robyn Carston and Seiji Uchida, eds., *Relevance Theory: Applications and Implications*, P&B NS 37 (Philadelphia: Benjamins, 1998), 298. For more detail, see chs. 3–4.

together has lost currency. Scholars now generally accept that they were composed with coherence and purpose.[194]

The author presented the book of Titus as a letter from Paul, which, in addition to any other approaches employed, calls for a reading strategy that wrestles constructively with the literary context and implied historical setting. If we presuppose that features of the text contribute more or less to a contextual argument, then exposing a pseudonymous writer's strategies for achieving credibility can only *partially* illuminate the rationale for including any portion (e.g., the Cretan quotation). Therefore, to the extent that scholars view features in the Pastorals, such as the Cretan quotation, as mere reinforcement for the ruse of Pauline authorship, they leave the question of meaning unanswered.[195]

---

194. Further, I have seen no evidence to suggest that 1:10–16 or any part thereof is an interpolation. Citing Norbert Brox, Faber writes, "The most radical interpretation of Titus 1:10–16 views the citation as interpolation. This view is advanced by Norbert Brox, who suggests that the quotation is inappropriate to scripture generally, and ill-suited to the Epistle to Titus." See Faber, "'Evil Beasts, Lazy Gluttons,'" 137; Brox, *Die Pastoralbriefe*, RNT (Regensburg: Pustet, 1963), 288. See also Van Nes's discussion of post-Pauline interpolation in the Corpus Paulinum, esp. George Barr's scalometric work, in *Pauline Language*, 130–34.

195. Several writers view concrete segments in the Pastoral Epistles, including the Cretan quotation, as serving mainly to evoke historical vividness (e.g., Dibelius and Conzelmann, *Pastoral Epistles*, 135–37; Cook, "Pastoral Fragments," 122–23; Vogel, "Die Kreterpolemik"). Donelson suggests that the scenario of Titus in Crete was invented based on Acts 27 (see *Pseudepigraphy and Ethical Argument*, 61). In contrast, Mounce contends that, if the Pastorals represent the generation after Paul handing down tradition, such assumptions do not adequately account for references in these letters that anticipate reunion between Paul and his delegates (*Pastoral Epistles*, lviii).

2
Relevance Theory: Insights for Biblical Interpretation

The discipline of biblical studies grows more eclectic every year, incorporating numerous tools and techniques from the fields of history, sociology, psychology, philosophy, literature, and linguistics, to name a few. In modern linguistics, few theories have more currency and prominence than relevance theory. In recent years, several biblical scholars have brought the insights of relevance theory to bear on their study of Scripture.

Relevance theory analyzes and explains the cognitive processes by which hearers correctly infer speaker intentions, given the inherent underdeterminacy of speech. In a sense, theorists reverse-engineer natural language processing to discover how readers arrive at their conclusions. By doing so, relevance theory helps scholars discern mismatches between speaker intention and audience uptake as well as critique and evaluate interpretations for their plausibility in an original context. Although conventional tools exist for similar functions, relevance theory offers a comprehensive theory and a consistent terminology. Relevance theory helps steer scholars toward better interpretations, first by critiquing flawed interpretations—relevance theory is a theory of communication, not a method of interpretation—and second by sensitizing scholars to the cognitive environment, salience, and other cognitive-linguistic factors with respect to the original audience.

Although we refer to speech, speakers, hearing, and listeners, it is recognized that relevance theory applies to written texts, as I explain briefly below. This chapter provides a more substantial introduction to relevance theory, especially to those insights that are most pertinent to interpreting Scripture.[1] Chapters 3–6 expand on its details while addressing their

---

1. For a list of some biblical scholars who provide fuller general introductions to relevance theory, see the introduction.

application to particular features of Titus. The description in this chapter elucidates the promise of a relevance-guided biblical hermeneutic.

Disambiguating Schools of Pragmatics

Because Titus takes the form of a letter, it calls for an interpretive approach that appreciates its communicative intent. I therefore base this study in the linguistic discipline of relevance theory, which shares the narrow scope of linguistic pragmatics that is regularly dubbed the "British-American" (sometimes "Anglo-American") model. I must note the definitional distinction between two broad schools of pragmatics to indicate the specific branch that informs my research. Stephen Levinson explains the Continental versus the British-American approaches, which each school calls *pragmatics*. The main difference is scope. The Continental school is broadly applied across psycholinguistic, sociolinguistic, anthropological, and other disciplines without sharp boundaries, while the British-American school is linguistics-focused.[2] For the sake of narrow focus and material appropriateness, this study is guided by the British-American model of linguistic pragmatics, of which relevance theory is a species.[3]

General Description

Relevance theory explains how humans come to understand one another when the logical and informational content of their speech is incomplete or not explicit. One of its fundamental premises is the underdeterminative character of speech—that spoken and written communication achieves its function in society in spite of being, in virtually all instances, incomplete. The task of linguistics, then, is to discern *how* or *why* speech works.

---

2. Stephen C. Levinson, *Pragmatics*, CTL (Cambridge: Cambridge University Press, 1983), ix, 1–34. Levinson explains that he writes his textbook on pragmatics with a focus on the Anglo-American approach because the Continental approach is broad and encompassing of disciplines outside linguistics proper and because the Anglo-American approach focuses more on linguistics and philosophical approaches toward "ordinary language."

3. Yan Huang and Billy Clark also discuss the distinctions and concerns of each model with more detail. See Huang, "Micro- and Macro-Pragmatics: Remapping Their Terrains," *IRP* 5 (2013): 129–62; Clark, *Relevance Theory*, 1–42.

The chief question is, How are listeners able to understand speakers in the absence of critical information?

Although relevance theory is now conversant with the broader cognitive disciplines and relies more and more on the hard sciences (e.g., neurology), it started in the domain of philosophical linguistics and still is at home answering the questions posed by a philosophy of language. More specifically, it is a species of linguistic pragmatics, a field of study first defined by H. Paul Grice in the 1960s during a lasting wave of philosophical linguistic developments that one might call the cognitive turn in linguistics. J. L. Austin and Noam Chomsky were fellow surfers.

Grice addressed the issue of underdeterminacy by positing a *cooperative principle*. That is, one could explain that human language has worked for so long by positing that communicators cooperate with one another in the making of meaning in such a way that successful communication benefits them cognitively, socially, and materially. More specifically, because Grice saw speakers as the producers and controllers of language, it was *their* behavior that most interested him. Grice articulated somewhat commonsense assumptions about the rules that speakers supposedly adhere to in the process of conversation. Foremost was the assumption that participants in a conversation observe certain unstated patterns of cooperation in order to make speech work. Under the cooperative principle, Grice defined several maxims (e.g., of quantity, of quality, of relevance, of manner) and submaxims that speakers appeared to follow. He reasoned that the principle of cooperation placed implicit obligations on the speaker to obey certain rules, such as "Do not use more words than are necessary" (maxim of quantity) or "Do not say something you know to be false" (maxim of quality). The true meaning of "what was said" (Grice's semitechnical term for utterances)[4] was not found in decoding the logical form of the sentence but in the *implicatures* of the utterance—that is, what the speaker intended to come of it. Importantly, an utterance is sentence-plus-context.

The architects of relevance theory, British linguists Dan Sperber and Deirdre Wilson, refined Grice's philosophy into a viable theory by smoothing out some inconsistencies and delineating a set of principles that placed Grice's maxim of relevance at the center of understanding why communication has worked for humans. Relevance theory was then able to explain and predict the success of natural language. For instance, the reason people

---

4. Clark, *Relevance Theory*, 167–68, 171.

did not use more words than necessary or say what they knew to be false was that such would not be relevant.[5] Sperber and Wilson argued that all of Grice's principles and maxims could be subsumed under the maxim of *relevance*, with its twin assertions—the cognitive and the communicative principles of relevance (see below).

Relevance theorists appreciate Grice's contributions to the philosophy of language, but they generally think that he did not go far enough in assessing the extent of inference required to interpret speech. Whereas Grice considered many implicatures to be conventional and many meanings to be intrinsic to semantic forms,[6] relevance theorists contend that inference is required even at the level of what seem to be explicit forms. Hence, they developed the concept of explicature—the implicit meaning of evidence made manifest by the speaker but not necessarily encoded semantically.

Explicature is a critical concept for understanding the process of utterance interpretation according to relevance theory. Sperber and Wilson's own definition may be helpful: "What we are calling the explicature is close to what might be commonsensically described as the explicit content, or what is said, or the literal meaning of the utterance. The less explicit the meaning, the more responsibility the hearer must take for the interpretation he constructs."[7] Green offers this technical definition: "The explicatures of an utterance consist of the information encoded in the sign system and all the information inferentially connected to it through reference assignment, disambiguation, and enrichment."[8]

In another critical development, Sperber and Wilson also reversed the theoretical orientation of natural language processing. Whereas Grice's starting point was an implicit contract between interlocutors that mainly influenced the *speaker's* behavior, relevance theorists approach utterance interpretation as a cognitive process from the *hearer's* perspective. This subtle difference is theoretically important. Relevance theory endeavors

---

5. Of course, as a comprehensive theory of language, relevance theory must also explain lying. See, e.g., Yong Liu, "A Study of Lying from the Perspective of Relevance Theory" (MA thesis, Huazhong Normal University, 2009).

6. Conventional implicatures are essentially form based, though more socially complex.

7. Dan Sperber and Deirdre Wilson, "Pragmatics," in *Oxford Handbook of Contemporary Philosophy*, OHO (London: Oxford University Press, 2007), 481.

8. Green, "Relevance Theory and Biblical Interpretation" (2013), 269.

to delineate how hearers think through language. The role of the hearer is crucial in Grice's scheme, but his key assumption of cooperation issues in a catalog of maxims that speakers supposedly follow. Most relevance theorists, although they appreciate Grice's groundbreaking legacy, insist that he did not adequately reckon the extent to which utterance meaning must be inferred. Instead of understanding the cooperative principle to place implicit obligations on the speaker, they understand that the principle of relevance requires the hearer to infer meaning and intention. So, communication is viewed as a cognitive-interpretive process that ascribes intention (approximating the speaker's) rather than a matter of producing sentences.

Relevance theory attempts to explain why hearers understand speakers to mean things or to *intend* things by their speech. Theorists reason that communication has worked for the species in the development of social, cultural, and material existence because hearers have been generally successful at discerning speaker intentions. So, they investigate how humans successfully comprehend utterances given the underdeterminacy of linguistically encoded semantic representations (i.e., sentences). Their task is to analyze and describe how humans in fact interpret natural language communication. They begin descriptively by examining successful instances of utterance interpretation and move inductively toward more encompassing claims about how language functions.

To support its economic theory of language, relevance theory makes two standard assumptions, one about human cognition and one about human communication. These two principles undergird the many particulars of the theory and set it apart from grammatico-semantic or decoding approaches. The principles are as follows:

1. the cognitive principle of relevance: human cognition is geared toward the maximization of relevance (that is, the achievement of as many contextual effects as possible for as little effort as possible)
2. the communicative principle of relevance: every ostensive stimulus communicates a presumption of its own optimal relevance[9]

---

9. These are standard definitions (see, e.g., Carston and Uchida, *Relevance Theory*, 29–34).

A few points about these two assertions are in order. Note the perspective of the principles; they refer to what happens in the mind of the hearer.[10] They are implicit assumptions that make communication work. It is why subjects were more likely to spend time and effort deciphering computer-generated gibberish sentences when they were told that humans produced them than they were to try to interpret human-composed poetry when they were told that a computer produced it.[11] Regina Blass, a student of Wilson, offers a helpful expansion of the communicative principle: "By demanding attention from the audience she [the speaker] suggests that the information she is offering is relevant enough to be worth the audience's attention."[12]

In the economy of cognitive effects, relevance theory recognizes what research on recall processing speed and early language development reinforces—namely, some speech requires more cognitive effort to grasp and some less. When hearers arrive at what seems to be a relevant interpretation, they stop processing (even if they have mistaken the speaker's intention). Most theorists would say that hearers follow the path of least effort and stop when their expectations of relevance are met.[13]

The importance of this insight for biblical studies, where modern readers are interpreting ancient literature, is readily apparent. Original audiences had access to cognitive content and cultural assumptions that modern readers are fortunate merely to approximate, requiring a careful (and, I would add, humble) process of inference. The assets by which natural language users (including the Bible's original audiences) interpret speech have been called their *cognitive environment*, which is inevitably mismatched between audiences. Constructing the cognitive environment of an ancient audience requires humility and keen attention to the speech itself, which makes manifest both requisite evidence and lacunae. According to relevance theorists, interpretation is a dialectical process that

---

10. Sperber and Wilson, "Pragmatics" (2007), 473.

11. Raymond W. Gibbs Jr. and Markus Tendahl, "Cognitive Effort and Effects in Metaphor Comprehension: Relevance Theory and Psycholinguistics," *M&L* 21 (2006): 388–89.

12. Regina Blass, *Relevance Relations in Discourse: A Study with Special Reference to Sissala*, CSL 55 (Cambridge: Cambridge University Press, 1990), 43.

13. See Sperber and Wilson, "Pragmatics" (2007), 474. For a summary of a "relevance-guided comprehension heuristic," which incorporates this concept, see Clark, *Relevance Theory*, 34–40.

involves mutual adjustment between intermediate conclusions and the contextual assumptions needed to arrive at them toward a final construal.

Relevance theorists understand that hearers ascribe intention to speakers in the process of communication. Without this assumption of cooperation, communication will not occur. That is why the specific stock and trade of relevance theory is *ostensive inferential communication*. *Ostensive* indicates that, even beyond the utterance, the speaker communicates an intention to be understood. *Inferential* indicates that the utterance cannot be understood solely by means of its logical-semantic form and must be processed by the hearer to derive meaning and intention. Because of this, the insights of relevance theory are consistent with an inductive (i.e., evidence-based) approach to Bible study. *Communication* indicates that language is a cooperative effort between human speakers and listeners to accomplish things, including making meaning, together.

According to Sperber and Wilson, hearers take the following actions in discerning utterance meaning: (1) construct an appropriate hypothesis about explicatures by developing the linguistically encoded logical form; (2) construct an appropriate hypothesis about the intended contextual assumptions (implicated premises); and (3) construct an appropriate hypothesis about intended contextual implications (implicated conclusions).[14] By *implicated premises* they do not mean what is implied by the utterance in an informational sense but rather the assumptions required to make sense of the utterance from the standpoint of cognitive effects. Contextual assumptions include implicated premises as well as basic knowledge from the shared cognitive environment required for comprehension. Billy Clark condenses the aforementioned list of actions: "working out explicatures, working out implicated premises, and working out implicated conclusions."[15] Theorists are careful to note that these steps are logically sequential but that they actually occur rapidly and virtually simultaneously in the human mind. The three insights that organize my study—(1) the inferential nature of communication, (2) the hearer's role in communication, and (3) the nonpropositional dimensions of communication—roughly correspond to the objects of these three actions—explicatures, contextual assumptions, and implicated conclusions.

---

14. See Sperber and Wilson, "Pragmatics" (2007), 479–84.
15. Clark, *Relevance Theory*, 144.

Importantly, theorists do not claim a specific ordering of these actions, and they outline several specific tasks that may be required in the process of utterance interpretation. These include disambiguation of terms, reference assignment, decoding deictic terms, determining explicatures, deciphering implicatures, interpreting vague expressions, and working out ellipsed material. All of these narrower tasks are logically discrete but virtually simultaneous and *pro re nata* (born for the present circumstance). Not all tasks are required in each instance of utterance interpretation. Clark speaks of these tasks as questions that might need to be answered, allowing that different utterances require different sets of questions or tasks.[16]

Theorists emphasize two critical facts about actual utterance interpretation: first, it is a dialectical process, such that necessary tasks are completed in dependence on the results of each; and, second, the necessary processes are generally rapid and intuitive. The tasks may be logically separable but are functionally codependent. Nevertheless, theorists base their outlines of processes on a narrow set of shared principles that generally vary only somewhat in detail and terminology.

Some features of relevance theory apply globally to all instances of interpretation, because relevance theory is based on patterns of human cognition. First, the hearer's assumption of relevance instigates a desire for worthwhile cognitive effects in the processing of an utterance. That is, a hearer seeks to derive cognitive effects that will satisfactorily reward the processing effort expended.[17] Second, interpretation involves a nonsequential, dialectic process that, from the standpoint of natural languages, is rapid, intuitive, and virtually simultaneous.[18] Therefore, cross-reference between the insights described below and developed further in chapters 3–6 is critical. Third, relevance theory elevates the importance of speak-

---

16. Clark, *Relevance Theory*, 22.
17. Huang, "Micro- and Macro-Pragmatics," 140–44. He writes, "Grounded in a general view of human cognition, the central tenet of relevance theory is that the human cognitive system works in such a way as to tend to maximize relevance with respect to cognition and communication. Thus, the communicative principle of relevance is responsible for the recovery of both the explicit and implicit content of an utterance."
18. Gibbs notes, "Introspection is an unreliable indicator of unconscious mental activity"; so we need insight into "the underlying cognitive mechanisms used in normal language understanding" ("Intentionalist Controversy," 196). Theorists have made tremendous progress both empirically and analytically in this regard. Gibbs further states, "Cognitive scientists are suspicious of conscious introspections as a source of data in theorizing about cognitive processes" (198).

ers, hearers, and the effects of the utterances on them over the semantics of words and structures in the process of interpretation. For these reasons, the introductory definitions provided below will be essential as well as free cross-reference, just as in human cognition, to relevance-theoretical principles.

Relevance theorists seek not only to understand how interlocutors comprehend one another but also to explain why they sometimes misinterpret utterances. Misunderstandings often involve a mismatch between the speaker's expectations of which assumptions the hearer should access and which assumptions the hearer actually does access. Difference in idiom as well as distance in time and space, and thus culture, can compound and exacerbate problematic mismatches between speaker assumptions and listener assumptions, as when modern readers interpret ancient documents.

The too often unrecognized difficulty with applying the theory to biblical studies is that it is not a method of interpretation. Rather, it is an explanatory framework for why specific audiences and readers come to their interpretations and a means of critiquing whether they have followed the rules expected by the speaker or writer. In many cases, relevance theory offers coherent and consistent explanations for faulty exegesis. Its native terms can help scholars explain why readers would come to an otherwise untenable conclusion—for example, a mismatch between the contextual assumptions of the author and the modern reader, a mismatch between what was salient (and thereby cognitively rewarding) for original audiences versus modern eavesdroppers.

This brief introductory description of relevance theory cannot cover every aspect. The best treatments of relevance theory in biblical studies provide an overview, but anyone serious about applying the insights of relevance theory to biblical studies should read the critical literature directly. With this basic, albeit incomplete, description of relevance theory, let us consider a handful of critical corollaries.

Relevance Theory and Literature

Relevance theory has always focused on natural language, but live speech is not its only domain of applicability. Several scholars have argued for and demonstrated the application of relevance theory to literature or written speech. For instance, Seiji Uchida explains that features appearing to be unique to literary texts (e.g., suspense and twist) actually accomplish communicative functions that parallel spoken language. He asserts that the basic explanatory claims of relevance theory (à la Sperber and Wilson's classic 1986 treatment) apply to written as well as spoken language.[19] According to Uchida, the human mind uses the same basic strategies and processes to interpret both live speech and literary texts. The cognitive principle and the communicative principle (defined above) apply to both, although the process with written texts can be slowed down and drawn out, as eyes can return where ears cannot. Because the biblical text is written language that ostensively conveys some meaning, relevance theory is a fitting discipline to apply.[20]

Blass argues that the linguistic features of written and spoken discourse do not fundamentally differ, so the interpretive insights of relevance theory are applicable to texts, including the Bible.[21] Anne Furlong asserts no decisive difference between the comprehension of written and spoken language: "An account of literary interpretation is best placed within a general theory of communication and cognition [i.e., relevance theory].... Literary interpretation is a special case of the interpretive strategies used in spontaneous comprehension, rather than a deviation from them."[22] Furlong provides several reasons why relevance theory is suited to literary interpretation and argues that relevance theory supplies an ideal framework for literary interpretation studies: "Relevance theory provides just the kind of coherent, unified approach that the field needs."[23] What is relevant to a context constitutes the key to explaining how hearers and readers arrive at their interpretations; because, as theorists hold, both hearers and readers follow one governing principle—relevance—in the process of interpretation.

Authorial Intention in Relevance Theory

Owing to trends in philosophical psychology, art criticism, and literary interpretation in the mid- to late twentieth century, it had become passé

---

19. Seiji Uchida, "Text and Relevance," in Carston and Uchida, *Relevance Theory*, 161–78. For the version of relevance theory that Uchida interacts with and makes claims about, see Dan Sperber and Deirdre Wilson, *Relevance: Communication and Cognition*, 2nd ed. (Oxford: Blackwell, 1996).

20. The relevance theory literature typically uses *ostensively*, as distinct from *ostensibly*, with regard to the connotation that an utterance conveys meaning of relevance to the hearer.

21. Blass, *Relevance Relations in Discourse*, 10; for her full argument, see 7–42.

22. Furlong, "Relevance Theory," 26. See also Anne Furlong, "A Modest Proposal: Linguistics and Literary Studies," *CJAL* 10 (2007): 323–45.

23. See Furlong, "Relevance Theory," 7.

a generation or two ago to assert a retrievable authorial intention. But cognitive linguists such as Raymond Gibbs Jr. examine the psychological and hermeneutical aspects of the question of intention and criticize the abandonment of speaker/author intention as a dubious consequence of philosophical approaches and a contradiction of overwhelming empirical evidence. Gibbs writes, "A widely-held assumption in contemporary cognitive science is that listeners'/ readers' recognitions of speakers'/authors' intentions is [sic] a crucial aspect of utterance interpretation."[24]

Although arguments for and against *Pauline* authorship may be inconclusive, readers can see that Titus has sufficient coherence in its canonical form to posit a purpose. In other words, we perceive that someone with intention authored Titus. Stephen Pattemore explains that relevance theory "does treat a text as a record of a genuine communication event."[25] Linguists reason that intention is pertinent, even necessary, to meaning, so interpreters must seek it to the extent that it is recoverable. The primary route into the meaning of Titus begins with its self-presentation and reception as a letter.

The most current work in pragmatics, and specifically relevance theory, assumes that communication involves ostensive intention and that it is not only a *worthwhile* objective to discern this intended meaning but an *achievable* one, too. Whereas, Gibbs notes, "Continental philosophers and literary theorists have proclaimed that authorial intentions do not constrain the interpretation of literary and philosophical texts," the current turn in cognitive linguistics has reaffirmed the importance of intention on the part of speakers and writers.[26] Due to current research, communication theorists reject the axiom that a speaker's or writer's intentions are either irretrievable (on account of diverse subjective factors in the hearer or reader) or irrelevant to the enterprise of discerning meaning. Noël Carroll recounts the history of mistrust in the enterprise of

---

24. Gibbs also explains, "My use of utterance refers both to oral and written linguistic acts." See Raymond W. Gibbs Jr., "The Intentionalist Controversy and Cognitive Science," *PP* 6 (1993): 182.

25. Pattemore, *People of God*, 28.

26. Gibbs provides the following example of the preceding turn *from* intention: "Many legal theorists argue that the interpretation of the Constitution does not depend on understanding something about the intentions of its original framers in 1787" ("Intentionalist Controversy," 184).

discerning authorial intention (i.e., the intentional fallacy) in the modern era and argues that it was misguided and self-contradictory.[27]

The starting premise of relevance theory is the observation that ostensive inferential communication has tended to be successful for humanity. Robyn Carston and Seiji Uchida explain that the three words of the technical phrase "ostensive inferential communication" signify speaker intention, hearer processing, and cooperative effort.[28] Because communication is inferential, hearers have a significant but delimited role. Because communication is ostensive, a retrievable speaker intention is assumed. Gibbs explains, "Authorial intentions provide the main criterion for textual interpretation that enables literary analysis to be objective.... Without authorial intentions there is simply too much indeterminacy and instability in the public linguistic conventions governing meaning, hence there is no stable object for literary study and criticism."[29]

Development of Relevance Theory

According to Yan Huang, pragmatics is "the study of language in use."[30] Levinson regards the pioneer of pragmatics as Charles Morris, who first coined the term *pragmatics* in reference to one aspect of semiotics. According to Levinson, one of Morris's major contributions to semiotics was his introduction of a trichotomy that included *semantics*, which deals with the relationship between signs and the things they represent; *syntax*, which deals with the relationships between signs; and *pragmatics*, which deals with the relationship between signs and their interpreters. Morris's conceptions were broad and nontechnical and did not constitute a theory of language.[31]

Grice applied pragmatics specifically to natural language use. His inquiries were sparked by the assumptions inherent in this critical

---

27. Noël Carroll, "Interpretation and Intention: The Debate between Hypothetical and Actual Intentionalism," *Metaphilosophy* 31 (2000): 75–95. Carroll's evaluation of growing streams of intentionalist interpretation concerns literature, making it pertinent to our inquiry. He argues that actual authorial intention is paramount to interpretation, especially when a text's meaning is contested or uncertain (see, e.g., 76, 89).

28. Carston and Uchida, *Relevance Theory*, 298.

29. Gibbs, "Intentionalist Controversy," 193.

30. Huang, "Micro- and Macro-Pragmatics," 130.

31. Levinson, *Pragmatics*, 2.

synthetic question: How are humans able to understand one another consistently and successfully, even when the linguistically encoded meanings of their utterances to each other are incomplete?[32] Linguistic pragmaticists recognize the inferential nature of human communication and, in semiotic terms, focus on the relation between signs and their interpreters.[33] Linguistic pragmaticists and relevance theorists have been critiquing, refining, and developing the discipline for nearly fifty years, but Grice's ideas are still considered both pioneering and influential in the field. One of his major contributions was proposing a philosophy and grammar for calculating and describing the gap between the linguistically encoded content of a statement and a speaker's intentions with the utterance, and for explaining how hearers successfully and consistently bridge that gap in natural languages.

Grice recognizes that natural language has an inferential dimension and that speakers and hearers, as well as writers and readers, are involved in a cooperative process—hence, his cooperative principle. Grice presents this principle as follows: "Make your conversational contribution such as is required, at the stage at which it occurs, by the accepted purpose or direction of the talk exchange in which you are engaged."[34] He understood much natural language to require inference, but later relevance theorists extended this pragmatic claim to say that linguistic communication is inherently inferential. Grice's maxims of quality, quantity, relevance, and manner with their submaxims give more specific parameters for what was assumed in his governing cooperative principle.[35]

Within a generation, a discipline within pragmatics arose, and Sperber and Wilson were its chief proponents and architects. They seminally argued that all of Grice's maxims could be subsumed under a single prin-

---

32. H. Paul Grice, "Logic and Conversation," in *Speech Acts*, ed. Peter Cole and Jerry L. Morgan, SS 3 (New York: Academic Press, 1975), 41–58. This text is a copyrighted reprint of Grice's William James Lectures at Harvard, 1966–1967. My synthetic question tries to draw out the thrust behind assumptions, inquiries, and conclusions that he does not succinctly state in a single place.

33. Levinson, *Pragmatics*, 2–3.

34. Grice, "Logic and Conversation," 45; see also Levinson, *Pragmatics*, 101.

35. It is not necessary for the sake of this study to describe Grice's maxims in detail. I comment on some as appropriate, but relevance theorists have refined and superseded his classic presentation. For a succinct outline, see Levinson, *Pragmatics*, 101–2.

ciple of relevance, properly and technically defined.³⁶ Hence relevance theory became a central extension of pragmatics, bringing technical precision to the broader discipline. They came to call it relevance theory, because it built on Grice's maxim of relevance: "Make your contribution relevant."³⁷ Two developments were crucial: First, relevance theory became a comprehensive theory of utterance interpretation built on a single principle of relevance, so that relevance theory is more properly dubbed a *species* of pragmatics than a subfield within pragmatics.³⁸ Second, relevance theory gave technical precision to several aspects of Grice's proposals. Such precision was necessary to make it a viable theory, whereas pragmatics had been a thoughtful (even historically pivotal) but inexact conception of how humans succeed in communicating through natural language.³⁹

For Sperber and Wilson, the chief maxim of pragmatics is that utterances must be relevant to the context in which they are spoken.⁴⁰ While relevance theory was still in its infancy during the 1980s, Levinson and other linguistic pragmaticists often appealed to the principle of relevance in working out implicatures.⁴¹ Relevance theory defines these with technical precision: an implicature is "an ostensively communicated assumption that is derived solely via processes of pragmatic inference."⁴² It is an implication of an utterance that the speaker intends to convey. Implicatures can be either weakly or strongly implied. Levinson also observed

---

36. Dan Sperber and Deirdre Wilson, "Pragmatics," *Cognition* 10 (1981): 282–83.

37. Levinson, *Pragmatics*, 102.

38. I use *species* to refer to relevance theory's relationship to pragmatics in agreement with a general recognition that relevance theory, in Furlong's words, "comes out of the linguistic discipline of pragmatics" ("Relevance Theory," 7).

39. A third development came later and more gradually—the shift from a purely philosophical discipline to a cognitive-linguistic discipline, wedding relevance theory to theories of the mind. A fourth development is current, which is the use of more neurological data in refining the theory.

40. Dan Sperber and Deirdre Wilson, *Pragmatics: An Overview*; CLCS Occasional Paper No. 16 (Dublin: Dublin University, Trinity College (Ireland), Centre for Language and Communication Studies, 1986), 16 and passim.

41. E.g., "Incidentally, exactly how the appropriate implicatures ... are to be predicted remains quite unclear, although the maxim of Relevance would presumably play a crucial role" (Levinson, *Pragmatics*, 111).

42. Carston and Uchida, *Relevance Theory*, 297; see also Clark, *Relevance Theory*, 78–79.

that relevance seemed to be the only maxim in Gricean pragmatics that could not be flouted for effect and that relevance has a binding effect on the other maxims.[43] It is not relevant to say something that is patently uninformative, something that is not of concern in the broader discursive enterprise, something that disregards the course of the discussion, something of no usefulness or interest to the audience, and so forth. I show how miso-Cretan interpretations of Titus 1:12 may contradict this fundamental principle.

Within the broader discipline of pragmatics, relevance theory provides a unified theory of utterance interpretation governed by a single, economic assumption: an assumption is relevant in a context to the extent that its contextual effects in the context are large and to the extent that the effort required to process it in the context is small.[44] This governing rule of relevance theory is a succinct articulation of the economy of cognitive effects. Sperber and Wilson argue that this explanatory framework makes it a complete theory, in contrast to Gricean pragmatics, which offers some broad, mostly philosophical insights about how language works but lacks a simple, cohesive explicative framework.[45]

From a Theory to a Method

To be clear once again, relevance theory is not a method of interpretation. It is a theory about how hearers successfully interpret (or fail to interpret) utterances when the linguistically encoded form is profoundly underdetermined. The success of natural language through human history is the theory's empirical bedrock. *That* natural language has tended to work for humans is taken for granted; relevance theory is interested in explaining *how*. Theorists have developed a "relevance-guided comprehension heu-

---

43. Levinson, *Pragmatics*, 111–12.
44. Carston and Uchida, *Relevance Theory*, 299, paraphrased.
45. Clark explains various aspects of the development of Grice's intuitions and philosophical linguistic speculations into a proper theory, acknowledging, as others have, that Sperber and Wilson were pivotal to clarifying and consolidating the discipline theoretically (Clark, *Relevance Theory*, 43, 67–68, 84). For their own articulation of these issues, see, e.g., Deirdre Wilson and Dan Sperber, *Meaning and Relevance* (Cambridge: Cambridge University Press, 2012), 1–27. Pragmatics and relevance theory bear an integral kinship, so I refer to concepts from either interchangeably when they are true of both.

ristic" with a well-defined set of tasks, but fluent language users accomplish them rapidly and practically involuntarily.[46]

Natural language comprehension is not typically self-conscious and deliberate, so relevance theorists endeavor to answer the critical, empirically based question, How are language users so adept at understanding one another? Theorists delineate the mental processes humans follow to arrive at meaning even though humans understand language *without* formally learning these processes.[47]

Even though relevance theory is not an interpretive method, scholars can strategically apply its valid and well-tested insights to biblical interpretation. I define the approach that I describe and demonstrate in this book as a strategic application of key insights from relevance theory to the linguistically and historically responsible interpretation of biblical texts. I label such an approach a *relevance-guided biblical hermeneutic*. Titus 1:12 is used as a test case. I now discuss the task of applying relevance theory to scriptural texts.

Relevance Theory and the Bible

The relevance-theoretical insights that structure this study are described below. But beforehand, some preliminary comments are in order with respect to applying relevance theory to biblical studies. Relevance theory has been applied to the Bible in two broad fields—Scripture translation and linguistics-oriented interpretation. While translation theory has utilized relevance theory widely and rigorously since the 1980s, biblical scholars (as distinct from translation scholars and practitioners) have incorporated it into an applied method only more recently. Throughout this study, in addition to the linguists whose ideas I engage, I also reference several scholars who have applied relevance theory to biblical studies. In my own research into this juncture of disciplines, finding works was one of the challenges, because no single search result sufficed. These comments and select bibliographic notes will acquaint readers with authors and works that exist in this space and provide a sense of the intersection of these disciplines, the possibilities, and the gaps. Relevance theory has informed the work of several biblical scholars, while some have misunderstood or mis-

---

46. Clark, *Relevance Theory*, 34–40, 119, and passim; Sperber and Wilson, "Pragmatics" (2007), 474.

47. Clark, *Relevance Theory*, 9.

applied the theory to disparate concerns. Several inaccurate or imprecise presentations of relevance theory are available to biblical scholars as well as works that extrapolate insights from relevance theory into concerns not native to the discipline (e.g., theology). It is nearly impossible to summarize the works in any subdiscipline within modern biblical scholarship exhaustively. More biblical scholars are working with this discipline each year. So, I have focused mostly on scholars whose field of investigation is proximate to my own, who have written significant works as Bible scholars or with major implications for biblical studies.

Translation studies was the first area of biblical scholarship to use relevance theory extensively, and the literature on the implications of relevance theory for biblical translation is sizable,[48] yet Kevin Smith, a scholar specializing in translation, conducted the only substantial relevance theory analysis of the book of Titus of which I am aware.[49] Biblical scholars working with relevance theory exhibit one of two general emphases: they introduce the theory to their audiences for its general hermeneutical insights, or they apply native insights from relevance theory to the interpretation of specific texts.[50] Most engage in both projects to an extent, as

---

48. Ernst-August Gutt is one of the earliest and most prolific writers at this juncture of disciplines. See, e.g., Gutt, *Translation and Relevance: Cognition and Context*, 2nd ed. (New York: Routledge, 2014). Regina Blass, Philip Goodwin, and Harriet Hill each model fine arguments for applying interpretive insights from relevance theory to translation. See Blass, *Relevance Relations in Discourse*; Goodwin, *Translating the English Bible*; Hill, *The Bible at Cultural Crossroads: From Translation to Communication* (Manchester: St. Jerome, 2006). Ernst Wendland is a translator and theorist who takes a more skeptical posture toward the promise of relevance theory for translation. See, e.g., Wendland, "Review of *Bible Translation Basics: Communicating Scripture in a Relevant Way*, by Harriet Hill, Ernst-August Gutt, Margaret Hill, Christoph Unger, and Rick Floyd," *BT* 63 (2012): 219–24.

49. Smith, "Bible Translation and Relevance Theory."

50. For examples of the former, see, Green, "Relevance Theory and Biblical Interpretation" (2009); Green, "Relevance Theory and Biblical Interpretation" (2013); Karen H. Jobes, "Relevance Theory and the Translation of Scripture," *JETS* 50 (2007): 773–97; Meadowcroft, "Relevance as Mediating Category;" Vilson Scholz, "Communication Models, Relevance Theory, Bible Translation, and Exegesis," in *The Press of the Text: Biblical Studies in Honor of James W. Voelz*, ed. Andrew H. Bartlett, Jeffrey J. Kloha, and Paul R. Raabe (Eugene, OR: Pickwick, 2017), 234–43; Margaret G. Sim, *A Relevant Way to Read: A New Approach to Exegesis and Communication* (Eugene, OR: Pickwick, 2016); and Benjamin Joel Wukasch, "Centered Fuller Communication: Sensus Plenior, Relevance Theory, and a Balanced Hermeneutic" (thesis, Trinity

does this study, but their work is generally clear about whether they are focusing on the theory or focusing on a specific text. Green presents some of the most insightful and reliable introductions of the theory and its various aspects. Pattemore presents some of the most accurate, consistent, and incisive applications to Scripture. Other scholars have contributed works that combine biblical studies with adjacent areas of linguistics.[51] Additionally, many have applied selected insights from relevance theory without it influencing their entire work.

Every description and application of relevance theory is distinct, as biblical scholars identify the dimensions of this comprehensive and multifaceted theory that they find most illuminating for the questions they ask or the material they examine. The present study is no different. Although the insights chosen to structure this study are native and global to relevance theory, they differ from those employed by other scholars, mostly in emphasis. The relevance-theoretical literature exhibits diversity of reasoning and conclusion, as does any discipline, but the present study demonstrates general continuity with other relevance-informed studies.

Biblical scholars widely agree that the literary, linguistic, and sociohistorical contexts in which the Bible was produced are pertinent to interpretation, but relevance theory holds that interpreting utterances (sentences in their contexts) demands such a specific set of assumptions that our encyclopedic knowledge of literature, semantics, and sociohistorical background can often be insufficient or misleading. Insufficient, because it lacks the extreme specificity of a given instance of communica-

---

Western University, 2015). Not all the work at this juncture of disciplines represents relevance theory accurately, coherently, or helpfully or applies it consistently or appropriately. Stephen W. Pattemore critiques one such effort in "Review of *A Relevant Way to Read: A New Approach to Exegesis and Communication* by Margaret G. Sim," *RBL* (2018), https://www.sblcentral.org/home/bookDetails/11354. For examples of the latter, see Casson, *Textual Signposts*; Yael Klangwisan, *Earthing the Cosmic Queen: Relevance Theory and the Song of Songs* (Eugene, OR: Pickwick, 2014); Nelson R. Morales, *Poor and Rich in James: A Relevance Theory Approach to James's Use of the Old Testament*, BBRSup 20 (University Park, PA: Eisenbrauns, 2018); Pattemore, *Souls under the Altar*; Pattemore, *People of God*.

51. Such works include, e.g., Richard S. Briggs, *Words in Action: Speech Act Theory and Biblical Interpretation* (Edinburgh: T&T Clark, 2001); Briggs, "How to Do Things with Meaning in Biblical Interpretation," *STR* 2 (2011): 143–60; and Kevin J. Vanhoozer, "Discourse on Matter: Hermeneutics and the 'Miracle' of Understanding," *IJST* 7 (2005): 5–37.

tion; misleading, because it includes a host of facts that are prominent to us but that may not have been prominent to ancient readers. Therefore, our best indications of which assumptions influenced particular instances of communication come from the text itself. Relevance theory offers a criterion for prioritizing and incorporating ideas from various fields. The principle of relevance compels audiences to derive meaning attuned primarily to the narrow scope of utterance context and only secondarily to the broader literary-historical environment, the semantics of lexemes and syntax, or purported historical backgrounds. Audiences draw on real-world knowledge as the literary context requires or suggests it.

Because relevance theorists base their claims in the observable success of human language, relevance theory offers a promising foundation for a reading strategy less prone to the dubious assumptions and problematic conclusions described in chapter 1. Instead of favoring specific indicators of meaning such as grammar, lexical definitions, or general sociohistorical knowledge, it sees language as functioning at the intersection of these and other factors in countless particular contexts. It reckons all matters of context within its explanation of how meaning is conveyed through language.

Relevance theory does not prescribe the creation or interpretation of utterances, but its insights, properly understood, illuminate the process of interpretation and sensitize interpreters to critical linguistic evidence, on the one hand, and expose faulty assumptions, on the other. In this sense, relevance theory can be the basis for a historically and linguistically responsible interpretive strategy appropriate to the biblical text as written communication.[52] Because it evaluates all factors affecting interpretation on the basis of one economic scale—relevance—it is especially suitable for illuminating the interpretation of difficult passages.

I previously described several problems with interpretations of Titus 1:12 and now identify the location of those errors, in semiotic terms, as between the text and its interpreters, not a misunderstanding of semantics or syntax. Some sensible corrections in syntactic and semantic understanding are needed as well, but pragmatics is my main concern. Specifically, I explain how relevance reveals where interpreters have erred and how it

---

52. Armin Baum explains reasons for understanding Titus in particular and the Pastoral Epistles in general as primarily *written communication* as opposed to the more oral (dictated to a scribe) style of the other letters in the Corpus Paulinum ("Semantic Variation within the Corpus Paulinum," 288–89).

points to evidence for deriving historically and linguistically responsible, contextually appropriate interpretations.

Three Key Insights

Although the development of relevance theory as a discipline incorporates many valuable concepts, I have found three insights to be key: the inferential nature of all communication; the role of the hearer in communication; and the nonpropositional dimensions of communication. These three represent central assumptions that theorists consistently advance. They differentiate relevance theory from other disciplines, and they complement one another. These insights are global to relevance theory and not logically sequential or hierarchical, so their applications overlap. On the basis of these relevance-theoretical insights, I explain both my interpretation of Titus 1:12 and the interpretive errors made by neglecting or violating these insights.

As indicated earlier, scholars recognize these three insights with different conceptual labels. For instance, Furlong identifies the writer's intention and the question of responsibility in interpretation as "those aspects most pertinent to literature." She then explains that these aspects involve (1) "vagueness and indeterminacy," which correspond to the inferential nature; (2) distinguishing "between interpretations produced in the search for optimal relevance (exegetical) from those produced in the search for actual or maximal relevance (eisegetical)," which corresponds to the hearer's role; and (3) literary or "poetic" effects, which correspond to the nonpropositional dimensions.[53] The centrality of these insights will become even clearer as I introduce them in conversation with prominent theorists.

1. The Inferential Nature of All Communication (Explicatures)

The underdeterminacy of linguistically encoded speech is the central assumption of pragmatics. Sperber and Wilson believed Grice had not gone far enough in recognizing the degree to which language was inferential. Grice was mainly concerned with the recognized deictic, referential, and ambiguous features of speech and explaining why hearers were able

---

53. Furlong, "Relevance Theory," 2. Listed in my order, not hers.

to discern the meaning of components such as pronouns, references to time, and nonliteral speech. He objected to pure semanticism in which the meaning of an utterance is held in the linguistically encoded forms to the neglect of the relationship between signs and their interpreters. He argued that people do not comprehend utterances simply by grasping the meanings of words (lexical semantics) and their relations to each other (syntax). Relevance theorists aim at explicating how hearers fill utterances with meaning (by means of inference) in order to arrive consistently at speakers' intended meanings.

Grice said that inferential processes were necessary once the propositional content of *what is said* had been clarified by means of a more conventional process of disambiguation, reference assignment, and clarifying ambiguities.[54] In other words, inference was necessary for deriving implicatures. Relevance theorists insist that language is inherently inferential and that deriving a speaker's explicatures as well as implicatures requires inferential processing. A speaker's explicatures include critical information about how linguistically encoded content is meant to be taken (e.g., as literal or figurative, as direct or indirect). Sperber and Wilson explain, "According to our account, the recovery of both explicit and implicit content may involve a substantial element of pragmatic inference."[55]

Since Grice, pragmaticists have been using the term *implicatures* in a technical sense, but Sperber and Wilson introduced the idea of *explicatures* to add precision to Grice's less technical label "what is said."[56] Furlong expresses the need for inference at every level of comprehension: "Even in establishing what is actually 'stated' rather than implied by a work, a substantial element of interpretation and inference is involved."[57] Sperber and Wilson explain how this development fit into the history of the discipline:

> A major development in pragmatics over the past thirty years (going much further than Grice envisaged) has been to show that the explicit content of an utterance, like the implicit content, is largely underdetermined by

---

54. To use ordinary language within the discipline, Grice and subsequent pragmaticists use non-technical-sounding terms (e.g., "talk exchange" and "what is said") to name specific linguistic phenomena. "What is said" is Grice's semitechnical term for the explicit, linguistically encoded content of an utterance (see, e.g., "Logic and Conversation," 44).

55. Sperber and Wilson, "Pragmatics" (2007), 481.

56. Clark, *Relevance Theory*, 167–68, 171.

57. Furlong, "Relevance Theory," 42.

> the linguistically encoded meaning.... Grice and others ... have tended to minimize the gap between sentence meaning and speaker's meaning.... Relevance theorists have argued that relevance-oriented inferential processes are efficient enough to allow for a much greater slack between sentence meaning and speaker's meaning, with sentence meaning typically being quite fragmentary and incomplete, and speaker's explicit meaning going well beyond the minimal proposition arrived at by disambiguation and reference assignment.[58]

The processes involved in Gricean pragmatics focus on how humans decipher referential speech and ambiguity, but relevance theory holds that *all* communication has an inferential character. The distinction between the linguistically encoded meaning of a sentence and the speaker's intended meaning in uttering it is crucial in both schemes, but relevance theory recognizes that speakers' observable linguistic behaviors convey signals about *how* to understand the sentences they utter, not just *what* those sentences mean. Disambiguation and reference assignment are nevertheless necessary components in the larger inferential program of human comprehension. Let us now look at those basic processes.

Basic Pragmatic Processes

Although relevance theory expanded the former boundaries of pragmatics, it recognizes the need for basic pragmatic processes in the interpretation of utterances. This basic processing involves a number of tasks that a hearer's mind employs selectively, *pro re nata*, without a prescribed sequence, rapidly, intuitively, and virtually simultaneously. Theorists logically delineate discrete tasks, but from a functional standpoint they are practically inseparable. A relevance-guided biblical hermeneutic would apply these processes as an initial step in evaluating and forming interpretations. They include resolving ambiguities, vaguenesses, and indeterminacies, assigning referents, decoding deictic terms, restoring missing or ellipsed material, and recovering implicit content.[59]

---

58. Sperber and Wilson, "Pragmatics" (2007), 470, 473.
59. Huang, "Micro- and Macro-Pragmatics," 138–39, 141; Sperber and Wilson, "Pragmatics" (2007), 478–84. Although these theorists include supplying contextual assumptions and naming presuppositions necessary for coherence as component processes, I focus on these later in ch. 4. They differ in kind from the basic processes listed here and involve more than enriching linguistically encoded content.

One of Grice's four maxims—a specific entailment of the cooperative principle—was his maxim of manner. The second submaxim under his maxim of manner is "Avoid ambiguity."[60] This more narrow expectation emerges from the assumption of cooperation but does not prevent speakers from using ambiguous expressions. It would be virtually impossible, or at least intolerable, to exclude all expressions that are inherently ambiguous (e.g., pronouns, prepositions). Rather, he meant that competent speakers tend not to use expressions that are ambiguous *to their hearers*. We could phrase the submaxim as a rule in the following way: do not use expressions that will be difficult for your hearer to disambiguate.

Assuming that a speaker or writer wishes to be understood, she will use expressions that are likely to be understood by her hearers or readers.[61] For that purpose, she may likely use expressions that are unconventional or would be ambiguous to a third party or an eavesdropper but are easily decipherable by the intended audience. Combining this flexibility of language with the particularity of conversational, historical, and situational contexts, it is easy to see how people who are not from the original audience, such as modern readers of ancient texts (eavesdroppers), can misunderstand. They do not share the same cognitive environment or situational context. Green explains how narrow the contextual particularity can be:

> According to RT [relevance theory], the *context* of an utterance is not all the information available from the discourse in which a sentence is embedded (such as a paragraph, a section of a book, or a book as a whole), the wider literary corpus of a particular author (such as the writing of Paul), nor the wider cultural context shared by communicators and their addressees (such as the history and cultures of the Jewish and wider Greco-Roman worlds). Rather, context is a subset of all the salient or available information to the communicator and the addressee, which is accessed in the communication of an utterance.[62]

---

60. Grice, "Logic and Conversation," 45–47. I do not focus on Gricean pragmatics but delineate its details when they are pertinent to the current discussion. His scheme is outlined succinctly by Clark, *Relevance Theory*, 57.

61. I employ the convention in relevance-theoretical literature of referring to a generic or hypothetical speaker in the feminine and her hearer in the masculine (see Clark, *Relevance Theory*, xvii). When referring specifically to the author of Titus, however, I use masculine pronouns.

62. Green, "Relevance Theory and Biblical Interpretation" (2013), 268.

Relevance theorists offer differing lists of interpretive tasks, not because they lack agreement but because they generally agree that interpreters cannot prescribe a sequence or standard list of necessary actions in the process of recovering meaning.[63] Nevertheless, certain tasks are commonly needed. Uchida provides the following list of basic pragmatic processes: "Three subtasks are involved here: (a) disambiguation, (b) identification of the reference of referring expressions, and (c) enrichment of the logical form or semantic representation of the sentence uttered."[64] As with other theorists, he does not intend this list to be exhaustive, detailed, or universal.

Theorists regard all of these processes as serving to clarify both explicit *and* implicit content and explain how a single principle of relevance governs their application in countless specific contexts. Comprehending explicit and implicit content and even accessing contextual assumptions require basic pragmatic processes. The discrete tasks into which theorists delineate these processes are essential; and they ground the comprehension of higher-level explicatures, to which I now turn.

Higher-Level Explicatures

Speakers are always communicating explicatures, which are assumptions necessary to understand the linguistically encoded content of their speech properly. According to Carston and Uchida, an explicature is "an ostensively communicated assumption which is inferentially developed from the incomplete conceptual representation (logical form) resulting from linguistic decoding."[65]

Suppose a commuter asks, "When is the train coming?" A listener might reasonably derive the explicature, *The speaker wishes to know* [when the train is coming]. Although this explicature cannot be semantically decoded from the sentence, it is not only reasonable but *necessary* to comprehend her communicative intent. If the truth conditions were right, responding verbally with "Three o'clock" might be appropriate. A hearer adept at dealing with open questions would recognize this. If the commuter utters this example sentence ("When is the train coming?") in a context in

---

63. See, e.g., Clark, *Relevance Theory*, 121.
64. Uchida, "Text and Relevance," 161–63.
65. Carston and Uchida, *Relevance Theory*, 297; see also Clark, *Relevance Theory*, 78–79.

which it is a rhetorical question, the adept hearer will need to recognize a different, higher-level explicature. According to Carston and Uchida, a higher-level explicature "involves embedding the proposition expressed by the utterance in a higher level description such as a description of the speaker's propositional attitude, a speech act description or some other comment on the embedded proposition."[66] Now, suppose everyone on the train platform is well aware of the time and the train schedule, but the train is quite late. Without any announcement, it is clear to everyone that the travelers are equally informed. Then, someone shouts, "When is the train coming?" [guttural exhale]. In such a context, a perfectly reasonable higher-level explicature might be *The speaker is agitated that she does not know* [when the train is coming] or *The speaker is frustrated that* [when the train is coming] *is no longer predictable.* An eyeroll and a grunt might be appropriate responses in this context, although they would be unacceptable responses to the open question in the former context. If one of the travelers responds with the scheduled arrival time (e.g., "Three o'clock"), thinking it to be an open question, he might receive a retort of laughter or ridicule. Additional explicatures are possible, and hearers tend to be remarkably adept at intuiting which are appropriate.

In the example above, the circumstantial context restricted interpretation. Settings can restrict interpretation as much as the semantics of words, but speakers often embed higher-level explicatures *verbally*. Suppose the traveler said, "I'm not asking, When is the train coming? anymore." The higher-level explicature might be *The speaker has given up her effort to find out* [when the train is coming] or *The speaker is frustrated that* [when the train is coming] *is no longer predictable.* These explicatures concern the *speaker's attitude* toward a statement, and they are necessary for understanding the meaning of that statement.

The speaker's attitude is crucial to interpretation, and it is an explicature—part of *what is said*, in Gricean terms.[67] Therefore, discerning the speaker's attitude is a necessary inferential task. When Clark lists the tasks

---

66. Carston and Uchida, *Relevance Theory*, 297; for further explanation, see also Clark, *Relevance Theory*, 208–11.

67. As noted earlier, *explicatures* in relevance theory overlap with "what is said" in Gricean pragmatics. They also overlap with *conventional implicatures*—linguistic forms that are not dependent on truth conditions or lexical semantics but are derived from shared conventions (e.g., "That is all I am saying," "You can...," or "They say that..."). See Levinson, *Pragmatics*, 127–31.

involved in recovering explicatures, he includes disambiguation, reference assignment, the recovery of ellipsed material, narrowing down the intended meaning of vague terms, and deciding whether thoughts represented are being entertained by the speaker or attributed to someone else.[68] Importantly, Sperber and Wilson also include the recovery of the speaker's attitude toward what is said in their list of tasks for pragmatic inference.[69] This recovery is paramount for understanding some kinds of speech, such as jokes, irony, and antagonistic rhetoric. Interpreters of Scripture who understand the array of inferential tasks that occur virtually simultaneously in a listener's mind can apply them systematically to Scripture as literature, because it constitutes a relatively fixed conversational contribution.

A speaker always communicates explicatures that convey her attitude toward what is said—that is, whether it is her own thought, whether it is her attribution of someone else's thoughts, and so forth. Recovering such information is critical. Ostensive inferential communication involves a speaker making her communicative intention manifest. This making manifest implies a desire on the part of the speaker for sympathy. Rather than express her own idea directly, the speaker may present another person's idea with an implicit judgment so that her hearer has the opportunity to make the same judgment.[70] Her judgment on an idea may be an implicature, but that the idea is not her own is usually an explicature. The speaker wants her audience to enter into her mental processes and conclude with her, feel with her, agree with her, be convinced with her, and respond with her. Paul trusts that his readers will share his conclusions, including his attitude toward the ideas he presents.

2. The Role of the Hearer (Contextual Assumptions)

Relevance theory shifts the focus from obligations communication presumes on the speaker or writer, à la Gricean pragmatics, to cognitive processes hearers and readers engage in to infer meaning. As

---

68. Clark, *Relevance Theory*, 166. Theorists use "missing or ellipsed material" and "implicit content" interchangeably (cf. Sperber and Wilson, *Pragmatics: An Overview*, 11).

69. Sperber and Wilson, *Pragmatics: An Overview*, 9.

70. I expand on this idea, which is foundational for irony from a relevance-theoretical perspective, in ch. 4 under "Higher-Level Explicatures."

Sperber and Wilson put it, "Relevance theory ... approaches verbal comprehension as a psychological process."[71] Like its kindred discipline, pragmatics, relevance theory views communication as a cooperative endeavor, but this assumption uncovers meaning from the perspective of the hearer. Why? Because hearers' success in human communication throughout history vouches for the success of speakers as comprehension completes the *talk exchange*.[72] Appreciating the role of the hearer is especially crucial in biblical interpretation, because modern interpreters differ from earlier audiences in language, culture, experience, and other factors. They therefore customarily have mismatched contextual assumptions and see different aspects of the text as salient, thus skewing interpretation. Let us now consider how interpreters may account for and ameliorate these divergences.

Mismatched Contextual Assumptions

Hearers must supply some of the material needed to fill the gap left by language's underdeterminacy. Theorists refer to this audience-supplied material as contextual assumptions. These assumptions combine with the utterance to yield enough cognitive effects to make the utterance satisfactorily relevant. The two main sources or types of contextual assumptions are the cognitive environment (informational) and implicated premises (logical). These assumptions differ between interpreters in proportion to various kinds of distance (e.g., space, time, culture, language).

If biblical interpreters sketch the assumptions that ancient interlocutors plausibly shared, they can then derive implicatures and conclusions based on assumptions closer to those held by original audiences. These processes are discussed and demonstrated in chapter 5. Here are introduced the two sources or types of contextual assumptions—cognitive environment and implicated premises—in more detail.

---

71. Sperber and Wilson, "Pragmatics" (2007), 495.
72. See Frank Brisard, "H. P. Grice," in *Philosophical Perspectives for Pragmatics*, ed. Jef Verschueren, Jan-Ola Östman, and Marina Sbisà, HPH 10 (Amsterdam: Benjamins, 2011), 113; H. Paul Grice, "Further Notes on Logic and Conversation," in *Reasoning: Studies of Human Inference and Its Foundations*, ed. Jonathan E. Adler and Lance J. Rips (Cambridge: Cambridge University Press, 2008), 41; Sperber and Wilson, "Pragmatics" (1981); Sperber and Wilson, "Pragmatics" (2007).

Cognitive Environment

A hearer's cognitive environment provides the informational assumptions needed to interpret an utterance. Specific historical-contextual information, from the macro (e.g., imperial) scale to the micro (e.g., domestic) scale, is included, but discursive context profoundly influences one's cognitive environment. Biblical exegetes normally bring historical facts and perspectives to bear on an interpretation—what was meant by what was said. Based on insights about human cognition, however, a relevance-guided biblical hermeneutic would accentuate two values: first, it would prioritize the evidence, recognizing that the discourse itself signals the comparative relevance of historical-contextual information; second, it would result in the evaluation of alternative interpretations on a consistent set of criteria.[73] Relevance theory essentially explains *how* hearers are able to understand utterances and, just as importantly, *why* nonoriginal readers might err. A fitting complement to the aim of explaining utterance interpretation is relevance theory's capacity to explain why certain interpretations are less satisfactory. The outcome of a relevance-guided hermeneutic is not only an interpretation but the evidential basis for evaluating one interpretation over another.

Carston and Uchida define *cognitive environment* as follows: "the set of assumptions which are **manifest** to an individual at a given moment."[74] This set of assumptions does not include the hearer's encyclopedic knowledge of their world or the sum total of their memory; it is constantly changing and limited by matters of cognitive accessibility, which can be increased and decreased, initiated or canceled by several factors, especially by the utterances themselves.

Communicators' minds are the fund, machinery, and product of their speech; so what is said represents what is on their minds more reliably than

---

73. From the perspective of literary theory, Stephen Bonnycastle explains some of the problems with assuming that an exhaustive knowledge of the historical background of a given writing is the best way to appreciate it. It is exhausting, impossible, and distracting. The response of "new criticism" to focus instead on the writing may be an overcorrection. See Bonnycastle, *In Search of Authority: An Introductory Guide to Literary Theory*, 3rd ed. (Orchard Park, NY: Broadview, 2007), 83–90. A relevance-guided biblical hermeneutic strikes a balance. Texts indicate to us what historical knowledge is critical.

74. Carston and Uchida, *Relevance Theory*, 295; see also Clark, *Relevance Theory*, 115. He builds a similar definition based on Sperber and Wilson, *Relevance*, 1986.

general knowledge of monumental politics, popular religion, grammar, and culture. Interpreters can sketch the cognitive environment of ancient communicators through close linguistic analysis and relevance-guided historical and interdisciplinary inquiry. Evidence from the discourse grounds a plausible representation of communicators' shared cognitive environment. This evidence includes suggestions of mutual, layered assumptions about each other's memory and environment. The starting point, then, is the discourse itself.[75] Interpreters take cues from the conversation as to which historical and other matters are pertinent rather than assuming that any particular historical fact was relevant ex ante.[76]

Scholars already endeavor to augment their knowledge of the ancient world in order to understand adequately the original circumstances of biblical texts and to interpret them with faithfulness to their historical and literary context (e.g., gathering topographic, monumental, inscriptional, and historical details on ancient Ephesus). It is impossible, however, to reconstruct fully the situational context of any biblical text. Guided by the principle of relevance, with sensitivity to the potential mismatch between audiences' contextual assumptions, interpreters should focus their historical and interdisciplinary inquiries on signals from the text as they discern which aspects of history and culture are relevant to a specific conversation.

Hearers intuitively enrich the meanings of otherwise underdeterminative, linguistically encoded speech with material from their cognitive environment. Adept speakers leverage their hearers' cognitive environment to fill the gaps. Factors such as recency of mention, salience, rhyme, homonymy, and topical relation significantly influence the availability of memories.[77] A common illustration of the power of these features of discourse to affect a hearer's cognitive environment is a statement such as, "Do not think about flying purple elephants." In spite of the linguistically encoded imperative meaning of the sentence, the hearer almost certainly has *flying*

---

75. Robert E. Longacre asserts that linguists and grammarians (interpreters in their own right) have not adequately taken "into account the natural function of context in resolving most ambiguities." See Longacre, *The Grammar of Discourse*, 2nd ed., TLL (New York: Plenum, 1996), 1.

76. Casson explains that the text provides the most important data for determining the relevance of historical background information (*Textual Signposts*, 40–45).

77. Clark, *Relevance Theory*, 104, 149; R. Reed Hunt, "Does Salience Facilitate Longer-Term Retention?," *Memory* 17 (2009): 49–53. Theorists highlight empirical studies of the Fodorian modularity of the mind hypothesis that have revealed factors that affect recall. See comments below on salience.

purple elephants on his mind. The sentence deliberately defeats itself. This power suggests, first, that the linguistically encoded meaning of a sentence is not a determinative indicator of utterance meaning; and, second, that a relevance-guided hermeneutic could help interpreters to apply knowledge of history and custom, words and syntax more strategically.

Historical information, grammatical analysis, and sociological inquiry help to eliminate or subordinate certain interpretations in favor of others, so lacking a detailed understanding of the exact circumstances behind each utterance does not entirely prevent us from making some reasonable claims about a text's meaning. The literary context of utterances within a biblical book or New Testament epistle is a rich, albeit incomplete, source of evidence for sketching the cognitive environment of original communicators. At the same time, the documents themselves reveal critical historical and situational knowledge. As Aageson points out regarding the Pastoral Epistles, "Perhaps no other set of documents in the NT points to such a broad range of conflicted issues in the early church as do the epistles of 1 & 2 Timothy and Titus."[78] These texts especially aid investigation into particular problems within the early church. This may be most profoundly evident as they stand between the apostle Paul and the contemporary church and render what the historical church has accepted as an authoritative interpretation and application of the Pauline apostolate. So, the utterances within their contexts in the form of the text that we have constitute the instance of ostensive inferential communication that interests relevance-guided biblical interpreters.

The objectives, processes, and outcomes of relevance-guided historical inquiry would be distinct from those of various forms of sociohistorical biblical interpretation. The ancient *world* is not the object of relevance-guided historical inquiry as much as the (context-specific) ancient *mind*, influenced by matters of language, social concern, everyday culture, political and economic circumstances. This kind of inquiry concerns itself with the thought world of writers and readers, focusing on evidence from the texts themselves. The propositional thrust of an utterance is logically founded on a combination of the explicatures, derived from the linguistically encoded form, and reasonable contextual assumptions.[79] A plausible sketch of the cognitive environment of

---

78. Aageson, *Paul, the Pastoral Epistles*, 16.
79. Clark, *Relevance Theory*, 141.

communication participants combines with implicated premises and a lexical-grammatical analysis of the logical form of an utterance to yield reasonable intermediate conclusions. But, for relevance theory, propositions are not final. The end product of comprehension is multidimensional, including the propositional as well as the social-behavioral, because what is truly *relevant* has real-world consequences.

In sum, the principle of relevance mediates the influence of monumental history and politics, archaeological and literary knowledge of daily life, lexicography and grammar upon interpretation. The text cues modern interpreters as to what aspects of history, language, anthropology, and so forth are pertinent to interpretation. Readers cannot assume ex ante that a city's status under the Roman Empire, broad cultural shifts, details of household social relations, market practices, coinage, inscriptions, or any other *prescribed* set of facts are equally or entirely pertinent to a passage under examination. Certain matters may be profoundly relevant, but the utterance within its context, rather than a general exegetical rule, controls whether, which, and to what extent. The text is that component of the ancient environment that interpreters can have the most confidence of affecting readers' perceptions of the world, their thinking, and their behavior.

Implicated Premises

Language is underdetermined not only informationally but also logically. Interpretation requires logical assumptions that cannot be derived solely on the basis of the linguistically encoded meaning of the sentence uttered. Whereas hearers fill informational gaps in the underdeterminacy of language by drawing on content from their cognitive environment, they also fill logical gaps by supplying implicated premises.[80] Levinson explains that, in order for a hearer to maintain the assumption of a speaker's cooperation, the hearer must assume some unstated premises, which the speaker takes for granted. As Levinson puts it, "It must be supposed that S think that q."[81] Many intermediate premises are necessary but do not carry the final communicative thrust of an utterance or reflect its nonpropositional dimensions.

---

80. Clark, *Relevance Theory*, 227.
81. Levinson, *Pragmatics*, 113; expanded below.

An illustration might be helpful: Nearing dinnertime, I shout upstairs, "You can get the drinks." Here is the enriched propositional sentence meaning after disambiguation, reference assignment, and some basic pragmatic processes: *You, Barnabas David Allen, have the functional capacity to retrieve drinks of some kind that are somehow distinguished from other things (by the definite article)*. If that is what my son honestly interprets my utterance to mean, he will be puzzled and fail to perceive the relevance of my statement. It is this presumption of relevance that drives hearers to interpret utterances with more success. In order to understand my utterance as relevant, my son will need to assume the premise that no drinks are at the dinner table yet, even though my statement does not include that information. His assumption of relevance causes him to trust my cognitive environment, which includes real-time knowledge of the table setting. Further, he will understand that my use of the definite article distinguishes the drinks he will get as the drinks our family will imbibe at this evening's dinner *as long as* he complies.

Levinson outlines the logic of implicated premises as follows:

1. S has said that p
2. there's no reason to think S is not observing … the co-operative principle
3. in order for S to say that p and be indeed observing the … co-operative principle, S must think that q
4. S must know that it is mutual knowledge that q must be supposed if S is to be taken to be co-operating
5. S has done nothing to stop me, the addressee, thinking that q
6. therefore S intends me to think that q, and in saying that p has implicated q.[82]

The speaker is a prime agent in Levinson's outline, but note how he describes the inferential process from the hearer's perspective. This logical outline of deriving implicated premises corresponds to the standard relevance-theoretical approach.

---

82. See Levinson, *Pragmatics*, 113–14. Because of the nonpropositional dimensions of communication (ch. 6), a statement of ability may only be relevant if the ability is employed, unless the purpose of the utterance was to implicate a judgment on the ability of the hearer.

The presumption of relevance combined with the fact that an utterance has been made can suggest certain implicated premises. Hearers infer both implicated premises and implicated conclusions dialectically employing "mutual enrichment processes"—that is, inferences at one level interact with linguistically encoded content to make inferences at the next level.[83]

A mundane example demonstrates the dialectic between sentence meaning and logical and informational contextual assumptions: Suppose that my wife and I share the assumption that I am waiting to take a shower. She says, "Barney is out of the shower." The sentence does not indicate that Barney was taking a shower, but any hearer would assume so, not because he derives it semantically or observes it contextually but because he infers it logically. Because I know that our house has a single shower, I bring this real-world knowledge to the comprehension process as a contextual assumption, and I conclude that the only shower in our house is now available to me. Her utterance is relevant, because it means that I can now take a shower. The sentence is uninteresting informationally; Barney, in fact, spends most of his life *out of the shower*. It is only satisfyingly relevant if I assume both what is logically implied and contextually known. With this explanation of the two types of contextual assumptions, informational and logical, I turn now to another major aspect of the hearer's role in communication—*salience*. Because it differs between cultures, salience demands the attention of relevance-guided biblical interpreters.

Original Audiences versus Modern Eavesdroppers

Because of the simple economy of comprehension, hearers accept interpretations that require the least effort as long as they yield appropriate cognitive effects and satisfy their expectations of relevance. Therefore, ideas that are *salient* can achieve greater relevance.[84] Several factors may

---

83. Uchida, "Text and Relevance," 161–62.

84. *Salience* is widely used by theorists but is a less technical term. The phenomenon I refer to by this label has also been called *isolation effect* or *prominence*. The effect has been reliably demonstrated and confirmed experimentally. See Hunt, "Does Salience Facilitate?" for discussion. See also Hámori Ágnes, "Illocutionary Force, Salience and Attention Management: A Social Cognitive Pragmatic Perspective," *ALH* 57 (2010): 53–74; Kevin Joel Apple, "The Role of Relevance and Salience in Detecting the Intergroup Bias" (PhD diss., Ohio University, 1997); Istvan Kecskes, "The Role of

contribute to salience in the mind of a hearer (e.g., recency, repetition, boldness).[85] To use an audiological metaphor, salient ideas have higher volume, because they speak more loudly than their less noisy neighbors within the context. In fact, they may be so loud that their less salient neighbors' voices recede. Unfortunately, modern interpreters hear statements at different volume levels from their original audiences. Consequently, modern readers may fulfill their expectations of relevance by taking as salient a different idea than the ancient writer had expected. What original audiences took as background information may sound more salient to modern audiences and vice versa.

This phenomenon corresponds to the problem of *figure* and *ground* ambiguity in Gestalt psychology. A hearer can accidentally or deliberately confuse the assertions that a speaker wants to convey with the background required to present them.[86] Typically, cooperative interlocutors in an original conversational context have no problem distinguishing between front- and background details, but modern eavesdroppers must be careful not to allow what is salient for them to drown out what the ancient speaker intended to convey.

Salience can accompany an isolation effect—that is, a contextual interruption that leads to additional processing and engraining. According to R. Reed Hunt, "Salience is a subjective experience that follows perception of an event that violates the prevailing context."[87] Speakers may achieve salience in various ways deliberately or accidentally. Concepts, claims, or connotations may stand out grammatically (e.g., a noun in a list of adjectives, unusual syntax), aurally (e.g., abrupt changes in sound), theoretically (e.g., seeming contradictions; cf. Prov 26:4–5), or socioculturally (e.g., taboos, embarrassment, icons).[88]

Salience in Processing Pragmatic Units," *ALH* 51 (2004): 309–24; Jobes, "Relevance Theory and Translation," 781–85, esp. 784.

85. Empirical studies show that humans have shorter recall times for topics, ideas, words, and domains that have been more recently contemplated, accessed, or stimulated, even if only in passing. See studies mentioned in Clark, *Relevance Theory*, 90–122; Hunt, "Does Salience Facilitate."

86. Levinson, *Pragmatics*, 177–81, esp. 180.

87. Hunt, "Does Salience Facilitate," 49.

88. Francisco Yus identifies means by which speakers achieve salience, including repetition of concepts. See Yus, "Relevance Theory and Contextual Sources-Centered Analysis of Irony: Current Research and Compatibility," in *Relevance Theory: Recent*

According to Sperber and Wilson's communicative principle, hearers presume the optimal relevance of an utterance.[89] Clark explains that this leads interpreters to "follow a path of least effort in deriving effects and ... stop when expectations of relevance are satisfied."[90] Modern readers interpreting ancient texts complicate this process. Biblical scholars know that their situational context in the modern world does not supply all of the cognitive material necessary for interpretation, so they deliberately augment their available store of knowledge and exercise tentativeness.[91] Such positive attitudes and behaviors ameliorate somewhat the tendency to interpret texts solely on the basis of a modern cognitive environment, replete though it may be with historical knowledge. It is nevertheless difficult for modern readers to escape the gravitational pull of a salient (to them) interpretation.[92] For example, the salience of *talent* as a word that has come to mean "ability," rather than an arcane unit of measure, may be hard to overcome when interpreting the parable of the talents (Matt 25:14–30). Or, consider the tendency to attach the sense of *religious giving* to Jesus's discourse on judgmentalism and forgiveness in Luke 6:27–42. The salience of *give* read as "tithes and offerings" is too powerful to resist even though it does not cohere with the discursive context. The church has bills to pay, for goodness' sake!

To interpret ancient texts well, modern readers must contend with the tempting salience of interpretations that emerge when Scripture collides with modern sensibilities. They do so by constructing reasoned estimations of ancient cognitive environments, which must be done with as much particularity and precision as the evidence suggests but with the tentativeness that our severe limitations require. The original audience's knowledge and intuitions are not available to us, but relevance theory illu-

---

Developments, Current Challenges and Future Directions, ed. Manuel Padilla Cruz, P&B NS 268 (Philadelphia: Benjamins, 2016), 158.

89. Sperber and Wilson, "Pragmatics" (2007), 474.

90. Clark, *Relevance Theory*, 37, 68–69, 120. Biblical interpreters often refer to the *meaning* of a passage, but hearers/readers are cognitively geared toward finding the *relevance* of an utterance. What readers take to be the *meaning* may simply be the *relevance* for them and not for the utterance in its original context, which might more properly be called the *meaning* of a text.

91. On tentativeness, which is critical and probably underrated, see Bauer and Traina, *Inductive Bible Study*, 6.

92. Furlong addresses problems with diachronic interpretation in "Relevance Theory," 196–97.

mines utterance interpretation in such a way as to allow us sensitively and systematically to follow the processes of natural language comprehension. As noted above, the end products of interpretation, according to relevance theory, are real-world outcomes, not mere propositions, so I now turn to the third and final insight that drives this study—the nonpropositional dimensions of communication.

3. The Nonpropositional Dimensions of Communication (Implicated Conclusions)

According to Kevin Vanhoozer, to comprehend Scripture in spite of our limitations is to recognize that "words demand things of us," regardless of our equivocations.[93] Language does more than convey information. Its inherent underdeterminacy suggests that information transfer may not even be the *primary* function of language. Scholars have indicated how prevalently speakers use language to accomplish other tasks.[94] Relevance theorists use the term *cognitive effects* as technical language for what utterances produce when adequately comprehended. The outcome of utterance interpretation is not merely a propositional form but a changed context.[95] So, communication is successful when its implications are recognized cognitively or even realized materially, not simply when its propositions are understood. A speaker's intention in ostensive inferential communication can rarely be reduced to a set of propositions. Hearers must recognize the real-world implications of utterances.

Grice rightly contended that the linguistically encoded form of an utterance stood in for a fuller sense of the speaker's meaning, but the interpretive end product he assumed was basically informational, propositional. He considered other language uses to be special. Even with reference to

---

93. Vanhoozer highlights Kierkegaard's concept of "procrastination"—"to busy oneself" with anything *but* the text on its own terms ("Discourse on Matter," 34, 36). Vanhoozer further urges that a text belongs to someone and conveys *their* meaning, which he further argues is retrievable (27). So, the reader is in a medial position with respect to the text. Although he does not speak in terms of relevance theory, his theological hermeneutic gives place to the hearer's inferential role and the nonpropositional dimensions of communication. See his entire conclusion (34–37) for full and nuanced argument.

94. In ch. 6, I discuss some pertinent ideas from speech-act theory.

95. Huang, "Micro- and Macro-Pragmatics," 149–52; Furlong, "Relevance Theory," 12.

speech acts, Grice taught that the implicatures of an utterance could ultimately be expressed in the form of enriched propositions.[96] In another development from Gricean pragmatics, relevance theory recognizes that every utterance involves expectations about how its propositional content will translate into attitude and action on the part of the hearer. To affect a hearer's mind is to change his world. Understood in this way, imperatives are not entirely different from declaratives; just the syntax makes the speaker's intentions more or less transparent.[97]

Sperber and Wilson describe three components of an *enrichment* process that hearers follow to derive implicatures and explicatures from an utterance. Their description illuminates the nonpropositional dimensions of communication. First, hearers develop the linguistically encoded logical form to arrive at explicatures; second, they discern the intended contextual assumptions (e.g., time of day, stakeholders, topic); and, third, they construct the implications of the utterance (i.e., implied content that is necessary for relevance and its actionable conclusions).[98] In natural language as empirically observed, these processes frequently lead to implications beyond the acquisition of knowledge. Actionable conclusions—major or minor—are almost always outcomes of the interpretive process.

Suppose that I instruct my teenager to mow the lawn while I am away. Days later, he lounges on the couch. He is displeased to hear me say, "The lawn has not been mowed." His displeasure does not result from receiving disappointing information that he did not have before I spoke. The essential function of my utterance is not informational. My son's displeasure comes from the *implications* of the utterance: my attitude of disapproval toward the proposition encoded by my statement and the inconvenience of apparently being expected to cease his current leisure to comply with my previous instructions. Other implications may be possible, but these seem strongly implied. My son might correctly arrive at actionable conclusions, but even his discomforting emotional response is a nonpropositional outcome of my utterance inasmuch as I intend or expect it.

---

96. See Grice, "Logic and Conversation," 53–54. For an alternative development of Grice's approach to noninformational language uses, see Joana Garmendia, "A (Neo) Gricean Account of Irony: An Answer to Relevance Theory," *IRP* 7 (2015): 40–79.

97. Robyn Carston, "Truth-Conditional Semantics," in Verschueren, Östman, and Sbisà, *Philosophical Perspectives for Pragmatics*, 286–87.

98. See Sperber and Wilson, "Pragmatics" (2007), 481. This is my simplified summary of their enrichment process.

Utterances can have greater or lesser nonpropositional dimensions, and an interpretive method that is informed by cognitive linguistics can help readers identify and appreciate them. So, let us now overview relevance theory's definition of cognitive effects—the actual outcomes of speech—and their customary social and behavioral correlates.

The Economy of Cognitive Effects and Processing Effort

Clark defines a cognitive effect as "a change in an individual's representation of the world."[99] Theorists identify three basic kinds of positive cognitive effects that hearers can derive: (1) a contextual implication, (2) strengthening an existing assumption, and (3) contradicting an existing assumption.[100] These cognitive effects are positive because they have a net impact on hearers' representations of the world, not because they benefit hearers. Cognitive effects involve net changes in a hearer's perception of the world. Hearers intuitively seek these effects, whether the consequence promises to be pleasant or unpleasant. Hearers act on their outward world based on these representations; therefore, internal cognitive effects indirectly but inevitably affect a shared material environment.[101] Modern readers of the Bible must deliberately seek to discern implicatures that would have led to cognitive effects satisfying to original audiences even if those effects do not interest the modern reader.

Hearers typically expend a level of energy commensurate with the anticipated power of the cognitive effect—greater effects should reward greater processing effort. So economy is a rule for deriving implicatures as well as for constructing utterances. Speakers can be more efficient, and thereby effective, by relying on accessible memories or prominent features of their shared cognitive environment to form implied prem-

---

99. Clark, *Relevance Theory*, 77–78.

100. See, e.g., Nam Sun Song, "Metaphor and Metonymy," in Carston and Uchida, *Relevance Theory*, 90; Clark, *Relevance Theory*, 364; Blass, *Relevance Relations in Discourse*, 44.

101. Although this comment treads on the sociocultural and cognitive-behavioral dimensions of pragmatics that I identified as outside the scope of my study, recognizing this boundary area that interpretation naturally leads toward is critical for appreciating that the task of interpretation does not end with a set of propositions but rather with a set of deeds.

ises; for, as Sperber and Wilson claim, hearers "follow a path of least effort."[102]

Theorists speak in terms of processing effort because relevance theory considers communication from the hearer's perspective.[103] When speech is straightforward, hearers can derive cognitive effects without much effort. Anaphoric referential speech, for example, requires less effort to process than cataphoric referential speech, because the antecedent reference is already in mind and requires no suspension or placeholding. Among the factors that affect processing effort, and thereby the relevance of an utterance, Clark lists, "recency of use, frequency of use, perceptual salience, ease of retrieval from memory, linguistic or logical complexity, and size of the context."[104] These factors affect the accessibility of contextual assumptions. So, vividness, brevity, and recency, for instance, are factors that can decrease processing effort. An adept speaker intuitively adjusts the economy of her utterances to avoid pitfalls that could make them less relevant. Too much vividness could distract; brevity could fail to supply critical details; and recency could confuse referents, for example. Modern readers of ancient texts cannot intuitively discern such fine-tuning with the same degree of success that original hearers presumably did. We need more conscious, deliberate practices.

Along with their principle of relevance, Sperber and Wilson describe certain hypotheses about the economy of cognitive effects. They claim, "Other things being equal, the more contextual implications a proposition has, the more relevant it will be, and that other things being equal, the greater processing effort it requires, the *less* relevant it will be."[105] So, in brief, the higher the quantity of contextual implications, the more relevant; and the more efficient (i.e., the less processing effort), the more relevant.

Reaching further back in memory, deciphering obscure references, untangling complex logic, or interpreting vague or ambiguous speech typically increases processing effort, but the expense can be worthwhile if the hearer derives sufficient cognitive payoff. Poetry, for instance, appears, on

---

102. See Sperber and Wilson, "Pragmatics" (2007), 474. This is the general mode and first step in what they call a "relevance-guided comprehension heuristic." For a summary, see Clark, *Relevance Theory*, 34–40.
103. See e.g., Clark, *Relevance Theory*, 106, 365.
104. Clark, *Relevance Theory*, 104.
105. Sperber and Wilson, *Pragmatics: An Overview*, 20.

the surface, to break some economic rules of communication.[106] Rather than being straightforward, it is typically elliptical and ambiguous. Yet it gives people many cognitive rewards.[107]

The economy of ostensive inferential communication is not a single-value system such that shorter statements are necessarily more relevant than longer statements or that perspicuous statements are necessarily more relevant than ambiguous ones simply because longer or more ambiguous statements require greater processing effort. The calculus has multiple factors. It is true that hearers tend to "follow a path of least effort,"[108] but hearers who expect the cognitive effects to be great enough will expend more effort. Hearers, however, do not consciously decide on how much effort to expend. According to the communicative principle of relevance, they work out the implicatures of ambiguous speech virtually involuntarily, because the assumption of relevance and the promise of cognitive effects are inherent in utterances.

This intuitive effort of comprehension involves a process of *mutual adjustment* whereby hearers negotiate the implications of explicit and implicit content. Mutual adjustment evokes the process's dialectic nature. Hearers adjust their understanding of an utterance's explicatures and implicatures until they infer conclusions that yield adequate cognitive effects. So, hearers accept the word meanings and speaker attitudes, for instance, that they must assume in order for their interpretation to achieve optimal relevance (i.e., the greatest available cognitive effects).[109]

Indirect or nonliteral speech typically requires more processing effort, but it can be potent, yielding greater cognitive effects than similar propositions uttered literally, making the expenditure worthwhile. Nonliteral speech can also provide hearers a shortcut to comprehension, actually decreasing processing effort. Many relevance theorists regard literal and figurative uses of language to be degrees on a scale.[110] The implicatures of figurative lan-

---

106. Poetry breaks rules of economy not in terms of word count but in terms of processing effort.

107. Regarding poetry, Gibbs and Tendahl acknowledge that "we are sometimes willing to spend quite a deal of effort in utterances with the expectation of gaining some extra benefits" ("Cognitive Effort and Effects," 389).

108. Sperber and Wilson, "Pragmatics" (2007), 474; Clark, *Relevance Theory*, 37, 69, 120.

109. Clark, *Relevance Theory*, 242.

110. Deirdre Wilson, "The Pragmatics of Verbal Irony: Echo or Pretence?," *Lingua* 116 (2006): 1722–43; Clark, *Relevance Theory*, 253–79.

guage are a subset of all possible implicatures of the same utterance, but interpreting a speaker's figurative use of language literally usually denies the hearer adequate cognitive effects. Therefore, natural language listeners are usually able to detect figurative use and interpret appropriately.

Consider an example: "Lance is my dog" and "Lance is my best friend" can both have literal and figurative meanings; they can also be synonymous when one is figurative while the other is literal. Either could stand in for *Lance is a pet canine that I care for and that belongs in my household* or *Lance is a human confidant with whom I have an affectionate relationship*.[111] Given the conversational context, a hearer will rapidly and virtually involuntarily arrive at the proper interpretation, deriving satisfactory cognitive effects. Increased personal knowledge is an inevitable result. Imagine the difference between a figurative use and a literal use. A literal use can increase social distance, while a figurative use can decrease it. A statement such as, "Lance isn't my dog; he's my best friend" can have multidimensional (e.g., social, cognitive) effects. It does not merely inform; it invites the hearer into the speaker's personal life, her affection for and valuation of a family member, thereby strengthening social bonds. Figurative language therefore has the potential to produce strong cognitive effects when deployed strategically, even though more direct, literal uses may be easier to process.

Relevance theorists regard cognitive effects as the primary outcomes of communication, but these *internal* effects in the hearer's mind have profound influence on interlocutors' *external* world. They are interpersonal, social, and frequently intended to affect behavior.[112] These may be indirect outcomes that the speech and the speaker cannot control, but they are not of secondary importance. A relevance-guided biblical hermeneutic must consider these nonpropositional dimensions of speech.

Social and Behavioral Outcomes

Cognitive effects are changes in how a hearer perceives the world in his mind. As at least one theorist has summarized, $context^1 + utterance = context^2$.[113] $Context^2$ essentially constitutes a new environment. The three basic

---

111. I take several intermediate assumptions for granted to derive these implicatures.
112. Additionally, although not germane to this study, theorists have been testing the neurological and physiological effects of speech.
113. I do not think that I originated this formulation, but I cannot recall where I may have encountered it. I retain it here nevertheless because of its illustrative power,

kinds of positive cognitive effects—contextual implications, strengthening existing assumptions, and contradicting existing assumptions—lead to commensurate, albeit indirect, external outcomes. A biblical writer's intentions toward such outcomes are often transparent, but natural language listeners are adept at perceiving them even when they are not semantically obvious.

Pertinent to my inquiry, speech-act theory, as first advanced by Austin, delineates logically distinct dimensions of speech as simultaneous acts. A *locution* is a direct act of speaking something that has sense and reference. An *illocution*, intrinsic to many (and some argue all) locutions, is an act accomplished by speaking the locution (e.g., inviting, arguing, promising, forgiving) in the right felicity conditions. A *perlocution* is generally accomplished by the speaker only with the hearer's cooperation or uptake (e.g., informing, convincing, surprising, grieving, as transitive acts).[114] Richard Briggs discusses the implications of speech-act theory for biblical studies. With respect to meaning-making agency, he presents speech-act theory mainly from the perspective of what speakers accomplish. Because perlocution is not guaranteed, it is not considered intrinsic to speech. So, Briggs elevates self-involvement as a critical criterion for identifying and understanding illocution.[115] Perlocution, as an indirect act, however, is commensurate with intention in speech. I address the relationship between speech-act theory and relevance theory in chapter 6. For now, my general point is that language not only affects the mind; it affects a shared world, even if indirectly.

Commonplace figures, devices, and modes of speech do more than simply inform. For instance, Nam Sun Song identifies some of the relational effects that obtain with the use of metaphor. He points out that some cognitive effects specifically reinforce social outcomes, such as implicit

---

not because it substantially affects the logic of my argument. In literary-theoretic terms, this formula evokes Bonnycastle's succinct statement: "Language does not merely *represent* the world; it also organizes the world" (*In Search of Authority*, 122). In context, Bonnycastle has structuralism in mind and develops ideas that deliberately separate author intentions from reader interpretations, but the expression is pithy and prima facie applicable. See also Furlong, "Relevance Theory," 12.

114. Helpfully summarized in Briggs, *Words in Action*, 38–43. See original proposal by J. L. Austin, *How to Do Things with Words*, 2nd ed., ed. James O. Urmson and Marina Sbisà, WJL (Cambridge: Harvard University Press, 1975), 83–108; see also Levinson, *Pragmatics*, 236. Whether they consider some or all locutions to carry illocutionary force depends on the theorist.

115. See Briggs, *Words in Action*.

affirmation, intimacy, and trust alongside the informational content of an utterance. Such effects can be rhetorically powerful.[116] In rhetorical terms, they may lead to increased ethos.

The Epistle to Titus provides examples where Paul's speech held crucial social implications. Consider his affectionate language in the greeting of Titus: "to [my] true son, Titus, according to [our] shared faith" (1:4). The communicative context, more than the semantics of the constituent words, conveys social intimacy; the first-person pronouns supplied in translation are meant to convey the effect. As a letter read before a gathered community, this is a public display of affection. Paul also effectively transferred a mantle of authority to Titus when he wrote, "These [things] teach and encourage and rebuke with every [degree of] sanction; no one [is to] disregard you" (Ταῦτα λάλει καὶ παρακάλει καὶ ἔλεγχε μετὰ πάσης ἐπιταγῆς· μηδείς σου περιφρονείτω, 2:15). Such a statement in its context does not merely transmit information; it bolsters confidence, courage, and accountability beyond the linguistically encoded semantic values. It implies Paul's authority vested in Titus.

Ambiguity and nonliteral speech require trust, because speakers must rely on hearers to derive the correct meaning. Ken-ichi Seto contends that irony, a mode of speech that presumably requires comparatively more processing effort, yields positive relational effects.[117] For example: suppose a speaker witnesses someone committing an idiotic act then says to her neighbor, "What a genius!" Her hearer feels invited into an inside joke and derives significant effects beyond the propositional payload. The speaker could simply say, "I think that person has done an idiotic act," but by doing so she would not also invite her hearer to enjoy a snicker with her. The cognitive effects or rewards of good utterance interpretation can involve a valuable connection with the speaker or other social outcomes.

Through the three key insights discussed above, relevance theory suggests why some interpretations are less plausible than others and why certain interpretations should be favored, without resorting to a confessional, emotional, or traditional appeal. Given that, as I argue, conventional interpretations of the Cretan quotation of Titus 1:12 are unsatisfactory, how can relevance theory illuminate interpretations of Titus 1:12? I explain and

---

116. Song, "Metaphor and Metonymy," 94.
117. Ken-ichi Seto. "On Non-echoic Irony," in Carston and Uchida, *Relevance Theory: Applications and Implications*, 244–45.

demonstrate the application of these key insights from relevance theory in the following chapters.

3
Basic Pragmatic Processes

Natural language users bridge a significant gap between the semantics of words and syntax in a sentence, on one hand, and the speaker's intended meaning, on the other. Huang explains, "In Anglo-American pragmatics, it has been widely accepted that the linguistically encoded meaning of a sentence radically underdetermines the proposition a speaker expresses when he or she utters that sentence. This is generally known as the linguistic underdeterminacy thesis."[1] Several scholars argue that relevance theory applies to written communication inasmuch as authors intend to affect readers just as speakers do hearers.[2] A major difference is the amount of time allowed for producing and processing text versus speech. Because the insights of relevance theory apply no less to interpreting textual communication than spoken, they illuminate biblical interpretation.

Linguistic pragmaticists recognize that communication involves inference. The words, syntax, and discourse features of what is said leave much for audiences to infer. "What is said" is Grice's semitechnical language for explicit speech (sentences as uttered), as distinct from "what is meant," which for him was a propositional form enriched by pragmatic processes.[3] The meaning of an utterance is not equal to the value of the words and syntax even in a semantically decoded propositional form. As Blass explains, "The grammars of natural languages fall far short of relating

---

1. Huang, "Micro- and Macro-Pragmatics," 153. For an iteration in the context of biblical scholarship, see Gene L. Green, "Relevance Theory and Theological Interpretation: Thoughts on Metarepresentation," *JTI* 4 (2010): 79. For an explanation pertaining to verbal irony, see Wilson, "Pragmatics of Verbal Irony," 1733.

2. Uchida, "Text and Relevance"; Blass, *Relevance Relations in Discourse*, 43–92; Silviu Serban, "Gricean Pragmatics and Text Linguistics," *ASHUJS* 12 (2011): 96–101.

3. See Grice, "Logic and Conversation," 44, 46, 51–52, 58, and passim.

utterances to the thoughts they were designed to convey."[4] Hearers must and in fact successfully do make countless inferences in order to comprehend utterances.

In chapters 3–4, I address two facets of this key insight: basic pragmatic processes and higher-level explicatures, respectively. These two facets correspond to a development in the discipline from Gricean pragmatics to Sperber and Wilson's relevance theory. According to relevance theory, hearers must make inferences not only at the linguistic decoding level but also at the second-order conceptual level. In fact, studies of language acquisition have shown that both levels are inherent to comprehension.[5] This chapter and the next explain and demonstrate the application of these two facets to the specific features of Titus 1:12. This application is grounded in relevance theory's insight regarding the inferential nature of all communication and fleshes out what I call a *relevance-guided biblical hermeneutic*. I start with basic pragmatic processes.

Sentences are formal and symbolic, composed of words and their syntactical arrangements apart from performative factors such as intonation and visual signals (e.g., eye roll, gesture). By *sentence*, relevance theorists technically mean the "linguistically encoded semantic representation" or the "logical form."[6] *Utterances* are sentences spoken or written within specific social and discursive contexts. In order to discern how hearers grasp utterance meaning, given the underdeterminacy of sentences, relevance theorists apply what I categorize as *basic* pragmatic processes to arrive at a propositional form. This artificial form expands the sentence's details and is as precise as the sentence allows and as open-ended as it requires. Clark explains, "Within relevance theory, the proposition expressed is the propositional form arrived at by fleshing out a linguistically encoded semantic representation."[7] Basic pragmatic processes are required to accomplish this fleshing out, but this procedure is not equivalent to interpretation, which involves more than semantic decoding.[8]

Relevance theorists observe that natural language comprehension is typically a real-time process that does not require intermediate steps. That

---

4. Blass, *Relevance Relations in Discourse*, 42.
5. See Clark, *Relevance Theory*, 171–92, 258–63; Levinson, *Pragmatics*, 282.
6. E.g., Clark, *Relevance Theory*, 200, 244, 299. See also Sperber and Wilson, *Pragmatics: An Overview*, 6–7, 32; Meadowcroft, "Relevance as Mediating Category," 622.
7. Clark, *Relevance Theory*, 200.
8. Huang, "Micro- and Macro-Pragmatics," 136, 152.

is, hearers do not go through two separate processes—one in which they decode a semantic representation into a full proposition, and another in which they interpret the proposition according to higher-level contextual assumptions. Audiences work on both levels simultaneously, dialectically. So, theorists distinguish *logically* between what I am calling basic pragmatic processes (Clark's "fleshing out") and second-order processing, that is, thoughts about thoughts or meta-analysis, of which higher-level explicatures are a type. Theorists do not, however, claim that these two levels are sequential.

As natural language users ourselves, we readily acknowledge the gap between sentence meaning and utterance meaning, and we recognize that hearers regularly bridge that gap to understand speakers successfully. For the sake of biblical interpretation, Green asks, "How, then, do we fill the gap between sentence and utterance meaning?" Pragmatic inference is the process by which humans fill the gap, and relevance theorists endeavor to define the tasks and constraints involved more precisely. Green continues, "The gap between sentence meaning and utterance meaning is filled by an inferential process constrained by the principle of relevance."[9] Through this principle, theorists articulate a simple, coherent framework for understanding how pragmatic processes function, especially when pragmatic steps conflict with one another—for example, when the cognitive effects on a listener of using an ambiguous statement outweigh the risks to the speaker of being misunderstood.

Basic pragmatic processes are tasks that must be accomplished in order to decode the logical form and to achieve higher-level (or second-order) comprehension. This necessity does not imply a rigid sequence. These aspects of comprehension occur dialectically but virtually simultaneously in real time. Hearers typically need to understand who and what pronouns refer to, what sense of a word the speaker uses, and so forth. So, pragmatic processes include disambiguation and reference assignment, as well as an array of tasks intended to resolve vagueness and indeterminacy or restore ellipsed material. These tasks include discerning the meaning of explicit and implicit logical connectives, analyzing lexical pragmatics, and deciding where to place items on the literal-figurative continuum.

In their seminal overview of pragmatics, Sperber and Wilson list the pragmatic tasks that are employed in the interpretation of utterances as

---

9. Green, "Relevance Theory and Biblical Interpretation" (2013), 267, 271.

follows: "The choice of an actual interpretation involves a variety of related tasks: disambiguation, reference assignment, resolution of vaguenesses or indeterminacies and restoration of missing or ellipsed material. These tasks are genuinely pragmatic and must be handled by a theory of utterance interpretation rather than a theory of sentence meaning [semantics]."[10] Over the past several decades, Sperber and Wilson have become leaders in the field of pragmatics and have refined their ideas but have made no substantial changes to what they list as the main tasks of pragmatics.[11] In the following sections, I apply select aspects of pragmatic processing as they are especially relevant for interpreting Titus 1:12. I cover the tasks indicated above under categories that fit the material under examination. The first category is referential and deictic speech.

Referential and Deictic Speech

Referentials are words and phrases that stand in for a more specific referent or target (e.g., *someone, it, what, she*). The meanings of *deictic* words depend on their conversational or discourse context (e.g., *now, I, that, here*). Both types of words are context dependent. With both reference and deixis, processing effort is crucial in weighing alternative interpretations, because these types of speech widen the gap of indeterminacy by supplying less specific semantic information. Take the following sentence, for example: "I like it, and so do they." In the second clause, *do* efficiently replaces the verb and object of the first. The words *it* and *they* also have a referential function. The referents are outside the sentence and would normally be in the conversational context. The adverb *so* has a deictic and a discursive function; it points to the kind of action and expresses a context-specific relationship of comparison between the two propositions.

Referential and deictic speech typically identifies a prominent element in the discourse or in the conversational context. This kind of speech is most often anaphoric. That is, the target has usually already been mentioned within the near context. Levinson describes anaphora as "where some term picks out as referent the same entity (or class of objects) that some prior term in the discourse picked out."[12] When speakers or writers use an alternative word or phrase to refer to or replace a word or phrase from *earlier* in

---

10. Sperber and Wilson, *Pragmatics: An Overview*, 2.
11. See Sperber and Wilson, "Pragmatics" (2007), esp. 478–84.
12. Levinson, *Pragmatics*, 67.

the context, it is anaphoric. Cataphoric references require more processing effort because they force the hearer to suspend the more ambiguous reference until he hears what it is pointing to later in the conversation. According to Dan Cristea and Oana-Dianna Postolache, "a cataphoric relation is given by a pair of coreferring mentions in which the first one introduces the referent and is information-poorer than the subsequent one."[13]

Michael Smith claims that cataphoric pronouns are not superfluous or ornamental but have a specific function. He compares the function achieved by "shell nouns" (an example is what grammarians refer to as *casus pendens*), which are also cataphoric. Smith's description of their linguistic function clearly expects greater-than-usual processing effort (i.e., suspending a mental space to await the referent). Speakers might use cataphora to catch hearers off-guard, to build suspense for effect, or to topicalize a subject; however, as Smith explains, "Cataphors are appreciably less common than anaphors."[14] Cristea and Postolache summarize a corpus analysis that shows "cataphorae" occurring fewer than one in 250 uses of referential speech.[15] Writers may use reference and deixis to avoid repetition, but their choice of which alternative to use frequently contributes to the meaning of its target by signaling *how* to conceive of it.

Because anaphora relies on a known target fresh from the preceding context, it requires significantly less processing effort. Empirical studies of language and neuroscience have demonstrated what linguists have hypothesized, namely, that "recency of use" decreases processing effort.[16] I now look more closely at these kinds of speech in Titus, starting with reference.

---

13. Dan Cristea and Oana-Dianna Postolache, "How to Deal with Wicked Anaphora?," in *Anaphora Processing: Linguistic, Cognitive, and Computational Modelling*, ed. António Branco, Tony McEnery, and Ruslan Mitkov, ASTHLS 263 (Philadelphia: Benjamins, 2005), 36.

14. See Michael B. Smith, "Cataphoric Pronouns as Mental Space Designators: Their Conceptual Import and Discourse Function," in *Cognitive and Communicative Approaches to Linguistic Analysis*, ed. Ellen Contini-Morava, Robert S. Kirsner, and Betsy Rodriguez-Bachiller, SFSL 51 (Amsterdam: Benjamins, 2004), 63. Smith regards cataphoric pronouns as a syntactic class with distinguishable patterns that Titus 1:12 does not exhibit. In fact, none of the pronouns of Titus 1:12–14 signal *placeholding* (as in the sentences, "I like *it* when…" and "The *ones who* ought to hear this are…"), as Smith describes it. As such, the pronouns of Titus 1:12–14 are even less likely to be cataphoric.

15. Cristea and Postolache, "How to Deal," 40.

16. See Clark, *Relevance Theory*, 104. He references studies of Fodoran modularity that tested information association and retrieval on the basis of structures proposed by

Reference

Referentials exhibit various kinds of ambiguity that can indicate or identify a more specific target in the world *outside* the text (e.g., a topic of conversation), *within* the text (e.g., a character), or created *by* the text (e.g., a logical claim or grammatical feature). This last kind may be labeled discourse referential. Elementary school students learn that speakers can use referentials for style and convenience, but choosing referentials over narrower descriptive terms or choosing one type of referential over another also has pragmatic effects. These choices contribute to meaning beyond simply replacing another more specific word. This section disambiguates several referentials in Titus 1:10–16 and argues that they consistently point to troublemakers in the Cretan church, not to Cretans in general. The pronouns of this passage are pivotal to understanding Paul's meaning. Although assigning referents is a relatively basic task, doing so correctly is a critical part of interpretation. Misconstruing a referent can lead to profound misinterpretation. Therefore, understanding where interpreters have assumed false referents and why those misconstruals seemed so apt is crucial to evaluating their interpretations.

Paul introduces a large group ("many [people]," πολλοί, 1:10) of presumptuous, unsanctioned leaders over whom he repeatedly expresses angst (1:11; 2:8, 15; 3:9–11).[17] The epexegetical phrase "especially those

---

philosopher and cognitive scientist Jerry Fodor. Although Fodor's proposals regarding the modular structuring of the mind are speculative and difficult to test directly, several indirect tests suggest that his ideas about processing speed and information retrieval have predictive power.

17. Although the effect on my thesis is negligible, one textual variant in Titus 1:10 deserves comment. It includes καί and reads as follows: Εἰσὶν γὰρ πολλοὶ καὶ ἀνυπότακτοι. It is one of the few plausible variants in this section of Titus. The καί appears in D, F, G, I, Ψ, 1739, and some other, especially Western and Byzantine, texts. The UBS[5] gives the text a C rating. The variant subtly affects Paul's introduction of the troublemakers. Without καί, πολλοί (1:10) is an attributive adjective, as most English translations convey. This variant phrase has more than one translational possibility. Bruce M. Metzger judges the alternative reading as either a case of awkward hendiadys (using two descriptors in a parallel construction to attribute a single compound quality—e.g., "nice and easy") or straightforward attributive speech. See Metzger, *A Textual Commentary on the Greek New Testament* (Stuttgart: Deutsche Bibelgesellschaft, 1994), 584–85. Marshall says that the variant reading results in pleonasm—using extra

of the circumcision" (μάλιστα οἱ ἐκ τῆς περιτομῆς, 1:10) refers not to the entire category of troublemakers but to a (probably numerically significant) portion of them.[18] Mounce cites ancient evidence that there was a significant number of Jews living in Crete in the first century CE.[19] Quinn recognizes that this phrase refers almost exclusively to Jewish Christians—Jewish in ethnicity, Christian in faith, and Cretan only in geographic residence. Yet he claims that Paul uses the Cretan quotation to target people of both ethnicities alike.[20] Although scholars are not confident that, historically speaking, Paul was addressing a problem of Jew-gentile relations within the Cretan church, he likely nevertheless used this phrase to activate the assumption that Jewish believers were *en force* among the troublemakers. Several statements in Titus strongly suggest that those who ascribed to and elevated features of Jewish religious culture were instilling a sense of ethno-religious inferiority in Cretan believers. This evidence is discussed in chapter 5 under "Cognitive Environment." Presumptuous leaders impressed on believers that those not adhering to the customs of Jewish religious culture were inferior. That teaching, of course, was contrary to Paul's gospel and "healthy doctrine" (1:9, 13; 2:1–2, 8); furthermore, it "upset entire households" (1:11). One cannot know the extent to which this represents a real historical issue, but the writer portrays it as one that comports with representations in other New Testament books.

---

words to describe the problematic offenders. He suggests that it may have been original but that it was dropped by scribes (*Critical and Exegetical Commentary*, 193). The main translational choice is between "there are many insubordinate ones" (accepted reading) and "there are many and insubordinate ones" (variant reading). To expand the variant reading for clarity: "there are people, who, because they are insubordinate, are [too] many" (i.e., more than there should be). Metzger prefers this latter understanding of the variant rather than the more awkward reading that the troublemakers were *both* numerous and insubordinate. See also Perkins, who delineates the three main grammatical options with or without the conjunction without passing judgment on which is preferred (*Pastoral Letters*, 252).

18. See Smith, "Bible Translation and Relevance Theory," 136, for an analysis that reads μάλιστα as possibly identifying the circumcision faction with the insubordinate ones without remainder.

19. Mounce, *Pastoral Epistles*, 396.

20. Quinn, *Letter to Titus*, 98. Hayne Griffin makes a similar claim. See Thomas D. Lea and Hayne P. Griffin, *1, 2 Timothy, Titus*, NAC 34 (Nashville: Broadman & Holman, 1992), 289–90.

Later in Titus, Paul does not transparently develop his ethical instruction on the vices identified in the Cretan quotation.[21] He does, however, consistently address issues that undermined the Cretans' moral and spiritual reputation. Influential people in Titus's Christian community and those sympathetic to their rhetoric questioned Cretan legitimacy, and troublemakers impressed a sense of religious and moral inferiority on ethnic Cretans. When Paul talks about components of Jewish religious culture, he does so in a way that diminishes exclusionary claims and relativizes the worth of customs as symbols of credibility or validity. Each time Paul mentions Jewish religious and cultural interests, he counters the notion that gentiles cannot be full-fledged members of the church without attending to certain traditions, circumcision (1:10) being chief among them.

The first pronouns that require disambiguation appear in the quotative frame: "someone from [among] them—a prophet of their own—said" (εἶπέν τις ἐξ αὐτῶν ἴδιος αὐτῶν προφήτης, 1:12a). This translation aims to convey in English the sense that the speaker belongs to whatever group Paul has been talking about. The partitive use of the genitive pronoun αὐτῶν, coupled with ἴδιος, emphasizes this belonging. Most commentators note the label *prophet* within the subject phrase as peculiar, but few satisfyingly address the unusual syntactic construction. Knight regards the phrase ἴδιος αὐτῶν προφήτης as emphatic of belonging and takes for granted that the group is ethnic Cretans.[22] Mounce asserts that the repetition of αὐτῶν is classical.[23] Marshall says that the τις ἐξ αὐτῶν is "typically vague."[24] In fact, it is difficult to translate the exact thrust into English.

Although a few constructions in Greek literature bear some similarity, this syntax does not seem to constitute an established idiom; it is unusual. Under the rubric of Grice's maxim of manner—namely, "be brief"—Levinson explains why speakers might not adhere to the maxim. He reasons, "Wherever I avoid some simple expression in favour of some more complex paraphrase, it may be assumed that I do not do so wantonly, but because the details are somehow relevant to the present enterprise."[25]

---

21. Although some scholars note subtle correlates (see Kidd, "Titus as Apologia"; Faber, "Evil Beasts, Lazy Gluttons").
22. Knight, *Pastoral Epistles*, 298.
23. Mounce, *Pastoral Epistles*, 399.
24. Marshall, *Critical and Exegetical Commentary*, 198.
25. Levinson, *Pragmatics*, 107–8. Note that relevance is essential to this explanation.

Nonconventional verbiage presumably signals special meaning. Let us examine more closely the referential components of this quotative frame.

Because of the partitive use,[26] let us address the first αὐτῶν and then return to the sequentially prior τις. This genitive plural pronoun in ἐξ αὐτῶν ("from [among] them," 1:12) references a group or category of people that probably corresponds with οἵτινες ("who[ever]," 1:11), which itself refers to the troublemakers mentioned earlier (1:10). Paul mentions another plurality of persons further from the context of 1:12, in the previous paragraph (τοὺς ἀντιλέγοντας, "the contradicting [people]," 1:9). No other references to a group of people commend themselves as the target of αὐτῶν. In terms of literary context, πρεσβυτέρους ("elders," 1:5) is distant and unlikely as a referent, because Paul shifts his focus from good leaders to bad in the paragraph that begins at 1:10.

Many commentators implicitly or explicitly take the referent of this pronoun (αὐτῶν, 1:12) to be Cretans.[27] Although the miso-Cretan reading assumes that Κρήτῃ ("Crete," 1:5) signals the target, Paul's mention of this place is not only distant but primarily geographical. Hearers typically expect referents to correspond substantially with their pronouns on a conceptual level, and referentials normally correspond in kind (e.g., number, gender, conceptual type) with their referents.[28] As it is a singular proper name for Paul's former and Titus's current location (1:5), Paul probably did not expect readers to suspend the place name in their mind while he discussed other topics and people for a stretch of eight finite clauses (seven verses) before referring to the people who dwell in that place as αὐτῶν.

---

26. Perkins, *Pastoral Letters*, 254.
27. E.g., Knight, *Pastoral Epistles*, 298–99.
28. Incidentally, all of Michael B. Smith's dozens of English and German examples follow this pattern. His examples, even of cataphora, reveal that when it functions, the referent is able to replace the cataphoric pronoun or noun with very little grammatical adjustment (Smith, "Cataphoric Pronouns"). One caveat with his study is that he was not examining all possible types of cataphors, but it suggests that similar rules are normal. Cristea and Postolache, with respect to the factors of referent resolution, note that grammatical equivalence can occasionally be a misleading indicator of resolution, so grammatical mismatches should not stand alone in dismissing a word or discourse unit as a referent ("How to Deal," 21–24). Their computational anaphora resolution engine would limit scans for referent expressions to ten sentences for coreferentials and three sentences for functional referentials, but they acknowledge that most referentials can be found within five sentences. Eight clauses seems to be the outer limit.

Cristea and Postolache provide a detailed technical description of the factors affecting reference resolution.[29] Although Koine Greek is not one of the languages they account for in their investigation, they make cross-linguistic claims about language cognition, so their findings are applicable to biblical literature.[30] Blass argues that relevance-theoretical observations are valid cross-linguistically and that languages that differ on the surface level of forms do not differ as much on the cognitive level.[31] One of the factors Cristea and Postolache identify for successful reference resolution under "positional features" is "intervening discourse units." They found "that the great majority of the anaphors can find an antecedent within this range," which they earlier identify as "a vicinity of five sentences."[32] Resolving a referent further away in the discourse typically requires the referent to be remarkably salient, another factor in reference resolution that these and other authors mention. *Crete* just does not seem to meet the criteria for salience in comparison to the intervening material between 1:5 and 1:12.[33]

Conventional, miso-Cretan readings of Titus 1:12 require unlikely syntactic maneuvers, taking the referent of αὐτῶν ("of them," 1:12, the second instance) to be either distant or cataphoric. On account of their linear (incremental) processing hypothesis, Cristea and Postolache are dubious of all purportedly cataphoric usage.[34] They suggest that when analysts suspect cataphoric usage, they should examine other referential alternatives before resolving a referring expression as such.[35] This suggests that "Cretans" (1:12b) is most likely *not* the proper reference assignment for αὐτῶν. A more appropriate antecedent is readily available in the pre-

---

29. Cristea and Postolache, "How to Deal," 21–25.
30. They assert, for example, that the "domain of referential accessibility is thought to be stable to language change" (Cristea and Postolache, "How to Deal," 25).
31. Blass, *Relevance Relations in Discourse*, 90.
32. Cristea and Postolache, "How to Deal," 23–24.
33. See ch. 5 under "Original Audiences versus Modern Eavesdroppers."
34. For details, see Cristea and Postolache, "How to Deal."
35. Cristea and Postolache, "How to Deal," 36–38. Their corpus analysis shows that there is usually some suggestion of the identity of referents within the few sentences prior to referring expressions. They address several complexities with referential language and, echoing other scholars, say, "In cases where a pronoun precedes a noun but the text contains an earlier more informative mention of the same entity, … the pronoun should be resolved against the preceding text as in ordinary anaphora" (37). I contend that Titus 1:10–16 features this pattern.

ceding context, and its proximity as an anaphoric referent makes it far more likely. The relevant subset of people who dwell in Crete and the referent of οἵτινες ("who[ever]," 1:11) are one and the same. Therefore, αὐτῶν probably refers to the troublemakers in the Cretan church.

No miso-Cretan reading of the personal pronoun (αὐτῶν, 1:12, the second instance) could be coterminous with Cretans in any normal sense (e.g., ethnic, geographic, political), nor could it refer narrowly to Cretan Christians, for none of the poets to whom such interpretations attribute the quotation lived during the Christian era. The context suggests a more straightforward reading. The presumptuous, troublemaking leaders— described as rebellious, idle-talking, deceptive, and especially from the circumcision (1:10)—are its most likely antecedent. Because Paul gives a relatively vivid description of that group, the idea that the pronoun refers to Cretans (either as a far-reaching anaphor or as an unusual cataphor) is doubtful. I argue that Paul was concerned with the out-of-place use of the supposedly famous refrain about Cretans and shows no interest in or awareness of its possible origins in Cretan literary history.

On the basis of natural language comprehension, a simple linear processing exercise should demonstrate how the tradition that the quotation is from Epimenides is superfluous to grasping Paul's use. Read the book of Titus through to the quotative frame (1:12a) but pause before reading the quotation itself (1:12b), then ask, simply on the basis of the text and not its history of interpretation, What do we know about the speaker to whom Paul refers? Does Paul convey sympathy or trust toward this speaker? The analysis below continues the examination of referentials and suggests an answer.

The pronoun τις ("someone," 1:12a) refers to a member of the group to which αὐτῶν refers.[36] As argued above, the group is not coterminous with ethnic Cretans or Cretan Christians generally, so a critical question is, What is the whole and what is the part? According to a typical iteration of the miso-Cretan reading, the whole is ethnic Cretans, and the part is a poet of Cretan descent, namely, Epimenides. This conventional reference assignment effectively excludes Jews, so we should reasonably

---

36. In 1 Tim 1:3–7, τις is used twice to refer to unnamed troublemakers who cause some of the same sorts of difficulty in Ephesus. Correlated ideas include "myths and genealogies" (see Titus 1:14, 3:9) and "meaningless talk" (see 1:10). The pronoun is common, but my point is that Paul refers anonymously to troublemakers in these contexts, suggesting that the referent of τις is one of them.

ask, Whence this concern with "circumcision" (1:10) and "Jewish myths" (1:14) in the surrounding material? The intuitive natural language exercise described in the paragraph above casts these assumptions about the identity of the whole and of the part into doubt. A more natural reading is that αὐτῶν (used twice for intensity) is anaphoric and refers to the presumptuous leaders. It was "from [among] them" (ἐξ αὐτῶν, 1:12a) that the quotation had (re)emerged with a new and ugly pejorative purpose, and Paul became aware of its currency. He may not have known or cared about the original attribution of this quotation. What mattered was that the unidentified troublemaker (τις, 1:12a) who employed the ghastly slur was one of those who presumed to be leaders and teachers among the congregation. One of their tactics in advancing and maintaining their status was utterly objectionable to Paul—that of accentuating the supposed ethno-religious inferiority of the Cretan populace. The author of Titus portrays Jew-gentile tensions as a significant issue in the Cretan church.[37]

The indefinite pronoun τις ("someone," 1:12) may be used to refer to someone whose identity is well-known in order to downplay the fame or importance of the individual, as in, "As *some* pop singer once said, 'Beat it.'"[38] The conventional reference assignment, however, assumes that Paul draws on Epimenides as an authority, which does not cohere with a choice to understate his importance. Therefore, I judge that this nontypical use of the indefinite pronoun does not apply in this case. Typically, τις is used when some feature of its referent (i.e., exact identity) is not known or not relevant. It is not clear that Paul knew the author of the quotation or its original poetic context. His use of τις corresponds to being uninterested or unable to identify with certainty the person or persons who were using it. He may not have known the quotation outside its tertiary (an echo of an echo) and inappropriate context—the Cretan church.

To whom does Paul credit the saying? Whether Epimenides authored the quotation at some point is not pertinent to Paul's use. He discloses scant to no knowledge of or interest in Epimenides. The near context

---

37. I discuss the themes of church leadership and Jew-gentile relations in Titus in ch. 5 under "Cognitive Environment."

38. Its plural form is used in 1 Tim 1:3 to instruct "certain people not teach different doctrines." These people certainly had a specific identity, and Paul certainly had specific objections to their doctrines, but he obscured their exact identity, likely because, as in Titus, it was the behavior that concerned him.

indicates that this τις was part of a troublesome group (1:10–12a). While natural language hearers process referential speech in real time, modern readers must look again to the context, especially the preceding verses, for the most likely referent. Evidence from context strongly suggests that Paul was concerned with someone from among the group of troublemakers, regardless of whether this τις was echoing the words of someone who came before, such as Epimenides. Although many interpretations of Titus 1:12 depend on assigning the quotation to this figure, pragmatic reference assignment does not commend the tendency.

Another word deserves attention: ἴδιος ("[their] own," 1:12a). Grammatically and morphologically, this word is an adjective, but it almost always has a referential function.[39] Taking adjectival forms, it matches the inflection of its head noun and not of its referent, which frequently obscures the number and gender of its target, requiring pragmatic inference on the basis of context. This feature makes it a prime example of the underdeterminacy of linguistically encoded speech. Every use of ἴδιος elsewhere in Titus is anaphoric, taking a referent from the preceding context (1:3; 2:5, 9). When this word appears in comparable New Testament epistolary literature to make reference to persons (as it does in 1:12; 2:5, 9), the use is also anaphoric.[40] When anaphoric, the referent typically appears in the immediate near context, never more than a few clauses away. Not only is ἴδιος typically anaphoric, but its referent is typically explicit, yet miso-Cretan readings require that the referent is implied and not explicit because no group or person that appears in the text is coterminous with what various iterations of the reading expect. This evidence, too, points to

---

39. Based on its referential function, some classify it alongside pronouns. See A. T. Robertson, *A Grammar of the Greek New Testament in the Light of Historical Research*, 3rd ed. (London: Hodder & Stoughton, 1919), 692; MM, 298. MM explains that grammarians who equate ἴδιος with the possessive pronoun are missing its often rich emphasis on belonging.

40. The instance in the epistolary greeting (Titus 1:3) would only be an exception if the target of ἰδίοις were taken to be λόγον and not ζωῆς or ἐλπίδι or any other preceding word, which would be an odd reading. The occurrences of ἴδιος in the Pastoral Epistles (1 Tim 2:6; 3:4–5, 12; 4:2; 5:4; 5:8; 6:1, 15; 2 Tim 1:9, 4:3), the undisputed Pauline corpus (Rom 8:32, 10:3, 11:24, 14:4–5; Gal 2:2, 6:5, 9), and Hebrews (4:10, 7:27, 9:12, 13:12) demonstrate that cataphoric use is rare. The listed occurrences are exhaustive of every use within their respective books, which are representative. In all of these examples, the referent appears in the preceding context. Miso-Cretan readings require unusual (unlikely) syntactical maneuvers.

the troublemakers of 1:10–11 as the group from which the speaker of 1:12 comes, as far as Paul seems to be concerned.

Finally, let us look at the immediate context following the Cretan quotation. The pronoun αὐτούς ("them," 1:13c) refers to the direct object of a severe reproof. Paul issues the command to reprove (ἔλεγχε αὐτοὺς ἀποτόμως, "rebuke them severely," 1:13c) on the basis of (δι' ἣν αἰτίαν, "on account of which reason," 1:13b) the evidence he presents (ἡ μαρτυρία αὕτη, "this testimony," 1:13a). The near proximity of the claim that someone was advancing the insult suggests that the demonstrative here (αὕτη, "this," 1:13a) refers to the testimony Paul gives concerning the troublemakers in Crete—namely, they are propounding a characterization of ethnic Cretans inconsistent with the gospel and social reality. For this reason, Paul commands Titus to rebuke *them* severely—that is, the troublemakers.

The miso-Cretan reading typically assumes either that Paul was instructing Titus to rebuke Cretans generally or that his command to rebuke resumed his concern with the troublemakers, which he supposedly suspended in 1:12–13a.[41] Although the latter of these assumptions, unlike the former, has the benefit of not being ridiculous, it ignores how connected the passage is by virtue of the density of referentials in verses 12–13. The relative pronoun (ἣν, "which," 1:13b) should not be separated from its referent to the extent this latter reading calls for. That is, the *reason* corresponds to the offenses Paul lists in 1:10–11, and the slur of 1:12 is one of the offenses. All of the offenses Paul lists constitute a single "testimony" or "reason" (μαρτυρία, αἰτίαν, respectively, 1:13) for rebuke. The quotation represents an egregious example. Evidence for this logic is described more fully under "Procedural and Logical Connectives and Particles" below. For now, let us consider deixis.

Deixis

Deictics, also known as *indexicals*, serve a pointing function. They link words and sentences to other things—features of time, place, person, status, discourse, and so forth—without necessarily replacing them as referentials do. In his discussion of deixis, Levinson includes discourse deixis (also known as text deixis), which is pertinent for interpreting Titus 1:10–

---

41. Towner is one of the few who does not see 1:12–13a as a digression (*1–2 Timothy and Titus*, 129–32).

16 and other biblical literature and for evaluating interpretations thereof. Discourse deixis points to a proximal or distal text or argument, linking components of the utterance to components of the broader discourse context. It points to other speech, not to actual or imagined objects. The following example is adapted from Levinson: "That's a rhinoceros; spell it for me."[42] The pronoun in the second clause does not refer to an animal in the world outside the discourse but to the *mention* of the animal within the discourse.[43] Mentions can become complex, because speakers may have in mind entire sentences, ideas, or ad hoc components of their speech. Speakers mention things to process, critique, or evaluate them. In the case above, the speaker asks the hearer to process (spell) *rhinoceros*. In the next chapter, I detail the technical use of *mention* in relevance theory.

"This testimony is true" (ἡ μαρτυρία αὕτη ἐστὶν ἀληθής, 1:13) presents interpreters with a neglected question: Does ἡ μαρτυρία αὕτη point to the world outside or the world inside the discourse? Commentators do not adequately address this important concern. Marco Rocha has developed a set of rules for determining the target of demonstratives.[44] In his corpus analysis, the largest percentage of successful demonstrative referent resolutions is discourse deictic. In other words, to grasp the meaning of the demonstrative in most cases requires *discourse knowledge* as opposed to any other strategy, such as collocation, "first-candidate search" (i.e., the closest prior noun), or "first-candidate chain" (i.e., preceding phrase or sentence).[45] Miso-Cretan readings suggest that "this testimony" (1:13) refers to the quotation about Cretans—that is, the preceding sentence. Some interpreters describe some nuance Paul added. For instance, he winked at the logical contradiction inherent in the liar paradox that would

---

42. Levinson, *Pragmatics*, 62–64, 85–86.
43. *Mention* has a technical meaning in linguistic pragmatics. See chapter 4 under "Higher-Level Explicatures" for more definition and detail.
44. See Marco Rocha, "Anaphoric Demonstratives: Dealing with the Hard Cases," in Branco, McEnery, and Mitkov, *Anaphora Processing*, 403–27. Rocha aimed for an extremely precise analysis because he wanted to program computers to execute a repeatable process for analyzing text. He provides valuable insights, even though he does not entirely succeed. The problem is that most computerized linguistics projects tie analysis to form so that the system can compute all instances, which makes relevance theorists balk. Rocha worked with corpora of English and Portuguese, and his analysis found similar patterns in both languages. He argues that his findings apply cross-linguistically and therefore reflect cognitive linguistics.
45. Rocha, "Anaphoric Demonstratives," 409.

obtain if a Cretan stated the quotation. Paul, tongue in cheek, affirms that it is true, thus deliberately creating a contradiction of his own. As Thiselton suggests, "The additional comment 'This testimony is true' is not a sign that the writer (or an editor) is oblivious to the nature of paradox; it is more likely to have been intended as a light touch underlining the absurdity of a regress *ad infinitum*."[46] I noted before, however, that this view depends on the attribution of the quotation to Epimenides, which is at least unassured if not doubtful. Alternatively, if Paul was primarily concerned with troublemakers in the Cretan congregation who used the quotation as a slur against Titus's missionary congregation, the demonstrative likely has a discourse deictic function. It points to Paul's testimony against the troublemakers, not to his agreement with a prejudicial assessment of the Cretans made outside the text. In chapter 5 under "Contextual Assumptions," I explain the cognitive framing and activation of Paul's courtroom language.

The near demonstrative pronoun οὗτος ("this," 1:13) was distinguished as the marker of proximity in classical Greek from ἐκεῖνος ("that"). By the era of the Greek New Testament, it might have lost some of its distinctive force in Koine so that it occasionally differed little from the personal pronoun αὐτός ("it") in usage,[47] but the NRSV translation, "That testimony is true" (1:13a), suggests an underlying *far* demonstrative. If one *assumes* that Paul is concerned with an ancient Cretan poet, then a far demonstrative would be appropriate, but the Greek does not lean in such a direction. If Paul is pointing, however, to his own exposure of a problem in his case against the troublemakers, then the near demonstrative we find in the passage is fitting. The author of Titus knows how to use both οὗτος ("this," 1:13) and ἐκεῖνος ("that," 3:7) distinctively, so it is reasonable to argue that they should be differentiated.

The author of 2 Timothy clearly knew how to distinguish between near and far demonstratives in discourse deixis, pointing to referents in the near discourse as οὗτοι ("these [ones]," 2 Tim 3:8) and the far discourse as ἐκείνων ("those [ones]," 3:9) to distinguish between οἱ ἐνδύνοντες ("the ones slyly entering," 3:6) and Ἰάννης καὶ Ἰαμβρῆς ("Jannes and Jambres,"

---

46. Thiselton, "Logical Role," 207.

47. Daniel B. Wallace, *Greek Grammar beyond the Basics: An Exegetical Syntax of the New Testament* (Grand Rapids: Zondervan, 1996), 318. The development was more complex and largely took place later than the New Testament. See Io Manolessou, "The Evolution of the Demonstrative System in Greek," *JGL* 2 (2002): 119–48.

3:8), respectively. To avoid confusion while skipping over another demonstrative to reach the target, the writer chose the far demonstrative in the second instance. This suggests that the near demonstrative in Titus 1:13 retains its proximity-marking force. The proposal that the same author wrote each of the Pastoral Epistles reinforces this claim.

If ἡ μαρτυρία αὕτη ("this testimony," 1:13a) points to a saying that had currency in the Cretan church and that Paul was affirming, then it depends on a truth-conditional proposition. Inquiries into historical (opinions about) Cretan malfeasance would, then, be understandable. Given that Paul identifies the subject of the predicate adjective *true* as a *testimony*, we reasonably ask, In what sense could the poetic saying be categorized as a testimony?[48] This question deserves attention. But, evidence suggests that Paul pointed to his own description of the troublemakers' malfeasance in Crete as a *testimony* that indicted them for their demeaning speech (1:12) and disrupting behavior (1:10–11). I contend that the deixis targeted Paul's own discourse, rather than some truth-conditional content in the outside world for which modern scholars should feel obliged to find corroborating evidence.

Social deixis is also relevant for interpreting the Bible. It involves aspects of language that encode the social identities of participants or the social relationships between each other or other persons referred to.[49] Writers, as well as speakers, regularly choose their words based on their propriety both to describe real-world objects (semantic appropriateness) and to describe them properly to specific hearers (social appropriateness). In languages with honorific systems and formalities, Levinson notes, "it is almost impossible to say anything at all which is not sociolinguistically marked as appropriate for certain kinds of addressees only."[50] Native speakers of any language (including English) are usually not conscious of the extent to which social deixis affects their seemingly intuitive choices of lexeme and syntax.

For example, consider how the following list of congratulatory phrases reflects various levels and registers of celebration as well as types of relationship between the speaker and the hearer: *I'm proud of you; I applaud*

---

48. In ch. 5 under "Contextual Assumptions," I explain the effect of activating a courtroom. It suffices here to note that αἰτία (1:13) can mean "a basis for legal action," which fits the context if Paul uses it metaphorically. See entry in BDAG, 31.

49. Definition based closely on Levinson, *Pragmatics*, 89.

50. Levinson, *Pragmatics*, 90.

you; I admire you; Yay! Each statement is appropriate to the same occasion but evokes different social arrangements. They may exhibit semantic differences, but their pragmatic differences are more significant.[51] Levinson explains, "Social deixis is concerned with the grammaticalization, or encoding in language structure, of social information."[52] Social deixis signals social roles such as differentiations between first, second, and third persons and the social categories among them as well as indications and invocations of privilege, deference, or disdain. Levinson observes that almost any utterance has social deictic features.

Paul's self-designation is an example of social deixis. He refers to himself as "a servant of God, an apostle, moreover, of Jesus Christ" (1:1). Thus he introduces the letter by signaling aspects of his vocation in relation to God and, implicitly, Titus and the church. He sets himself as an authority representing the "unlying God" (1:2). So, when he sanctions Titus to execute certain authoritative actions (e.g., "appoint," 1:5; "rebuke," 1:13), he invokes multiple layers of social obligation—for instance, when he says, "I desire you to insist on these [things]" (3:8).

Does Paul use the honorable title "prophet" (προφήτης, 1:12) to refer to a pagan poet, Epimenides? As far as Acts 17:28 is concerned, Paul knew how to say *poet* when referring to a pagan author.[53] If Paul agreed with the quotation and wanted to elevate the status of its originator, he might have done so by naming him a *prophet*. His usage, however, seems to suggest special marking, which is often signaled by noncustomary usage.[54] Towner thinks that Paul's use of this inappropriate, honorific title is likely

---

51. Social deixis also relates to material in ch. 6, "The Nonpropositional Dimensions of Communication."

52. Levinson, *Pragmatics*, 93.

53. Craig S. Keener incidentally suggests that Epimenides was also a possible source for a phrase of Paul's poetic quotation in Acts 17:28, which may have been an amalgam (note the plural source, *some ... poets*). See Keener, *Acts: An Exegetical Commentary* (Grand Rapids: Baker Academic, 2012), 3:2657. Because none of Epimenides's works survive, this can only be conjecture. Keener's footnotes show that these attributional claims are secondhand in nature. Several references fail to corroborate the attribution of the Acts quotation to Epimenides but are merely ancient literary mentions of Epimenides. The vagueness about who Epimenides was and when he lived is discussed in ch. 1, where every reference that Keener cites is addressed.

54. See Steven E. Runge, *Discourse Grammar of the Greek New Testament: A Practical Introduction for Teaching and Exegesis*, LRBS (Peabody, MA: Hendrickson, 2010), 61–68; Levinson, *Pragmatics*, 307–8.

sarcastic.[55] It had distinct significance in a Jewish ethno-religious context; as Quinn notes, "Prophetic credentials were found and valued among the Jewish Christians."[56] A descriptive use would have flattened its significance. After describing the troublemakers (1:10–11), Paul downplays the speaker's importance ("someone from among them") then plays up the speaker's credentials ("prophet"). This is a standard tactic in irony, as when friends observe someone's ridiculous choice or behavior and remark, "What a genius!"[57]

Paul subverts the normal meaning of the descriptor by pointing snidely to an impudent leader who only poses as a prophet in the scenario recounted in Titus 1:10–12. Only in the questionable company of the troublemakers, and perhaps in his own mind, is the speaker of this quotation considered a prophet. To have such a prophet as this—now that Paul has exposed him—is a source of shame. Suwon Yoon explains how honorific titles can be deployed subversively to achieve dramatic pragmatic effects.[58] In the case of Titus 1:12, *prophet* is actually not an honorific title but a sarcastic dismissal.

The Cretan quotation may have evoked a liar paradox in its original setting, and Paul may deliberately accentuate the logical contradiction involved. Following Thiselton, however, the contradiction is even more dramatic and effective if it exposes the failure of third parties (i.e., the presumptuous leaders) to speak anything objectively true by taking up this quotation as a slur.[59] According to the miso-Cretan reading, part of the validity structure for Paul is that the quotation emerged from within the

---

55. Towner, *Letters to Timothy and Titus*, 700, 742.
56. Quinn, *Letter to Titus*, 109.
57. See, e.g., Wilson, "Pragmatic of Verbal Irony"; Yus, "Relevance Theory and Contextual Sources-Centered Analysis"; Seto, "On Non-echoic Irony." See fig. 4.2, where I explain irony in more detail.
58. Suwon Yoon, "Semantic Constraint and Pragmatic Nonconformity for Expressives: Compatibility Condition on Slurs, Epithets, Anti-Honorifics, Intensifiers, and Mitigators," *LangSci* 52 (2015): 46–69.
59. See Thiselton, "Logical Role," 207–23. He develops his interpretation from arguments of linguists J. L. Austin, J. R. Searle, and others (esp. 218–21). As I have suggested, his is one of the best and most nuanced treatments of this passage in history. His great contribution was in calling attention to the gross mistreatment of this passage on the basis of flawed historical inquiry. In the end, however, his conclusion is not convincing because it requires a specific and fragile set of contextual assumptions (implicated premises, to be exact; see my ch. 5) that are not reasonable to expect.

Cretan community (i.e., first-person reference), but it could only be true if it were used from without (i.e., third-person reference). Perhaps, however, the troublemakers, rather than Paul, leaned on this validity structure, whereas Paul exposed the absurdity of the quotation in their mouths by pointing to their dubious logic—they relied on a lie to tell what they purported to be a truth.

Procedural and Logical Connectives and Particles

Titus 1:12 and its context have discursive features that require inferential processing, and the discipline of discourse analysis is especially helpful for discerning the logical connections between sentences and discourse units *as encoded* in language. Linguist Robert Longacre developed one of the earliest methods of discourse analysis (or "discourse grammar") applied to the Hebrew Bible. He analyzed the stable, discourse functions of words and phrases and considered objectivity and reliability to be important strengths of the method. It straddles the domains of semantics and pragmatics, stripping numerous erroneous semantic accretions away from formal components of language while asserting their stable functional core.[60] Because it is now practiced by a broad array of interpreters and linguists, it exhibits diversity in method, philosophy, and level of precision.

Describing two broad trends within discourse analysis should clarify its relation to relevance theory: one broad grouping of discourse analysts emphasize formal and code-driven phenomena, ameliorating some of the subjective tendencies of interpretation. So, it is about decoding what an author has encoded by observed patterns of cohesion, coherence, and development. The attraction of discourse analysis for these interpreters is its presumed objectivity since it is based on disinterested verifiable textual data rather than on impassioned, rhetorical readings. For example, Steven Runge claims that each Greek connective "brings to bear a unique *semantic* constraint to the relationship of the clause that follows with some other portion of the discourse."[61]

Further, he insists on Epimenides as the referent, which I have shown is uncertain. My final interpretation is more plausible.

60. Longacre, *Grammar of Discourse*, 1–6.

61. See, Runge, *Discourse Grammar*, 51, emphasis added; see also 19. Stanley E. Porter and Andrew W. Pitts regard the objectivity of discourse analysis as an asset in finding ways to locate variant-unit boundaries for text criticism. See Porter and Pitts,

Analysts in the other grouping emphasize that the patterns they observe do not place semantic constraints on utterances as much as trigger pragmatic inferences. For example, Mira Ariel writes, "Hence, we cannot simply argue for or against specific semantic analyses based on prevalent discourse patterns, for the correct account for the pattern may be pragmatic, rather than semantic."[62] Along these lines, Blass explains, "Discourse is not a purely linguistic notion, and can therefore not be investigated in purely formal linguistic terms."[63]

This breadth of opinion and method is actually illuminating. Linguists such as Runge and Blass, representing different perspectives on the role of discourse analysis, provide nuanced discussions of how formal components of language affect discourse interpretation. Analysts from the semantic maximalist strain emphasize stable encoding, whereas analysts from the pragmaticist strain emphasize flexibility and context dependence. These emphases parallel the dialectic that relevance theory holds to be essential to comprehension. Discourse analysis complements relevance theory in that it demonstrates the linguistic encoding of some pragmatic functions while also appreciating the influence of context. The meaning of ἀλλά, for example, is not contained in an English word that glosses it, such as *but* or *rather*. Instead, ἀλλά pragmatically signals a context in which an audience is to expect the correction of an inadequate or incomplete view— namely, the view that the speaker articulates in the immediately preceding clause.[64] So, the pragmatic and semantic features of language combine.

Consider the extended ἵνα purpose clause contained in Titus 1:13–14. The intention of the stern rebuke (1:13) is to refocus attention away from "Jewish myths and commandments of humans who are turning from the truth" (1:14). These diversions, however, are not clearly related to the content of the quotation in 1:12. Do such myths and commandments cause generalized moral failure? The substance of the quotation cannot be the

---

Fundamentals of New Testament Textual Criticism (Grand Rapids: Eerdmans, 2015), 80–86.

62. Mira Ariel, "What Discourse Can(not) Teach Us," *IRP* 6 (2014): 181–210. See also Blass, *Relevance Relations in Discourse*, 7–42.

63. Blass, *Relevance Relations in Discourse*, 41.

64. Runge, *Discourse Grammar*, 55–57. See also Shawn Craigmiles, "Pragmatic Constraints of ἀλλά in the Synoptic Gospels" (PhD diss., Asbury Theological Seminary, 2016), 353–70. Although Craigmiles's study focuses on the Synoptic Gospels, the conclusions are pertinent, esp. with regard to the discourse passages.

reason for the rebuke. Addressing gluttony or laziness, for instance, would not accomplish the ends described above in any transparent way. If the church in Crete were exercising excessive austerity (e.g., fasting) under the influence of "Jewish myths and commandments of humans," as some commentators hold,[65] it is difficult to understand how rebuking them for *gluttony* would solve the problem. If, however, Paul wanted Titus to rebuke insolent leaders for advancing a degraded view of Cretans, then one of the results of rebuking them could be that they cease teaching their corrupt doctrine, which involved "Jewish myths and commandments" (implying ethno-religious superiority). These presumptuous leaders, not the Cretans in general, were the "people who are turning from the truth" (1:14).[66] Although they were in the church, their doctrine and social concourse did not agree with Paul's. If Titus was supposed to rebuke Cretans for general and intrinsic moral failure, it would not transparently lead away from paying attention to these myths and commandments. Rather, it might just as likely lead them toward finding in such regulations a remedial system for their supposedly inherent faults. The instrumental connection that Paul envisaged between the imperative and its stated purpose would be extremely weak.

Consider also Paul's use of ἀλλά in 1:15. Greek writers typically use this conjunction to correlate two ideas while making a *correction* or *completion* in the second clause (the one beginning with ἀλλά) and usually keeping the principal claim from the first clause intact.[67] Titus 1:15 may be translated as follows: "to the clean [ones], all things [are] clean; while to the defiled and faithless ones, not one thing [is] clean; instead, both their thinking and conscience [are] defiled" (πάντα καθαρὰ τοῖς καθαροῖς· τοῖς δὲ μεμιαμμένοις καὶ ἀπίστοις οὐδὲν καθαρόν, ἀλλὰ μεμίανται αὐτῶν καὶ ὁ νοῦς καὶ ἡ συνείδησις). While leaving the principal claim intact that "not one thing [being] clean" pertains to persons who "have been defiled and are unfaithful," the ἀλλά clause completes this idea by explaining why. It is crucial, therefore, to understand to whom Paul is referring as "clean [ones]," "unclean [ones]," and related designations. The play on words suggests a

---

65. E.g., Aageson, *Paul, the Pastoral Epistles*, 80; Barrett, *Pastoral Epistles*, 127, 132, 145; Bassler, *1 Timothy*, 27–28; Mounce, *Pastoral Epistles*, 402; Twomey, *Pastoral Epistles*, 224.

66. The canonical portrayal of the Cretans, in contrast, is of a missionary population that was turning *toward* the truth.

67. Runge, *Discourse Grammar*, 55–57.

religio-cultural distinction or conflict. Paul places the very people who advance Cretan unworthiness on the wrong side of this poignant comparison, drawing as it does on religious connotations salient for Jews.

Let us consider two conjunctions (δέ and γάρ) side by side for reasons that will soon be apparent. The coordinating conjunction δέ is part of the connecting tissue of Titus, appearing in the letter relatively frequently. It has a range of possible nuances, but it consistently advances the argument. This conjunction marks development and comparison (with contrast, when appropriate) between concepts. In vernacular terms, δέ basically indicates that not enough has been said, so it signals *I must add something more* and could be paraphrased, "What's more...." The need to say more is not so much a logical necessity as an authorial compulsion; in order to satisfy the communicative intention, the author must add what follows the δέ.[68]

The logical conjunction γάρ is used to strengthen or confirm a previous proposition. Although it can, in context, have a causal force, that force derives from the nature of the material introduced by γάρ, not by the semantics of the conjunction itself. According to Runge, γάρ "adds background information that strengthens or supports what precedes."[69] The notion of background information is critical in discourse analysis because one of the discipline's key insights is that authors place things in the background as a means of accentuating and enriching the *focus* (i.e., what summons audience attention). Typically, γάρ marks these logical relationships between major components of an argument at the sentence level or larger. When γάρ marks a causal relationship, component A (the first unit) is the effect, outcome, or principle claim, and component B (the clause or paragraph containing the conjunction) is the cause, reason, or support.[70] Some Greek authors tended to use γάρ at the more macro level for major argument components, and some deployed γάρ so frequently that demarcating argument components becomes difficult.[71] Titus exhibits the former of these two usage tendencies.

Although δέ does not appear in Titus 1:12 according to the NA[28] accepted text, it does appear there in fourth-century Codex Sinaiticus

---

68. Incidentally, δέ and γάρ, as postpositive conjunctive particles, never appear as the first word in their clause.
69. Runge, *Discourse Grammar*, 52.
70. See Casson, *Textual Signposts*, 61–122.
71. Runge describes uses of this conjunction in line with my description here (*Discourse Grammar*, 51–54).

(original hand). The quotative frame therein builds on verse 11, adding δέ, and may be translated, "moreover, someone from them—a prophet of theirs—said" (1:12a).[72] This same variant appears in ninth-century codices F and G, eleventh-century codex 81, and a few other minor witnesses. Although Sinaiticus is a significant witness, the total evidence for this variant is not strong, and the preferred reading (without δέ) is probably original. Nevertheless, this variant suggests that early scribes and interpreters saw continuity and development between Titus 1:11 and 1:12, rather than divergence. Twelfth-century codex 103 inserts γάρ in the place where δέ appears in these others. This variant may have been an interpretive move and suggests that the scribe saw continuity between the verses and logical support for 1:11 in 1:12. That is, "someone speaking" (εἶπέν τις 1:12) the quotation coincides with "disrupting households" and "teaching what they ought not" (1:11).

Greek authors often abutted sentences without explicit connectives. This asyndeton can also be a conjunctive strategy. Runge explains that asyndeton—"linking clauses without the use of a conjunction"—is the default means of conjoining clauses in Koine Greek.[73] By *default*, he does not mean the most common but the most unmarked. Writers often used it when the connection between clauses is obvious on the basis of context, not primarily when they change topics. The clauses that meet between Titus 1:11 and 1:12, according to the favored NA[28] reading, do not feature an explicit conjunction. What could this asyndeton mean? Wilson and Sperber write, "A conjoined utterance is presented as a unit, encouraging the hearer to process the two utterances jointly and in parallel, looking for implications derivable from both."[74] The author chooses not to make the linkage explicit but to allow the context of the conjoined clauses to signal

---

72. For high-quality photographic scans of the original manuscript, see "See the Manuscript," Codex Sinaiticus, https://codexsinaiticus.org/en/manuscript.aspx. In her discussion of quotation theory, Kujanpää explains that Paul, like any author, was deliberate about how he framed quotations, signaling how he wanted them to be taken. "He tailors the introductions to his argumentative needs" (Kujanpää, "From Eloquence," 195; also see 186).

73. Runge, *Discourse Grammar*, 20–21.

74. Deirdre Wilson and Dan Sperber, "Pragmatics and Time," in Carston and Uchida, *Relevance Theory*, 19. Wilson and Sperber also point to Diane Blakemore, *Semantic Constraints on Relevance* (New York: Blackwell, 1987). She suggests the same effect of conjoined pairs, namely, that both are required for a full interpretation. The second-order processing requires greater effort, but it yields greater cognitive effects.

their relationship because, as Runge puts it, "the writer judges that the implicit relation between the clauses is sufficiently clear."[75]

A sentence tends to follow one of two broad logical-semantic directions after asyndeton: first, the sentence could break with the previous material, typically forming a new paragraph; second, it could develop the previous material through an implicit logical relationship, exhibiting more or less continuity. When authors take the second direction, the implicit relationship tends to be one of particularization.[76] As I have shown, Titus 1:12–14, especially the referential material, builds and depends on 1:10–11. The asyndeton does not signal a level of discontinuity that constitutes a break here. Rather, the quotation with its frame logically develops Paul's description of the troublemakers. Specifically, 1:12 presents a particular example of their behavior, so the relationship between the major clauses that abut at the juncture of verses 11 and 12 seems to be one of particularization. That is, uttering the insult is a specific example of the troublemakers' behavior that had been resulting in "upsetting entire households" (1:11b) and that should be addressed by the implicit injunction "[someone] ought to silence [them]" (οὓς δεῖ ἐπιστομίζειν, 1:11a).[77] Therefore, Paul's use of the Cretan quotation has a primarily argumentative function rather than a descriptive function. He is not interested in describing the Cretans but is both exposing an incriminating example of leadership malpractice and rendering a verdict with damages (to echo Paul's courtroom imagery).[78]

This common use of asyndeton as a move from general to particular with essential continuity between clauses is exhibited in several more specific logical-semantic relationships. Stephen Levinsohn lists other common relationships that correlate to asyndeton: "orienter-content, ... generic-specific, ... conclusion-grounds," all of which would comport with the interpretation I have been suggesting.[79]

Wilson and Sperber offer a helpful way to understand the pragmatic effect of conjoined clauses without an explicit conjunction. They say that

---

75. Runge, *Discourse Grammar*, 20.
76. See Runge, *Discourse Grammar*, 23.
77. Literally, "whom [someone] ought to silence" or "gag" (although this second gloss is likely more belligerent than fitting). See Bassler, *1 Timothy*, 190.
78. Discussed in ch. 5 under "Cognitive Environment."
79. Stephen H. Levinsohn, *Discourse Features of New Testament Greek: A Coursebook on the Information Structure of New Testament Greek* (Dallas: SIL International, 2000), 122. I have simplified Levinsohn's formatting.

the speaker sometimes raises a question in the first part of the utterance that she answers in the second part. What question does Titus 1:10–11 raise, and how does 1:12 answer it? Because Paul portrays the troublemakers and the fruit of their work in such general terms in 1:10–11, the question of what exactly they were teaching and how exactly they were upsetting households remains until 1:12. It seems natural, then, that he would answer the question with an example of their most egregious or representative offense. Thus, he frames and echoes the quotation that exemplifies the troublemakers' whole attitude toward the Cretan people, not least of all those in the congregation.

Observing the asyndeton between 1:12 and 1:13 is also a starting point for grasping the relationship between the quotation and its frame and the consequences Paul begins to describe.[80] The referential and deictic features described above suggest a significant level of continuity, not a change in topic, but by using asyndeton Paul does not explicate the kind of relationship these verses have to each other. Hearers must infer it from context. Given its deictic reference, I think that "this testimony is true" (1:13a) is most likely an explanatory comment on verse 12 as a whole. It explains the entire verse; the Cretan quotation itself is merely an embedded clause within the sentence. A consequential imperative tightly follows this comment—"for which reason, rebuke them severely" (1:13b). We may infer, then, that the relationship between verses 12 and 13 is one of explanation with hortatory causation. So, Paul instructs Titus to rebuke the insolent leaders severely because of the trouble they are causing stemming from attitudes exemplified by the quotation. Let us now consider a third and final basic pragmatic process—disambiguation on the basis of lexical pragmatics.

Lexical Pragmatics

Individual word meaning depends on usage in context. This context includes the entire communicative environment—both spoken words *and* social circumstances.[81] Lexical pragmatics is the area of relevance

---

80. I address only instances of asyndeton that appear immediately before and after the Cretan quotation. It is not surprising to see several more instances in Titus. Runge judges that asyndeton is the default approach for conjoining clauses in NT epistolary and speech material (*Discourse Grammar*, 17–26, esp. 20–23).

81. See Green, "Lexical Pragmatics and the Lexicon"; Patricia Kolaiti and Deirdre Wilson, "Corpus Analysis and Lexical Pragmatics: An Overview," *IRP* 6 (2014): 211–39.

theory that deals with questions of word meaning. I explore two basic concepts regarding lexical pragmatics that have particular bearing on the interpretation of Titus 1:12: literalness versus figurativeness and words as ad hoc concepts.

Whereas lexical semantics concerns the intrinsic and stable meanings of words, lexical pragmatics concerns the meaning of words as they appear in particular utterances in natural language.[82] Clark explains that, upon hearing a word, an audience accesses three kinds of conceptual information: (1) lexical information, which includes the technical specifications of a word, word type, where the word fits into a language, and so forth; (2) logical information, such as what concepts the word contributes to the sentence and the role (including grammatical) of the word in the sentence; and (3) encyclopedic information that comes from an individual's understanding and associations involving that word and the real world.

Everyone has a different set of encyclopedic information to access, and the senses of words differ in both degree and quality, so the variations of meaning for a given word are virtually innumerable.[83] In order to understand a speaker's intended meaning, a hearer engages in a quest for cognitive effects. Relevance theorists refer to this process as mutual adjustment and enrichment. Upon hearing the encoded form, hearers engage in a dialectic (*mutual*) process and *adjust* their assumptions based on the level of cognitive effects that they derive from a particular meaning (*enrichment*).[84] Therefore, the process is not completely open-ended but is "constrained by the principle of relevance," like a gravitational pull toward the speaker's intended meaning.[85] With this basic understanding of lexical pragmatics, let us consider how hearers discern where words fall on the literal-figurative continuum.

---

82. Lexical semantics is not confined to dictionaries, but lexicographers endeavor to incorporate as much semantic content as forms convey, even though contemporary usage makes this goal an ever-moving target. The same holds for grammars and grammarians as they attempt to account for various uses and combinations of words. Every new utterance expands possible meanings because it is spoken from a new context.

83. Clark, *Relevance Theory*, 244–52.

84. This process is developed further in ch. 5 under "Contextual Assumptions" and "Implicated Premises."

85. Green, "Lexical Pragmatics and the Lexicon," 325. Clark details this process in *Relevance Theory*, 240–52.

The Literal-Figurative Continuum

The advertising announcer says, "We'll be there in no time." She does not intend her hearer to take this common statement literally (i.e., "company representatives will be present instantaneously"). Relevance theorists do not hold, as Grice did at first, that literalness is the default mode of speech.[86] Clark explains,

> Relevance theorists have always assumed what is sometimes called "the continuity hypothesis" on which loose, hyperbolic, and metaphorical utterances are not different in kind or processed in significantly different ways from literal utterances. On this view, literalness is a matter of degree, and utterances may be more or less literal. Full literalness is not the norm but an exception at one end of the range of possibilities.[87]

Literalness or figurativeness can have humorous, ironic, sarcastic, and other connotations when extended to either end of the spectrum. Patricia Kolaiti and Deirdre Wilson explain, "There is no clear cut-off point between literal use, approximation, hyperbole and metaphor, but merely a continuum."[88] So, a more appropriate question to ask than *whether* a writer's words are literal or figurative is, What kind or degree of literalness or figurativeness does the writer exhibit here?

Although relevance theorists have since updated Grice's concepts, his analysis of nonliteral speech can be helpful to biblical interpreters. According to Grice's intuitions, when someone hears a sentence that obviously does not conform to the maxim of quality—that is, a sentence that is false, strictly speaking—he does not dismiss it as senseless. Instead, he gets to work at understanding what the speaker could mean in an alternative, nonliteral sense that she conveys by "flout[ing] the maxim."[89]

---

86. See Kolaiti and Wilson, "Corpus Analysis," 219–21; Sperber and Wilson, "Pragmatics" (2007), 485–90; Garmendia, " (Neo)Gricean Account," 42.

87. Clark, *Relevance Theory*, 251.

88. Kolaiti and Wilson, "Corpus Analysis," 222.

89. Grice, "Logic and Conversation," 53–54. Garmendia explains, defends, and corrects Grice's account of nonliteral speech, specifically his treatment of irony (*making as-if to say*), which inherently entails a negative judgment toward the thought expressed ("[Neo]Gricean Account," 42, 58, and passim). According to her, one can still subscribe to Gricean pragmatics without holding to the idea that literalism is the default mode of speech (42–43).

Relevance theorists prefer a more direct explanation for nonliteral communication. This preference corresponds to the aim of *explaining* the functional success of natural language rather than *prescribing* a method of interpretation. The speed with which hearers typically intuit figurative use necessitates a real-time model that corresponds to the rapidity of natural language comprehension.[90] Grice's procedure nevertheless may be conceptually useful because it divides interpretation into logically discrete steps.[91] Relevance theorists would not expect an original audience to engage in such an effort-intensive process, but modern interpreters of the Bible have little choice. Grice correctly reasoned that statements that are untrue from a literal standpoint are not thereby considered meaningless or false; hearers engage in a process for interpreting their nonliteral meaning. His two-step process for interpreting utterances—finding the literal meaning and then canceling it and considering others—has its shortcomings, but it helps interpreters to appreciate the reasoning behind a relevance-guided hermeneutic.

Consider again Paul's use of the word "prophet" (προφήτης, 1:12). We do not have access to the author's tone of voice, but evidence we do have suggests that Paul used *prophet* not only nonliterally but ironically. Expectations of poetic style and divine inspiration are often commensurate with the label *prophet* in the New Testament, even when the label is misapplied. Paul, however, was not referencing Israel's classic prophets whose written works were featured in the canon of Jewish Scripture, and he was not referencing New Testament–era contemporaries in the church who exercised corresponding gifts of inspired speech (cf. *prophet* in 1 Cor 12:28–29; 14:29, 32, 37–38; Eph 2:20; 3:5; 4:11; 2 Pet 2:16) or other categories associated with *prophet*. Conventional readings of Titus 1:12 assume that he was using the word in a more generic sense: a person with the capacity to speak a poignant truth that defies or surpasses the wisdom, knowledge, or convention of the culture of which he or she is a part. Certainly, Paul could draw on non-Jewish and non-Christian authorities to vouch for a teaching that he wished to advance, but why do interpreters think that Paul was doing so in Titus 1:12? Certainly, the hexameter style suggests that the quotation emerged outside and prior to Titus, yet I suspect that its history

---

90. I discuss the cognitive effects of figurative speech in ch. 6 under "The Economy of Cognitive Effects."

91. Grice provides an explanation of his basic scheme for understanding not-literal speech in "Logic and Conversation," 46–49.

of interpretation influences the assumption that Paul looked to its originator with authentic deference.⁹²

The common view that Paul deliberately vested the originator of the quotation with authority by labeling him a prophet is doubtful. First, it presumes the attribution of the quotation to a Cretan, Epimenides—a dubious assumption on literary-historical and grammatical grounds. Second, it requires that Paul advanced the substance of the Cretan quotation in toto, which has the problematic sociohistorical implications and literary-canonical contradictions explained in chapter 1. Third, it assumes a topical break within the paragraph that is unsustainable on the basis of connective, referential, and deictic language throughout the context. Fourth, nothing else in the context suggests that Paul views the speaker, whom he refers to using the indefinite pronoun τις ("someone," 1:12), to be a trustworthy source. Fifth, Paul's theological and moral concerns in the rest of the book do not find expression in the quotation itself, whereas reporting the quotation as an example of the disruptive behaviors of a contingent of impudent leaders in the church does correspond to concerns he consistently raised in Titus.

A pragmatic sense for *prophet*, derived ironically from a literal sense, would have had special significance for a target with a Jewish background. The speaker stood in a cohort of presumptuous leaders *within* the church. Rather than achieving the title of *prophet* honorably, however, he wears it illegitimately. Paul ridicules the untrustworthy, self-appointed, and self-satisfied speaker by calling him a prophet ironically. Negative implications carry over to any wheedling, head-nodding, self-approved troublemakers who endorse such slurs. The redundant third-person pronouns coupled with the marked syntax of the quotative frame serve to distance the speaker from Paul and convey that this prophet is not so much *one of ours* as *one of theirs*. He is a *prophet*, but *to them* (i.e., the troublemakers), not *to us* (i.e., Paul, Titus, and faithful Cretans).

---

92. Other New Testament epistolary literature reveals that referring to someone as *prophet* was not necessarily positive. The apostle Paul acknowledges that not all who are seen or who see themselves as prophets should be recognized as such, especially when their speech results in disruption (1 Cor 14:37–38). Furthermore, calling a person a prophet is not automatically an endorsement (2 Pet 2:16).

Words as Ad Hoc Concepts

Without denying that words inherently contain some semantic information, Sperber and Wilson argue that every instance of a word differs from every other instance of that same word. Humans create an ad hoc concept every time they perceive an object or infer the meaning of a semantic representation.[93] Clark explains this lexical pragmatic doctrine: "Pragmatic processes create 'ad hoc' concepts, derived by modifying the encoded concepts in order to find interpretations which satisfy their [hearers'] expectations of relevance."[94] This involves concept broadening and narrowing. Theorists understand that virtually every concept or every word that encodes a concept has some flexibility or looseness and needs adjustment within the context of the utterance. For example, to say "Thelma is a princess" involves understanding that Thelma exhibits some qualities of a princess and that not all princesses possess every pertinent quality. Thus, broadening and loosening frequently occur at the same time.

For example, a technical definition of *flat* might be "consisting of all points on a plane without interruption or omission." To say "Kansas is flat" means that one understands *flat* to include things that are not completely flat. Clark points out that the concept encoded by the word *flat* is not something that anyone actually experiences in the world, so every time we use that word we are adjusting the concept.[95] Therefore, Kansas can be *flat*, and a person's haircut can be a *flattop*, and a tire, although primarily round, can be *flat* when it lacks sufficient air pressure for driving.

Other concepts or words have equally strict definitions but are derived on historical, cultural, or other bases rather than scientific or mathematical. As Green observes, "Ad hoc concept formation occurs on every page of the biblical text."[96] Some critical words in Titus derive their meaning on the basis of legal or religious practice, such as *prophet* (1:12), *testimony* and *accusation* (1:13), *clean* and *defiled* (1:15).

According to the lexical-pragmatic analysis of Kolaiti and Wilson, hearers furnish sufficient inferences to understand what meanings speakers intend. Kolaiti and Wilson argue that differences between the lexical-semantic assumptions that one hearer holds versus another do

---

93. Sperber and Wilson, "Pragmatics" (2007), 485–90.
94. Clark, *Relevance Theory*, 252 (quotation marks with italics original).
95. Clark, *Relevance Theory*, 248; I expand on his discussion of *flat*.
96. Green, "Lexical Pragmatics and the Lexicon," 323.

not present obstacles to comprehension; because speakers presumably provide sufficient information to disambiguate, narrow, and specify what they mean.[97] In instances of effective communication, hearers bring contextual assumptions that maximize their perception of relevance.[98] So, a speaker can draw an idea from "left field," while the listener understands the "heart" of the matter. Why? Because, in acts of communication, as opposed to mere verbal exercises or noncommunicative sonic acts, both parties are interested enough in accomplishing a shared meaning that they cooperate in their respective processes.[99]

The word *prophet*, as a survey of its uses demonstrates, is flexible and must be understood in its specific context. Kolaiti and Wilson conclude "that lexical narrowing and broadening are highly flexible and context-dependent processes which can combine in the interpretation of a single word, and support the view that there is a continuum of cases between literal, approximate, hyperbolic and metaphorical use."[100] Distance in time, space, language, and culture separates modern interpreters from first-century Christians, and our respective signaling systems are not entirely compatible. Because what was intuitive for them is not intuitive for us, our task is to listen for the clues that help to disambiguate the concept of prophet. Our knowledge of the ancient world and of the basic linguistically encoded meaning of words is only a starting point. *Prophet* activated something for Paul's intended listeners that satisfied their expectations of

---

97. Kolaiti and Wilson, "Corpus Analysis," 228–29. By *presumably*, I mean *in an effective act of communication*. Writers may fail at their part of the communicative enterprise, rendering the recovery of authorial intention abortive. But this happens with specific instances of attempted communication, not with language in general. Therefore, we proceed under the assumption that Paul thought that he had provided sufficient clues to disambiguate his meaning.

98. Kolaiti and Wilson, "Corpus Analysis," 230.

99. Hence Grice's cooperative principle ("Logic and Conversation," 45).

100. Kolaiti and Wilson, "Corpus Analysis," 234. They also offer a disclaimer about "the pragmatic intuitions we have relied on in analysing our corpus data." It reflects why the conclusions of biblical scholars can be confident but also tentative: "On the one hand, these intuitions are about actual utterances, produced in actual situations. On the other hand, those utterances were not addressed to us, which puts us in the position of overhearers rather than actual addressees. As a result, the pragmatic intuitions they give rise to are still to some extent about hypothetical pragmatic facts, and are open to error or influence by our prior theoretical commitments. This seems to be an unavoidable feature of the use of corpus data in lexical pragmatics" (236).

relevance and increased their cognitive effects as they understood the sentence within its conversational context.[101]

Paul certainly does not use the word *prophet* literally in the sense that it points the speaker out as either an ancient Hebrew prophet or a spiritually gifted Christian. *Prophet* here is a metonym that is only coterminous with the speaker of the quotation when the word is adjusted in contextually relevant ways. Song quotes Anna Papafragou: "The speaker ... wants to indicate ... the appropriateness of the metonymy to name the referent of a non-lexicalized *ad hoc* concept."[102] With Papafragou, Song contends that the speaker's purpose is to name the referent appropriately when the actual referent does not have an exact lexicalized concept available. Speakers limit the directions in which processing may proceed. Although a word's meaning differs with each utterance, several factors—including lexical norms, verbal context, topic, theme, and personality—provide boundaries to word meaning even as they present trajectories on which word meaning can vary.

Commentators frequently note how peculiar Paul's use of *prophet* (1:12) is in this context. Barrett suggests that labeling the speaker of this quotation a prophet is like the epithet ascribed to Caiaphas in John 11:51— not necessarily a personal compliment but a circumstantial fact.[103] Ceslas Spicq, also assuming the attribution of the quotation to Epimenides, associates the original speaker with Balaam's ass because neither of them was conscious of the truth they told.[104] Calvin attributes qualms about applying the title prophet to pagan writers as superstitious scruples; "All truth is from God," after all.[105] These suggestions explain the odd usage by assuming, first, that Paul was referring to the original author of this quotation and, second, that Paul agreed with its contents. It is not certain, however,

---

101. See Clark, *Relevance Theory*, 249.

102. Song, "Metaphor and Metonymy," 98, where he cites Anna Papafragou, "Metonymy and Relevance," *UCLWPL* 7 (1995): 157. He disagrees with Papafragou that metonymy is *necessarily* echoic. He argues that expanding the notion of echo to this extent is unhelpful. This distinction does not affect the insights I am pointing out regarding *prophet* as metonymic. Papafragou argues that metonyms may go through stages of conventionalization with frequent use but that one-off metonyms, as I argue *prophet* is, have full pragmatic effect. See Papafragou, "Figurative Language and the Semantics-Pragmatics Distinction," *LL* 5 (1996): 179–93.

103. Barrett, *Pastoral Epistles*, 131.

104. Ceslas Spicq, *Les Épitres Pastorales*, EBib (Paris: Gabalda, 1969), 2:609.

105. Calvin, *Commentaries*, 247–48.

that Paul was doing either. It is worth noting again that extant ancient references to Epimenides never call him a prophet. Paul appears to have been creating an ad hoc usage for *prophet* applicable to his circumstance and intention.

As noted, Paul uses a marked construction for the quotative frame (1:12a).[106] Quinn claims that it intensifies the individual's belonging to a group, but he assumes that it is a group of ethnic Cretans.[107] In my reading, however, it seems that Paul was intensifying the speaker's belonging to the contingent of troublemakers (1:10–11). The troublemakers were Paul's reason for the instructions of 1:5–9 (note the logic signaled by the conjunction γάρ in 1:10). While advancing this slur, the prophet held elevated status within a contingent that presumed to lead the Cretan church. Even if the title does not literally apply to the originator of the quotation, it is appropriate for use within a community, such as the Cretan church, that subscribes to notions of status derived from Jewish and ancient Christian religious culture. Thus, we disambiguate a label that the original audience would have rapidly recognized as elevated, figurative, ironic, and even ridiculous.

Basic pragmatic processes are necessary to relevance-guided biblical hermeneutics, but they only bring the reader to a point of grasping the *conceptual representation* or *logical form* of the linguistically encoded sentence.[108] That is, they help to accomplish the essential step of decoding semantic values, but utterance interpretation requires other levels of comprehension. An audience has only grasped a speaker's meaning when it grasps the higher-level explicatures of her utterance. To this we now turn.

---

106. Marked language illuminates speaker attitude. Levinson calls this the *m-principle* and explains: "Indicate an abnormal, nonstereotypical situation by using marked expressions that contrast with those you would use to describe the corresponding normal, stereotypical situations" (quoted in Clark, *Relevance Theory*, 88).

107. Quinn, *Letter to Titus*, 109.

108. The italicized phrases are virtually interchangeable in relevance theory for the [intermediate] end product of applying basic pragmatic processes to a sentence. For example and explanation, see Clark, *Relevance Theory*, 298, 306; see also Uchida, "Text and Relevance," 162.

4
Higher-Level Explicatures

Grice reasoned that bridging the gap between sentence meaning and utterance meaning involved completing basic pragmatic processes like those discussed in chapter 3; once a hearer had resolved ambiguities and assigned references based on the logical form, it only remained to infer what the speaker *meant* but did not *say*.[1] Huang recounts how pioneering relevance theorists Sperber and Wilson recognized the need for pragmatic inference to interpret even some explicit features of utterances.[2] In other words, speakers overtly signal critical cues to meaning that are not either lexicalized or grammaticalized; these are nevertheless recoverable on the basis of explicit features of language, so they coined the term *explicature*. In live speech, these features may include facial expressions and vocal inflections; in written discourse, readers must examine contextual indicators.[3]

Let us have a working definition for *explicature*. According to Gibbs and Markus Tendahl, explicatures are "elaborations of the expression's logical form that respect speaker's intentions."[4] Green says that an explicature "is the linguistically encoded meaning in addition to the information linked to it that is pragmatically inferred from context."[5] Theorists distinguish between strong and weak explicatures based on how critical the explicature is for understanding a speaker's intended meaning and how

---

1. Although the words *meant* and *said* do not sound technical, Grice uses these terms consistently in his writing to refer to implicit, inferentially enriched speech and explicit, linguistically encoded speech, respectively ("Logic and Conversation," passim).

2. Huang, "Micro- and Macro-Pragmatics," 153–54.

3. Nevertheless, relevance theory research suggests that nonverbal clues are typically supportive of indicators, particularly for irony, that already occur in the verbal context (see Yus, "Relevance Theory," 152–53).

4. Gibbs and Tendahl, "Cognitive Effort and Effects," 392.

5. Green, "Relevance Theory and Theological Interpretation," 79.

prominent the speaker has made it.[6] For this study, I speak of explicatures as all of the information that a hearer derives on the basis of formal features of an utterance, even those that require some level of inference in addition to basic semantic decoding.

To understand how complex speech-types, such as irony, operate through a relevance-theoretical model, we must realize that a speaker always communicates higher-level explicatures—that is, those explicatures that convey her attitude toward *what is said*.[7] Higher-level explicatures reveal whether a statement is the speaker's own thought or her attribution of someone else's thought—whether sentences render a positive or negative judgment or serve a dismissive hearsay function, for instance. These explicatures also regard how deeply layered the assumption of reciprocal knowledge is (i.e., *the speaker thinks that the hearer knows that the speaker believes that the hearer desires that…*). Utterances communicate more than the sum of the words and syntax in their linguistically encoded sentences because an utterance is *sentence plus context*. One of the most important facts about an utterance that hearers must determine is the speaker's attitude toward what she is saying. In fact, unless we understand the speaker's attitude, we fail to interpret her statement correctly.

The Speaker's Attitude toward a Sentence

A speaker communicates both propositional content and her attitude toward it, which pivotally affects the meaning of sentences. Recognizing this impact is nowhere more crucial than when the speaker has a disassociative or critical attitude toward a statement. Even Austin, the original speech-act theorist and a contemporary of Grice, considered the importance of ascertaining speaker attitude toward a sentence. Without the refined categories of later theorists, Austin recognized that sentences do not unambiguously carry meanings apart from a speaker's intentions. In short form, one of the ways he expressed this hypothesis was in his claim

---

6. See, for instance, Clark, *Relevance Theory*, 309.

7. Grice used "what is said" to refer to everything that speakers explicitly convey ("Logic and Conversation," 44 and passim). Benson Goh applies the concept of explicatures to biblical studies in "Honoring Christ, Subverting Caesar: Relevance-Historical Reconstruction of the Context of Ephesians as an Honorific Discourse Praising Jesus the Great Benefactor" (PhD diss., Asbury Theological Seminary, 2017), 30–43.

that saying "*p*" does not imply "I believe *p*."[8] Each utterance involves the speaker's choice to express her own thoughts or to present the thoughts of another. Theorists refer to these as *descriptive* use and *interpretive* use, respectively. In the second type, rather than her own thoughts, the speaker expresses her attitude toward other (sometimes fabricated or supposed) ideas or persons. Relevance-guided interpretation must interrogate the attitude Paul conveys toward what he says when he employs irony, metonymy, and other types of interpretive rather than descriptive language use.[9]

The pragmatic difference between "Sue is so beautiful" and "Sue thinks she is so beautiful" is the nature of the explicature. It pertains to the attitude of the speaker toward the proposition "Sue is beautiful." All-important to the truth-conditional content of the first utterance is whether, by the measure implied in the relationship between speaker and audience, Sue actually is so beautiful, but such is not important to the truth-conditional content of the second utterance. Only the attitude of the speaker is. The *semantic* difference resides in the word *thinks*, which does not in itself imply a negative attitude, but it does remove the notion *Sue is so beautiful* from the speaker herself. This distancing leads the rational hearer to infer two explicatures: that the speaker is not expressing this as her own thought and that she has a critical attitude toward the embedded sentence. More than the semantic content of the sentence, the pragmatic effect of the utterance is subject to truth-conditional evaluation. The extent of Sue's beauty is likely not relevant. The hearer must infer the speaker's attitude or fail to comprehend. A hearer would not understand either utterance properly without ascertaining the attitude of the speaker toward the statement, even if he had exhaustive semantic

---

8. J. L. Austin, "The Meaning of a Word," in *J. L. Austin: Philosophical Papers*, 3rd ed., ed. James O. Urmson and Geoffrey J. Warnock (New York: Oxford University Press, 1979), 63–64.

9. Most relevance theorists view irony as an echoic use of language (see Clark, *Relevance Theory*, 280–94; Wilson, "Pragmatics of Verbal Irony," 1722–43). Others hold to the original Gricean position that irony is pretense. See Gregory Currie, "Why Irony Is Pretence," in *The Architecture of the Imagination: New Essays on Pretence, Possibility, and Fiction*, ed. Shaun Nichols (Oxford: Oxford University Press, 2006), 111–33; Garmendia, "(Neo)Gricean Account." A particular view of irony is not essential to my thesis. My point is the fact of Paul's irony, not the type. Goodwin discusses the important distinctions and functions of *descriptive use* and *interpretive use* in *Translating the English Bible*, 44–45.

knowledge of the lexemes and syntax in use and even if he could reliably ascertain Sue's beauty.[10]

Grice was not far from recognizing the importance of what relevance theorists now call *explicature*. Clark writes, "Perhaps the key thing to notice here, given its importance in the development of RT [relevance theory], is that Grice is assuming that working out what is being communicated involves making rational inferences about the communicator's intentions."[11] So, authorial intention is crucial to meaning.

Are not speaker intentions passé in a postmodern literary-critical environment? As Gibbs notes, "There has been heated debate in many areas of philosophy, anthropology and literary theory as to whether intentions play a significant role in the interpretation of both oral and written discourse."[12] Gibbs describes three views about speaker intention within cognitive linguistics: (1) the independence view, in which utterance meaning emerges from a two-step process of linguistic decoding, then encyclopedic enrichment; (2) the constructivist view, in which the speaker's utterance forms ideas within the hearer's mind that fluidly incorporate both semantic and real-world information; and (3) the intentional view, in which the hearer takes sentence meaning and encyclopedic information into account but arrives at a meaning in harmony with the speaker's intentions based on common knowledge, beliefs, and attitudes.[13] In contrast to the independence view, the intentional view holds that speaker intention is also a necessary category of information for utterance processing. In contrast to the constructivist view, the intentional view holds that speaker intention is an essential constraint on what semantic and encyclopedic information is appropriate to utterance interpretation. The intentional view coincides with the importance of the dialectic of speaker attitude in relevance theory as both content and constraint.

Gibbs surveys fascinating empirical research on textual communication that found people willing to spend significant time trying to analyze

---

10. Discerning the writer's attitude corresponds to Schleiermacher's intuitions, who, in David W. Tracy's words, emphasized "the interpreter's need for 'empathy' and 'divination' of the original author's feelings and intentions." See Tracy, "Interpretation (Hermeneutics)," in *International Encyclopedia of Communications* (Oxford: Oxford University Press, 1989), 344.

11. Clark, *Relevance Theory*, 61.

12. Gibbs, "Intentionalist Controversy," 183.

13. Gibbs, "Intentionalist Controversy," 185–86.

anomalous (nonsensical) sentences if they believed them to be produced by a poet rather than a computer. Subjects quit deciphering difficult sentences more quickly if they believed them to be produced by a computer rather than a human. This research suggests that authorial intention is pivotal even to a hearer's decision to invest effort in interpreting an utterance. In relevance theory, utterances, as ostensive inferential communication, *definitionally* involve intention.[14]

Against fashionable claims, especially within criticism of art and literature, that meaning is not constrained by authorial intent, I quote Gibbs at length explaining the position of cognitive linguistics:

> On the one hand, critics of the intentional view often conceive of literature and other texts as having a life of their own and consequently claim they should not be interpreted under the constraints of any possible communicative intentions of the producer(s) of that text. This "autonomy of meaning" position views linguistic interpretation as a critical practice that can be extended in time beyond that associated with understanding of everyday speech and writing to exploit the multitude of possible meanings that are "in the text." Cognitive scientists, on the other hand, mostly assume that language understanding refers to immediate psychological and linguistic processes that occur in real-time to derive speakers'/authors' primary communicative intentions. Understanding, under this view, is a goal-oriented, unconscious mental activity that seeks to recover communicative intentions within the time-frame in which everyday speech and writing are ordinarily comprehended.[15]

In contrast to many hypermodern/postmodern literary studies, relevance theorists expect that speaker intention is not only recoverable but essential to interpretation. Without authorial intent, we have mere augmented self-expression, not authentic interpretation. Utterances provide both explicit and implicit indications of a speaker's attitude toward what she said.[16] Often, retrieving and understanding this attitude is as crucial to interpretation as any other information, but successful retrieval depends on a hearer's attention to contextual indicators that can become opaque to secondary audiences. These indicators are both discourse contextual and situation contextual, both linguistically encoded and

---

14. Gibbs, "Intentionalist Controversy," 190.
15. Gibbs, "Intentionalist Controversy," 183–84.
16. Sperber and Wilson, *Pragmatics: An Overview*, 3.

pragmatically inferred. In the case of Titus, historical-contextual and canonical-contextual evidence, when used with discernment, helps to reconstruct some of these indicators.

We do not claim to possess exclusive insight into the author's identity or make unverifiable assertions as to his psychological state when we endeavor to ascertain Paul's attitude toward sentences in Titus.[17] We merely try to discern, on the basis of linguistic evidence that is readily available to any careful examiner, whether and in what way Paul has implicated his own attitude toward a statement. Discerning intention or attitude does not require sophistication or inordinate effort. As Furlong states, "Ordinary hearers have some mechanism (generally successful, as far as we know) for recognizing speakers' intentions."[18]

The peculiar quotative frame (Titus 1:12a) seems to implicate Paul's attitude not only toward what is said but also toward who said it as a higher-level explicature of distance and disapproval. It serves a disassociating function and appears to be *hearsay functional*. A colloquial paraphrase would be as follows: "one o' the boys—some 'prophet' of theirs—even said." Obviously, this is not a literal translation, but it expresses the thrust of Paul's distancing language. It is difficult to capture the thrust of the quotative frame in English without grasping for an idiom to convey the distance and possible contempt. Reiko Itani calls hearsay an indicator of "diminished speaker commitment."[19] Such higher-level explicatures imply the degree of a statement's trustworthiness or lack thereof.

In ostensive communication, speakers make their communicative intention manifest. This making manifest involves the speaker's desire for sympathy. By plainly recounting an objectionable behavior (1:12), Paul trusted his readers to conclude what he concluded, just as he had. He distanced himself from the quotation and its speaker. This approach suggests that he was not expressing his thoughts about Cretans as such; he was testifying that some troublemaker was saying unacceptable things about them. In this way, he invited his hearers to perceive the offense plainly.

---

17. See Gibbs, "Intentionalist Controversy," 195. He does not discuss the Bible specifically, but I apply his arguments to utterances in Titus.

18. Furlong, "Relevance Theory," 45.

19. Reiko Itani, "A Relevance-Based Analysis of Hearsay Particles: With Special Reference to Japanese Sentence-Final Particle *Tte**," in Carston and Uchida, *Relevance Theory*, 48-49. English has several means for signaling hearsay, such as "was like [quotation]" and "[quotation] or whatever."

Use versus Mention

Relevance theorists distinguish between a speaker's *use* and her *mention* of a statement. One speaker may *use* "Yeah, right," to convey the linguistically encoded content of an answer in the affirmative. Another may *mention* "Yeah, right," while expressing distance or disassociation from the statement. In the latter instance, she is speaking ironically, and her meaning happens to be virtually the opposite of the linguistically encoded meaning of the words she speaks. Speakers may convey numerous degrees of distance along the continuum between sympathetic *use* and disassociative *mention* (see fig. 4.1); these nuances can be complex, especially with multiple layers of indirect speech. Every utterance involves some implication of the speaker's attitude toward the sentence; *use* and *mention* are relevance theory's technical designations for naming this fundamental distinction.[20]

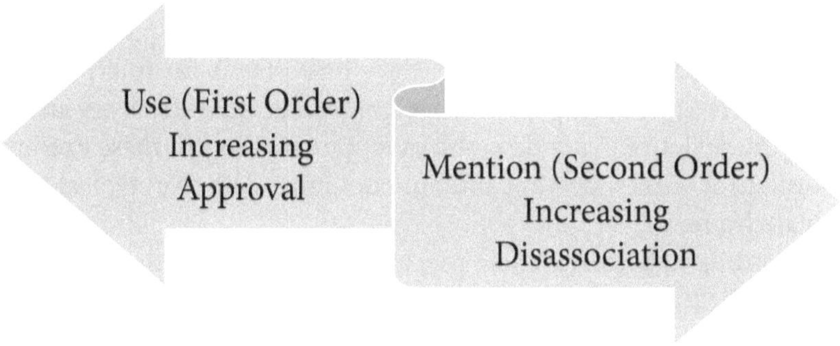

⬅ Use (First Order) Increasing Approval   Mention (Second Order) Increasing Disassociation ➡

Fig. 4.1. Use/mention continuum

The distinction between *using* (sorts of) language and *mentioning* (sorts of) language—between using sentences and mentioning sentences—is important for understanding echoic speech. An utterance that uses a sentence reflects the speaker's own thoughts, whereas an utterance that mentions a sentence reflects another person's thoughts (actual or imagined) or the speaker's thoughts from another time. Relevance theorists usually call this second type of speech *echoic*. Echoic speech resembles

---

20. *Use* and *mention* parallel distinctions in relevance theory between *description* and *interpretation*, respectively, italicized to indicate their technical sense.

and references utterances, rather than persons, places, or objects in the real world.

The following example demonstrates the scaling back of linguistically encoded indicators for recognizing echoic speech. Suppose a parent endures an hour-long wait for her teenager after being told that it would only be a five-minute wait. The parent grumbles, "'Five minutes,' she says; 'Five minutes'!" The echo is explicit, as is the subject (*she*), the speaker's daughter. Suppose the parent mutters, "'Five minutes,' huh?!" This, again, is an echo of her daughter's utterance with the same level (although a slightly different kind) of disassociation but without the linguistically encoded subject to indicate that the words were not the parent's own. Typical adult English-speakers would discern that she implicitly critiques someone else's speech because of the distancing mechanism in her echoic utterance.[21] The mother could adequately convey an ironic sense by muttering, "'Five minutes'?!" The parent holds the phrase "five minutes" up for criticism. Connotations include, *My daughter is making me wait longer than she admits.* The identity of the original speaker of the phrase and the exact phrase itself are both of secondary importance for interpretation. What matters according to a relevance-guided hermeneutic is her attitude toward the sentence. Of course, the exact punctuation in these examples substitutes for vocal inflection and provides more data than typical Greek quotative frames.

According to Seto, in echoic use, a speaker mentions the thoughts of another while leaving the interpretive nature of the representation implicit. So, the interpretive nature of irony typically remains implicit.[22] Seto quotes Sperber and Wilson regarding echoic mentions: "Some have their source in actual utterances, others in thoughts or opinions; some have a real source, others an imagined one; some are traceable back to a particular individual, whereas others have a vaguer origin. When the echoic character of the

---

21. Kujanpää explains, "When speakers indicate that they are quoting, they distance themselves from the contents of the quotation" ("From Eloquence," 188). This distancing could intend to allow a statement to speak with a different (presumably greater or more credible) authority than the speaker herself. It could also intend to allow listeners to join the speaker in evaluating the statement as something she does not truly endorse. Kujanpää explains that, according to the theorists she dialogues with, quotations are frequently deployed when expressing a thought that could be awkward, offensive, or delicate (188–89, 200).

22. See Seto, "On Non-echoic Irony," 239–40.

utterance is not immediately obvious, it is nevertheless suggested."[23] Paul was not using the term *prophet* (1:12) in a literal or descriptive sense, and he seems to have been speaking echoically. Paul was *echoing* the supposed designation of the speaker that his fellow troublemakers would have given him (perhaps in Paul's imagination).

A common but dubious assumption when interpreting this passage is to ascribe to Paul (even tacitly) a sympathetic attitude toward the speaker of the quotation. Although, as Gibbs states, "experimental evidence demonstrates that readers can easily distinguish irony that is speaker-intended from irony that is not speaker-intended," he explains that interpreters who are removed from the original social context of an utterance—and are thereby eavesdroppers—are especially susceptible to the error of misattributing attitudes to speakers who do not hold those attitudes but rather other, contrasting attitudes.[24]

Echoic language is not direct but attributive. The speaker engages in a metarepresentative mode of speech that implicitly attributes statements to another speaker or to herself at another time. A speaker using attributive language *can* be sympathetic toward her statement, but she implies that the word or idea is not her own. For instance, upon experiencing an unanticipated influx of bad fortune, a speaker may say, "When it rains, it pours." She may or may not consciously trace this slogan back to the early twentieth-century Morton Salt Company advertisement or other folk origins, but she is probably cognizant that she did not invent it and that her hearers also know this. Her speech is echoic and attributive, yet she affirms the substance of the slogan in her usage. This maneuver, however, often disassociates the speaker from the statement and allows her to convey, even while she makes the statement, a critical attitude toward its content. In this example, the critical attitude might be toward the inappropriateness of spouting pithy slogans when a crisis is afoot or toward a pessimistic outlook that might otherwise squelch her optimism.[25] Wilson contends

---

23. Seto, "On Non-echoic Irony," 240, quoting Sperber and Wilson, "Pragmatics" (1981), 309–10.

24. Gibbs, "Intentionalist Controversy," 194.

25. Users of the English quip "You are what you eat" certainly recognize that it is a well-known aphorism, that they did not invent it, and that their hearers will likely understand both facts. The effect of their utterance relies on such. It also relies on the hearer realizing that the speaker is not committed to its trustworthiness but takes it only to be a simplification if not a ridiculous proposition. The pithy proverb does not

that irony is primarily accounted for as an echoic use of language, and she says that two actions are typical: echoic attribution to another person or group of people or to people in general and conveying disapproval toward the statement.[26] Paul does these very two actions. First, he makes it known that the words he states are not his own by attributing the quotation to *someone* among *them* (1:12). Second, he conveys his disapproval of attitudes represented by such words by, for instance, instructing Titus to rebuke *them* (1:13). The next aspect of speaker attitude to consider involves the dynamics of insult language in Titus 1:12.

In-Group and Out-Group Insult Language

It matters *who* says things. Just imagine the difference in implications between Nas and Brad Paisley singing each other's lyrics.[27] It would take little effort to grasp the difference in meaning of the same words. As Sperber and Wilson explain, hearers seek "an interpretation of the speaker's meaning that satisfies the presumption of optimal relevance" while following "a path of least effort."[28] Paul spoke of a situation that Titus needed little effort to comprehend. Paul assumed that Titus knew of an ethno-religious superiority contest within the Cretan church. Readers can determine this fact without making any particular commitment to the interpretation of Titus 1:12. The historical circumstances of Pauline mission in the gentile world and Paul's downgrading religio-cultural practices and concerns that corresponded to Jewish interests in the epistle (1:10, 14; 3:9) reinforce the perception that the church exhibited ethno-religious tensions along Jew-gentile lines.[29] More specifically, a false sense of ethno-religious inferiority was a problem for the Cretan church and for the gospel on the island. In the context of a leadership discussion (1:5–16), Paul exposed one of the prime examples of malpractice. The presumptuous leaders were inferiorizing the Cretan people. No wonder Paul calls for a stern rebuke (1:13)!

---

lose its impact simply because the speaker and hearer fail to attribute it to Feuerbach's "Der Mensch ist, was er isst." See Ludwig Feuerbach, *Das Wesen des Christentums*, 2nd exp. ed. (Leipzig: Wigand, 1848), 267.

26. Wilson, "Pragmatics of Verbal Irony," 1735.

27. E.g., Nas, "Be a N—r Too," on [untitled album], The Jones Experience; Def Jam, 2008; Brad Paisley, "Accidental Racist," on *Wheelhouse*, Arista Nasvhille, 2013.

28. Sperber and Wilson, "Pragmatics" (2007), 474.

29. The issue of religio-cultural tension is expanded in ch. 5 under "Literary Context."

Regardless of the particular interpretation one holds, the Cretan quotation represents an insult (whether playful, ironic, or caustic) in some select context. Linguists have recently become more prolific about the social effects of disparaging humor and devoted a significant amount of scholarship to the various ways speakers employ insult language.[30] Such usage often retains the content not only of its target but also of the archetypal user of the insult or slur. For instance, the racial slur "n—r" does not simply carry ethnic semantic content; it also carries the situational content that reproduces the archetypal social relation between people when the word is used. The user of the slur relates to the target of the slur as a white plantation owner and recreates the social context that makes the speaker a social superior and the target a social inferior. Even when appropriated for more positive in-group uses as a term of affection, speakers still echo some of its original social dynamics, which is one reason that it is not an appropriate cross-group epithet. Thus, insults reproduce not merely semantic content but also socio-pragmatic content.[31] Lauren Ashwell argues that certain slurs have no "neutral correlate," meaning that they are not, properly speaking, a pejorative alternative but rather an inherent debasement of the referent.[32] Yoon argues that this fact operates across languages and is a macro-linguistic reality.[33]

If Paul intended to reproduce the situational content of the quotation as from a trustworthy Cretan source, his choice to refer to the speaker with an indefinite pronoun (τις, "someone," 1:12a) would subtly undermine this goal. Rather, Paul downplays the original social context of the quotation (as from Epimenides, for instance, assuming he knew the origin) in order to emphasize the tertiary contemporary context of the quotation as it concerns Titus's vulnerable congregation. *Somebody*—presumably considered to be a prophet among the people with whom Paul has voiced concern—was propagating the sentiment expressed in this quotation. By attesting

---

30. E.g. Donald A. Saucier, Conor J. O'Dea, and Megan L. Strain, "The Bad, the Good, the Misunderstood: The Social Effects of Racial Humor," *TIPS* 2 (2016): 77. They survey recent studies and conduct original cognitive-linguistic research.
31. I.e., nonpropositional dimensions. See ch. 6.
32. Lauren Ashwell, "Gendered Slurs," *STP* 42 (2016): 228–39, passim.
33. See Yoon, "Semantic Constraint," 47. He presents research on the reproduction of social relations in Korean and English.

to the quotation's currency among the troublemakers, Paul exposes the deeper problem of ethno-religious bigotry and bullying.[34]

In historical contexts of bigotry, where members of high-status categories use slurs and insults to target members of low-status categories, people from the latter group occasionally adopt (i.e., *appropriate*) slurs with which to refer to themselves. Because *who* is speaking affects the significance of degrading language, attribution of the quotation is pivotal. Several miso-Cretan readings assume that Paul drew it directly from Epimenides's own in-group banter, but I have already cast doubt on the helpfulness or accuracy of this attribution. If the quotation originated with Epimenides, Paul either may not have known or may have downplayed its origin, possibly because the troublemakers were using Epimenides's Cretan credentials as an excuse to insult the Cretans.

Assuming Paul's sympathetic attitude toward the quotation by pointing to its dubious historic attribution has more recent analogies. To illustrate: in November 2016, controversy surrounded US president-elect Donald Trump's announcement that Steve Bannon would be his chief strategist, because Bannon had provided a platform for alt-right and white-supremacist political voices on his Breitbart News Network. Notice how his successor at Breitbart, Joel Pollak, defended him in this excerpt from an interview with Steve Inskeep:

> INSKEEP: And let me ask another thing. And this is another Bannon quote, and we can pull out quotes. But it's a quote that he made in a 2011 radio interview that gets to maybe what he wants to do inside the country. He criticized feminists. He said, "Women that would lead this country would be pro-family. They would have husbands. They would love their children." And I'm just reading the quote here—"They wouldn't be a bunch of dykes that came from the Seven Sisters schools." What's he driving at there?
> POLLAK: I don't know. But there is a political correctness in this country that would say that if you said that once on a radio show, that you should be drummed out of public life. I would defy you to find a person in the LGBTQ community who has not used that term either in an endearing sense, or in a flippant, jovial, colloquial sense. I don't think you can judge Steve Bannon's views.[35]

---

34. Paul uses the terms μισέω ("hate," 3:3) and πλήκτης ("bully," 1:7) to refer to corresponding ideas in Titus.

35. Steve Inskeep, "Breitbart Editor Joel Pollak: Trump Strategist Steve Bannon Is

Pollak's defense was that Bannon used terms that people within "the LGBTQ community" themselves use. Essentially, he supposes that insider use grants permission for anyone to use such language. This logic is tacitly accepted in much of human society, as when someone asserts, *I can say this; I heard it from a* [term for a member of an ethnic, racial, gender, or other group]. Conventional interpretations imply that Paul relied on this logic, but it seems to me more likely that his opponents did.

Another recent analogy of the misuse of in-group banter comes from fictional manager Michael Scott on the television series *The Office* (US version). In the episode "Diversity Day," Scott mimicks a famous sketch by real-life comedian Chris Rock called "N—s vs. Black People," in which Rock explains, "I love black people, but I hate n—s."[36] What makes Scott's impression of Rock such a painful fiasco is that he is attempting to pull it off without irony, as though he were Rock. It all comes off as a horrible lampoon to anyone with the kind of social sense Yoon says humans have about the distastefulness of co-opting in-group insult language.

Ashwell highlights another problematic dimension of out-group parties co-opting in-group banter: out-groups recreate offensive pragmatic content, whether intentionally or not. This is in part because "paradigmatic slurs … do not have neutral correlates."[37] Echoing slurs risks reconstructing the social prejudices that form their conceptual frame.[38] The disclaimer could be as simple as "I'm from the South, so I can tell this joke." But now notice the single layer of additional separation in the following setups: "I heard this one from a friend who's [ethnicity]," or, "My wife is blonde, so I can say [offensive statement]." Disparaging speech reinforces stereotypes and the social status quo, nonpropositional effects that I discuss in chapter 6.

In a survey of research on the psychology of humor, Donald Saucier, Conor O'Dea, and Megan Strain explain why humans generally apply

---

A Conservative 'National Hero,'" transcript, *Morning Edition from NPR News*, November 16, 2016, https://tinyurl.com/SBL4832a.

36. Chris Rock, "Niggas vs. Black People," on *Roll with the New*, DreamWorks, 1997; *The Office*, "Diversity Day," directed by Ken Kwapis (written by B. J. Novak), March 29, 2005, on NBC. See an extended quotation of Rock's performance in Adam M. Croom, "The Semantics of Slurs: A Refutation of Coreferentialism," *Ampersand* 2 (2015): 30–38. Croom argues that Rock's liberal use of the epithet "n—a" invites such copycats.

37. Ashwell, "Gendered Slurs," 239.

38. I discuss such frames in ch. 5 under "Literary Context (Macro and Micro)."

different expectations to insiders versus outsiders for either's use of in-group language. Some speakers attempt to use racial humor subversively to defy social hierarchy, but such attempts have the potential of reinforcing that structure, whether intentionally antisocial or misunderstood as such.[39] Miso-Cretan reading assumptions virtually require that Paul presumed permission to use disparaging in-group banter. If we pay close attention to the attitude Paul expresses toward the quotation, we are not likely to arrive at this odd antisocial conclusion.

Any original, prebiblical literary context for the quotation is lost, and whether it was intended in its first use to be humorous or ironic is moot; advanced by any non-Cretan, it serves to introduce or reinforce an ethnic stereotype. Rather than advancing the quotation at face value, Paul indicates that he uses the quotation to serve a logical function (δι' ἣν αἰτίαν, "on account of this accusation," 1:13). He either leans on its content (i.e., *because Cretans are reprobate*) or presents it as evidence (i.e., *because troublemakers degrade Cretans*). The latter makes sense because, by exposing *someone* for disparaging the Cretans' intrinsic nature, he anchors his case against the troublemakers in a verifiable, concrete act that clearly contradicts his life-transforming gospel (3:3–7).[40] Paul did not use the disparaging quotation as an end in itself. For him, this kind of speech is no joking matter.

Stereotypes are difficult to undo. Even when a speaker is trying to counteract or contradict a stereotype through humor or ridicule, hearers have difficulty grasping anything but the superficial meaning of the stereotype she critiques. In the research that Saucier, O'Dea, and Strain highlight, people tended to grasp only the superficial message of a satirical television show rather than understand its subversive irony. They explain that with the subversive use of racial humor, "the humor may appear to advocate for the truth of those racial stereotypes," and "the deeper subversive message may be missed."[41] The stereotype "Cretans are ... evil brutes"

---

39. Saucier, O'Dea, and Strain, "The Bad, the Good," 75–85. For example, some studies exposed subjects to humor intended to subvert racial stereotypes and found that many of them did not grasp it as such.

40. As Vogel reasons, if the quotation were strictly true, then there could be no such thing as a Cretan Christian ("Die Kreterpolemik," 254). Such a teaching is contrary to Paul's gospel as expressed in Titus.

41. Saucier, O'Dea, and Strain, "The Bad, the Good," 80–81. Audiences watched Comedy Central's *The Colbert Report*, which subverts conventional political scripts by delivering American liberal talking points through a satirical American conservative

appears in Titus 1:12, but readers often miss the evidence that Paul did not hold this view.

Insulting language may seem innocuous, especially when it is *just a joke*, but there are social outcomes. One who invokes an ethnic insult through sly humor or a clever jab can react to objections with, "What's wrong? I was only kidding!" The stakes are low for the speaker but high for the target. But the Cretan quotation occupies a more complex context. It does not appear simply to suggest that stereotypes of Cretans are funny, acceptable, or even true. Rather than having a terminal function in the discourse, the quotation serves a secondary function either as a claim (the miso-Cretan reading; i.e., Cretans are reprobate) or as evidence for a claim (my relevance-guided reading; i.e., troublemakers were disparaging the Cretan missionary population), other rhetorical functions notwithstanding.

People generally sense that playful jabs used by in-groups are unacceptable insults when used by out-groups.[42] So, interpreters need to pay close attention to *who* is speaking and particularly whether she is speaking as a member of the target group or as an out-group individual. Claudia Bianchi explains why interpreters who are not part of the immediate audience have difficulty recognizing speakers' disassociative attitudes: "The crucial point is that out-groups lack unmistakable public means of making their dissociative attitude manifest. Even when their addressees know their nonracist or nonhomophobic opinions, bystanders and eavesdroppers (especially if they are members of the target group) may mistake an echoic (ironic) use for a derogatory one."[43] Bianchi describes what I believe has been happening with the Cretan quotation. Because Paul "lack[s] unmistakable means of making [his disassociative] attitude man-

---

mouthpiece. Viewers became *more* sympathetic to conservative policies and positions after watching *The Colbert Report* than they had been before watching.

42. Targeted groups appropriate insults for many reasons. According to tradition, the quotation was leveled by an in-group poet. Could the quotation itself have been an appropriation, intended to disarm insults against Cretans? Was it later reappropriated by out-groups to restigmatize Cretans? For relevance theory research on appropriation in general, see Claudia Bianchi, "Slurs and Appropriation: An Echoic Account," *JPrag* 66 (2014): 35–44.

43. Bianchi, "Slurs and Appropriation," 42–43. *Disassociative* is the alternate spelling chosen throughout the present volume and in much of the literature. *Dissociative* is more common in psychology than in linguistics. Bianchi uses both spellings elsewhere in the aforementioned article.

ifest," modern readers have mistaken his *mention* of derogatory words as his *use* of them.

Another reason interpreters need to pay close attention to *who* is speaking is that representations of *others* are always artificial. Select portions of reality or previous representations are reconveyed (hence, *re-presented*) to formulate reality for an audience.[44] The audience that accepts the representation feels obliged to see the world in such a way as to perceive empirical evidence conforming to their beliefs, unless or until the fault of the representation becomes too glaring to ignore. The troublemakers certainly viewed Cretans in this way, regardless of one's reading of Titus 1:12. Several interpreters who take the quotation at face value engage in a quest to reinforce their highly selective knowledge of ancient Cretans with additional facts, even when those facts are in most other ways irrelevant.[45] This practice is opposed to what Paul was trying to accomplish. He wants those *re-presenting* the Cretans as "evil" (κακά, 1:12) to be "silenced" (ἐπιστομίζω, 1:11), not justified or excused. He indicates how he would deal with those troublemakers, "whom [someone] should silence" (οὓς δεῖ ἐπιστομίζειν, 1:11).

Margaret Villanueva discusses this problematic kind of anthropological representation of otherness: "'Representation' in this sense means to re-present, to present again, carefully selected elements of reality from a singular perspective. A constant re-presentation of particular images and experiences as 'real,' even in the forms of jokes and cartoons, poses the danger that this will become 'reality for us,' that facile reification may be accepted as 'just the way things are.'"[46] Research shows a consistent correlation between an individual's racial attitudes and comfort level with prejudicial expressions. Multiple studies show that people who have less positive attitudes toward out-group individuals and who ascribe to negative stereotypes have a significantly higher comfort level with the use of racial slurs. Such people also tend to perceive the offensiveness of racial epithets as less severe than people who have positive attitudes toward out-group individuals.[47] These findings comport with general intuitions, but

---

44. See Margaret A. Villanueva, "Ethnic Slurs or Free Speech? Politics of Representation in a Student Newspaper," *AEQ* 27 (1996): 168–85.

45. See, e.g., Baugh, "Titus," 502, 504; Mounce, *Pastoral Epistles*, 397–99. Note also the scathing critique of this practice in Thiselton, "Logical Role."

46. Villanueva, "Ethnic Slurs," 169.

47. Conor J. O'Dea et al., "Out of Bounds: Factors Affecting the Perceived Offensiveness of Racial Slurs," *LangSci* 52 (2015): 155–64.

they also reinforce the correlation between the troublemakers' doctrine of an ethno-religious pecking order, on the one hand, and explicit insults toward Cretans, on the other. The reality of this tendency has troubling implications for the comfort level many interpreters have with some miso-Cretan readings. Samuel Bénétreau, for instance, finds Paul's supposedly bigoted remarks in Titus 1:12b to have been acceptable for the era but indelicate nowadays. Rather than critiquing the assumptions of this reading, he gives this caveat: "This is certainly not the tone to recommend in modern debates."[48]

Commensurate with a miso-Cretan reading, this passage's modern history of interpretation has exhibited what Christian Crandall and Amy Eschelmann call the justification-suppression model of prejudice.[49] Interpreters follow the impulse to either justify what appears to them to be prejudicial speech or to suppress it. The miso-Cretan reading assumes that Paul was co-opting in-group banter to shame the Cretans into shaping up morally, but this very offense appears to be what he was accusing the presumptuous leaders of doing. To these insolent leaders, the Cretans were not good enough as they were; their pedigree was a moral and religious liability. Therefore, the Cretans needed to convert more fully by observing the religio-cultural practices that the troublemakers prescribed. The pressure was upsetting entire households (1:11); and, when those presumptuous leaders discovered (or invented) the apropos Cretan stich (1:12b), their bullying became intolerable to Paul.[50]

When Paul identifies the troublemakers as "especially those from the circumcision" (1:10), he evokes a flawed ethno-religious dichotomy without endorsing it. According to the dichotomy, there were two types of people—Jews and gentiles. Cretans were a subset of the latter. The troublemakers' insults did not need to reflect specific faults of actual Cretans as

---

48. Samuel Bénétreau, *Les Épîtres Pastorales 1 et 2 Timothée, Tite*, EFTE (Vaux-sur-Seine: Édifac, 2008), 298. In French: "Ce n'est certes pas le ton à recommander dans des débats modernes." There was no debate. It was simply insulting, even as Bénétreau perceives it.

49. Christian S. Crandall and Amy Eshleman, "A Justification-Suppression Model of the Expression and Experience of Prejudice," *PB* 129 (2003): 414–46.

50. *Pace* Aída Besançon Spencer, *2 Timothy and Titus*, NCCS (Eugene, OR: Cascade, 2014), 25. Besançon Spencer suggests, "The Jews who were overturning whole households might have been promoting their Cretan heritage" without adequate explanation of how such a strategy would work.

much as to scorn an ambiguous class of people—those on the wrong side of this artificial divide.

Similarly to Ashwell, Adam Croom argues that ethnic slurs are not coextensive with descriptors and are therefore different in content. To explain the correlation between slurs and descriptors, he introduces the notion of *conceptual anchors*.[51] The Cretan quotation, in the mouth of a troublemaker, was not actually coextensive with ethnic or geographic Cretans but primarily referenced gentiles, whether converts or not, whose ethno-religious inferiority was highlighted on the basis of otherness from a privileged group of people who promoted Jewish interests over against gentiles or who found acceptance and approval among those who did. In other words, those advancing the quotation believed that Cretans were inferior qua gentiles, not qua Cretans.[52] Paul forces a conceptual reversal aimed at this very religio-cultural arrogance when he accuses the troublemakers of being "unclean," "defiled," and "unfit for any good work" (1:14–16) after they had labeled the Cretans as "evil," "defiled," and "nonworking" (1:12).

Croom demonstrates that slurs and descriptors do not necessarily have the same referential extension.[53] This linguistic reality suggests that the *Cretans* who were being disparaged by the quotation did not strictly correspond to a group identified by the geographic or ethnic label *Cretan*. More likely, *Cretan*, among the troublemakers in the church, is code for church members who are inferior by virtue of being gentile. Croom argues that pejoratives require a conceptual anchor that is not literally synonymous or coextensive with any appropriate, nonpejorative descriptor. *Cretan* has sadly *become* (!) a pejorative word itself. Paul and Titus seem to have been among the first to recognize this problem and address it as a contradiction of the gospel.

Croom explains that slurs not only refer but also pass judgment. He provides a formula for the pragmatic enrichment of conceptual anchors that I parallel: based on the book context of Titus, wherein the ethno-

---

51. Croom, "Semantics of Slurs," 31–37.

52. Wilson and Sperber explain, "The thought that is the object of the ironical attitude need not be identical to the proposition expressed by the ironical utterance but may merely resemble it in content" (quoted in Bianchi, "Slurs and Appropriation," 40).

53. Croom, "Semantics of Slurs." Ashwell's research also supports such claims ("Gendered Slurs").

religious tensions described here feature prominently, the conceptual anchor for *Cretans* would actually be something like *ethnically, and thereby religiously, inferior, and despicable on account of it, gentile*.[54] It might be uncomfortable for Titus to hear Paul disparaging his young congregation (as per a miso-Cretan reading), but it would be socially jarring for Paul to report his awareness of and negative opinion toward what the troublemakers were trying to get away with. Paul exposes the problem of bigotry in the church by introducing the statement as having come from one of the troublemakers, an issue that Titus may have known but been too timid to address (see Titus 2:15).[55]

It may be that Paul or his speaker (εἶπεν τις, "someone said," 1:12) appropriated the statement "Cretans are always liars" (with a few added epithets) from Callimachus's third-century BCE *Hymns* (1.8–9) or from an earlier source (e.g., Epimenides). A Cretan would have had the in-group credibility to render social commentary or to use the words ironically to subvert insults from out-group individuals, but using the quotation to assert its surface meaning silences this credible, subversive voice. So, we recognize two conflicting possibilities that many miso-Cretan readings tacitly hold: first, that a Cretan spoke it, which means that it is ironic, even paradoxical, in-group banter; and, second, that Paul asserts it, which means that the in-group voice has been silenced. I propose a third possibility: even though the troublemakers may have deferred to Epimenides's Cretan in-group credentials, Paul perceived how they were mis-*re-presenting* Cretans.

The relevance-guided reading I am suggesting has an analogy in Gal 2:15–21, in which Paul, in the dialogue between himself and Peter, corrects a pattern of thinking that elevates Jews above gentiles. When Paul uses the phrase "gentile sinners" in Gal 2:15, rather than disparaging non-Jews, as his old way of thinking dictated, he is merely ironically echoing (and thereby critiquing) the fault in that way of seeing the human population.[56] It sees the world as *us* and *them*. The terms by which people of status tend to distinguish themselves from others

---

54. See Croom, "Semantics of Slurs," 31–37.
55. I explain my use of *troublemakers* more in ch. 5 under "Literary Context."
56. See, e.g., discussion in Daniel C. Arichea and Eugene A. Nida, *A Handbook on Paul's Letter to the Galatians*, UBSHS (New York: United Bible Societies, 1976), 44–45; Marion L. Soards and Darrell J. Pursiful, *Galatians*, SHBC (Macon, GA: Smith & Helwys, 2015), 87; Jae Won Lee, *Paul and the Politics of Difference: A Contextual*

constantly change. Essential to Paul's new view of the world was a radical realignment of valuation that considered people equal before God, regardless of ethnicity, achievement, gender, religion, or other factors.[57] I now look more closely at specific ways Paul defends the Cretans from biased verbal attacks.

Paul's Reversal of Religious Designations

Regarding irony, Grice taught, "I cannot say something ironically unless what I say is intended to reflect a hostile or derogatory judgment or a feeling such as indignation or contempt."[58] Wilson refines Grice's general view, explaining that writers convey critical or derogatory attitudes toward sentences by producing utterances that would be pragmatically inappropriate if literally understood. Hearers' proven ability to distinguish appropriately between *use* and *mention* makes irony successful.[59]

Irony derogates ideas more than persons or behaviors. Titus 1:12 derogates the *idea* that ethnicity (and its commensurate religio-cultural appurtenances) is a criterion of being worthy of or exempt from status with God. The preceding verses suggest that Paul does not hold the speaker in 1:12 to be a reliable witness. I quote Wilson at length as she explains the echoic use of irony, which I see applying to 1:12: "The speaker in irony does not *use* the proposition expressed by her utterance in order to represent a thought of her own which she wants the hearer to accept as true, but *mentions* it in order to represent a thought or utterance she tacitly attributes to someone else, and which she wants to suggest is ludicrously false, under-informative or irrelevant."[60]

Study of the Jewish-Gentile Difference in Galatians and Romans (Eugene, OR: Pickwick, 2014), 70–72.

57. John M. G. Barclay draws out this rhetorical move in his paraphrase of Gal 2:15–21. See Barclay, *Paul and the Gift* (Grand Rapids: Eerdmans, 2015), 371.

58. Quoted in Wilson, "Pragmatics of Verbal Irony," 1727. Without discarding Grice's notions, Wilson critiques his early assumption that irony was primarily a matter of *pretense* or *making as-if to say*. For her, Grice's explanation was inadequate, a rearticulation of classical rhetoric dressed up in modern garb. She regards *echo* as the stock form of irony (1723).

59. See Wilson, "Pragmatics of Verbal Irony," 1727–28. Normally, such success assumes that the audience is contemporary with the speaker. In biblical interpretation, impediments to such comprehension arise.

60. Wilson, "Pragmatics of Verbal Irony," 1728.

Sperber and Wilson list three criteria that hearers intuitively use to spot irony: (1) recognition of the utterance as echoic, (2) identification of the source of the opinion echoed, and (3) recognition that the speaker's attitude toward the opinion echoed is one of rejection or disapproval.[61] Interpreters of Titus must note that the second criterion can include sources that are ambiguous and that the third criterion usually requires a measure of reasonable inference to ascertain the speaker's attitude.

I suggest three relevance-guided assumptions for interpreting irony based on Sperber and Wilson's three intuitive signals and developed from additional work by relevance theorists: First, a common-sense account of the statement would judge that the speaker is not saying it on her own behalf. In this sense, the speaker echoes the idea as if it were from another. Second, an account of the statement that appreciates its verbal context and life context would reason that the relevance of the statement to its contexts is a function not of its linguistically encoded content but of the speaker's power to convey her own attitude toward its content. Third, such an account of the statement would also perceive that the speaker's attitude toward the statement is one of disassociation in the form of ridicule, disdain, criticism, or some like attitude.[62]

The first assumption requires readers to appreciate the general theme of church leadership in Titus 1:5–16 and the specific topic of problematic leadership in 1:10–16. If Paul intended to expose the offenses of a divisive group in the community and to prescribe a remedy—which seems to be the case in 1:10–11 and 1:13—then we are compelled to ask, How does

---

61. Summarized in Seto, "On Non-echoic Irony," 240; derived from Sperber and Wilson, *Pragmatics: An Overview*, 29–32. For detailed explanation, see Wilson, "Pragmatics of Verbal Irony," 1734–38. For a countervailing assessment of irony with some adherents in relevance theory, see Grice, "Logic and Conversation," 49–53. Whether echo or pretense, my argument stands; the speaker's attitude is implicated as rejection or disapproval.

Seto disagrees with their first criterion, presenting instances and categories of irony that he claims are not echoic. His proposal does not affect my thesis; because even if irony is pretense, as Grice originally taught, it still involves the speaker's disassociative attitude toward the sentence (see Seto, "On Non-echoic Irony").

62. Based on a synthesis of common arguments from Wilson, "Pragmatics of Verbal Irony"; Currie, "Why Irony Is Pretence"; Seto, "On Non-echoic Irony"; Garmendia, "(Neo)Gricean Account"; Dan Sperber and Deirdre Wilson, "Irony in the Use-Mention Distinction," in *Radical Pragmatics*, ed. Peter Cole (New York: Academic Press, 1981), 295–318.

verse 12 fit in? The second assumption is critical for a relevance-guided hermeneutic. The literary context and Paul's life context (whether historical or literary-canonical) suggest that his attitude toward the statement would be more relevant than the content of the statement. Regarding the third assumption, the context signals that Paul opposes the kind of attitude represented by the content of the quotation; he instructs Titus to "rebuke them severely on account of [this] accusation" (δι' ἣν αἰτίαν ἔλεγχε αὐτοὺς ἀποτόμως, 1:13). This rebuke is aimed at troublemakers for whom the sentiment expressed in the Cretan quotation validates an ethno-religious social hierarchy with theological implications contrary to Paul's gospel. The specific points of irony I explore below include Paul's use of the title *prophet* to refer to the speaker of the quotation and Paul's reversal of Jewish religious language to shame the presumptuous leaders.

Prophet or Sloganeer?

Comprehending nonliteral language does not require a two-step process in which the literal meaning is first deciphered and then discarded for a *special* sense; it is rapid and synchronic. Theorists refer to this processing as *on-line comprehension*. Gibbs discusses empirical research that shows how quickly hearers discern "the meanings of words during on-line comprehension" based on judging "a speaker's probable intentions."[63] Paul introduced a group of impudent leaders in the verses preceding the quotation (1:12b), which suggests that these troublemakers (1:10–11) were the group from which the prophet (1:12a) came. This tight sequence of discourse would have influenced the original audience's perception of Paul's intentions. Titus and his community knew Paul's attitude toward the presumptuous prophet immediately. The quotation was an example of objectionable behavior.

The near context indicates that Paul was concerned with leadership malpractice; the syntax indicates that the speaker came from the company of presumptuous leaders; the broader context reveals no interest in gluttony or laziness; and the quotation harmonizes with the overall ethno-religious thrust of the unhealthy doctrine that Paul addresses elsewhere in Titus. These statements are all explicatures, because they are based on visible, verifiable evidence, although not strictly on the *semantic* value of

---

63. Gibbs, "Intentionalist Controversy," 191.

particular words (as might be represented in a lexicon) or syntax (as might be represented in a grammar).

According to Levinson, hearers reject implicatures if the discourse context negates them; because, unlike logical inferences, pragmatic presuppositions are *defeasible*. That is, unlike logical implications or entailments, they are susceptible to negation by added contextual evidence.[64] Hearers reject the presupposition that Paul uses the term *prophet* to honor or even to label the speaker objectively, because the discourse context casts doubt on the speaker's trustworthiness.

I have generally referred to irony as an echoic use of language, but relevance theory offers two major proposals for understanding irony. First, there is Grice's classic *irony as pretense* or *making as-if to say*.[65] Along these lines, Greg Currie explains that, in irony, "one pretends to be doing something which one is not doing: speaking seriously and assertively, seriously asking a question, seriously expressing distaste" while targeting "a restrictive or otherwise defective view of the world."[66] The second proposal, *irony as echo*, is currently more common among theorists. These accounts are not entirely incompatible. Wilson appreciates pretense accounts of irony, such as Currie's, but also critiques them.[67] For her, irony is essentially communicative, not expressive. Communicative speech—the stock and trade of relevance theory—focuses on audience comprehension, whereas expressive speech does not.[68] Both the echoic and pretense accounts nevertheless have explanatory power for a variety of irony types, and both hold that the speaker conveys a critical or mocking attitude toward her statement.

Paul seems to use the title *prophet* ironically, because he portrays the speaker as an untrustworthy source. For Paul, the speaker to whom he refers is only a prophet in his own mind and among the company of presumptuous leaders. Paul is allowing the speaker and the listener to look on

---

64. Levinson, *Pragmatics*, 169–70, 186–91, esp. 190.
65. Grice typically used nontechnical terms to refer to features of language (see "Logic and Conversation," 49–50). Wilson critiques Grice partly on the basis of his definitional imprecision and partly because even he did not appreciate irony's full pragmatic dimensions (Wilson, "Pragmatics of Verbal Irony," 1725–26).
66. Currie, "Why Irony Is Pretence," 116.
67. See Wilson, "Pragmatics of Verbal Irony," 1735.
68. For detailed examination of additional distinctions, see Wilson, "Pragmatics of Verbal Irony," 1735; Garmendia, "(Neo)Gricean Account;" Currie, "Why Irony is Pretence."

with ridicule as someone makes a labeling error. Paul invites his audience to sneer at such an inappropriate title for such an offensive and misguided person. Paul and Titus know the destructive effects of bigotry; and, as everyone in the Cretan church must learn, prophets speak gospel truth, not insults.[69]

Currie nuances his account by explaining that the pretense is not based on the mode of utterance. A comedy or a tragedy, being entirely pretended, is not also entirely ironical. Rather, departures from the normal mode of utterance signal ironic moments that can be humorous, caustic, or otherwise. Pretense itself is not ironic; it has to pretend to hold *a perspective of things* that is faulty from the authentic perspective of the speaker.[70] Further, according to Currie and others, framing irony with explanation defeats or nullifies it. He writes, "The kind of pretense we naturally label ironic generally requires a context that contains no explicit or conventional signals that what is said or done is pretense."[71]

Readers may not have access to real-time signals such as tone of voice, but they nevertheless can see linguistic cues in word choice and context that Paul is engaged in second-order metarepresentation. By *second-order*, Currie and other linguists mean the abstract thinking that humans engage in every day whereby they evaluate the semantically decoded content of utterances in alignment with the attitudes speakers demonstrate toward it. In other words, Paul is conveying thoughts about thoughts. Natural language practitioners use second-order processing intuitively and reliably, typically without being conscious of it.[72] This points to the subtlety of irony. According to Grice: "To be ironical is, among other things, to pretend..., and while one wants the pretense to be recognized as such, to announce it as pretense would spoil the effect."[73] Readers understand that Paul speaks ironically without using explicit, mechanical words or

---

69. Consider the culminating description of the depraved and unredeemed in Titus 3:3, "hating one another," before the "epiphany" of "the kindness and love of God our Savior" (3:4).

70. Currie's fuller but more complex definition: "Irony is a matter of pretending to a limited perspective in a way which is expressive of a view you have about the limitations of some suitably related perspective, where those limitations compromise, to some degree, the reasonableness of the perspective" ("Why Irony Is Pretence," 124).

71. Currie, "Why Irony Is Pretence," 124.

72. See Currie, "Why Irony Is Pretence," 127.

73. H. Paul Grice, *Studies in the Way of Words* (Cambridge: Harvard University Press, 1989), 54; see also Clark, *Relevance Theory*, 287.

phrases by which to explicate, for example, "Now, I'm being ironic here." His audience realized that labeling the speaker a prophet could not have been taken as literally true or descriptive.

Paul's use of the title *prophet* in Titus 1:12 is a case of metonymy, which Song says is related to its referent by way of contiguity, whereas metaphor is related to its referent by way of resemblance.[74] It is not simply a straightforward replacement. Metonymical interpretations are *associatively activated* by the expressions that replace the reference. In the words of François Recanati, metonymy is "sensitive to the linguistic and extralinguistic context in which the expression which receives the metonymical interpretation occurs."[75] Paul distanced himself from a group of people and then quoted someone from that group, so uttering the word *prophet* immediately triggered a negative association. The hearers had no difficulty in discerning that Paul intended the referent—a person who had been built up as having distasteful associations—to be taken as an unreliable witness. The label comes as a punch line immediately before the quotation (εἶπέν τις ... προφήτης· Κρῆτες, "[so] said some ... prophet, 'Cretans'"), grammatically unnecessary, suggesting that it is the overextension of Paul's disassociative reference to the speaker of the quotation.

Paul could not point to a preexisting, fully lexicalized referent, so he employed the label of prophet to refer to a category of people he described as not very prophetic (i.e., not truth tellers). In the absence of an exact lexicalization of what Paul had in mind, he used *prophet* to convey a complex of ideas, including his own attitude toward *them*. This higher-level explicature includes the notion that he was not necessarily the person who placed the label *prophet* on the speaker of the quotation. The metonym is echoic—Paul attributes the labeling to *them*. Masa-aki Yamanashi observes that ironic utterances often involve a switch in register or style.[76] Seto describes this as a heightening of intensity.[77] Certainly, the use of the word *prophet* is an elevation of formality or status, even a heightening or hyperbolic (and sarcastic) attribution of religious status. It is like when the swaggering Han Solo refers to the persnickety Princess Leia as "your worshipfulness."

---

74. See Song, "Metaphor and Metonymy," 95–96.
75. Quoted by Song in "Metaphor and Metonymy," 96.
76. Masa-aki Yamanashi, "Some Issues in the Treatment of Irony and Related Tropes," in Carston and Uchida, *Relevance Theory*, 277.
77. See Seto, "On Non-echoic Irony," 239.

Levinson highlights a crucial contention of the *correspondence theory* of metaphor, originally articulated by Max Black: effective metaphors typically combine two conceptual fields such that the effect of the metaphor is spoiled to the extent that it is explained.[78] Not all domains are equally compatible; however, stronger correspondence between domains leads to more effective metaphors. Metaphors in which the target (the object defined) and the symbol (the object defining) have conceptual, phonetic, or other correspondences can be especially strong. *Prophet* held cultural currency for Titus's community. Quinn recognizes the significance of the title, writing, "Prophetic credentials were found and valued among the Jewish Christians."[79] It appropriately refers to a *speaking* participant. In the social and conversational contexts of Titus, the conceptual correspondence would be strong, so the metaphor works smoothly and effectively.

Another indicator of irony, according to Seto, is known as topicalization. Theme and focus are two kinds of topicalization. Focus topicalization appears in Paul's use of the word *prophet*. Seto uses the following sentence as an example: "A fine friend she turned out to be."[80] That the statement is ironic is signaled by the topicalization of *friend* and the implied false complimentary attitude. Similarly, "prophet of their own" may function as a topicalization of the purveyor of this quotation, further suggesting Paul's disassociative attitude toward him. In Titus 1:12a, Paul employs several kinds of emphasis, including topicalization, the exaggerated honorary title, and the emphatic phrase of belonging, "one of their very own." Combining this with Paul's apparent disassociative attitude toward the group out of which this speaker comes yields a strong case for irony—suggesting that Paul's use of this quotation by no means advances the substance of what was said.

Philip Goodwin argues that relevance-centered biblical translation should convey the pragmatic thrust of an expression, especially when the semantics of a phrase could mislead readers.[81] To capture the irony

---

78. Levinson, *Pragmatics*, 159–60. Although this contention may not have concerned Max Black in his original articulation of the theory (*Models and Metaphors*, 1962), it coincides with the rapidity of natural language comprehension, because it does not posit a complex, multistep process for interpretation.

79. Quinn, *Letter to Titus*, 109. He cites Acts 13:1; 15:22, 32; 1 Cor 12:28–29; Eph 2:20; 4:11.

80. Seto, "On Non-echoic Irony," 247.

81. Goodwin, *Translating the English Bible*, 18 (see also 148, where he expands the argument and categorizes emphases as grounds for pragmatic translational choices; and 224, where he offers contextual translational alternatives for προφήτης [in Luke]).

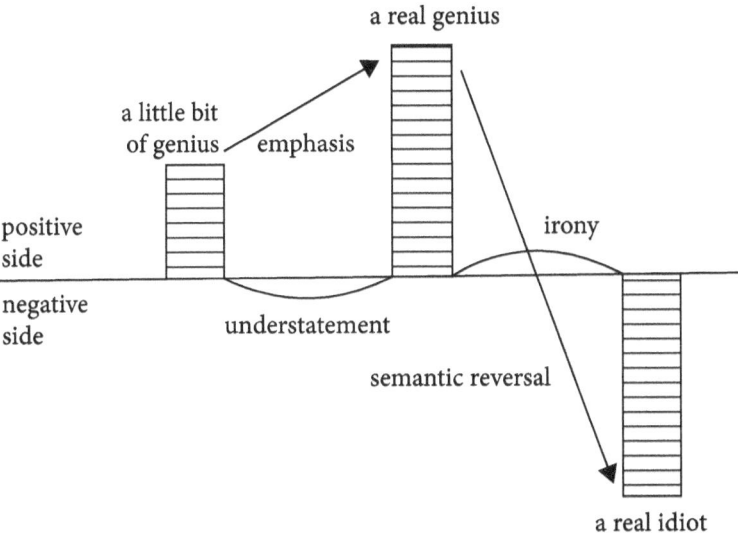

Fig. 4.2. Graph adapted from Ken-ichi Seto, "On Non-echoic Irony," in *Relevance Theory: Applications and Implications*, edited by Robyn Carston and Seiji Uchida, P&B 37 (Philadelphia: Benjamins, 1998), 245.

in an English idiom, I might render ἴδιος αὐτῶν προφήτης in Titus 1:12 as "their own resident sloganeer." This translation could lessen the cognitive effort of working through the irony of calling him a prophet and make the intended implications more accessible, which may be necessary for modern-day readers. Of course, "sloganeer" does not capture the ethno-religious thrust of *prophet*.

Seto uses a graph (reproduced above) to visualize how ironic metonymy (e.g., name-calling) works. He diagrams a horizontal baseline with a positive field above the line and a negative field below it. In the case of personal descriptions, the positive field represents a scale of compliments; the negative field represents a scale of insults. Seto argues that the degree of irony and the greatness of cognitive effects emerge from the measure of distance between what the speaker means and the propositional content of the utterance as linguistically encoded.[82] Seto claims that the characteristic function of verbal irony is to present an original thought and to show the speaker's critical attitude toward that thought. Ironic speech invokes an idea for the purpose of implicit ridicule. While irony is inherently com-

---

82. See Seto, "On Non-echoic Irony," 244–45, esp. fig. 18.

plex, it is still highly economical, because hearers can derive a significant cognitive-effect bang for their processing-effort buck.

Gibbs and Tendahl argue that metaphor does not necessarily require or reward more cognitive effort than literal speech. Appropriate metaphors can be the most efficient and effective way to convey a meaning.[83] The inherent complexity of irony has to do with the fact that it requires second-order processing (thinking about thoughts). This is irony: to hold up a thought for implicit criticism. Expressions that are within the mildly positive domain that Seto graphs are not typically considered ironic. Seto writes, "We would have to increase the voltage of meaning in order to make good ironic statements."[84] Seto recognizes and shows in his examples that most echo markers (which include signals of irony) involve highly charged or overcharged *positive* modifiers (either at the sentence or word level) that would not be used if the speaker were merely communicating their own positive attitude toward the subject. So, for example, when someone does something stupid and a speaker refers to them by saying, "[So-and-so] is a genius," it is overcharged. If *So-and-so* had actually done something smart, the speaker might normally have been expected to compliment them by saying something closer to "[So-and-so] is smart." Positive exaggeration (e.g., "prophet") is, therefore, a signal of echoic and ironic use. We now look at one last example of Paul's use of irony—the category reversal found in the surrounding context of the Cretan quotation.

Category Reversal

Another point of irony worth noting is Paul's remapping of the Cretan quotation's insulting language onto a constellation of concepts laden with religious valuations that Jewish congregants likely respected. If the Cretan church was developing in an ethno-religious environment such as the book of Titus seems to portray, then they would have recognized the extent to which the quotation's claims were loaded with religious freight in the mouth of contemporary Jews that they might not have been in the mouth of an ancient Cretan (e.g., Epimenides). Paul placed the speaker and his supporters on the wrong side of their own valuations. In the final two verses of the passage (1:15–16), not long after the hexameter quota-

---

83. See Gibbs and Tendahl, "Cognitive Effort and Effects."
84. Seto, "On Non-echoic Irony," 245.

tion (1:12b), Paul waxes poetic himself, using parallelism and religious imagery to expose the hypocrisy of the people who were advancing the doctrine of Cretan (i.e., gentile) inferiority within the community. Hoklotubbe recognizes, "These rival teachers, according to the author, embody the worst qualities of Cretans as portrayed in an apparently well-known saying."[85]

Although Paul does not develop the negative qualities ascribed to Cretans by the quotation (e.g., deceit, laziness, gluttony) as moral issues later in Titus, its contents are not totally irrelevant. The quotation has an existential thrust—that is, it concerns moral *being* more than moral *doing*, but Paul uses it as a foil against which to parody the troublemakers. The troublemakers were the true "nonworking bellies" (γαστέρες ἀργαί 1:12), desiring "disgraceful gain" (αἰσχροῦ κέρδους χάριν, 1:11; cf. μὴ αἰσχροκερδῆ, 1:7) but "unfit for any good work" (πρὸς πᾶν ἔργον ἀγαθὸν ἀδόκιμοι, 1:16b). Whereas the speaker referred to Cretans as "evil beasts" (κακὰ θηρία, "unclean," 1:12), Paul uses "having been defiled" (μεμιαμμένοις, 1:15) and "detestable" (βδελυκτός, 1:16) to refer to the troublemakers. Words for "clean [ones]" (καθαροῖς, 1:15) and cognates also contrast with such features of the quotation. Paul packs epithets that evoke central notions of Jewish religious purity into the passage. He compares and contrasts their actual behavior and speech with the insinuations leveled against the Cretans in the quotation. So *bellies* and *brutes* (1:12), as metonyms, would seem to miscategorize their target and be more applicable to the speaker's faction.[86] Paul, in turn, labels them *defiled* (1:15) and *detestable* (1:16). He seems to be accentuating a contradiction between the moral superiority implied in the condemnation of others and the actual moral condition of people who would purvey such ideas.

The hearer who infers such ironic speech appropriately receives tremendous payoff. By mentioning the quotation, Paul offers evidence for his hearers to judge even as he had to judge it. By use of echoic irony, Paul carries his audience along better than he could have by direct and explicit argumentation alone, for he demonstrates trust that they will understand his message, which will yield his audience what relevance theorists now call positive cognitive effects. Hearers who interpret irony well can derive a deeper connection with the speaker.

---

85. Hoklotubbe, "Civilized Christ-Followers," 371. With this I agree, but I disagree that Paul was affirming the quotation.
86. See Song, "Metaphor and Metonymy," 97–100.

A sentence uttered ironically, according to Wilson, "is more or less obviously false, irrelevant or under-informative."[87] Paul distances himself from the surface meaning of the quotation, just as would be expected of a person speaking ironically, and instead reverses its judgments back against its purveyors. Paul accomplishes what Wilson describes as the pragmatic function of irony: "The main point … is to express the speaker's dissociative attitude to a tacitly attributed utterance or thought … based on some perceived discrepancy between the way it represents the world and the way things actually are."[88] Speaker intention has been a significant concern for this chapter, but one of relevance theory's major developments from pragmatics is a focus on utterance interpretation as a process in the *hearer's* mind. To this focus we now turn.

---

87. Wilson, "Pragmatics of Verbal Irony," 1730–31.
88. Wilson, "Pragmatics of Verbal Irony," 1724. *Dissociative* is an alternative spelling of *disassociative* in the literature. *Disassociative* is chosen in the present volume because it is more common in linguistics and in the US. See "disassociative, adj.," OED Online.

5
The Role of the Hearer in Communication

Relevance theorists focus on how hearers arrive at meaning. This focus is commensurate with the evolution of the discipline of linguistic pragmatics. Whereas Gricean pragmatics is speaker-oriented, relevance theory is hearer-oriented. This chapter spells out some of the implications of recognizing the hearer's role in communication for interpreting utterances and applies them to Titus.

Grice taught that when a hearer observes a superficial violation of the cooperative maxims (in his words, "flouting the maxims"), he nevertheless assumes the speaker's deeper adherence to them.[1] Levinson explains, "Grice's point is not that we [speakers] always adhere to these maxims on a superficial level but rather that, wherever possible, people will interpret what we say as conforming to the maxims on at least some level."[2] Note the agency of the hearer in Levinson's explanation. Relevance theorists view interpretation as a cognitive process in the hearer. Furlong emphasizes the spontaneous and intuitive nature of the hearer's comprehension process as she contrasts relevance theory with reader-response criticism.[3] This contrast is important. Both systems hold the reader to be central to interpretation, but relevance theory explains how readers contribute to an interpretive process grounded in *speaker* intentions. Evaluating interpretations as valid or invalid cannot be the unilateral task of the reader; for, as Furlong notes, a reader "is not necessarily an authority on his own interpretive process."[4] Thus, the formulation of meaning is not entirely dependent on the subjectivity of the hearer. The objective of uncovering speaker intention constrains the practice of inference in natural language

---

1. See Grice, "Logic and Conversation," 53–54.
2. Levinson, *Pragmatics*, 102–3.
3. See Furlong, "Relevance Theory," 43–46.
4. Furlong, "Relevance Theory," 44.

exchanges.[5] As Tim Meadowcroft points out, "reader responsibility" does not devolve into "unrestrained privilege."[6]

Relevance theorists also hold that speakers do not utter sentences merely to convey information that hearers can ascertain through a process of comprehension. Sperber and Wilson see comprehension as too passive and proposition-oriented to be the ultimate task of pragmatics. They write, "It is utterance-interpretation, not utterance-comprehension, that is the natural domain of pragmatic theory."[7] Relevance theorists recognize that hearers play an active, not a passive, role in formulating meaning.

Further, speakers use utterances to accomplish effects in addition to and aside from comprehension. Speakers aim to alter their environments by affecting listener behavior and assumptions, social relations, and so on.[8] The interpretation of an utterance can be efficient and relevant, even when the informational payload of the utterance is uncertain or miniscule from the perspective of a third party (e.g., modern readers). In this chapter, I explain two key aspects of the hearer's role in communication and apply them to interpretations of Titus 1:12: I discuss contextual assumptions, which are composed of a hearer's cognitive environment (conceptual) and implicated premises (logical); and I discuss salience, which affects the relative prominence and accessibility of contextual assumptions.

Mismatched Contextual Assumptions

Hearers infer explicatures based on observable linguistic features in a discourse context, especially what the speaker has produced (i.e., not the entire material environment). Explicatures must be combined with contextual assumptions in order to arrive at utterance meaning. Contextual assumptions, although largely shared between a speaker and a hearer, are the content a hearer contributes to inferential interpretation. That is, they are a necessary ingredient for interpretation that neither the words of a speaker nor the material environment, on their own, supply. Clark explains, "Explicatures, which are based on encoded linguistic meanings of linguistic expressions, plus contextual assumptions, which are based on

---

5. See ch. 4.
6. Meadowcroft, "Relevance as Mediating Category," 627.
7. Sperber and Wilson, "Pragmatics" (1981), 283.
8. I discuss these nonpropositional dimensions of communication in ch. 6.

life experience and the situational context of the conversation, combine to equal implicatures, which constitute the meaning of an utterance."[9]

I focus on two broad kinds of contextual assumptions, one conceptual and one logical. A hearer's cognitive environment is a constantly changing, complex, and information-rich yet incomplete conceptual world. Implicated premises are assumptions that are logically necessary to conclude the correct (i.e., relevant) meaning and derive adequate cognitive effects.

Clark's diagram (fig. 5.1) represents an objective and repeatable process. It is especially helpful for meta-pragmatics—the process of interpreting utterances in which the interpreter is not a partner in the conversation (e.g., modern scholars reading ancient texts)—because it illuminates points at which interpreters might diverge from original audiences by making inappropriate assumptions. Clark writes, "In meta-pragmatics, … we imagine what might be available to an individual; and, of course, our model of the relevant set of contextual assumptions is radically impoverished compared to what is available to an actual individual at a specific time."[10]

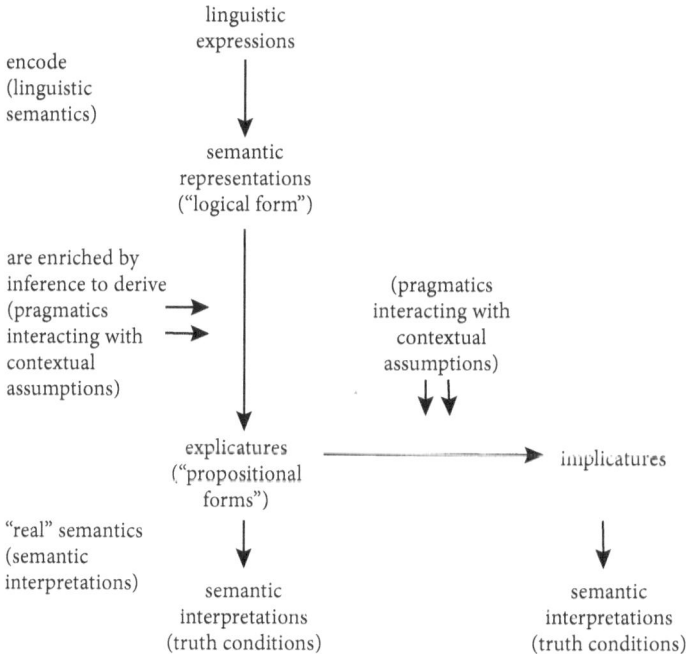

Fig. 5.1. Graph adapted from Clark, *Relevance Theory*, 299.

---

9. Clark, *Relevance Theory*, 141.
10. Clark, *Relevance Theory*, 333.

Clark bases this diagram on Wilson and Sperber's arguments that pragmatic inference is not only necessary to arrive at implicatures, as Grice taught, but that it is also necessary for deriving explicatures, as the diagram portrays. The most significant difference between this relevance-theoretical scheme and a more classic (Gricean) one is the presence of inference at all levels of the process. This section focuses on the center of this diagram, where contextual assumptions contribute to arriving at both final utterance meaning (implicatures) and logically intermediate sentence meaning (explicatures). As stated before, explicatures are only *logically* intermediate because processes of natural language interpretation occur so rapidly, intuitively, and virtually simultaneously that intermediate steps cannot be practically observed in a natural environment. For our purposes, however, this diagram helps to visualize the interplay of explicatures and contextual assumptions.

To discern the meaning of utterances, according to Sperber and Wilson, "implicated conclusions must be deducible from explicatures together with an appropriate set of contextual assumptions."[11] Modern interpreters of Titus, however, tend to introduce anachronistic or otherwise inappropriate assumptions into the interpretational process. Because a disparaging statement appears in Titus 1:12b, they assume that Paul affirms the substance of the saying in spite of evidence in the broader context of Titus that he was trying to ameliorate ethno-religious tensions, especially those that diminished the dignity of gentiles. In order to construe 1:12 as an insult leveled or endorsed by Paul, one must introduce assumptions that fail to cohere with the thrust of the letter as a whole or the sense of statements in the near context (1:10–16). I suggest that such a construal would have surprised original hearers. Blass recognizes the need for interpreters to grasp what was on the mind of original hearers, asserting, "The discourse analyst has to know some of the hearer's assumptions, no matter in what culture the analysis is done."[12] Here it is necessary to clarify how the contextual assumptions of original and modern interpreters can become mismatched and indicate contextual assumptions that original hearers of Titus plausibly held. I begin with an explanation of how the hearer's cognitive environment contributes to these assumptions.

---

11. Sperber and Wilson, "Pragmatics" (2007), 482.
12. Blass, *Relevance Relations in Discourse*, 13.

Cognitive Environment

A speaker expects her hearer to contribute what he already knows to the meaning of an utterance, and she signals which pieces of his store of knowledge are relevant. This subset of all of the hearer's knowledge is his *cognitive environment*. Clark provides the following definition: "The cognitive environment of an individual is a set of assumptions that are manifest to him."[13] Whether an assumption is manifest depends on various contextual factors—the utterance itself being one of the most important—but the test is whether the hearer "is capable at that time of representing it mentally and accepting its representation as true or probably true."[14] Note that this definition implies that cognitive environment is particular to individual people at specific times and can never be fully replicated.[15] It changes with every experience, word, and thought. In this section, I describe factors that contribute to an assumption being manifest. In order for readers of ancient writings to align their assumptions most reliably with those of original audiences, literary context is the chief factor.

Consider the task of disambiguation. Modern readers of biblical texts can properly disambiguate a reference only if the referent emerges from what could plausibly be construed as the original hearer's cognitive environment. If interpreters draw on information that is likely outside the cognitive environment of original hearers, they err.

To reconstruct a cognitive environment for interpreting Titus 1:12, I describe three considerations: encyclopedic knowledge, constraints on relevance, and literary context. These considerations logically develop

---

13. Clark adjusts Sperber and Wilson's definition by using *assumptions* in place of their *facts* (see Clark, *Relevance Theory*, 115). See also, Green, "Relevance Theory and Biblical Interpretation" (2013), 272.

14. Sperber and Wilson, quoted in Clark, *Relevance Theory*, 115. Pattemore also builds on Sperber and Wilson's definition, writing, "Context in RT [relevance theory] is a cognitive concept—a set of propositions that we hold to be true or probably true. The sum of all such ideas is our *cognitive environment*." See Stephen W. Pattemore, "On the Relevance of Translation Theory," *RevExp* 108 (2011): 267.

15. Some scholars have applied relevance theory to biblical studies in an attempt to reconstruct the cognitive environment of ancient authors and audiences and thus to illuminate interpretation. See, e.g., Joseph D. Fantin, "The Lord of the Entire World: Lord Jesus, a Challenge to Lord Caesar?" (PhD diss., University of Sheffield, 2007), examining specific passages in the undisputed Paulines; and Goh, "Honoring Christ, Subverting Caesar," examining Ephesians.

from one another. Encyclopedic knowledge is the complete set of available information. Constraints on relevance limit this to a more narrow, manageable, and accessible set for cognitive processing. Literary context is that most reliable, and therefore critical, subset for modern readers of the Bible. Green points out that *context* in relevance theory is a subset of all the information available to hearers from their environment. The aspect of the original hearers' cognitive environment that modern readers have access to with the most detail and certainty is the text of Scripture.[16]

Encyclopedic Knowledge

Hearers' cognitive environments include encyclopedic knowledge that differs for each individual. Biblical scholars may add to our store of knowledge but cannot predetermine what information is most relevant to an utterance. Blass writes, "It is a mistake to assume that context is something given in advance."[17] We risk confusing our knowledge of the ancient world, especially ancient literature, monumental history, and archaeology, with the cognitive environment of ancient interlocutors. Cognitive environments differ from person to person and, in one person, from time to time. One's cognitive environment is contextual.

So, modern interpreters must evaluate the relevance of encyclopedic knowledge carefully. We acquire a surplus (but also a deficiency) of facts about the world, facts of history and human behavior, lexical and grammatical facts, social and religious facts. Green refers to the ideal collection of facts as "all the information we need to process an utterance."[18] The hardest set of facts to ascertain is the exact and detailed, local and momentary sociohistorical situation of writing and reading. Grammars, lexica, encyclopedias, archaeological digs, monographs, and other such apparatuses build our encyclopedic knowledge. But it will never be complete, and it will always be askew due to the distorted perspective of monumental history and the

---

16. See Green, "Lexical Pragmatics and the Lexicon," 327. I do not say, "with exact detail" or "absolute certainty." As Blass applies relevance theory to a corpus of Sissala transcripts and refers to the contextual assumptions required to interpret meaning, she writes, "My analysis ... is not necessarily a representation of what was *actually thought* ... but how the interpretive process might have gone" (*Relevance Relations in Discourse*, 13).

17. Blass, *Relevance Relations in Discourse*, 41.

18. Green, "Lexical Pragmatics and the Lexicon," 327.

arbitrary nature of archaeological discovery, not to mention editorial biases. This kind of study is still necessary, but a relevance-guided hermeneutic counteracts a false sense of confidence in general knowledge by prioritizing evidence drawn from linguistic context in evaluating relevance.

For biblical studies, canonical facts—that is, how the canon portrays situations dealt with in biblical texts—are critical components of this encyclopedic background knowledge. Some Pastoral Epistles scholars argue that this kind of knowledge is especially critical for these books, because they view their composition as predicated on knowledge of the canonical Paul as a literary figure. Brevard Childs believes that these letters were written with a knowledge of the canonical Paul and that original audiences would have had this conception of Paul in mind. They then read and interpreted them in light of this preconception about Paul. In Childs's words, "The Pauline corpus was further developed by the Pastoral Epistles, which actualized the normative role of Paul's teachings in his apostolic witness to the gospel for the future generations of the Christian church."[19] In other words, these books rely on readers, in the first instance, knowing the backstory of Paul and his companions, adventures, and concerns from previous encounters with writings that were already known in first-century churches.

None of these sources of knowledge are new to biblical studies. They are a commonplace for various historical-critical approaches to interpretation. But, even as we attend to these sources of encyclopedic knowledge, relevance theory helps us to understand the narrower subset of knowledge that is most pertinent to interpretation and how its boundaries are formed. The accumulated knowledge of modern datasets not only is a blessing but could also be a curse if modern scholars encumber interpretations with irrelevant data. So, we now examine factors that constrain the relevance of encyclopedic knowledge so that hearers can process utterances economically.

Constraints on Relevance

Even though communication depends on the contextual assumption of encyclopedic knowledge—basically an arbitrary, immeasurable, and ever-

---

19. Brevard S. Childs, *The Church's Guide for Reading Paul: The Canonical Shaping of the Pauline Corpus* (Grand Rapids: Eerdmans, 2008), 192; see also discussion of Pastoral Epistles on 94–96. For a complementary *canonical* approach to the Pastoral Epistles, see also Wall and Steele, *1 and 2 Timothy and Titus*.

developing collection—natural language users are still able to comprehend one another. This is because relevance places several constraints on what hearers can or do access. So what hearers assume within a discourse is a subset of the immense store of knowledge theoretically at their disposal. Theorists emphasize three main constraints on relevance: (1) *mutuality* or shared knowledge, (2) *accessibility* or knowledge that requires the least effort to access, and (3) conversational *context*.[20] The third constraint includes two kinds of context, setting and discourse. The latter kind (discourse) mediates modern readers' access to the former.[21] Therefore, I emphasize the importance of literary context.

Mutuality

From his store of encyclopedic knowledge, a hearer accesses that which is shared with the speaker. If the knowledge is not shared, it does not yield a relevant assumption. A speaker judges which assumptions are needed based on countless subtle evaluations and triggers them accordingly. Her utterance is as lean as possible, adding only what is needed to accomplish her intentions. The greater the familiarity between interlocutors, the more efficient the discourse and, consequently, the less comprehensible to outsiders. Karen Jobes suggests this calculus: "The higher the degree of communication intended by implication, the smaller the intended audience."[22]

Speakers form utterances on the basis of second-order assumptions about hearers' cognitive environment. Further, relevant assumptions are not just mutually known but *mutually manifest*, thus involving second-order thinking. Each instance of communication depends on both speakers and hearers making assumptions about each other's minds. The less the speaker judges the hearer to know, the more she feels obligated to say, and vice versa. Mutually held contextual assumptions can be numerous and

---

20. Some linguists also study neurological phenomena of language that doubtless have bearing on the question of what constrains the knowledge that hearers access. I am not studying these phenomena directly.

21. Goh sensitively gathers clues from the discourse of Ephesians in order to reconstruct the shared cognitive environment of author and audience. From this close examination of what was transparently on their minds, he is able to interpret passages in Ephesians with greater clarity ("Honoring Christ, Subverting Caesar," 44–98).

22. Jobes, "Relevance Theory and Translation," 790.

subtle, and biblical interpreters must appreciate how heavily original interlocutors relied on shared knowledge to understand one another.

A conversational example from Gibbs illustrates this point:

> Joe: "Are you going to the big dance tonight?"
> Sue: "Didn't you hear that Billy Smith will be there?"[23]

Semantically, Sue's response holds no transparent relevance to Joe's question, but the quest for relevance drives him to infer a meaning from which to derive adequate cognitive effects. Joe uses his lexical, grammatical, and rhetorical knowledge, as well as encyclopedic knowledge of the real world, including his situational context. But he will not arrive at Sue's meaning if he does not grasp what Sue assumes to be common knowledge—namely, her attitude toward Billy Smith. If they both are correct about the other's assumptions, Joe will arrive promptly at Sue's intended meaning. Of course, what she intends to do with her speech is more than to inform. In fact, if she assumes that Joe knows Billy Smith will attend the dance, then she has not *informed* Joe of much at all. She has, however, entrusted Joe with sensitive knowledge, demonstrated familiarity, credited him with personal understanding, and other such relational outcomes.

Not just problematic passages but countless everyday interpretations of biblical texts exhibit a disjunction between the contextual assumptions that ancient audiences brought to an utterance and those of modern audiences. Gibbs explains that a shared cognitive environment and attention to speaker intention is just as instrumental to the interpretation of written texts as they are to live speech: "Both forms of communication [speech and writing] can vary in their degree of contextualization. Certain kinds of oral language, such as formal speeches, assume little common ground information between speakers and addressees. Many forms of written discourse, such as private letters, presume a rich common ground between author and reader."[24]

Access

A hearer's cognitive environment is also constrained by the accessibility of encyclopedic knowledge. Several factors affect this access either neg-

---

23. Gibbs, "Intentionalist Controversy," 186.
24. Gibbs, "Intentionalist Controversy," 190.

atively (e.g., distance in memory, multistep processing, or obscurity) or positively (e.g., recency of mention, simplicity, or prominence). Tomoko Matsui argues the congruence of scenario-based activation and relevance, and this relation helps to understand how an utterance can stock a hearer's cognitive environment, thereby increasing access to certain encyclopedic knowledge. Matsui argues that both activation and inference are required to interpret certain kinds of referential speech—namely that which leaves an inferential gap to be "bridged."[25] Paul uses this kind of speech in the context under investigation (Titus 1:10–16) when, for instance, he refers to those who are "unclean" and "defiled" (1:15). Paul's hearers were able to bridge the semantic gap between these ideas and "beasts" (1:12); because, in the right scenario, each idea evoked religious valuations, as did "circumcision" (1:10) in the near context.

Context

Context particularizes the cognitive environment, and speakers influence what portion of encyclopedic knowledge hearers access. Hearers think about what speakers talk about. Utterances place unique constraints of relevance on a vast set of ideas. Green explains, "Context is not a preset and well-defined body of information but, rather, consists of all the information that is relevant for the interpretation of a particular utterance. As such, context is a psychological construct."[26] As modern readers have limited access to the exact social situations of biblical writers and their audiences, the most reliable source of evidence for ascertaining their cognitive environment is the discursive context, which also illuminates the social.[27]

---

25. This type of speech is called *bridging reference assignment*. Tomoko Matsui highlights a distinction between herself and Clark, who claims that a hearer makes an inferential bridge to assign a referent rather than having the idea activated immediately. This is a minor distinction, but Matsui's explanation seems appropriate to natural language interpretation because, as she argues, it requires less processing effort. See Matsui, "Assessing a Scenario-Based Account of Bridging Reference Assignment," in Carston and Uchida, *Relevance Theory*, 123.

26. Green, "Relevance Theory and Biblical Interpretation" (2013), 268.

27. Furlong interchanges (as I do at times) *context* with the relevance-theoretical designation *contextual assumptions* ("Relevance Theory," 60–63). As Carroll puts it: "The best evidence for what an utterer, artist, or author intends to say or mean is the utterance or artwork itself" ("Interpretation and Intention," 77).

Lexica, grammars, atlases, and histories are common tools of biblical interpretation, and every generation introduces additional resources to the panoply. Such resources provide a glimpse into the original interlocutors' cognitive environment, particularly encyclopedic knowledge, but this general knowledge must be constrained and adjusted by relevance. A book's discursive context exercises this fundamental constraint. What is in the context is likely to be on the mind. Considerations of relevance govern and constrain which facts about the ancient world and what information concerning lexemes and syntax are applicable within a conversational context. Gibbs writes, "The context for understanding verbal discourse lies within the set of beliefs, knowledge and presuppositions that speakers/authors and listeners/readers mutually share."[28] Literary context is the most important indicator available to biblical scholars of what constitutes this mutually shared cognitive environment. As eavesdroppers, modern readers must infer utterance meaning on the basis of reconstructed contextual assumptions.[29] So, because a careful examination of literary context is the most reliable means for modern readers to discern what was in the cognitive environment of original audiences, I now detail specific evidence as it influences the interpretation of Titus 1:12.

Literary Context (Macro and Micro)

Discourse itself indicates which contextual assumptions are relevant. As Clark explains, "Contextual assumptions used in understanding an utterance need not be known to the hearer before the utterance is produced."[30] As Yael Klangwisan puts it, the "mutual cognitive environment" is a context that "evolves as the text unfolds."[31] In other words, the text is the reader's guide to relevance. Literary context is the best evidence modern readers have for reconstructing the cognitive environment of ancient readers, especially when a text's *Sitz im Leben* is uncertain or contentious. I delineate two aspects of literary context: structural, and thematic and topical.

---

28. Gibbs, "Intentionalist Controversy," 186.
29. Blass cites several scholars as she argues the centrality of literary context. She establishes the more objective nature of reconstructing contextual assumptions on the basis of literary context rather than on subjective third-party assumptions (Blass, *Relevance Relations in Discourse*, 13).
30. Clark, *Relevance Theory*, 226.
31. Klangwisan, *Earthing the Cosmic Queen*, 24.

Table 5.1. Selected structural outlines of Titus

Author						
Barrett	1:1-4 Address	1:5-16 Development of Christian work in Crete	2:1-3:2 The way of Christian obedience (subdivided as 2:1-8; 2:9-10; 2:11-3:2)	3:3-11 Salvation		3:12-15 Personal conclusion
Bassler	1:1-4 Salutation	1:5-9 Appointment of elders	1:10-16 Warnings about rebellious people	2:1-15 Instructions for various groups (subdivided as 2:1-10, exhortations proper; 2:11-15, doctrinal foundations for exhortations)	3:1-8 Instructions for the church (subdivided as 3:1-2 Exhortations proper; 3:3-8 Doctrinal foundations for exhortations)	3:9-11 Final exhortations concerning opponents	3:12-15 Travel arrangements and greetings
Marshall	1:1-4 Opening salutation	1:5-16 The appointment of elders and the danger from opponents	2:1-15 Teaching for the church—how believers are to relate to one another	3:1-11 Teaching for the church—how believers are to live in society	3:12-14 Personal instructions	3:15 Closing greeting
Mounce	1:1-4 Salutation	1:5-9 Qualities necessary for church leadership	1:10-16 Description of the problem in Crete	2:1-3:11 Instructions and theological basis for godly behavior (subdivided as 2:1-10, instructions; 2:11-15, theological basis; and 3:1-11, continued call)		3:12-15 Final greeting
Besançon Spencer	1:1-4 Introduction	1:5-16 Paul left Titus behind (5-9 appoint godly elders, 10-14 correct many, 15-16 defiled mind and conscience)	2:1-3:11 Teaching what is consistent with healthy doctrine (2:1-15, elders, youth, and slaves; 3:1-8, godly lives; 3:9-11, avoid divisive people)		3:12-15 Conclusion
Towner	1:1-4 Opening	1:5-16 To Titus	2:1-3:11 To the church	3:12-14 Personal notes	3:15 Final greetings and benediction

Structural

The literary context of Titus is our access point to discerning meaning at the level of *what is said*, and structure is the first feature of literary context to examine. Below, the logical and topical divisions of Titus, its book-level units, and their relation to one another are described. I also demonstrate that 1:5–16 has a unified theme and that observable boundary-making features signal the section's beginning, ending, and internal shifts, then explain how this structure influences the interpretation of 1:12. Table 5.1 (facing page) presents a summary, comparison, and analysis of the logical structures ascribed to Titus by prominent Pastoral Epistles scholars.[32]

Köstenberger states, "The various proposals regarding the structure of Titus … reveal a certain amount of consensus."[33] My own outline of Titus (table 5.2) is neither innovative nor controversial with respect to its main contours. It recognizes the following as major divisions: 1:1–4, 1:5–16, 2:1–15, 3:1–11, and 3:12–15.

Table 5.2. Structural outline of Titus 1:1–3:15

1:1–4 Epistolary opening, testimony, and greeting	1:5–3:11 Main body—"straighten out what remains and appoint elders" (1:5)			3:12–15 Epistolary closing, travelogue, and greeting
	1:5–16 Particular instructions regarding leaders; the contrast between good (5–9) and bad (10–16)	2:1–15 Particular instructions for several specific social categories within the household of God—i.e., the church (1–10) with theological substantiation (11–15) and λάλει *inclusio* (1, 15)	3:1–11 General and substantiatory instructions for all Christians	

---

32. Not all commentators give attention to logical structure—e.g., Huizenga's outline for Titus follows: ch. 1, "Rungs on the Social Ladder"; ch. 2, "Staying in Your Place"; ch. 3, "Orderliness Is Next to Godliness." The titles are pithy and clever but do not illuminate the letter's logic as much as locate types of objectionable material for readers (see Huizenga, *1–2 Timothy, Titus*, viii). Attention to a letter's native structure enables one to grasp a writer's message. The table is not to scale. Outlines in the table are from Barrett, *Pastoral Epistles*, 37; Bassler, *1 Timothy*, 9–10; Marshall, *Critical and Exegetical Commentary*, ix, 24 (table 6); Mounce, *Pastoral Epistles*, cxxxvi; Besançon Spencer, *2 Timothy and Titus*, 4–5; and Towner, *Letters to Timothy and Titus*, xii.

33. Köstenberger, "Hermeneutical and Exegetical Challenges," 15.

Discourse features in the Greek text reinforce these major breaks in Titus. The body (1:5–3:11) begins after a relatively substantial salutation (1:1–4) with the standard features of a Greco-Roman epistolary opening. The break between 1:4 and 1:5 is clear based on the conclusion of the salutatory blessing (1:4b), the topicalization affected by the left-dislocation of 1:5a ("This is the reason I left you in Crete," Τούτου χάριν ἀπέλιπόν σε ἐν Κρήτῃ), and the topical resumption of the following ἵνα clause ("in order that," 1:5b). The contextual features that denote the coherence of 1:5–16 include the overarching topic of leadership problems and solutions, the complementary nature of paragraph subtopics (i.e., leadership, good and bad), and the logical connection marked by the conjunction γάρ ("for," 1:10). Further explanation of these features will clarify.

First, the theme of addressing leadership problems holds this section together. On the one hand, 1:5–9 portrays a vacuum of good leadership that Titus must fill by sanctioning leaders of impeccable character. On the other hand, 1:10–16 portrays the harmful influence of people who have presumed the prerogatives and social position of leaders but without proper accountability, scruples, or healthy doctrine. Whereas Paul instructs Titus to deal with the broader church population under the rubric of a household code in 2:1–10, in the present section (1:5–16), Paul addresses leadership as a discrete issue. Not only the whole but also the parts of 1:5–16 address specific leadership-related matters. Thus, any interpretation should make clear how each piece, including the Cretan quotation, correlates to this obvious concern.

Second, the two paragraphs that comprise 1:5–16 describe two kinds of leaders by contrasting them along corresponding lines. The following list of features is not exhaustive, but it demonstrates thematic coherence—a continuous concern for good and bad leaders and what to do about them:

- Paul says that a good leader's children should not be prone to the accusation of being "insubordinate" (ἀνυπότακτα, 1:6), then his first accusation toward the impudent leaders is of being "insubordinate" (ἀνυπότακτοι, 1:10).
- Maintaining the household theme, Paul instructs Titus that elders are to "have faithful children" (τένκα ἔχων πιστά, 1:6), and then he refers to the troublemakers as "faithless" (ἀπίστοις, 1:15).
- Whereas Paul compares an elder to "God's household steward" (θεοῦ οἰκονόμον, 1:7), he accuses the troublemakers of "disrupting entire households" (ὅλους οἴκους ἀνατρέπουσιν, 1:11).

- Good leaders, among other things, are not to crave "shameful gain" (μὴ αἰσχροκερδῆ, 1:7), but "for the sake of shameful gain" (αἰσχροῦ κέρδους χάριν, 1:11) was precisely why the troublemakers took up leadership roles.
- Whereas Titus's elders were appointed in order to engage in "teaching" (διδαχὴν ... ἵνα ... διδασκαλίᾳ, 1:9), the main disruption in Crete resulted from the troublemakers "teaching" (διδάσκοντες, 1:11).
- Whereas good elders are to hold to the doctrine of the "faithful word" (πιστοῦ λόγου, 1:9), the troublemakers are "empty[-word]-speakers" (ματαιολόγοι, 1:10).
- One of the chief responsibilities of properly sanctioned leaders is to "rebuke" (ἐλέγχειν, 1:9) "those who contradict"; and the first opportunity in the letter to do so comes after the quotation, where Paul tells Titus to "rebuke" (ἔλεγχε, 1:13) "them sternly."
- Sanctioned leaders need to be able to encourage the church "in healthy teaching" (ἐν τῇ διδασκαλίᾳ τῇ ὑγιαινούσῃ, 1:9), and the hope for duly corrected troublemakers is "that they might be healthy in the faith" (ἵνα ὑγιαίνωσιν ἐν τῇ πίστει, 1:13).
- Paul's final, biting judgment against the troublemakers starkly contrasts with the "love for good" (φιλάγαθον, 1:8) that elders are to exhibit; he says that such menaces deny God by their "works" (ἔργοις, 1:16) and are themselves "unfit for every good work" (πᾶν ἔργον ἀγαθὸν ἀδόκιμοι, 1:16).

These correlations should suffice to demonstrate the strong complementary nature of these two pericopes (1:5–9 and 1:10–16). Each clear point of comparison illuminates the meaning of its counterpart.

Third, the conjunction γάρ (1:10) marks a clear logical relationship between the two pericopes (1:5–9 and 1:10–16). I call this relationship *hortatory substantiation* after Bauer and Traina.[34] In other words, the material governed by γάρ (probably 1:10–12) is the reason Paul presents for his prior instructions (1:5–9). The conjunction γάρ can govern a small or large amount of material from a single clause or sentence to a paragraph. Here it seems to be connecting multiple verses. The presence of these troublemakers and their activity (1:10–12) are the explicit bases for placing elders of

---

34. See Bauer and Traina, *Inductive Bible Study*, 107.

Paul's description in each town (1:5–9). In Titus, γάρ marks logical relationships between units that begin at 1:7, 10; 2:11; 3:3, 9, and 12. In each instance, it accompanies an argument in which support of some kind follows after critical instruction.[35] I now discuss three structural-contextual issues with the interpretation of Titus.

Structure-Based Mismatch

The general consensus on the simplicity of Titus does not prevent interpreters from making structure-based errors. Interpretive preconceptions can introduce mismatches between the contextual assumptions of ancient and modern readers that manifest structurally. The NRSV, for instance, places an editorial division between the quotative frame of 1:12a and the quotation proper of 1:12b, but this break is misleading. Separating the quotation from the rest of the text presumes that Paul defers to its authority, but this choice obscures evidence that he critiques it.

In the Greek text on which the NIV is based, a major editorial paragraph break begins after 1:12a. The Cretan quotation appears in a separate paragraph that divorces 1:12b–16 from its literary context and obscures the strong logical development, thematic unity, and other connecting tissue of the larger section on good and bad leaders (1:5–16).[36] No objectively discerned boundary of the passage suggests a strong break where the NIV Greek text places it. Although the English translation of the NIV does not carry this peculiar formatting forward, it makes perhaps an even more egregious embellishment by translating the quotative frame εἶπέν τις ἐξ αὐτῶν ἴδιος αὐτῶν προφήτης as "One of Crete's own prophets has said it" (1:12a). The NIV's dynamic-equivalence translation philosophy notwithstanding, this sentence seems more influenced by the history of interpretation than by the language of the passage.

The NIV translates ἡ μαρτυρία αὕτη ἐστὶν ἀληθής as "This saying is true" (1:13a). In English, *said* (1:12a) and *saying* (1:13a) are cognate, but

---

35. This observation of Paul's usage in Titus is congruent with the analyses of Runge, *Discourse Grammar*, 51–54; and Casson, *Textual Signposts*, 61–122. The conjunction γάρ appears less frequently in Titus than δέ (1:1, 3, 15, 16; 2:1; 3:4, 9, 14) and ἵνα (1:5, 9, 13; 2:4, 5, 8, 10, 12, 14; 3:7, 8, 13, 14), which tend to govern smaller portions of material and, of course, with their own nuances.

36. See Richard J. Goodrich and Albert L. Lukaszewski, eds., *A Reader's Greek New Testament*, 3rd ed. (Grand Rapids: Zondervan, 2015).

the underlying Greek words—εἶπέν (1:12a) and μαρτυρία (1:13a), as they appear in the text—have quite different roots and senses. The NLT translates this Greek sentence, "This is true"; and Eugene Peterson's *The Message* has "He certainly spoke the truth." Each of these translations obscures both pragmatic and semantic features of the underlying Greek sentence in order to sustain an assumption that derives from the history of interpretation and not from the text itself. Relevance-guided biblical interpretation detects such mismatches and constructively illuminates texts through careful contextual observation. I base the remaining two structural-contextual points on such observation.

Leaders and Leadership Malpractice

Paul instructs Titus to address leadership problems within the Cretan church vigorously throughout Titus 1:5–16, so an appropriate interpretation of 1:12 should demonstrate how the Cretan quotation is contextually relevant to this general intention. Two paragraphs comprise the unit—1:5–9, which concerns the appointing and qualification of good leaders, and 1:10–16, which concerns the presumptuous leaders who disrupt the church in various ways, for various reasons, and with various results. Under the influence of a miso-Cretan reading, it is difficult to see how the Cretan quotation fits into this otherwise coherent discussion. Thorvald Madsen surprisingly limits the leadership section of Titus to 1:5–11, supposing the Cretan quotation to belong to the section that addresses the general church population. This choice is mistaken for reasons I have already presented but also because Madsen is not consistent. He says that the rebukes of 1:14–15 are aimed at the "would-be apostles" (presumptuous leaders), but this claim ignores the structural boundary he indicates for the passages.[37]

Reconstructing the audience's cognitive environment must take into account this context of leadership problems. Paul describes the church's problems and the troublemakers' actions in terms of leadership. For example, they lead, though astray ("misleader," φρεναπάτης, 1:11a); they teach, albeit wrongly ("teaching that which [they] ought not," διδάσκοντες ἃ μὴ δεῖ, 1:11b) and with wrong motives ("for the sake of shameful gain,"

---

37. See Thorvald B. Madsen II, "The Ethics of the Pastoral Epistles," in Köstenberger and Wilder, *Entrusted with the Gospel*, 225–26.

αἰσχροῦ κέρδους χάριν, 1:11c); and they make value judgments between persons, even when wrongly justified ("Cretans [are] always liars," Κρῆτες ἀεὶ ψεῦσται, 1:12; cf. "confess ... deny," ὁμολογοῦσιν ... ἀρνοῦνται, 1:16).

Exemplifying the miso-Cretan reading, Barrett assumes that Paul was concerned with Cretan reprobation more than leadership malpractice. He misidentifies the source and nature of the problem, writing, "Opposition ... exists, arising partly out of the notoriously bad character of the Cretans themselves." Barrett identifies "Jewish gnostics" as the other source of opposition.[38] Evidence in Titus is probably too ambiguous to support the identification of a specific group. The divisions insolent leaders were causing troubled Paul, not their proto-Gnosticism, Jewishness, or ethnicity per se. A better case can be made that disruptions of the Christian mission in Crete, rather than supposed Cretan notoriety, prompted Paul's concerns.

Some scholars have shown that the Pastoral Epistles are concerned with the respectable behavior of Christians as a lifestyle apologia.[39] This being the case, the Cretans are not especially notorious, because Paul evidently was just as or more concerned with the morality of the Ephesian churches that Timothy oversaw under these terms (e.g., "piety," εὐσέβεια). Paul's concern with behavior does not explain why he would endorse a quotation that denounces the Cretans as incorrigible. The claim that the Cretan quotation advances the cause of positive public testimony ignores its immediate context within a leadership discussion and its book context, in which Paul shows almost no concern to address issues of laziness or gluttony.

Later in Titus, Paul speaks explicitly of a "divisive person" or "heretic" (αἱρετικός, 3:10), but the issue of division stems from impudent leadership, which he addresses in 1:10–16. The actions and attributes ascribed to Cretans by the quotation are not heretical (lit. "divisive"), but the behaviors of the troublemakers are. Among the most divisive could be this slur against the Cretans, accusing them of overall reprobation. The three epithets of this quotation could be considered a synecdoche for general reprobation and worthlessness, highlighting various aspects of corruption—speech ("liars," ψεῦσται), being ("evil," κακά), and action ("unworking," ἀργαί). It is indeed tremendously offensive and literally dehumanizing ("beasts," θηρία). Paul enjoins rebuke (1:13) in a context where, although he does not

---

38. Barrett, *Pastoral Epistles*, 127.
39. See Hoklotubbe, *Civilized Piety*; Kidd, "Titus as Apologia."

yet name heresy, he nevertheless identifies aspects of bad leadership that have dimensions of heresy (i.e., causing divisions). He thus describes "misleaders" (1:10), "upsetting whole households" (1:11), "contradicting" (1:9; cf. 2:15), and "attending to Jewish myths and commandments of people who abandon the truth" (1:14; cf. 3:11).[40]

The divisiveness was not theoretical but social, yielding a framework of superiority and inferiority. The base moral delinquency expressed in the quotation was not the cause of division. The act of attributing such reprobation to Cretans by spreading this slur against gentiles in Titus's congregation, however, was highly divisive. It called for a "stern rebuke" (ἔλεγχε ... ἀποτόμως, 1:13b) precisely in alignment with Paul's concern about leadership malpractice.

Leaders were de facto teachers, and teachers were de facto leaders. Problems with speech were problems with leadership, and vice versa. Paul describes the troublemakers' behavior and its consequences in speech-related terms. Huizenga observes that disruptive speech was their central behavior: "[Paul] describes their behavior in several strongly negative ways; in particular he condemns their speaking and teaching for 'upsetting whole families.'"[41] Harmful speech was the very problem Paul identifies as characteristic of the presumptuous leaders whom he calls "empty-talkers and deceivers ... whose mouths must be stopped" (1:10–11). This description raises the question, What were they saying that was so objectionable? Paul answers by quoting what "someone said" (εἶπέν τις, 1:12a). Speech and leadership in the church were integrally connected. The troublemakers were not vicious in a generic moral sense; their disruptions ("upsetting entire households," 1:11) constituted leadership malpractice. In such a context, Paul exposes one of their most disruptive, divisive, and misleading declarations—the Cretan quotation (1:12b).

Assuming that Paul affirms the miso-Cretan meaning of the quotation entails a significant, unexplainable literary-contextual interruption. In an otherwise logical and cohesive discussion of leadership issues in Crete (e.g., divisiveness, evil speech, and presumptuous leadership malpractice), Paul supposedly rails against the general Cretan populace. Such a disruption might betoken an interpolation, but no textual support for one

---

40. In this summary of leadership malpractice, Paul offers more detail concerning problems (i.e., heresy) in Crete than commentators generally acknowledge.
41. Huizenga, *1–2 Timothy, Titus*, 138.

currently exists.⁴² The miso-Cretan interpretation virtually requires one to see it as a tangent of some sort rather than as pertinent to Paul's argument. Towner writes, "The citation of the Cretan saying is almost an aside, and at first glance it appears primarily to disparage the Jewish-Christian teachers. Indeed, it does this; but ... [such] Cretan echoes ... also prepare the way ... to engage the Cretan social-religious world."⁴³ Such assumptions do not solve the problem of how it functions within its paragraph context, which, the supposed internal rupture aside, coheres well with the book context and the rhetorical development of Titus. It is therefore reasonable to assume instead that Paul's use of the Cretan quotation is relevant to the context. Paul does not change the topic of 1:5–16 when he presents the quotation. The pronouns he uses to introduce it seem to refer to the presumptuous leaders.⁴⁴

Recognizing the straightforward structure of Titus, it seems out of place for Paul either to disparage the Cretans abruptly or to raise moral issues such as gluttony and laziness that he does not address in greater detail later on. Additionally, a couple of the topics are not even morally specific but simply slurs about existential attributes (e.g., "evil," "brutish," 1:12b).⁴⁵ It is no wonder that many careful scholars have wrestled with this passage's coherence. The Cretan quotation does not need to be read as an interruption, however. Paul was addressing a leadership issue in the Cretan church. A number of impudent individuals had emerged in Titus's missionary congregation, and Paul instructed him to appoint the right kind of leaders and to rebuke the wrong kind of leaders while identifying particular problems. Madsen describes the problem that the epistle envisages: "Several would-be apostles—or, at any rate, several aspiring

---

42. Faber cites Norbert Brox as advancing what Faber calls the "radical" proposal that an interpolation occurs here (Faber, "'Evil Beasts, Lazy Gluttons,'" 137; Brox, *Die Pastoralbriefe*, 288).

43. Towner, *Letters to Timothy and Titus*, 699.

44. Henry Swete comments that "at first sight" ἐξ αὐτῶν appears to refer to οἱ ἐκ τῆς περιτομῆς. He does not say why he dismisses this possibility (see Theodore, *Commentary* [1882], at Titus 1:10–12). Jerome also intuitively identifies the speaker of the quotation with those "especially of the circumcision." Following Clement of Alexandria, however, he attributes the quotation to Epimenides, Crete's most famous poet (Jerome, *Comm. Tit.* 1.10–12).

45. *Pace* Faber, who attempts to show how Paul developed these themes throughout the letter, but I am not convinced that the moral issues raised by the quotation are significant concerns for Paul ("'Evil Beasts, Lazy Gluttons,'" 135–45).

VIPs—have risen up with eccentric doctrines and practices that efface the gospel and factionalize the churches."[46]

Table Turning

Within the paragraph that focuses on bad leaders (1:10–16), one of Paul's corrective strategies is to echo themes from the Cretan quotation as a means of characterizing the troublemakers instead. Towner observes, "These teachers (hyperbolically) embody all that is deplorable in Cretan culture."[47] He is right about the thematic echoes in Paul's critique of the troublemakers, but he takes for granted that Paul accepts the quotation as an apt description of the Cretans as opposed to a vicious stereotype. Toward the end of chapter 4, I identified various ways that Paul turns the troublemakers' insults back on them under the heading "Category Reversal." Here I specifically address how this rhetorical maneuver affects structure and context.

Paul's original readers were cognizant of the ethno-religious nature of the contentions in Crete and thus would not have been oblivious to the irony of the associations Paul made. Grasping the significance of these conceptual associations for Crete's Jewish Christians (1:10, 14) in particular is critical for modern readers. Paul exposes the ones who call the Cretans "liars" (ψεύστης, 1:12b) and characterizes them as "people who reject the truth" (ἀλήθεια, 1:14). He prepared original readers with his epistolary greeting, where "truth" (ἀλήθεια, 1:1) appears in reference to Paul's message and where "not lying" (ἀψευδής, 1:2) appears in reference to God's character. Whereas the troublemakers regarded the Cretans with disdain as "evil beasts" (κακὰ θηρία, 1:12b), which has implications of uncleanness, Paul says that it is rather "to the defiled" (μιαίνω) "and faithless" that "nothing is clean" (1:15) and that these troublemakers, barring restoration (1:13b), are "detestable" or "abominable" (βδελυκτός, 1:16).[48] The phrase "barring restoration" is used because restoration seems to have been the goal ("in order that they may be healthy," ἵνα ὑγιαίνωσιν, 1:13b); that is, Paul did not intend to leave the troublemakers in their malignant condition.

---

46. Madsen, "Ethics of the Pastoral Epistles," 225.
47. Towner, *Letters to Timothy and Titus*, 703.
48. Compare the use of μιαίνω ("defile") in LXX Deut 21:22–23, a passage that the apostle Paul demonstrates his familiarity with in Gal 3:13. The same concept of defilement appears in Titus 1:15. Compare also LXX Ps 17:25–26.

Instances of βδελυκτός ("detestable") in the LXX illuminate the thrust of Paul's use in Titus 1:16.[49] In the prayer of Jonathan, Nehemiah, and the returned exiles (2 Macc 1:23–30, esp. 1:27), βδελυκτός labels diaspora Jews who had been subject to gentile rule as a result of judgment. This usage suggests that the designation would have evoked negative ethno-religious associations. Paul fittingly evokes Jewish wisdom topics as well. Proverbs 17:15 (LXX) exhibits a striking conceptual analogy: "whoever judges the righteous [to be] unrighteous or the unrighteous [to be] righteous is unclean [ἀκάθαρτος] and detestable [βδελυκτός] before God." In addition to sharing critical lexemes with the proverb, Titus 1:15–16 also echoes the conceptual predicate structure of judgment on someone who pronounces that which is righteous and clean to be "evil" (κακά, 1:12b). As far as faithful Cretans are concerned generally, the ensuing discourse views them as made "righteous" and "clean" (2:11–15 and 3:3–7, esp. δικαίως in 2:12 and καθαρίσῃ in 2:14; cf. λουτροῦ in 3:5).

Thematic and Topical

In addition to literary structure, thematic and topical aspects of context influence an audience's cognitive environment. Linguists do not always or consistently distinguish between theme and topic.[50] For the sake of clarity, I use *topic* to refer to what the speaker is talking about—the matter at hand, even when expressed in figurative language.[51] I use *theme* to refer to the

---

49. The apostle Paul used a cognate participle to refer to his fictional interlocutor's assumed attitude of abhorring idols (ὁ βδελυσσόμενος τὰ εἴδωλα, Rom 2:22).

50. The scholarly ambivalence about differentiating these terms does not reflect disagreement at the philosophical level. First, linguists divide material along different conceptual lines, calling for different terms. Second, these terms (and others that have been proposed) and the concepts themselves are vague or multivalent. Runge, for example, regards *theme* as the given part of information structure, whereas *rheme* is newly asserted, focus information; he uses *topic*, however, in a less technical sense as whatever the speaker talks about (*Discourse Grammar*, 200–201). Maria Gómez-González writes, "Studies in this area have been characterised by terminological profusion and confusion because very different positions have been taken on the appropriate criteria for the definition and identification of the notions of Theme/Topic." Gómez-González, *The Theme-Topic Interface: Evidence from English*, P&B 71 (Amsterdam: Benjamins, 2001), 4.

51. Some object that the convenient term *topic* is too vague to be useful. Blass writes, "The notion of topic has no adequate theoretical definition and should there-

way the speaker is talking about it. A theme represents an implicit association that the speaker makes between various topics and higher-order schemas. Themes can be real-life or imaginary overlays that speakers apply across topics to make implicit conceptual connections. A theme structures information by implying relationships between things. It places multiple semantic components in relation to one another over portions of material. The semantic values of words, phrases, and sentences do not themselves convey themes. Themes cross boundaries between the semantically given and the pragmatically inferred. Semantic representations do, however, signal topics, which require less inferential processing effort to recognize but yield fewer cognitive effects. Some overlap exists between these categories of context. Themes and topics both shape and are shaped by their context dialectically; they are not disconnected ideas.

With regard to the linguistic function of topics, María Gómez-González describes two major perspectives. First, some linguists argue that any supposed function of language (in this case, topicality) must have corresponding formal features whereby it can be recognized. Second, others argue that topicality is required for comprehension; thus, it is intrinsic to language and will be present with or without formal indicators.[52] Relevance theorists, coming from a cognitive-linguistic perspective, tend to favor the second view, but several linguists, and especially discourse analysts, try to identify formal clues that frequently signal topics. These approaches are not absolute or mutually exclusive.

The topics and themes identified below are prominent regardless of specific formal criteria, but they are typically accompanied, if not signaled, by recognizable features. These features include the presence of multiple words that activate the same type-scene or conceptual frame; the simple recurrence of lexemes, cognates, synonyms, and antonyms; left-dislocation and resumption; and subject-predicate order reversal, which is a marked construction.[53] I introduce and explain each of these features

---

fore be dispensed with in theoretical accounts of textuality and comprehension" (*Relevance Relations in Discourse*, 41).

52. See Gómez-González, *Theme-Topic Interface*, 12–13.

53. See Gómez-González, *Theme-Topic Interface*, 15–16. This list of formal features that accompany (or signal) theme and topic corresponds to various conceptual approaches to theme and topic function. For example, left-dislocation is syntactic while recurrence is semantic, and type-scene or frame activation organizes informa-

as they pertain to the specific topics and themes I name below. First, I explain what is meant by type-scene or conceptual frame activation.

Type-scene activation (aka frame semantics, frame or scenario evocation, and conceptual frame activation) makes it possible for hearers to grasp specific meanings of ambiguous words (aka bridging reference assignment), because it allows for narrow contextual comprehension of words without lengthy qualifications.[54] Speakers can use such activation with any degree of literality or figurativeness, and they can make associations on numerous bases (e.g., scenario, synonym, rhyme, homonym, bridge term). Unfortunately, because of the economy of type-scene activation, nonoriginal audiences may activate the incorrect conceptual frame or not activate one at all, which leads to either a failure of comprehension or a nonrelevant interpretation.

Mike Borkent provides a succinct definition of *frame semantics*. He writes that frames include "the broad experiential knowledge necessary for understanding even simple words, since a frame is 'any system of concepts related in such a way that to understand any one of them you have to understand the whole structure in which it fits.'"[55] A hearer does not need to know every detail of a type-scene, just enough to build the frame.

The cognitive-linguistic notion of frame activation is crucial for understanding the role of themes and topics in interpretation. Words can *activate* entire conceptual worlds when they are used within the signaling environment established by a genre. As Barbara Dancygier writes, "Linguistic expressions prompt conceptualizations."[56] These conceptualizations may be referred to as *frames*, but they are not static and are themselves subject

---

tion. Marked constructions can vary according to language, but these concepts are cross-linguistic.

54. See Barbara Dancygier, José Sanders, and Lieven Vandelanotte, "Textual Choices in Discourse," in *Textual Choices in Discourse: A View from Cognitive Linguistics*, ed. Dancygier, Sanders, and Vandelanotte (Amsterdam: Benjamins, 2012), 185–91. They explain, "As cognitive linguists point out, the meaning of an expression owes as much to the specific semantics of the lexical items used as to the meanings prompted through syntactic form and frame evocation" (185–86). See also Matsui, "Assessing a Scenario-Based Account."

55. Mike Borkent, "Illusions of Simplicity," in Dancygier, Sanders, and Vandelanotte, *Textual Choices in Discourse*, 9. He quotes, in part, from Charles J. Fillmore's "Frame Semantics," in *Linguistics in the Morning Calm* (Seoul: Hanshin, 1982), 111–37.

56. Barbara Dancygier, *The Language of Stories: A Cognitive Approach* (Cambridge: Cambridge University Press, 2012), 19.

to pragmatic adjustment. No one can predetermine which components of a frame are necessarily present in the cognitive environment of a listener once a word is spoken, but the conversational context is key to uncovering which aspects of the frame are crucial.

Depending on context, the single word *yard*, for example, can also activate the conception of *house*, *grass*, and *fence*—all of which may be necessary for understanding a particular use of *yard*. However, if a speaker mentions *field*, then *house*, for instance, is not automatically activated, even though in some instances *yard* and *field* are synonymous. When a speaker mentions the word *restaurant*, then *waitstaff*, *tables*, *chairs*, *kitchen*, and so forth enter the listener's cognitive environment. She can then use generic verbs and nouns (e.g., *bus*, *tub*, *tip*, *order*, *check*, *wait*) in a sentence but still be understood in a very specific sense, because these more ambiguous words have relevance to the frame that she has activated. Type-scene activation allows a speaker to use language more efficiently by invoking specific components of a type-scene or conceptual frame and relying on the hearer to conceptualize relevant aspects from a bank of encyclopedic knowledge about the world. Jobes points out that frames can differ across cultures, and she explains some implications for translating Scripture: "Simply plugging in the equivalent words more often than not will fail to preserve the implicatures intended by the original language to the extent that the cultural frames of the original audience differ from those of the target audience."[57]

Linguists commonly use the frame of commercial transfer as an example: a hearer cannot comprehend the word *buy* without understanding the interactions of people involved in commercial transfer. Thus, Charles Fillmore, who introduced frame semantics, argues that using a single word (e.g., *buy*) often activates a cluster of other ideas and associations that are necessary for interpreting the word.[58] Empirical studies of mind modularity have shown that related ideas are activated together for natural language speakers so that recall time is measurably decreased for words related by a conceptual frame.[59] Further, the words used to activate a given frame can also indicate which perspective the speaker is favoring. For instance, a speaker's choice to use *buy* instead of *sell* to describe a transaction that inherently involved

---

57. Jobes, "Relevance Theory and Translation," 789.
58. As explained in Dancygier, *Language of Stories*, 32–33.
59. See discussion of studies of cognition and Fodorian mind modularity in Clark, *Relevance Theory*, 91–97, 346–49.

both actions expresses her wish to favor the perspective of the buyer rather than the seller (not that other options must always occur to the speaker).[60]

We will examine several themes and topics in Titus in a sequence and level of detail commensurate with how they illuminate each other. Each one is critical for appreciating how context shaped the audience's cognitive environment. We start with the thematic frame that Paul activated of a courtroom with its related topics.

Courtroom

In the first chapter of Titus, several words and information structures suggest that Paul is activating the type-scene of a courtroom. He uses words from a judicial domain (e.g., *testimony, true, accusation, convict,* 1:13; *confess, deny,* 1:16) and structures information forensically. The sequence establishes both his own and the troublemakers' character (1:1–4, 10–11), makes an accusation (1:12), swears an oath (1:13a), and then renders a verdict and a sentence (1:13b).[61] Establishing pathos for specifically forensic purposes may be one of the reasons the epistolary introduction of Titus is remarkably longer than the other Pastoral Epistles.[62] By evoking a legal proceeding in a semi-official correspondence (perhaps modeled after imperial *mandata principis*) that would be read aloud and intentionally overheard by the named addressee's community, Paul makes the trial public.[63] Marshall explains that, although Titus features a salutation to an

---

60. According to one cognitive theory of quotation, Kujanpää explains, "Quotations do not describe the situation but 'demonstrate' it from a certain point of view" ("From Eloquence," 187). A quotation recollects an original occasion of speech, but speakers choose which aspects of the original occasion to include in their quotative framing, depending on their intentions (187). Listeners experience the quotation more vividly than if the speaker merely expressed the thought in her own words. Listeners are a step away from the original event of speaking (188, 190).

61. Craig S. Wansink describes components of legal proceedings and forensic rhetoric that are seen in the NT, especially in Paul's undisputed epistles, and we see several in Titus 1. See Wansink, "Roman Law and Legal System," *DNTB*, 984–91.

62. Commentators note the relative length of Titus's epistolary introduction (1:1–4) and offer various hypotheses. Marshall critiques the hypothesis that it was written to introduce a faux collection: "This hypothesis depends completely on prior assumptions" (*Critical and Exegetical Commentary*, 112 n. 3).

63. Wall points out that the closing greeting, which uses a plural pronoun (ὑμῶν, 3:15), "indicates the congregational scope of the exhortations and instructions

individual, the letter is transparently written "for the church for which he is responsible."[64] Although addressed to an individual, the anticipated audience is actually that addressee's gathered religious community.[65] Within the performance of a letter in a certain genre (e.g., *mandata principis*, which originated in the domain of imperial politics), a speaker can activate themes that evoke other type-scenes (e.g., a trial).

Paul demonstrated some knowledge of Greco-Roman legal proceedings, and the abundance of judicial language in Paul's undisputed epistles illuminates the use in Titus.[66] Paul was appearing in court as a witness on behalf of the Cretans. L. Ann Jervis explains that coming to another's defense was a custom of responsibility and honor in Roman courts.[67] The custom also comports with Jewish standards of honor and integrity regarding witnessing on others' behalf (Lev 5:1, Deut 19:15-21). Paul could bring testimony, oath, opinions of a council (πρεσβύτερος, 1:5-9), and a version of magisterial orders (*mandata principis*) to bear in building his case.

---

addressed to the [singular] apostolic delegate [Titus]" (Wall and Steele, *1 and 2 Timothy and Titus*, 373). Johnson discusses the genre of *mandata principis* as it is proposed for Titus (*First and Second Letters*, 137-42). For examples of the genre, see Stanley Kent Stowers, *Letter Writing in Greco-Roman Antiquity*, LEC 5 (Philadelphia: Westminster, 1986), 103-4.

64. Marshall, *Critical and Exegetical Commentary*, 111.

65. Christopher Forbes explains that the plural address of the majority of Paul's undisputed letters is unconventional. His survey of ancient letters indicates "the remarkable rarity of plural or communal address in Greco-Roman letters. Letters with a plural or communal address are ... far from common.... The Pauline congregational letters, with their communal mode of address, stand out as remarkable in this context." See Forbes, "Ancient Rhetoric and Ancient Letters: Models for Reading Paul, and Their Limits," in *Paul and Rhetoric*, ed. J. Paul Sampley and Peter Lampe (New York: T&T Clark, 2010), 157.

66. Peter Lampe believes that the Pastoral Epistles, as deutero-Pauline writings, exhibit the features of rhetoric, including forensic rhetoric, because they were possibly written as rhetorical exercises on the basis of a Pauline school. See Lampe, "Rhetorical Analysis of Pauline Texts—Quo Vadit? Methodological Reflections," in Sampley and Lampe, *Paul and Rhetoric*, 15. On the use of testimony in ancient forensic contexts and by Paul in 2 Corinthians, see Fredrick J. Long, *Ancient Rhetoric and Paul's Apology: The Compositional Unity of 2 Corinthians*, SNTSMS 131 (Cambridge: Cambridge University Press, 2004), 47-49, 211-12. On the legal system in Paul generally, see Wansink, "Roman Law," 989. On forensic rhetoric as it sometimes appears in Paul, see Thomas H. Olbricht, "Aristotle, Aristotelianism," *DNTB*, 119-21.

67. L. Ann Jervis, "Law/Nomos in Greco-Roman World," *DNTB*, 634.

These are among the forms of forensic evidence Fredrick Long lists in his detailed survey of proofs in conventions of ancient forensic rhetoric.[68]

Paul indicated that Christians should not seek satisfaction from law courts but should judge matters themselves (1 Cor 6:1–11).[69] Craig Wansink indicates that Christians taking others to trial subjected the parties to all of the inequity and corruption of secular courts. By judging matters within the community, the church could ensure fairness between those of higher and lower status.[70] Rather than shunning judicial proceedings entirely, Paul transports them from the power-differentiated secular sphere into the community of the faithful.[71] Paul was not threatening to press charges in some higher court; he was enacting the type-scene of a courtroom by invoking allusions to judicial proceedings and by shaping his discourse according to the conventions of forensic rhetoric.[72]

The logical phrase that connects the "testimony" (1:13a) with Paul's command to "rebuke them sharply" (1:13c) is δι' ἣν αἰτίαν ("on account of which reason," 1:13b). This phrase can be idiomatic, but the noun αἰτία also had the more specific meaning of "accusation" or "a basis for legal action" in judicial contexts.[73] There seem to be three possible candidates as the *reason* ("accusation," αἰτία) for rebuke. In order of probability: (1)

---

68. See Long, *Ancient Rhetoric*, 47–49.

69. James S. Jeffers, *The Greco-Roman World of the New Testament Era: Exploring the Background of Early Christianity* (Downers Grove, IL: IVP Academic, 1999), 158–59.

70. See Wansink, "Roman Law," 988–89.

71. The church was (ideally) a place where power and status differentials were negated by the cross (Gal 3:26–28). Regarding this Galatians passage, Barclay writes, "All the pairings cited by Paul are strongly endowed with hierarchical assumptions. For Jews, to be Jewish is not just 'different' from being 'Greek,' but self-evidently superior to it—and vice versa for 'Greeks'" (*Paul and the Gift*, 397).

72. In this way, Paul demonstrated what he was asking Titus to do—prosecute illegitimate teachers and leaders. See the often collocated themes of imitation (-μιμ- words) and example (-τυπ- words) in 1 Cor 4:16, 11:1, Phil 3:17, 4:9, 1 Thess 1:6–7, 2 Thess 3:9, 1 Tim 4:12, and in Titus 2:7.

73. See "αἰτία," BDAG, 31. The use depends on context. Generic examples include Luke 8:47 ("the reason why she touched him," δι' ἣν αἰτίαν ἥψατο αὐτοῦ) and Acts 22:24 ("the reason why they were thus shouting against him," δι' ἣν αἰτίαν οὕτως ἐπεφώνουν αὐτῷ). Examples in a judicial context include Acts 23:28 ("and wanting to ascertain the charge for which they were accusing him," βουλόμενός τε ἐπιγνῶναι τὴν αἰτίαν δι' ἣν ἐνεκάλουν αὐτῷ), where the syntax differs, and Acts 28:20 ("for this reason therefore I have asked to see you and speak to you," διὰ ταύτην οὖν τὴν αἰτίαν παρεκάλεσα ὑμᾶς

the copulative statement "this testimony is true," (2) the "testimony" itself, or (3) the list of reprobate attitudes and behaviors the quotation articulates concerning the Cretans as per the miso-Cretan reading. For several of the aforementioned reasons, and on account of its proximity as an antecedent of the relative pronoun, the best candidate seems to be the first. The reason for the rebuke is the veracity of the testimony.

When Paul mentions "testimony" (μαρτυρία, 1:13), he activates witnesses, judges, offenders, and prosecutors in a sort of gestalt complex cognitive entity. Paul is evoking key components of this type-scene. Because the conceptual frame of judicial proceedings is in plain view, his assertion of "true" (ἀληθής, 1:13) acquires a more specific thrust than it would without other components of the frame. Pragmatically, it becomes a verdict. Paul introduces the secondhand quotation as from an unreliable witness of whom he has already established the untrustworthy character. Paul is the μάρτυς ("witness") of the μαρτυρία ("testimony"). Thus, Paul claims to bear witness and to swear on his own report that someone was disparaging Titus's missionary congregants. So, I suggest, it is *Paul's* witness, not the so-called *prophet's*, that he asserts as true. Long argues that "laws and testimony" were "the two most forceful" forms of evidence in ancient judicial rhetoric as identified in his survey of "artificial proofs." He adds, however, that "Quintilian (*Inst.* 5.7.1) attributed testimony the highest place of honor for a case."[74]

Some prominent interpretations assume that the "testimony" (1:13) Paul pronounces as true is that borne by a Cretan poet. They infer that Paul ratifies the substance of the quotation—that Cretans in fact are intrinsically morally defective. But in what sense is this assertion a testimony when one considers the legal domain in which this word is at home? Such interpretations gloss over the semantic thrust of μαρτυρία ("testimony," 1:13) and the courtroom frame that Paul was activating. Quinn recognizes the courtroom language of the letter here, but he says that Paul was joining a Cretan poet—in Quinn's paraphrase, "one of their own countrymen"—as a second witness against the ethnic Cretans.[75] According to Mounce, by these words Paul "adds his personal stamp of approval" to the

---

ἰδεῖν καὶ προσλαλῆσαι). Most contexts are generic (e.g., 2 Tim 1:6, 12). Perkins notes that ἡ μαρτυρία "refers to something as a piece of evidence" (*Pastoral Letters*, 254).

74. Long, *Ancient Rhetoric*, 49.
75. Quinn, *Letter to Titus*, 107.

quotation.[76] It was Paul's "way of giving apostolic authority to something said by a non-Christian."[77] It is not plain, however, that Paul was deferring to the authority or vouching for the trustworthiness of the saying's originator. Assuming so, Harrill wonders, "What exactly, however, warrants confidence in the Cretan prophet is not explained beyond the apostolic trustworthiness of the author's own 'Pauline' voice."[78]

The NEB translation of 1:13a as "and he told the truth!" obscures the underlying referent embedded in the phrase. These may be examples of mismatched assumptions. A more fitting dynamic equivalent translation might be, "I'm telling the truth!" If the signals of courtroom proceedings mean that Paul is presenting arguments against a group of unsanctioned leaders and essentially accusing them of misdemeanors against other believers, then this meta-comment probably refers to Paul's own testimony. Allow me to paraphrase and embellish 1:13 to capture this thrust: "I hereby verify the testimony that I have presented to you regarding these troublemakers who have slurred the Cretans, and on account of this accusation the consequence is a stern rebuke."

Paul presents a case against the most shocking and blatant offenders among the troublemakers—those who justified their presumption on the basis of age-old ethnic stereotypes. Paul is not saying that all of the leadership problems in Crete center on this issue, but bigotry is a stinging example. Somehow, Paul received enough evidence to render this accusation against someone from among the troublemakers. It is plausible that the author heard about the nature of these problems from sources in the Cretan church. After all, we know that Paul was able, for instance, to receive impeaching information about distant congregations privately from sources official or unofficial (e.g., 1 Cor 1:11, 5:1).

The simple recurrence of the topic of truth and lies in Titus accentuates the courtroom scene contextually, because occurrences cluster in 1:10–16 and because concerns with truth and falsehood correspond in specific ways to the setting of a courtroom. Within the quotation, Cretans are called "liars" (ψεύστης, 1:12), but Paul discloses the most salient disagreement between truth and reality in the crescendo of his remarks about

---

76. Mounce, *Pastoral Epistles*, 397.
77. Mounce, *Pastoral Epistles*, 398.
78. Harrill, "'Without Lies or Deception,'" 452. Harrill's argument depends on the attribution to Epimenides as the origin of Paul's "bitter invective against Cretans" (453).

the troublemakers—"they profess to know God, they nevertheless deny [him] by their works" (1:16). Idiomatically, Paul's audience could infer: Who do they think they're calling liars?! It is as the proverbial pot calling the kettle black. Whereas Paul calls his testimony "true" (ἀληθής, 1:13), he characterizes some of the troublemakers' "actions" (ἔργον, 1:16) as the commandments of people who reject the "truth" (ἀλήθεια, 1:14). Overly concerned with peripheral religious works, they nullify their capacity to do "any good work" (ἔργον, 1:16) by their harassment of the Cretans. These collocated contrasts are striking. Paul reveals that this topic of truth telling and lying was already on his mind when he uniquely opened the Epistle to Titus with his own salutation as a servant of the "unlying" (ἀψευδής, 1:2) God, whose purpose includes spreading the knowledge of the "truth" (ἀληθείας, 1:1).

The correlation between truth, lies, and a court of law is intuitive but has scriptural precedent. Consider Rom 3:4—"Let God be *true* [ἀληθής], though everyone [else] be a *liar* [ψεύστης], just as it is written, 'So that you may be *justified* [δικαιωθῇς] in your words, and conquer when *you judge* [κρίνεσθαί σε].'" The context of this verse shows the natural relation of more general-purpose words such as *true* and *liar* with the narrower concepts of acquittal and judgment in the context of Paul's judicial-style confrontation of bias and bigotry against gentiles.[79] In sum, Paul is prosecuting bigotry, not participating in it. I now examine a major topical aspect of context that would have shaped the original audience's cognitive environment—Jewish religious culture and customs.

Jewish Religious Culture and Customs

In the material surrounding the Cretan quotation, Paul addresses controversies regarding several Jewish concerns. Mounce writes, "This passage [1:10–16] clearly shows that the teaching was primarily Jewish."[80] Barrett observes that the heresy in Crete "undoubtedly contained a Jewish

---

79. Further examples of this cluster of ideas, in particular swearing of oaths and testifying in a court-of-law-like setting, include John 3:32–33; 8:13–18; 19:35; 21:24; Rom 3:21; 9:1; 1 Cor 15:15; 2 Cor 11; Gal 1:20; 3 John 12. See also LXX Exod 23:1; Deut 19:15–21, treated below.

80. Mounce, *Pastoral Epistles*, 395. He may overstate the evidence when he continues, "and taught asceticism and guidelines for ritual purity and defilement."

element," citing Titus 1:10, 14; and 3:9.[81] He claims that the cluster of heretical concerns in 3:9–11 represents "Jewish Gnosticism."[82] Although I think Barrett overstates the presence of gnostic elements, he rightly sees that these concerns have Jewish roots. Aageson writes, "In Titus 1:10–16, the Jewish character of the opposition in Crete is identified in general terms."[83] The opponents were not all Jewish even though "the ones from the circumcision" (1:10) were prominent among them.[84] Few interpreters recognize that the troublemakers' disdain for the Cretans probably intensified Paul's concern in Titus. Stegemann, for instance, considers these as separate issues: "On the one hand it is maintained that these negative characteristics are particularly or primarily (μάλιστα) applicable to 'those of the circumcision' (οἱ ἐκ τῆς περιτομῆς). Shortly afterwards a warning is given not to subscribe to Jewish fables (Ἰουδαϊκοῖς μύθοις). On the other hand, the 'opponents' are also identified with negative prejudices concerning the Cretans."[85] Given the referential language and literary context, it would be reasonable to say that the opponents were not merely identified *with* but *as* the promulgators of these prejudices!

Although Jewish religious culture clearly featured prominently among the troublemakers of the Cretan church, that is not to say that Paul found Jews themselves or Judaism itself problematic. Mounce points out that,

---

81. Barrett, *Pastoral Epistles*, 12. Under the influence of Pastoral Epistles amalgamating tendencies, he emphasizes the presence of Gnosticism in Crete. He regards "Jewish myths" (1:14) and "genealogies" (3:9) as primarily gnostic despite such interests being at home in nongnostic Jewish cultural contexts. I do not fully argue against Gnosticism or Barrett's "Jewish Gnosticism" (14–15) being an issue in Titus, although others have (e.g., see discussion in Aageson, *Paul, the Pastoral Epistles*, 65, 150, 161). Paul may have revealed affinity with a *gnosis* orientation when he identified his apostleship as "according to knowledge of the truth" (1:1, κατὰ ... ἐπίγνωσιν ἀληθείας), acknowledged that "once, even we were ignorant" (3:3, Ἦμεν γὰρ ποτε καὶ ἡμεῖς ἀνόητοι), or instructed Titus to "put aside stupid controversies" (3:9, μωρὰς δὲ ζητήσεις ... περιΐστασο·). Several references could be construed as having a gnostic outlook in view. My argument does not depend on particular theological details of heresy.

82. Barrett, *Pastoral Epistles*, 145.

83. Aageson, *Paul, the Pastoral Epistles*, 79.

84. Guthrie claims that several pieces of evidence "clearly [show] that the heresy in this case had a Jewish origin." He continues, "It is evident that in Crete some form of Jewish controversies of an entirely speculative and irrelevant nature had arisen" (*Pastoral Epistles*, 44–45).

85. Stegemann, "Anti-Semitic and Racist Prejudices," 278; see also Huizenga, *1–2 Timothy, Titus*, 139.

although the divisive element in Crete "was primarily Jewish," not everything "must have centered on the law."[86] Paul was combating distortions of Judaism as much as of his Christian gospel.[87] He decried corruptions of Jewish faith as much as (or qua) distortions of Christian faith. Even though the controversy surrounded concerns of a Jewish provenance, Paul did not see Judaism as inherently contrary to Christianity.

Mounce distinguishes the problematic element in the Cretan church as "aberrant Judaism."[88] Marginal or ancillary matters had become central for Paul's opponents; and, instead of bearing fruit of a religious or spiritual nature, their behaviors had produced ethno-religious class stratification. The problems that Paul addressed had significant social dimensions. The epistle portrays a vacuum of leadership (1:5); and some Cretan Christians felt pressured to attend to various interests of a Jewish (Ἰουδαϊκός, 1:14) religious provenance (1:10, 14; 3:9–11), while Titus was to advocate Paul's transformative gospel to the gentiles (2:11–15, 3:3–7). The conflict in Crete was ethno-religious at core;[89] and, in the Cretan quotation, Paul saw a smoking gun.

Although several scholars consider some of Paul's contentions in Titus to be anti-Semitic, they still recognize "the Jewish nature of the problem in Crete."[90] The letter context of Titus suggests that alienating or factionalizing currents in the Cretan church stemmed from the comportment of a Jewish contingent (1:10, 14; 3:9–11).

---

86. Mounce, *Pastoral Epistles*, 396.

87. The apostle Paul saw himself as being true to Judaism even as he defended the gospel (e.g., Phil 1:7, 3:5).

88. Mounce, *Pastoral Epistles*, lxi.

89. According to Barrett, "Judaizers of the old kind no longer threaten the peace, and even the existence of the Church, and the place of Gentiles is so comfortably assured that the author seems unaware of the theological struggles and revolutions which preceded their admission." It is hard to see how he can read Titus in this way without amalgamating it with the other Pastoral Epistles. Any attentive reader of Titus can see the struggles Barrett denies. He claims that the old ethno-religious contests of the mid-first century gave way to gnostic heresies in the Pastoral Epistles that interest him more. Reading Titus on its own, apart from 1 and 2 Timothy, the ethno-religious contestations appear clearly (see Barrett, *Pastoral Epistles*, 32–33).

90. Mounce uses these words (*Pastoral Epistles*, 379), whereas others might see it as the anti-Semitic nature of the problem in Paul. Huizenga is among such critics (*1–2 Timothy, Titus*, 139, 140, 188, and passim); see also Stegemann, "Anti-Semitic and Racist Prejudices," 271–94.

Jewish interests in Titus have two levels of specificity: First, some items directly and explicitly refer to Jewish matters on the semantic level, such as "circumcision" (περιτομή, 1:10), "Jewish" and "commandment" (Ἰουδαϊκός and ἐντολή, 1:14; see also "quarrels about the law," μάχας νομικός, 3:9). Second, some items indirectly but plausibly refer to Jewish interests on the basis of context, such as "genealogy" (γενεαλογία, 3:9), "prophet" (προφήτης, 1:12), and "detestable" (βδελυκτός, 1:16; cf. LXX Lev 18:30, Rom 2:22). Both levels contribute to the overall sense that ethno-religious divisions were central to problems in the Cretan church. Notice that all of these items appear in near proximity in the two main sections where Paul directly addresses issues regarding troublemaking opponents (1:10–16; 3:9–11).[91]

I argued in the previous chapter that Paul uses the honorable designation *prophet* (1:12)—a significant title in Jewish religious contexts—sarcastically. He does the same with "commandments" (1:14). The "prophet" was only a truth teller in his own mind and among the like-minded.[92] Paul compares the behaviors and attributes of the false leaders with the insults of the quotation.[93] Especially in their central flaw—deceit—these leaders were no different from their caricature of Cretans. Regarding the quotation, Towner writes, "Paul now springs the rhetorical trap that will vilify the opponents in a way most appropriate for the Cretan church."[94] Not incidentally, deceit (with corresponding notions of truth and lies) is the only moral issue from the quotation that Paul transparently develops elsewhere in the letter, primarily in its first chapter.

Apparently, some Jewish believers and their sympathetic associates instilled the Cretan believers with an ethno-religious inferiority complex analogous to congregations that Paul had dealt with elsewhere in the New Testament (see Acts 15:1–2, 7–9; Rom 2:25–29; 4:14; Gal 2:14–16; 3:2–5, 8,

---

91. Mounce notes that Paul addressed problems of a "Jewish nature" in two particular sections (1:10–16, 3:9–10; see *Pastoral Epistles*, lxix–lxx; cf. 453–54). Literary context and comparisons with texts such as LXX Lev 22:5, 8 and Num 19:13, 20 reveal that seemingly generic terms, such as καθαρός ("clean") and μιαίνω ("defile") in 1:15, could have profound salience for anyone with Jewish religious sensibilities.

92. Towner similarly judges the title to be dismissive (*Letters to Timothy and Titus*, 691).

93. Several scholars have discussed this comparison. See, e.g., Christopher A. Porter, "Chapter 18: Titus," in *T&T Clark Social Identity Commentary on the New Testament*, ed. J. Brian Tucker and Aaron Kuecker (New York: T&T Clark, 2018), 470–71.

94. Towner, *Letters to Timothy and Titus*, 694.

25–29; 5:6–12; Phil 3:2). This is a topos known to readers of the New Testament.[95] The essential substance of their message was that those who would not attend to certain features of Jewish religious culture (e.g., "circumcision," Titus 1:10; "Jewish myths and commandments of humans," 1:14; "vain controversies" and "genealogies," 3:9) could not be Christians of the first order.[96] Paul was primarily concerned with attitudes and practices that were used to denigrate gentile Christian religious status. To gain a following, the troublemakers even deprecated the people whom Paul left Titus in Crete to nurture (1:5). According to miso-Cretan readings that assume a contextual disjunction, Paul abruptly shifted from his concern with these impudent leaders to lambaste the general Cretan populace himself!

Paul labels a significant contingent of the troublemakers in Crete "those from the circumcision" (1:10), but he does not explicitly indicate that they insisted on gentile converts becoming circumcised (as in Gal 6:12–13). Circumcision is, of course, a central marker of Jewish identity. Mounce explains that "from the circumcision" was "a circumlocution for 'Jewish'" used elsewhere by Paul "of Jews (Rom 4:12) and Jewish Christians (Gal 2:7–9, 12; Col 4:11…)."[97] Paul uses the phrase as an ethno-religious designation to refer to Jews. Perhaps, secondarily, it could refer to sympathetic gentiles who had embraced aspects of Jewish religious culture as a means of attaining acceptance or status. The group's specific composition may elude us, but it is clear that patently ethno-religious factors measured and mediated contests of status in the Cretan church.[98]

We discover elsewhere in the New Testament that being an uncircumcised gentile was a key feature of Titus's (canonical) identity (Gal 2:1–5). Wall suggests that his gentile identity is essential to understanding the book regardless of whether he was a historical or merely literary figure

---

95. See Marshall, "Pastoral Epistles," 284.

96. Note that the author does not directly implicate the troublemakers with abuses of Torah (see 1 Tim 1:7–9, Titus 3:9); only certain, mostly peripheral, aspects of Jewish religious culture were in view.

97. Mounce, *Pastoral Epistles*, 396. Mounce also cites ancient evidence from Josephus and Philo that "there were large numbers of Jews in Crete" (p. 396). Evidence includes Josephus, *Ant.* 17.12.1; *J.W.* 2.7.1; *Life* 76; Philo, *Legat.* 282. Quinn discusses uses of the term and phrase "from the circumcision" in *Letter to Titus*, 16, 98.

98. Barclay claims that the issue Paul addressed in Galatians and his other undisputed works was the misperception that Jews intrinsically held a privileged religious status (*Paul and the Gift*, 162). The same issues of privilege and status are visible in Titus.

in the Epistle to Titus. Wall refers to the Paul on which the author of the Pastorals based his inscribed writer as the "canonical Paul," understanding that if the Pastorals were written on the basis of a proto-canon, then information from undisputed works must illuminate their meaning. We should not, then, disregard other New Testament texts that portray Titus, because this information was likely within the cognitive environment of the writer and original readers of the Epistle to Titus. The "canonical Titus," then, illuminates the Titus of Titus.[99] Wall writes, "Titus represents God's approval of Paul's 'mission to the uncircumcised' and so of Jerusalem's decision to initiate faithful Gentiles into the covenant."[100] So, Paul's instruction to "let no one despise you" (2:15) parallels the correction Titus is supposed to make on behalf of his gentile congregants.[101] Paul has instructed Titus to "speak and encourage and rebuke" (λάλει καὶ παρακάλει καὶ ἔλεγχε, 2:15)—a summary of actions Paul instructed him to perform with different constituencies earlier in the letter. In particular, a form of ἐλέγχω ("rebuke") appears surrounding the Cretan quotation in 1:9 and 1:13. The household code (2:1–10) instructs Titus to teach a set of alternative-to-Torah—but not contrary-to-Torah—standards of personal, interpersonal, and communal behavior. While Titus did this, he was to assert and rely on his authority among the churches of Crete by virtue of Paul's commission. Unlike Timothy, the problem Titus faced was not dismissal on the basis of age (1 Tim 4:12) as much as ethnicity—the same basis on which the troublemakers disparaged the Cretans.

On the hearers' minds was not only the clawing for social prominence but the pivotal role of ethnic and religious identity within that contest. John Barclay's construal of the historical situation of Galatians is relevant to what we see in Titus.[102] Before Paul mentions the quotation, he evokes the ethno-religious composition of the troublemaking constituency. Concerning such social contests among the Galatians, Barclay writes, "A central token of cultural capital within the Jewish tradition [circumcision] is here [Gal 2:1–10] acknowledged to be disposable in the mission to

---

99. See Wall and Steele, *1 and 2 Timothy and Titus*, 34.

100. Wall and Steele, *1 and 2 Timothy and Titus*, 343.

101. Based on its placement in the household code's sequence and structure (Titus 2:1–10) and on the theme of imitation elsewhere, it is clear that Paul portrays Titus as a model (τύπον, 2:7) for the entire congregation. It seems that Paul wants Titus to defend himself as much as his predominantly gentile congregation.

102. See Barclay, *Paul and the Gift*, 334.

Gentiles—certainly not because that mission is of less significance, or the status of Gentile converts lower than that of Jews, but because *God is at work* as much in one form of the mission as in the other."[103] The troublemakers in Crete would likely not accept such a proposition. Concerning such contests, Barclay later writes, "At issue is not simply the adoption of this or that Jewish practice, but the capacity of the Christ-gift to refound and reorient life by a logic that challenges every other attribution of value."[104] In light of the gospel material of Titus 2:11–14 and 3:3–7, might this also describe Paul's contention with Crete's troublemakers?

Echoing the Old Testament—the Scripture of the church (2 Tim 3:16)—is commonplace in the New Testament, although some commentators minimize the extent to which the Pastoral Epistles do this. Richard Hays proposes seven tests to detect, confirm, and interpret such echoes. Of his seven criteria—availability, volume, recurrence, thematic coherence, historical plausibility, history of interpretation, and satisfaction—the two that have remarkable correspondence to relevance theory, especially the idea (below) of implicated premises, are thematic coherence and satisfaction.[105] Simply echoing Scripture might not be of significance, but some echoes correlate particularly with the Cretan quotation and the topic of Jewish religio-cultural interests.

The Cretan quotation conveniently echoes a Jewish way of referring to people as worthless (i.e., not worthy to live). In the Deuteronomic law,

---

103. Barclay, *Paul and the Gift*, 363.

104. Barclay, *Paul and the Gift*, 399. Angela N. Parker identifies a similar parallel: "Paul wrestles with Jewish identity in relationship to Galatian identity." See Parker, "On Womanist's View of Racial Reconciliation in Galatians," *JFSR* 34.2 (2018): 30. With respect to the situation that the epistle to Titus envisions, we might say that the church was wrestling with the relationships of Jewish identity and Cretan (gentile) identity. See also discussion of correlations between Galatians and Titus in Aageson, *Paul, the Pastoral Epistles*, 78–82.

105. Richard B. Hays, *Echoes of Scripture in the Letters of Paul* (New Haven: Yale University Press, 1989), 29–33. A fine line differentiates *satisfaction* from the "affective fallacy" (i.e., accepting what *seems* to be the right interpretation), but relevance theory adds precision to this critically valuable criterion. According to relevance theory, "cognitive effects" are not intermediate (means) to the discovery of meaning (as *satisfaction* might imply); they are the purpose (ends) of communication. Nevertheless, evaluating or interacting with critiques of Hays's methodology is beside my purpose. His concepts and categories are well-known and therefore readily understood labels for what I see in Titus.

Israelite parents could take their rebellious son to the elders and call him "stubborn and rebellious ... a glutton and a drunkard" (Deut 21:20 NRSV). This was a premise for stoning the offender with the aim to "purge the evil from your midst; and all Israel will hear, and be afraid" (Deut 21:21 NRSV). This alone does not speak to *Paul's* intention, but the following verses in Deuteronomy illuminate a remarkable correlation with Titus. The goal of this punishment was that "you will drive out evil" (ἐξαρεῖς τὸν πονηρὸν, LXX Deut 21:21; cf. 1 Cor 5:13), and the remaining discussion says that if the Israelites leave dead bodies exposed after execution, they will "defile" (μιαίνω, LXX Deut 21:23) the land. These concepts and even some lexemes have strong correspondence not only to ideas but to their sequence in Titus 1:10–16. The charges that Israelite parents would bring against their rebellious son compare with the insult of the quotation against the Cretans. The moral condition of the troublemakers ("defiled," μιαίνω, Titus 1:15) parallels the fate of the land if Israelites leave dead bodies out postexecution. What seems to contrast sharply are the outcomes that the accusers expect (namely, ostracism, death, and perhaps defilement) and the outcomes that Paul enjoins for the troublemakers (namely, healthy doctrine and restorative justice).[106] This scripture from Deuteronomy could have been within the cognitive environment of Paul's audience.[107]

Within the near context of the Cretan quotation, Paul identifies "Jewish myths and commandments of people who reject the truth" (1:14) as matters to which duly rebuked people will cease to (mis)direct their attention. Aageson claims that "the problem of the commandments apparently turns on the issue of purity, associated with refraining from certain practices and from eating certain foods.... According to the text of Titus, the nature of the opposition is limited to these problems."[108] Paul directly links these issues to the rebuke he enjoins (1:13). If Aageson is right, then it is most fitting for the quotation to be in the mouth of a presumptuous leader whose logic dictates: if Cretans, by birth, are unclean (beasts and gluttons), then they can only enter into right relationship with the God

---

106. See ch. 6 on the redemptive nature of "sound doctrine" in Titus.

107. Other correspondences include the qualification that elders not have children accused of rebellion (Titus 1:6) and that Deut 21:23 is adjacent to the passage that talks about the curse of the person hung on a tree, which Paul references in Gal 3:13. The phrase is also echoed in the gospels (Matt 11:19, Luke 7:34), suggesting that this Torah reading might have been common in the early church.

108. Aageson, *Paul, the Pastoral Epistles*, 80.

revealed in Torah and live the most privileged form of Christian faith by a thorough conversion, which includes reforming dietary practices, renouncing their own identity, and embracing fitting religious observances.[109] Aageson, for one, acknowledges that "the theological structures of Galatians and Titus have one thing [this concern] in common." Aageson dismisses the scale of what he calls the "nagging judaizing tendency" in Crete, but it nevertheless appears to be one of Paul's chief concerns in Titus.[110]

---

109. Philo of Alexandria (ca. 20 BCE–ca. 50 CE), Jewish philosopher and contemporary of Paul, representing a widespread sensibility in Judaism, assessed that God's favor accrued to Jews on account of their adherence to a universal set of values and ordinances. Philo wrote that gentiles' instructors (from their nurses to their philosophers) "impress inextricable error" (ἐνεχάραξαν πλάνον ἀνήνυτον) on them but that God could "initiate" (συνάγων καὶ μυσταγωγῶν) into his ways any who were so inclined (*Virt.* 178). Gentiles, by virtue of "low birth" (δυσγένειαν), were misled "by foreign laws and unbecoming customs" (ἐξ ἀλλοκότων νόμων καὶ ἐκθέσμων ἐθῶν) but could turn to that "of which truth is the governor and overseer" (ἧς ἔφορος καὶ ἐπίσκοπος ἀλήθεια, *Virt.* 219). When gentiles converted to Judaism, they converted to the eternal and universal truth. For Philo, one could be "born" (φύντας ἐξ ἀρχῆς, lit. "issuing from the start") or "converted" (προσηλύτους), but "choosing to embark on piety" (πρὸς εὐσέβειαν ἠξίωσαν μεθορμίσασθαι) made one superior (*Spec.* 1.51). Converts to Judaism were evidence of its superiority and universality. Converting to true piety corresponded to serving the "truly living [One/God]" (τοῦ ὄντως ὄντος, *Spec.* 1.309). Philo, Paul, and others used "piety" (εὐσέβεια) to denote observant (Jewish/Christian) faith. Hoklotubbe explains that its currency in the Greco-Roman world made it a handy crossover term (*Civilized Piety*). Philo had to allegorize Judaism to universalize it, but he exemplified a common Jewish trope that the purported primacy, universality, and instrumentality of (idealized) Jewish doctrine implied its superiority. In Barclay's assessment, Philo thought, "What Jews observe on a daily basis is not some ethnically particular legislation, still less some arbitrary collection of customs, but the tangible instantiation of the order of the cosmos. To keep the law is to follow the grain of the universe: those who do so are obviously most pleasing to God and most worthy of his gifts" (*Paul and the Gift*, 233). Philo represented but one stripe of Judaism in which this attitude obtained. See Gregory E. Sterling, "'A Law unto Themselves': Limited Universalism in Philo and Paul," *ZNW* 107 (2016): 30–47. Translations of Philo here follow *Philo*, 10 vols., trans. Francis H. Colson and George H. Whitaker, LCL (Cambridge: Harvard University Press, 1929–1962).

110. Aageson, *Paul, the Pastoral Epistles*, 80–81. Aageson interprets Galatians as arguing against a theological "covenantal nomism" and does not fully address the social dimensions of Paul's concern in Galatians or Titus. Aageson focuses on Paul's legal arguments, concluding (or confirming) that the Epistle to Titus is not concerned with improper

Opponents who considered the Cretans to be gluttons might have advised them to observe an ascetic diet. They might have even shamed and ridiculed them. This scenario comports with Barrett's view of "Jewish Gnosticism" in the Pastoral Epistles,[111] but the quotation is on the wrong lips in Barrett's scenario. It only works if the Cretans' opponents uttered it, not if a Cretan uttered it, as Barrett assumes. The quotation may have had a life of its own centuries before Titus; Paul's contemporary opponents, however, were unconcerned with this history since it conveniently served their doctrinal purposes when taken out of its original context. Barrett identifies the content of the troublemakers' teaching as "apparently ascetic, representing a combination of Jewish food laws and dualistic rejection of the material."[112] This conception of how the quotation was functioning contextually leads to the equation between laziness, gluttony, and vice, on the one hand, and Jewish food laws and asceticism, on the other. This is an example of how the amalgamation of the Pastoral Epistles has introduced an artificial mismatch between the contextual assumptions held by ancient and modern readers. Are they too ascetic or too indulgent?!

When Paul articulates the redeeming purpose of Jesus's self-giving work (Titus 2:11–15; see also 3:3–7), he expresses the logic of the gospel that undergirds his whole vision of human redemption—the reason he can see Jews and gentiles as equals before God. Paul explains key aspects of Christian conversion that correspond verbally and conceptually to aspects of the tension he describes in 1:10–16. Thus, 2:14 reads, "[Jesus] who gave himself on our behalf, in order that he might redeem us from every lawlessness and might cleanse unto himself a distinct people, eager for good works." Verbal correspondences include "cleansing" (καθαρός, 1:15; καθαρίζω, 2:14) and "good works" (ἔργον ἀγαθὸν, 1:16; καλῶν ἔργων, 2:14; see also 2:7). Conceptual correspondences include the idea of the work of Christ being the basis of one's status and the idea that the result of this christological work is a (singular) distinct people, not a divisive compound. So, Paul's saying "to the clean [ones] all things are clean" (1:15) is a critique that questions the redemptive status of anyone who would take it on themselves to call other believers "evil beasts" (1:12)—that is, "unclean"—regardless of their excuse. If a person has trusted Christ for

---

interpretations of the law, whereas Galatians is. Barclay argues the narrowness and misleading nature of the "covenantal nomism" designation (*Paul and the Gift*, 115–58).
    111. See Barrett, *Pastoral Epistles*, passim.
    112. Barrett, *Pastoral Epistles*, 132.

redemption, then they do not need to follow Jewish dietary regulations or other laws. Insolent leaders "defied" (ἀνυπο[τασσω], 1:6, 10), "contradicted" (ἀντιλέγω, 1:9, 2:9), "rejected" (ἀποστρέφω, 1:14), and "denied" (ἀρνέομαι, 1:16) this message.

Paul left-dislocates "ones who are defiled and unbelieving" (1:15), suspending them in a δέ development clause. By means of this topicalization, he accentuates the self-condemning effects of judging people's redemptive status on an ethno-religious basis. It is only those sorts of people who find that "nothing is clean" (1:15). Simply reversing the order without changing the grammar yields a more syntactically neutral or unmarked way of organizing the information: "nothing is clean to ones who are defiled and unfaithful." But Paul placed the information in a cause-and-effect order. So why did the troublemakers see their Cretan brothers and sisters as unclean? It was because the troublemakers themselves were defiled and unfaithful. Grammatically, "nothing is clean" is the predication, but pragmatically, "ones who are defiled and unfaithful" is the predication. To convey the effect of this topicalization, I render it, "It is to those who are defiled and unfaithful that things are unclean." One senses the biting allegation when so phrased.

Exposing and correcting these troublemakers was not a form of bigotry—as though the history of interpretation should shift from seeing Paul as anti-Cretan to seeing him as anti-Semitic. Several dynamic facts make church discipline, not bigotry, the most appropriate designation for Paul's interest in and speech concerning the Jewish opponents. First, Paul never renounces or denounces Judaism or condemns Jews as such. Second, he says that the ethno-religious composition of the opponent group is mostly (but not necessarily all) Jewish; Jews did, after all, have a significant place in the early formation of the church. Third, the issues he mentions as being "foolish," "empty," or "useless" (1:10, 14; 3:9) were not central to Judaism. Fourth, and perhaps most importantly, the troublemakers were trying to exploit and expand a power differential by driving a wedge of bigotry and hierarchical social status between Jewish and Cretan Christians within the church. So, Paul was concerned for the members of his vulnerable missionary congregation as well as for the integrity of the gospel. If the Cretan quotation seems simply repugnant and appalling, that was Paul's point.

Division or Heresy

The foregoing observations suggest the prevalence of ethno-religious tensions in the Cretan church. Further, a theme of division is present throughout the epistle, even though Paul does not mention a "divisive person" (αἱρετικὸν ἄνθρωπον, 3:10) until later in the letter. The concept of division, us/them distinctions, in/out contests, and the dynamics of superiority and inferiority were on the audience's minds. We derive the English word *heretic* from the Greek word αἱρετικός that Paul uses to label that kind of troublemaker, but a set of propositional beliefs that contradict another set of propositional beliefs does not appear to be what primarily ailed the Cretan church. The ethno-religious social tensions could not be ignored. As suggested above, Titus himself was likely a collateral target of such prejudices (2:15).

That Paul does not more explicitly define the "false beliefs" against which he contends frustrates several commentators, but the Pastoral Epistles themselves do not necessarily maintain that a wrong set of ideas is at issue. For example, Huizenga writes, "We should be suspicious of the author's labels imposed on those who disagree with his teachings, especially since he does not describe or engage their ideas in any constructive way."[113] Bassler is disappointed that "the author's refusal to engage his opponents in a substantive debate does not allow us to identify their theology with any precision."[114] Stegemann contends, "We shall not be able to extract the beliefs and teachings, or praxis, of the Christians who are so sharply rejected here, from the Pastoral Epistles. They have disappeared in the sea of polemic."[115] In historical retrospect, commentators can reconstruct forms of heresy as they appeared to evolve, but these reconstructions are based on a limited and arbitrary selection of available texts. Most commonly, scholars compare gnostic Christian writings with the ideas Paul refutes in the Pastorals,[116] but the heart of the problem in Crete does not

---

113. Huizenga, *1–2 Timothy, Titus*, 179.

114. Bassler, *1 Timothy*, 189; see also Vogel, "Die Kreterpolemik," 255. Conventionally understood, the Cretan insult does not help readers grasp the supposed heresy. If, however, Paul was rebuking its use, then the heresy is comprehensible. Given what Titus and his community knew, they needed no further explanation.

115. Stegemann, "Anti-Semitic and Racist Prejudices," 279; see also Twomey, *Pastoral Epistles*, 218–23. This frustration seems in part to be an outcome of viewing the Pastoral Epistles as an amalgam.

116. For example, Bassler, *1 Timothy*, 27–28; Barrett, *Pastoral Epistles*, 12, 14–15, 32–33, 127, 145; Twomey, *Pastoral Epistles*, 224; Mounce, *Pastoral Epistles*, 396, 402. For examples of countervailing judgments on this very issue, see Faber, "'Evil Beasts, Lazy Gluttons,'" 141 (also 137–38); Benjamin Fiore, *The Pastoral Epistles: First Timothy, Second Timothy, Titus*, SP 12 (Collegeville, MN: Liturgical Press, 2007), 14–15.

seem to have been a matter of lining up theological ideas in the wrong fashion. It was the social and behavioral outcomes of division that were unacceptable. The gospel that Christ accepts people without regard to conventional tokens of status confounds the attempts of superiority groups to place additional demands on converts. Christ is the agent of acceptance, and his ruling cannot be overturned: Jews and gentiles are equals in grace.[117]

Establishing *us* and *them*, also known as *othering*, is a way of defining boundaries around cultures and ethnicities. In the religious matrix of "clean" versus "unclean" (1:15), an epithet of "evil beasts" (1:12) has strong *in* and *out* implications. Marianne Bjelland Kartzow explains that "The Pastoral Epistles construct opponents through 'othering' them in various ways.... The Pastoral Paul's polemic is built on a technique where previously influential insiders are made through degradation to be outsiders."[118] Othering occurs when speech distances people from the speaker, who is normally the implicit protagonist of natural language communication. Ascribing inferiority (e.g., intellectual, moral, hereditary, doctrinal) is an act of othering. Today, othering is almost invariably suspect, making it difficult for interpreters to read texts in sympathy with writers. Yet othering may be a linguistic-pragmatic tool that can be wielded in both just *and* unjust ways. The Cretan quotation certainly exemplifies negative, othering speech. By echoing comparable negative categories for the troublemakers (e.g., unclean, defiled, turning from the truth), Paul uses othering speech to affect correction, accountability, and restoration.

With certain exceptions, insiders in such a framework perceive the other as tacitly inferior in some way. As expressed in Titus 3:3–5, a Christian convert might view the former self as other. But the categories of difference that were once available for ethnic and cultural othering are no longer applicable to this new status in Christ. This inapplicability seems central to the epistle. Contradictions of this new reality seem to parallel what Paul contended with in Galatians. As Barclay says of the issue in Galatians, "The Christ-event [is] subversive of normative systems of worth." Circumcision and even uncircumcision (Gal 6:15) may have been "tokens of superiority" or "the object of public pride," but they had no cur-

---

117. The wording of concepts from the previous sentences owes much to Barclay, *Paul and the Gift*.

118. Marianne Bjelland Kartzow, *Gossip and Gender: Othering of Speech in the Pastoral Epistles*, BZNW 164 (New York: de Gruyter, 2009), 15.

rency in the household of God.[119] "The Christ-event" in Titus is signified in the language of *epiphany* (2:11, 3:4). "Tokens of superiority" (i.e., signs of participation in a superior group),[120] such as circumcision, observance of visible ceremonies, or adept participation in controversy may have been means of establishing status, but Paul repeatedly instructs subjection, not self-aggrandizement, within the household of God. The anthropological prevalence of such tiered thinking and social arrangement reinforces the notion that the troublemakers were leveraging existing "tokens of superiority" to form primitive social structures, falsely dividing the Cretan church into superior and inferior groups. Titus was to challenge the tiers.

If heresy causes or exacerbates division and animosity, then in this sense the Cretan quotation is an expression of heresy even though its semantic representation does not strike the modern reader as holding much theological content. *Heresy* has come to mean straying from an established dogma, but heterodoxy is only one aspect of division. The modern impulse to identify this or that particular heresy from a known lineup of heterodoxies is anachronistic.[121] We cannot tell precisely what theological propositions the troublemakers taught, because Paul expresses his concern with them in terms of their social effect on the church (e.g., "upsetting whole houses," 1:11). Paul hopes that Titus can restore the erring leaders ("in order that they might be healthy in the faith," ἵνα ὑγιαίνωσιν ἐν τῇ πίστει, 1:13b).[122] He is protecting the community's tenants as much as the community's tenets!

---

119. Barclay, *Paul and the Gift*, 394. The household was a metaphor for the church in the first century (e.g., Gal 6:10; Eph 2:19; 1 Tim 3:4-5, 15; 2 Tim 2:20-21; Titus 2:5; 1 Pet 4:17).

120. Barclay, *Paul and the Gift*, 394.

121. Suspecting that canonized literature represents an inherently oppressive orthodoxy is also anachronistic. See Bart D. Ehrman, *Lost Christianities: The Battles for Scripture and the Faiths We Never Knew* (New York: Oxford University Press, 2003), 181. He claims, "Written attacks of the proto-orthodox on Christians of other persuasions" led to the tragic loss of so-called heretical writings due to campaigns of eradication that have distorted history, thus "the polemical literature from the period looks completely one-sided."

122. In his undisputed works, Paul commonly addressed divisions of various kinds. See Rom 11:17-21; 14:1-4; 1 Cor 1:10; 11:18; 2 Cor 11:4; Gal 1:6-7; 4:17, 29; 5:15; Phil 2:1-2; 4:2; less so but still present in 1 Thess 5:13; however, apparently not Philemon. See also Eph 2:11-13, 21-22; 4:1-6; Col 2:16; 3:15; 2 Thess 3:6, 14-15; 1 Tim 1:3-4; 6:3-5; 2 Tim 4:3-4, 16.

Paul gives specific instructions to Titus in dealing with "a divisive person" (3:9–11). Such persons correspond to the main category of troublemakers that concern Paul. They divided and were divided from the Pauline church—outcomes that correspond to the troublemakers' actions (1:10–12). Stegemann perceives the association: "The author of the letter understands [the antagonists] as a sort of 'party' (cf. Titus 3:10) within the Christian communities of Crete.... These negative characteristics are particularly or primarily (μάλιστα) applicable to 'those of the circumcision' (οἱ ἐκ τῆς περιτομῆς). Shortly afterwards a warning is given not to subscribe to Jewish fables (Ἰουδαϊκοὶ μῦθοι)."[123] Paul seems, then, to be concerned with one main category of troublemakers, some of whom expressed their divisiveness through pithy ethno-religious insults.

Moral Topics

The Cretan quotation represents a different set of moral concerns than Paul himself addresses in the rest of Titus, where gluttony, laziness, and general debauchery are not even broached. Hoklotubbe argues that Paul's concern in Titus has to do with a cluster of ethical and religious behaviors that corresponded to the general rubric of piety (εὐσέβεια, 1:1).[124] The contingent most likely to disparage Cretans on allegations of general moral faults was one that advocated strict food laws and proto-gnostic moral scruples.[125] So, whereas Paul addresses one set of character traits, his opponents were preoccupied with another, which happens to be reflected in the quotation. Scholars such as Kidd and Riemer Faber have attempted to correlate the moral concerns of the quotation with the broad moral concerns of the book, but the connections are tenuous.[126] When Paul speaks in his own voice (that is, not in words he attributes to another), a specific set of issues repeatedly concerns him. At the center are practices of right teaching (1:9 [twice]; 2:1, 3, 7, 10) and submission (below), the personal qualities of σώφρων ("sensible," 1:8; 2:2, 5; cognates in 2:4, 6, 12) and σεμνός ("serious," 2:2, 7), and a number of φιλο- root words ("loving [appropriately]," 1:8 [twice]; 2:4

---

123. Stegemann, "Anti-Semitic and Racist Prejudices," 278.
124. Hoklotubbe, *Civilized Piety*.
125. See Twomey, *Pastoral Epistles*, 224; Mounce, *Pastoral Epistles*, 402; Bassler, *1 Timothy*, 27–28; Barrett, *Pastoral Epistles*, 127, 145.
126. See Kidd, "Titus as Apologia"; Faber, "'Evil Beasts, Lazy Gluttons.'"

[twice]; 3:4, 15).[127] The spread of these virtues across every social category that Paul addresses yields a remarkable comparison among the expectations of each group. In other words, what Paul expects of one category of people has a high degree of correspondence to what he expects of otherwise contrasting groups, including leaders and slaves, women and men, young and old, Jew and gentile.[128] If Paul were truly concerned with gluttony or laziness, he knew how to address those issues (see Rom 14:20–21; 16:18; 1 Cor 5:11; 8:8–13; 10:7; 11:20–22, 33–34; Gal 6:9; Eph 4:28; 1 Thess 2:9; 4:9–12; 5:14; 2 Thess 3:6–15; 1 Tim 5:13), but he does not do so in Titus.[129]

Paul shows some concern in the rest of Titus with general morals, but the issue he exposes through the quotation is bigotry—not gluttony, laziness, or general wickedness. A troublemaker enacted bigotry by deploying the quotation, which Paul exposes and rebukes. Bigotry is not in the semantics of the quotation; it is in the pragmatics. The quotation they propagated and its subsequent history of interpretation make the Cretans out to be much worse than Paul's instructions in the rest of Titus suggest as he calls them to thoughtfulness, self-control, devotion, submission, love, and so forth.

Submission

One of the strongest themes throughout Titus is submission. This theme emerges from the portrayal of social relationships evoked by many

---

127. Marshall says that Titus 2:12 provides the clearest and most complete clustering of cardinal Greek virtues in the Pastoral Epistles (σωφρόνως καὶ δικαίως καὶ εὐσεβῶς; see Marshall, *Critical and Exegetical Commentary*, 183–84). Furthermore, Paul's Hellenistic Judaism bridged this cluster between standard virtues of gentiles and Jews in the church, so his summary strategically invoked a conception of goodness that would resonate with his entire audience.

128. It is revealing but unnecessary for reconstructing the audience's cognitive environment, and therefore beyond the scope of this chapter, to examine the overlap of moral expectations among groups. It echoes such a core Pauline doctrine as the radical equality of persons before God seen in 1 Cor 12:13, Gal 3:28, even Col 3:11 and Rom 10:12. This correspondence is particularly visible through an explicit comparative connective adverb that Paul uses in Titus to move from one category to another (ὡσαύτως, 2:3, 6).

129. When needed, the apostle Paul could call a congregation to cease and desist from numerous kinds of wrongdoing. In addition to passages above, consider 1 Cor 6:8, Eph 4:25, Col 3:8–9, Acts 20:33–35.

occurrences of Greek words that feature -ταγ- roots (ἐπιταγή, "command" [noun], 1:3, 2:15; διατάσσω, "command" [verb], 1:5; ἀνυπότακτος, "insubordinate," 1:6, 10; ὑποτάσσω, "submit," 2:5, 9; 3:1) and from specific words sharing that semantic domain such as ἐνκρατής ("disciplined," 1:8), ἐξουσία and πειθαρέω ("authority [figure]" and "obey," 3:1).[130] The theme of submission does not follow a superiority-and-inferiority scheme but an *equals-in-humility* program that applies to the entire constituency of the church, including Paul himself. Unlike the social dynamic that the troublemakers pushed, where others are inferior, an ethic of submission commits all uses of power and freedom to the service of others.[131]

After discussing the need and criteria for good leaders, Paul introduces the prime leadership problem he perceives in the Cretan church: "For many are insubordinate" (Εἰσὶν γὰρ πολλοὶ ἀνυπότακτοι, 1:10).[132] Paul is concerned with obedience and submission throughout Titus, and leaders themselves are to model these qualities. Although hierarchy is assumed, every level of church member is supposed to be submissive. These troublemakers, however, saw themselves as above it all.

The troublemakers may have looked at Titus's gentile ethnicity as an excuse not to show him deference (2:15). To them, he was inherently an inferior and an unacceptable leader. The underlying prejudice of the Cretan quotation made any gentile unacceptable as a leader. Titus was

---

130. This list could be even larger. Paul discourages being "enslaved" (δουλόω, 2:3) by wine; says that "serving" (δουλεύω, 3:3) various passions and pleasures characterized Christians' former life; refers to "commandments" (ἐντολή, 1:14), which imply expectations of obedience. The words listed fall into one of three semantic domains shared with ὑποτάσσω (2:5, 9; 3:1), the most frequent word of this kind in Titus. The domains are 33F Command, Order; 36C Obey, Disobey; and 37A Control, Restrain, as delineated in L&N. I acknowledge critiques of their philosophy and method regarding semantic domains, but the point remains that concerns for submission are remarkably prominent in Titus with respect to all populations.

131. David Lyon proposes that postmodern shifts toward hermeneutics of retrieval (discussed below) help readers to recognize their moral responsibility to "anyone who has valid claims on us." My relevance-guided interpretation reclaims this feature of Titus that I describe in terms of submission. See Lyon, "Sliding in All Directions: Social Hermeneutics from Suspicion to Retrieval," in *Disciplining Hermeneutics: Interpretation in Christian Perspective*, ed. Roger Lundin (Grand Rapids: Eerdmans, 1997), 112–13.

132. The presence of a variant that includes καί in this text (discussed earlier, in ch. 3, under "Basic Pragmatic Practices, Reference") does not affect my point that the initial problem Paul points to is insubordination among the presumptuous leaders.

no better than a Cretan, because the troublemakers seemed to disfavor Cretans qua gentiles, not qua Cretans. It seems that in the Cretan quotation his antagonists had laid their hands on a conveniently specific popular saying.

Unsurprisingly, Paul places instructions regarding slaves where they would normally appear in a household code—at the end (2:9–10).[133] And, as might be expected, submission is a requirement for slaves. Although 2:1–10 is indeed structured as a household code, several familial relations are absent. The only explicit relations mentioned are between older and younger women (2:3–4), between younger women and their own husbands and children (2:5), between Titus and younger men (2:6–7), and between slaves and their own masters (2:9). Paul could take for granted that Titus thought slaves within a household should be obedient and "not talk back" (μὴ ἀντιλέγοντας, 2:9; see 1:9), but his discussion of slaves evokes other associations and the places of people within the "household of God"—a recognized metaphor for the church.[134] In this way, the literal household code reinforces the metaphorical environment of God's household and the call toward specific dispositions (prominently, submission) in all types of relationships as articulated elsewhere in Titus.[135]

Regarding the theme of submission, note the initial prominence of Paul as a "slave" (δοῦλος, 1:1) of God and leaders pictured as "household stewards" (οἰκονόμον, 1:7, a category of slave or servant). Notice also that attributes customarily associated with subordinates, such as slaves, are expected even of leaders in God's (ideal) household. For instance, sub-

---

133. See David E. Aune, *The New Testament in Its Literary Environment*, LEC 8 (Philadelphia: Westminster, 1987), 196; Jeffers, *Greco-Roman World*, 86–87, 228–29.

134. Much has been made of the prevalence of this metaphor as distinctive of the Pastorals. The Greek phrases translated "household of God" actually appear in Eph 2:19 (οἰκεῖοι τοῦ θεοῦ), 1 Tim 3:15 (οἴκῳ θεοῦ), and 1 Pet 4:17 (τοῦ οἴκου τοῦ θεοῦ). Cf. Gal 6:10 (τοὺς οἰκείους τῆς πίστεως, "the household members of [the] faith"). The community of faith portrayed as a household is more of a theme in Titus than a set phrase, but it was a ready metaphor throughout Scripture, and the household was a go-to metaphor for leadership structures in Greco-Roman society. See, e.g., Aristotle, *Pol.* 1.1253; Dionysius of Halicarnassus, *Ant. rom.* 2.24.3–2.27.4.

135. The troublemakers' behaviors occupy the preconversion end of the submission-insubordination continuum. Being "disobedient" (ἀπειθής) and "serving" (δουλεύω) "all kinds of passions and pleasures" characterized "us," even Paul, before "the kindness and love of God our savior appeared" (ἐπιφαίνω) and prior to "rebirth" (παλιγγενεσία). See Titus 3:3–7.

mission, ungreediness, and not-talking-back all appear as expectations of the general church population. These qualities appear both in the household code for slaves (2:9–10) and in the leadership discussion (1:7–10) as desired traits. The troublemakers, however, exhibit the opposite qualities, being "contradictory" and "insubordinate" (ἀντιλέγω, 1:9; ἀνυπότακτος, 1:10). When Paul says, "Slaves should be submissive … pleasing … and not talk back" (Δούλους … ὑποτάσσεσθαι … εὐαρέστους εἶναι, μὴ ἀντιλέγοντας, 2:9), he is repeating several of the key qualities expected of those who would lead with integrity. They are to instantiate the values of submission and sensibility, just as Titus is to be a model for them (τύπον, 2:7; see 1 Tim 4:12, Phil 3:17, 2 Thess 3:9, 1 Pet 5:3).

Paul's expectations of slaves and his general expectations of all Christians parallel each other remarkably. In the section of Titus regarding general instructions for all Christians, Paul urges "showing all gentleness" (πᾶσαν ἐνδεικνυμένους πραΰτητα, 3:2); while in the section of the household code regarding slaves, he urges "showing all good faith" (πᾶσαν πίστιν ἐνδεικνυμένους ἀγαθήν, 2:10). This code in Titus 2:1–10 has an additional layer of significance. The portion regarding slaves submitting does not complete an otherwise comprehensive code, but it shows that the expectations of every member of the household are parallel with the requirements of good leaders. The comparison demonstrates that Paul expects the Christian community to exhibit submission from the top to the bottom of the social ladder—an attitude the presumptuous leaders in Crete did not share. The requirements of a true leader are precisely those of servanthood—another contrast with the aggrandizing behavior of the antagonists. The code applies comparable values to all people—even Paul, who begins the letter by identifying himself within this category of "slave" (δοῦλος, 1:1; see 2:9). Paul indicates that submission, noncontentiousness, and ungreediness are specific qualities to look for among those in higher-status positions. Titus's leadership section (1:5–16) and household code (2:1–10) feature striking correspondences between submission or the lack thereof (ὑποτάσσω, 2:9; see ἀνυπότακτος, 1:10), talking back or contradicting (ἀντιλέγω, 2:9; see 1:9), and inappropriate gain (νοσφίζομαι, 2:10; see αἰσχροκερδής, 1:7; αἰσχροῦ κέρδους χάριν, 1:11). "Servants must be good; despots [δεσπόται, 2:9] ought to be gooder!" or so to speak.

Postcolonial interpretations of household codes and δοῦλος language in the New Testament often note that the apostles did not go far enough in condemning, resisting, or overturning slavery and other oppressive institutions.¹³⁶ I do not disagree, but, in examining Titus within its own setting, apart from the developments of modern history, I would highlight how Paul subverts and partially diffuses—not just rhetorically and spiritually—the inherent inequality of these social arrangements. Understanding how the concept of submission functions in Titus, it is not simply as Ralph Broadbent, exhibiting the tendency to amalgamate the Pastoral Epistles, summarizes: "The Christian communities involved are being encouraged to follow the hierarchical rules of empire, with the emperor and other local rulers at the top and women, slaves and children at the bottom. In between come the male leaders of the Christian community."¹³⁷

We have now covered several critical themes and topics for understanding the audience's cognitive environment as well as pertinent structural matters. The other kind of contextual assumption that readers bring to interpretation are implicated premises, which they must logically infer.

Implicated Premises

As we have seen, words and ideas within a hearer's context—from encyclopedic real-world knowledge to topics and themes emerging within the discourse—shape his cognitive environment and delimit his contextual assumptions. In relevance theory, implicated premises represent another kind of contextual assumption. Such premises are that subset of all possible contextual assumptions that are logically necessary in order to derive adequate cognitive effects for the processing effort expended, thereby arriving at a satisfactory interpretation of the utterance and concluding what the speaker intends.

Implicated premises are not contained in the sentence uttered or in the hearer's knowledge base; thus, they are not within the hearer's cognitive environment. Implicated premises are grounded, first, in the presumption of relevance and, second, in that an utterance has been made.¹³⁸ The logi-

---

136. E.g., Ralph Broadbent, "The First and Second Letters to Timothy and the Letter to Titus," in *A Postcolonial Commentary on the New Testament Writings*, ed. Fernando F. Segovia and R. S. Sugirtharajah, BP 13 (New York: T&T Clark, 2007), 323–28, esp. 325.

137. Broadbent, "First and Second Letters," 327.

138. See Clark, *Relevance Theory*, 227–28, 238–39. Note correspondences to Hays's satisfaction criterion in *Echoes of Scripture*, 31.

cally intermediate steps required to infer the meaning of an utterance are numerous (e.g., speaker dialect, word sense). Relevance theorists cannot be exhaustive but delineate selected intermediate steps for illustrative and explanatory purposes. Gibbs underscores the broad scope of such premises: "These assumptions range from recognition of the mutual belief that both author and reader are reasonably competent speakers of the same language up to very specific mutual assumptions about particular linguistic and conceptual knowledge from which readers can draw inferences about what is meant."[139]

Audiences must combine contextual assumptions with explicatures to arrive at utterance meaning. They must bridge numerous gaps unaided by the semantics of the sentences uttered. Although hearers cannot consciously evaluate all possible implicated premises (e.g., whether a speaker uses English), certain premises will either be necessary or more strongly implicated. In natural language, hearers do not need to identify these premises; they just need to assume them. Modern interpreters of the Bible, however, must have various means for evaluating the strength of implications. The three key means are hearer intuition, satisfactory coherence, and cognitive effects. Brief explanations follow.

Hearer intuition. Interpretations and the premises that contribute to them should not violate hearer intuitions. When people who share a natural language have a conversation, their inferential intuitions are generally reliable. Of course, there are multiple kinds and degrees of separation when modern readers interpret Scripture, so great care, humility, and tentativeness are in order. Nevertheless, in a closing chapter on testing pragmatic theories, Clark quotes Recanati, describing the "Availability Hypothesis: In determining whether a pragmatically determined aspect of utterance meaning is part of what is said..., we should always try to preserve our pre-theoretical intuitions on the matter."[140] This yields a general rule: if an interpretation contradicts our intuitions about what an utterance *could* mean, then it is suspect, or we should at least have other strong grounds for accepting it. In this light, some miso-Cretan interpretations seem unsustainable because, for one thing, to "rebuke them" (ἔλεγχε αὐτούς, 1:13),

---

139. Gibbs, "Intentionalist Controversy," 190.
140. See Clark, *Relevance Theory*, 333; quoting from François Recanati, "The Pragmatics of What Is Said," *M&L* 4 (1989): 310. See also Furlong, "Relevance Theory," 143, who advises that a reader "is not necessarily an authority on his own interpretive process."

meaning either a specific ethnic group in the church or its host nation, sounds absurd.

Satisfactory coherence. An implicated premise should yield a more coherent reading, so an utterance's becoming more coherent on the basis of a given assumption is evidence for its acceptance. If we assume that the Cretan quotation is being spoken by someone of status within the group of troublemakers, then Paul's concern with it is immediately apparent. If we do not assume this, then it is difficult to make sense of its placement in Titus 1:12. It seems a non sequitur and has puzzled many readers.

Cognitive effects. One can compare the cognitive effects of interpretations that either include or exclude a given premise. In chapter 6, I discuss cognitive effects in more detail, but let us consider them briefly here. Relevance theorists delineate three basic kinds of cognitive effects: (1) strengthening an existing assumption, (2) contradicting an assumption, and (3) synthesizing new information from new and old assumptions that could not be derived from either alone.[141] If Paul used the Cretan quotation to expose and address bigotry in the church, then the cognitive effects could be enormous. That Paul intended this effect is plausible; and his original audience would arrive at it if they grasped the implicated premise that Titus 1:12 serves Paul's purpose of exposing the gospel-denying, mission-destroying bigotry of the troublemakers rather than of repeating an overworn trope about Cretan delinquency. Imagine, by analogy, the cognitive effects that extended to Corinthian Christians who had just realized that the apostle Paul knew of, objected to, and chastened the church regarding incest (1 Cor 5:1).

Let us examine the implicated premise that Paul's utterance in Titus 1:12 aims at serving the purposes of the Christian community in Crete by exposing the character and behavior of troublemakers on the bases of intuition, coherence, and effects. Intuition suggests that Paul's concern in the epistle is a Christian community that includes ethnic Cretans and Jews as well as the troublemakers among them. That is, these troublemakers are within the church. Barrett holds this premise explicitly: "The *objectors* are not outside the Church, but within it; the author would not have found it necessary to deal with the heathen in this way."[142] Unfortunately, Barrett does not carry the implications forward into his interpretation, conclud-

---

141. Abbreviated from Clark, *Relevance Theory*, 102; for fuller discussion, see 99–104.
142. Barrett, *Pastoral Epistles*, 130.

ing that Paul had a high view of the speaker of the quotation and a low view of Cretans generally, irrespective of their relation to the church.

One piece of evidence for accepting the implicated premise that Paul's use of the Cretan quotation was part of intra-community, as opposed to extra-community, paraenesis is the *target* of the rebuke—that is, *whom* it addresses. As throughout the New Testament, the paraenesis is aimed within the community, not at the wider world. Paul's instructions make sense on the basis of this implicated premise. He does not address the character and the sins of those outside the church, except as regards believers' responses to them. Paul instructs Titus in what to do with the troublemakers (1:13–14), not with Cretans in general. One specific instruction that is central to the context (1:10–16) and is repeated within the letter is Paul's sanction to "convict" or "rebuke" (ἐλέγχω, 1:9, 13; 2:15)[143] those who "contradict" (ἀντιλέγω, 1:9; see 2:9). This instruction corresponds closely to that of "admonishing a divisive person" (αἱρετικὸν ἄνθρωπον ... νουθεσίαν, 3:10). The reason Paul initially says that elders must be able to "rebuke" (ἐλέγχω, 1:9) those who contradict is "because" (γὰρ, 1:10) of the presence and activity of troublemakers. So, Titus's "rebuke" (ἔλεγχω, 1:13) is directed at those troublemakers and *not* at the Cretans in general. Barrett recognizes that the antagonists, "rather than heathen" in general, are a part of the Christian community; yet, because he does not carry this premise into his interpretation, he maintains that ethnic Cretans merit a rebuke on the basis of 1:13—a classic mismatch between the contextual assumptions of the original audience and a modern interpreter.[144]

In Titus, Paul enjoins different kinds of rebuke (ἐλέγχω in 1:9, 13; 2:15; ἐπιστομίζω in 1:11; νουθεσία in 3:10) but always toward the same kind of target. He refers to antagonists in general terms (e.g., 1:9; see 2:8), but the original recipients of the letter were likely able to correlate Paul's descriptions to recognized individuals or groups according to the character, behavior, and attributes mentioned. An implicated premise that original recipients of the letter likely inferred was that identifiable troublemakers causing known problems were behind Paul's discussion of such things. In other words, their cognitive quest for relevance would have automatically triggered correspondences between items in Paul's speech and items in their world. Modern readers automatically do this, too, but with an

---

143. See "ἐλέγχω," BDAG, 315.
144. See Barrett, *Pastoral Epistles*, 130.

unavoidable mismatch. For the historical author and recipient, the references would be to a more closely shared set of persons and circumstances.

The explicit *purpose* of the rebuke provides additional evidence for accepting the implicated premise that the Cretan quotation is commensurate with intracommunity paraenesis. Although interventions for this serious issue were to be conducted "sternly" (ἀποτόμως 1:13), they were generally restorative and aimed to bring the offending party into a "healthy" (ὑγιαίνω and cognates in 1:9, 13; 2:1–2, 8) relationship with both the truth and the congregation. Barrett judges correctly: "The word [ὑγιαίνω] suggests not only freedom from error, but also teaching which is able to impart healthiness, that is, salvation."[145] Huizenga also details the concept of ὑγιαίνω and cognates being causal and not merely stative, especially as used by ancient philosophers.[146] The goal was restoration for the sake of the entire community, including the troublemakers. The aim of Titus's rebuke can be called *restorative* in that the purpose (ἵνα, 1:13) is "well-being" (ὑγιαίνω, 1:13). The intention is that the presumptuous leaders will be themselves sound in the faith, just as was expected of elders (1:9), older men (2:2), and Titus himself (2:1, 8). Those within the church who stirred up strife and misled entire households were not to be utterly and finally shunned. They could be restored as long as they heeded Titus's stern rebuke (1:13; see 3:10).[147]

The purpose of Titus's rebuke is not to turn those dastardly Cretans toward the right way of thinking and living. Such a view does not appreciate the implicated premise that Paul is engaged in intracommunity paraenesis and also fails on the basis of intuition and coherence. It neglects to reckon with the real problems of going on a wholesale campaign to transform a population without any reference to the gospel. Assuming a miso-Cretan reading of the quotation leads Mounce to wonder whether "the description ... might also include non-Christian society in Crete."[148] This question is unnecessary because, in Titus, Paul expresses a doctrine of Christian transformation that is incompatible with a description of converts as intrinsically reprobate, regardless of ethnicity (2:11–15, 3:3–7). Titus is not being instructed to rebuke Cretans in general but a group

---

145. Barrett, *Pastoral Epistles*, 130.

146. See Huizenga, *1–2 Timothy, Titus*, 146–48.

147. Margaret Davies also makes this connection. See Davies, *The Pastoral Epistles*, NTG (Sheffield: Sheffield Academic, 1996), 92–93.

148. Mounce, *Pastoral Epistles*, 398.

quite distinct from that description—those who reinforced the doctrine that Cretans had an inferior status as gentile believers. The goal is restoration within the community of all constituents of the community.[149]

I challenge the common contextual assumption that Paul regarded this quotation as authoritative due to its supposed provenance from a Cretan poet—namely, Epimenides—and that therefore it was not censorious for Paul to use it.[150] Modern commentators normally take it as an implicated premise, but should remnants of this premise be added to a Bible translation for clarification to non-Cretans, so that they will have all of the relevant assumptions at their disposal needed to interpret properly (i.e., according to miso-Cretan assumptions)?[151] Or, as I argue, is this premise a convenient later interpretive conjecture?

Detailed Process Outline

Sperber and Wilson delineate the logical process of moving from linguistically encoded semantic representations through explicatures to implicatures. The process involves forming and testing hypotheses, and they present models that relevance theorists sometimes reproduce to explicate interpretive processes.[152] At the end of this section, I produce a detailed model that outlines hypotheses formed in the process of understanding Titus 1:12–14.[153] Even though the process is rapid, intuitive, and virtually simultaneous for natural language users, we logically delineate the following inferential tasks for interpretation: hearers enrich the semantic representation (logical form) by inference to derive explicatures; they then combine those explicatures with contextual assumptions, including implicated premises, to arrive at propositional interpretations (implicatures or implicated conclusions).

---

149. The Pastoral Epistles feature restorative justice. Paul imposed discipline to instruct, not condemn: "whom I have handed over to Satan in order that [ἵνα] they might be taught" (1 Tim 1:20). Barrett says of this passage, "This may mean that they were to be restored by some kind of disciplinary process" (*Pastoral Epistles*, 22).

150. *Pace* Guthrie, *Pastoral Epistles*, 200.

151. Kevin G. Smith answers positively ("Bible Translation and Relevance Theory," 232).

152. See Sperber and Wilson, "Pragmatics" (2007), 482. For variations developed from their conceptualizations, see Clark, *Relevance Theory*, 297–99.

153. For an example of such models, see Clark, *Relevance Theory*, 224 (example 24). I base my process on a schematic that Clark uses repeatedly.

In the three examples below (Titus 1:12a, 13a–b, 13c–14), I outline these tasks sequentially from top to bottom for transparency. I begin with the linguistically encoded semantic representation from a reference in Titus. I draw out reasonable explicatures in propositional form. Then I summarize some critical contextual assumptions. According to relevance theory, hearers infer meaning from the interaction of items in these middle two sections; so, last, I present relevant implicatures.[154] As noted, it is impossible to capture every intermediate logical step on the way to an interpretation, so the examples are illustrative. I go through this process with three example passages to demonstrate one transparent approach to the process of a relevance-guided biblical hermeneutic.

Titus 1:12a

Logical Forms: linguistically encoded semantic representation
εἶπέν τις ἐξ αὐτῶν ἴδιος αὐτῶν προφήτης
"Someone from among them—a prophet of theirs—said:"

Explicatures: the proposition expressed
An unnamed person who belongs to a previously mentioned group, who is considered a prophet within that group, has said the words that follow.

Contextual Assumptions: including implicated premises
- Paul does not claim ownership of the statement he is about to utter, but he emphatically refers to the speaker as one of *theirs*.
- The trustworthiness of the quotation depends on that of the group referred to as *them*.
- The group that Paul describes in the immediately prior context of several verses was composed of *troublemakers*.
- For a person to be considered a *prophet* among such a group is no compliment at all.
- The speaker therefore is not trustworthy, and Paul does not share or endorse his opinion.
- The context should illuminate Paul's actual reason for mentioning the quotation given that he does not sympathize with it.

---

154. See Clark, *Relevance Theory*, 228.

- In the context, Paul describes character, behavior, and motivations of the troublemakers in contrast to good leaders.
- Paul is now disclosing a statement that he has heard that these troublemakers entertain.

Implicatures: propositional interpretation
Paul is framing a quotation with which he does not agree that comes from a group of people whom he opposes in order to expose the character, behavior, and speech of troublemakers in Crete in stark contrast to the kinds of leaders the church needs. He is about to reveal objectionable words that have been spoken among this group.

Titus 1:13a–b

Logical Forms: linguistically encoded semantic representation
ἡ μαρτυρία αὕτη ἐστὶν ἀληθής. δι' ἣν αἰτίαν ἔλεγχε αὐτοὺς ἀποτόμως
"This testimony is true. On account of which reason, rebuke them severely."

Explicatures: the proposition expressed
Paul swears on the veracity of the evidence he has presented. The claim that Paul has just made is true; and, because the accusation that Paul has made is true, Paul orders Titus to convict the offending group severely.

Contextual Assumptions: including implicated premises
- Paul refers to what he has just said as a *testimony*.
- The last sentence Paul says is clearly framed as a quotation of someone else's words.
- That sentence is proverbial, not testimonial, and it is embedded in a hearsay clause.
- Paul's own voice is heard in the framing of the Cretan quotation, from which he distances himself as he mentions it.
- Paul is referring to his full claim that someone has uttered the Cretan quotation as his *testimony*.
- Context indicates that Paul describes the troublemakers' character and behavior, which includes speaking slurs and falsehoods.
- Paul refers to his claim as an *accusation* that calls for Titus to *convict* the group from which such speech emerges.

- As a mentor who takes the health of the church seriously, this suggests that Paul objects to the sort of behavior he describes (i.e., dredging up old, offensive stereotypes and using them to denigrate a missionary population).

Implicatures: propositional interpretation

Paul objects so severely to the kind of behavior that the troublemakers engage in, exemplified by the currency of the Cretan quotation among them, that he uses the sharp, courtroom language of "testimony," "accusation," and "conviction" to convey the seriousness of the problem that Titus is to address and to spur commensurate action.

Titus 1:13c–14

Logical Forms: linguistically encoded semantic representation

ἵνα ὑγιαίνωσιν ἐν τῇ πίστει, μὴ προσέχοντες Ἰουδαϊκοῖς μύθοις καὶ ἐντολαῖς ἀνθρώπων ἀποστρεφομένων τὴν ἀλήθειαν.

"in order that they might be sound in the faith, not attending to Jewish myths and commandments of people who turn from the truth"

Explicatures: the proposition expressed

- The envisioned result of the aforementioned corrective action toward the group that concerns Paul includes being healthy in faith, which contrasts with paying attention to Jewish myths and to the commandments of people who turn from the truth.

Contextual Assumptions: including implicated premises

- A result is a change in circumstances; therefore, the previous state of the relevant group probably contrasts in significant ways from that envisioned.
- Both behaviors that Paul thinks would end as a result of the rebuke explicitly involve religio-cultural interests of a Jewish nature ("Jewish myths," "commandments"), so the behaviors that Paul objects to and wants Titus to correct emerge from such interests.
- The Cretan quotation does not suggest that its targets (ethnic Cretans) have any problem with overadherence to "Jewish myths and commandments"—far from it; the very opposite seems true.

- The description of Cretans in the quotation corresponds to some Jewish sensibilities about the nature of gentiles in the world.
- This quotation, if accepted, provides ample grounds to promote the austerity and restraint that might come from adhering to aspects of Jewish religious culture, even if such would be contrary to Paul's gospel.
- Therefore, the rebuke is aimed at such people as might hold to and advance the contents of the quotation; namely, troublemakers, who have been described as having Jewish affinities.
- The rebuke Paul orders is meant to counteract the bigoted purveyance of the quotation and does not directly address problematic behaviors of ethnic Cretans.

Implicatures: propositional interpretation

By obeying Paul and correcting those who have kept the Cretan quotation current among them, Titus will nurture healthy faith among his ethnically diverse Christian community and curb the divisive influence of status-driven doctrines that frame fellow believers as aliens and inferiors on the basis of empty (ματαιο-, 1:10, 3:9) and misguided (φρεναπάτης, 1:10) comparisons of value.

The middle sections (Explicatures and Contextual Assumptions) of these examples could contain numerous intermediate explications and assumptions, so this is just a transparent example of my own process. Despite the force with which I present my argument, I hold it tentatively. The example of the process is more important than the particular points.

Interpretation involves a complex combination of implicit and explicit information, and the logical form provides only an *indication* of speaker meaning. Sperber and Wilson write, "The hearer's task is to use this indication, together with background knowledge, to construct an interpretation of the speaker's meaning, guided by expectations of relevance raised by the utterance itself."[155] Albeit generically, they describe Titus's task as he processed Paul's instructions. In summary form, the model above outlines this process.

Let me now summarize key explicatures and plausible contextual assumptions we have discerned: Paul is concerned with church lead-

---

155. Sperber and Wilson, "Pragmatics" (2007), 481.

ership throughout Titus 1:5–16. He has just described good leadership (1:5–9) and has moved on to address bad leadership (1:10–16). The quotative frame Paul uses (1:12a) follows directly from his succinct description of problematic leaders (1:10–11), yielding the contextual assumption that he is about to tell Titus something that one of those people had said. The several pronouns in this context (οὓς, οἵτινες, 1:11; αὐτῶν, 1:12 [twice]; αὐτούς, 1:13) have no clearer referent than the troublemakers. The "prophet" is a prophet in *their* eyes, not necessarily in Paul's. Ethno-religious tensions existed in the Cretan church (or at least the literary representation we have of such). These tensions involved the illicit elevation of persons with Jewish affinities over against ethnic Cretans. Paul's descriptions of such correspond to Titus's local, real-world evaluation and previous knowledge of circumstances in the Cretan church. An implicated conclusion emerges from these assumptions: it is natural to think that Titus expected Paul to address the issue of ethno-religious bigotry in the Cretan church in such a way as to shun it and chart a more peaceful way forward.

Having demonstrated how contextual assumptions critically influence interpretation and how they may be mismatched between ancient audiences and modern readers, let us now consider a crucial factor that affects what readers assume—salience. Interpretations sometimes differ because salience differs between ancient audiences and modern readers.

Mismatched Salience

Why has *Cretan* come to mean "reprobate" in Titus 1:12 if that is not what Paul originally intended? Here the role of the hearer is pivotal. The miso-Cretan interpretation probably has more salience for modern readers than for those in the original context, even when modern readers resist the most damaging implications of the interpretation.[156] The quotation is striking and brash; and readers who are removed from the original context, where Paul's critique of known acquaintances would have been mortifying, easily arrive at the miso-Cretan interpretation, because it requires less effort for

---

156. Tracy explains a critical component of Hans-Georg Gadamer's argument: "The fact is that no interpreter in any discipline approaches any text or any historical event without prejudgments formed by the history of the effects of the interpreter's culture" ("Interpretation [Hermeneutics]," 344). I have pointed out the effects of dubious attribution and the history of interpretation for many readers of Titus.

them.[157] Such salience can put faulty interpretations on the fast track for modern minds. Furlong makes an important point about why relevance theory needs to be applied to literary interpretation: "Communication creates a presumption of optimal relevance. However, ... there is no guarantee that an interpretation that satisfies the reader's expectation of relevance is in fact the intended interpretation."[158] The interpretation that rewards modern-day readers with cognitive effects may not be the interpretation that gave sufficient cognitive effects to ancient readers within Titus's community and vice versa.

One consequence of the rapidity of natural language comprehension is that whatever is salient for a given audience tends to dominate their attention and disproportionately influence interpretation.[159] According to Kevin Joel Apple, salience intensifies evaluations.[160] In contemporaneous conversations, this tendency makes communication and comprehension both effective and efficient. But it can lead to unfortunate misunderstandings for readers who are not from the original audience. Salience, by definition, draws attention to important features of an utterance, making real-time decisions easier for the hearer. We must make the humble and critical recognition that what is salient to modern-day readers may differ from what was salient to original audiences. We can explain this difference in part as a result of the human mind intuitively applying normal processes of contemporaneous comprehension to the reading of (non-contemporaneous) ancient literature. Gibbs discusses the nature—rapid

---

157. As Paula Fredriksen explains, "Ancient people make sense first of all to one another rather than to us." See Fredriksen, "What Does It Mean to See Paul 'within Judaism'?," *JBL* 141 (2022): 380.

158. Furlong, "Relevance Theory," 76. Here, a distinction between natural salience (e.g., a cut) and nonnatural salience (e.g., a word), by analogy to Grice's natural meaning (e.g., that of a found photograph) and nonnatural meaning (e.g., that of a deliberate report, perhaps of the same event), may be helpful. Because hearers search for the meaning of ostensive communication, they give signals of nonnatural salience more weight in interpretation, even if they pick up the wrong signals.

159. See Furlong, "Relevance Theory." Although when she talks about *salience* she is referring to discourse prominence (138–44), she does talk about *intentional* versus *accidental* salience, which corresponds more to my usage of this relatively fluid term in relevance theory. What corresponds more to my usage is the contrast she makes between a hearer's quest for *optimal* relevance, which she calls *exegesis*, and his alternative quest for *maximal* relevance, which she calls *eisegesis* (54–56).

160. Apple, "Role of Relevance," 33.

and unconscious—and some of the consequences of natural language comprehension:

> All language interpretation takes place in real-time ranging from the first milliseconds of processing to long-term reflective analysis. This temporal continuum may roughly be divided into moments corresponding to linguistic comprehension, recognition, interpretation and appreciation. Comprehension refers to the immediate moment-by-moment process of creating meanings for utterances. These moment-by-moment processes are mostly unconscious and involve the analysis of different linguistic information (e.g. phonology, lexical access, syntax) which, in combination with context and real-world knowledge, allows listeners/readers to figure out what an utterance means or what a speaker/author intends.[161]

Salience corresponds to a type of neural activation called semantic priming. Jobes describes this phenomenon as she correlates relevance theory and neuroscience: "Because neural activation is not a conscious process, one cannot avoid semantic priming that leads either to correct understanding or to misunderstanding in language comprehension."[162] To this effect, Jobes quotes Wilson and Sperber: "Our perceptual mechanisms tend automatically to pick out potentially relevant stimuli, our memory retrieval mechanisms tend automatically to activate potentially relevant assumptions, [and] our inferential mechanisms tend spontaneously to process them in the most productive way."[163]

According to Green, "The principle of relevance predicts that when contemporary readers intuitively interpret a biblical text by drawing upon salient information from their own cognitive environment, they may skew the meaning of the biblical author's utterance.... Therefore, RT [relevance theory] not only describes what occurs in successful, but also in unsuccessful communication."[164] Green also shares Harriet Hill's insight: "This observation also accounts for the way Scripture, written during another era in a different cultural context, is often misunder-

---

161. Gibbs, "Intentionalist Controversy," 196–97.
162. Jobes, "Relevance Theory and Translation," 784.
163. Wilson and Sperber, *Relevance Theory*, 611; quoted in Jobes, "Relevance Theory and Translation," 784.
164. Green, "Relevance Theory and Biblical Interpretation" (2013), 269.

stood, because contemporary readers often supply salient information from their own highly accessible context."[165]

The Cretan quotation appears in the midst of a conversation about the presumptuous and disruptive behavior of troublemakers and provides an example of speech that Paul finds objectionable, but the salience of the ethnic insult causes us to ignore Paul's agenda so that *he* becomes the bigot. Hámori Ágnes demonstrates how the salience of a statement can jar listeners into paying attention to a narrow segment of dialogue when they failed to follow the rest of the context.[166] Perhaps interpreters may relinquish long-held or favored interpretations when offered historically and linguistically plausible and relevant alternatives.

Mounce observes that most people bring questions of concern to themselves when they approach the Pastoral Epistles.[167] There is some validity to reading the Bible this way—for instance, as Scripture for the Christian community. It does not, however, promise to lead modern readers closer to historical meanings. Modern interests can unmoor contemporary readings from an author's intention, especially if readers do not recognize their interests as foreign to the original conversational context.[168] For twenty-first-century readers of the Pastoral Epistles, the most crucial questions seem to be authorship and views about women. Other interests, of course, exist, but several scholars identify these as at the forefront of modern concern.[169] This is why Dibelius and Conzelmann can read the Cretan quotation and conclude that its purpose was to preserve the ruse of Pauline authorship. Such a conclusion does not help interpreters understand the quotation in its context—historical or literary. Preoccupied with

---

165. From Hill's 2003 PhD dissertation, "Communicating Context" (44–51); quoted in Green, "Relevance Theory and Theological Interpretation," 84.
166. Many of her examples come from political speeches (see Ágnes, "Illocutionary Force"). I discuss illocutionary force in ch. 6.
167. See Mounce, *Pastoral Epistles*, x.
168. I am focusing on the hearer's role, taking speaker competence as a constant for the sake of the argument. According to their abilities and preferences, speakers say what they think is relevant enough for the effort of the hearer, but the calculus does not always work. See Wilson and Sperber, "Pragmatics and Time," 8–9. They list reasons that an utterance may be less relevant than expected. Among them: "The speaker may not have the information that the hearer would find most relevant; she may be unwilling to give it, or unable to think of it at the time.... Lack of time, lack of ability or stylistic preferences may prevent her expressing herself in the most economical way."
169. See, e.g., Mounce, *Pastoral Epistles*, x; Collins, "Pastorals."

signals about authorship, Paul's intentions become secondary.[170] Many readers begin with questions in their minds that likely did not concern Titus's earliest readers, and their sensibilities are triggered by a different set of sociocultural concerns than original audiences held. This is not to say that modern concerns or valuations of sociohistorical matters are inferior to ancient ones but simply to point out that difference can lead to divergence and thus dubious interpretations.

If salience, like a squirrel to a dog, can cause modern readers to attend to a different set of concerns from those that interested original audiences, we must understand two things to mitigate this tendency: What factors lead to salience, and what can modern readers do to recover what was salient for ancient audiences?

Means of Salience (Discourse Prominence)

Accessibility, intensity, and conspicuousness contribute to the salience of a concept. Within a hearer's cognitive environment, certain contextual implications are more accessible than others. Studies of Fodorian modularity of mind have shown that people recall words more quickly when they have heard either those words or related words recently.[171] These studies have been tested repeatedly with confirmatory results, showing that recency is a factor in making implied assumptions accessible.[172]

---

170. Authorship is often a settled question prior to interpreting Titus. See, e.g., Dibelius and Conzelmann, *Pastoral Epistles*, lviii; and comments in my conclusion under "Implications for Canonical Esteem."

171. Relations between words may be semantic, syntactic, grammatical, aural, or idiosyncratic.

172. Clark, along with Sperber, Wilson, and others, identifies relevance theory with commitments to Jerry Fodor's modularity-of-mind hypotheses. Clark writes, "Relevance theory is Chomskyan in that it assumes that the linguistic system is independent of other kinds of knowledge and Fodorian in that it assumes a modular architecture" (*Relevance Theory*, 347–49). Fodorian modularity basically posits that the mind, with general but as-yet largely unexplored correlations to the brain's neurological architecture, is made up of functional modules that accomplish discrete processes related to sound, patterns, memory, reason, etc. For explanation of the correspondence between relevance theory and Fodor's hypotheses as well as discussion of specific experiments, see Clark, *Relevance Theory*, 91–97; see also Ernst-August Gutt, "Relevance and Translation," in *In the Mind and across Minds: A Relevance-Theoretic Perspective on Communication and Translation*, ed. Agnieszka Piskorska,

Another important factor in making contextual assumptions accessible is the prominence of the contextual assumption. Relevance theorists tend to use *prominence* and *salience* interchangeably, but *prominence* can have the added sense of being conspicuous or unavoidable, whereas salience is usually a conceptual designation.

I adapt here an illustration from Clark about the salience of a child's cut finger in determining that a speaker's utterance has to do with the results of the injury. Because the mother and the son share the assumption that the boy is wailing on account of his cut finger, the boy is poised to interpret whatever she says as relevant to this inescapably salient concern. So, if she says, "You're not going to die," then he does not take this as an absolute prediction that he will defy the fate of all living things. Neither does he regard it simply as a *nonrelevant* prediction that he will not die in the near future; although this is closer to the truth, it is otherwise *nonrelevant*.[173] Rather, he understands, by way of implicature, that she is telling him that *he will not die in the near future as a result of this cut, so do not overreact!* By her talking about death in the face of a minor flesh wound, she is echoing his overreaction ironically and thereby critiquing it. When something is prominent enough in a hearer's mind, its salience triggers contextual assumptions of relevance that factor into interpretation, eclipsing other, less salient possibilities.[174]

A salient concept saves a hearer time and processing effort and increases relevance; thus, when a concept is salient for an individual hearer—even though it was not expected to be so by the speaker—the risk of misinterpretation increases. The miso-Cretan interpretation of Titus 1:12 leans on the salience of the quotation as an insult. It sticks out so much to modern readers that they lose track of the grammatical, topical, rhetorical, and social contexts in which it appears. In other words, its intensity as an insult increases its salience for modern audiences. The divergence between what

---

Marta Kisielewska-Krysiuk, and Ewa Wałaszewska (Newcastle: Cambridge Scholars, 2010), 296.

173. I use the term *nonrelevant* in place of *irrelevant* because I am speaking more technically about the failure of an interpretation to satisfy the requirements of relevance dictated by relevance theory.

174. For Clark's less dramatic version of the cut finger illustration, see *Relevance Theory*, 151–52. Clark explains how salience potentially decreases processing effort, thereby increasing relevance. For his discussion of factors that decrease processing effort, see his fourth chapter (123–55).

was salient for the original audience and what is salient for a modern audience can cause interpreters to succumb to a red herring. This explains why many accept readings that, upon closer examination, appear misguided.

For the epistle's original audience, Paul uttering the insult as a topic of conversation would not have been nearly as salient as his accusation that exposed the offenses of members within their community against their fellow believers and against his gospel. Removed from this singular ancient social context, modern readers accentuate the residual salience of the insult.

Interpreters accept various miso-Cretan readings because, apart from the conversational context, the quotation itself is salient as an expressive insult. Expressives can convey a speaker's attitude toward what she says unambiguously. They have a pragmatic effect beyond their semantic meaning; they can jar listeners by heightening emotional intensity. Yoon (also quoting Christopher Potts) explains, "The hallmark of expressives is that when uttered, they have 'an immediate and powerful impact on the context.'"[175] The Cretan quotation features negative expressives (e.g., θηρία, "beasts," with reference to humans, is expressive degradation), which explains why it leaps out to modern readers as salient, but to the original audience its salience may have been no greater than a hackneyed stereotype in comparison to the shaming effect of Paul bringing this closed-door speech to light and taking the troublemakers to court (as described above).

In addition to the difference in the modern reader's mind of what is salient, the modern tendency to read and interpret shorter, disconnected passages of Scripture contributes to distortions of meaning. We disallow the broader context to illuminate meaning, and we are gripped by a different set of interests.

All of the contextual assumptions delineated above in this chapter have implications for what was salient to the ancient readers. For instance, Paul's designation of the troublemakers as "abominable" (βδελυκτοί, 1:16) had strong religious overtones. It turned the tables on the Cretans' critics. Paul uses this word with a cluster of other religiously charged words to describe the true economy of "clean" (καθαρός, 1:15 [thrice]) and "defiled" (μιαίνω, 1:15 [twice]). This rearrangement of religious designations exposes the troublemakers' misalignment with Paul's gospel. For the Cretan church, conversant with Jewish religious culture as they apparently were, the connotations of this kind of speech would have been salient. According to the troublemakers, the

---

175. Yoon, "Semantic Constraint," 48.

Cretans were unfit for Christian community and good works, but Paul strikingly reorients the means of religious and social value on these presumptuous leaders—it was *they* who were unfit, defiled, unfaithful, abominable, and unworthy (1:15–16), but by virtue of their behavior, not their nature. With some understanding of *how* to identify what is salient, let us consider some possible ways to recover salience for original audiences.

Recovering Salience for Ancient Readers

How can we recover what was salient for original audiences? Hermeneutical approaches that are geared toward amplifying stifled voices could be an asset to relevance-guided biblical hermeneutics. Such approaches recognize that the comfortable bourgeois modern interpreter's own intuitions are prone to self-interest and disregard for the voices of the disenfranchised.[176] In the ears of modern interpreters, the voices of original authors and audiences are often the last to have a hearing. Two complementary hermeneutical approaches that may illuminate the ethnically charged text of Titus and interpretations of it are a hermeneutic of retrieval and a hermeneutic of suspicion. I call them approaches because they are not methods in a technical sense. A common criticism of these approaches is that they lack consistency and precision when applied by various scholars.[177] We may use them, nevertheless, to illuminate ancient sensibilities regarding what was salient and what was relevant.

---

176. Kune Biezeveld, along with the pioneers of "reading other-wise," Gerald O. West and Musa Dube, advises that it is crucial to "reckon with one's own subjectivity as a biblical scholar." See Biezeveld, "The Role of 'The Other' in the Reading of the Bible: Towards a New Roadmap for Bible Reading in the Western World," in *African and European Readers of the Bible in Dialogue: In Quest of a Shared Meaning*, ed. Hans de Wit and Gerald O. West, SRA 32 (Leiden: Brill, 2008), 134; Gerald O. West, ed., *Reading Other-Wise: Socially Engaged Biblical Scholars Reading with Their Local Communities*, SemeiaSt 62 (Atlanta: Society of Biblical Literature, 2007). Eric Anum encourages "the biblical interpreter to become aware of his or her own hidden preconceptions or antipathies." In the practice of reading other-wise, we do this through dialogue with a culturally different person. How else can we see our own blind spots? See Anum, "Collaborative and Interactive Hermeneutics in Africa: Giving Dialogical Privilege in Biblical Interpretation," in de Wit and West, *African and European Readers*, 149.

177. See the critique by Werner Kahl in "Growing Together: Challenges and Chances in the Encounter of Critical and Intuitive Interpreters of the Bible," in West, *Reading Other-Wise*, 147–58.

Hermeneutics of retrieval are typically approaches that endeavor to recover the voices of populations stifled by patriarchal or, using Elizabeth Schüssler Fiorenza's term, *kyriarchal* interpretations.[178] Such approaches do not need to have a prechosen "ideological position" by which to yield "advocacy readings."[179] In the case of Titus, I contend that Paul's, Titus's, and the Cretans' voices have been stifled by previous hegemonic interpretations.[180] In contrast to typical retrievals, I aim to recover these and so have traced some of the interpretive misdemeanors regarding Titus to assumptions introduced by the history of interpretation.

A relevance-guided biblical hermeneutic attempts readings that are sensitized to unheard voices and ambivalent to dominant interpretations. The aim must include "the retrieval of forgotten perspectives" (e.g., through theological dialogue).[181] When David Tracy, a pioneer in hermeneutics of retrieval, originally spoke about the forgotten perspective of the "classic" text as the "other" that we come to encounter, what he meant largely by *retrieval* was the retrieval of the meaning of texts, liberated from the distortions of convention, interpreted through dialogue with diverse persons. Later scholars developed from Tracy a foundation for retrieving more and more nuanced layers of forgotten (not presumed) meaning.[182]

I ask, in the interpretation of Titus, whose perspective is more forgotten than that of ancient Cretan Christians? Tracy urges that interpreters have a responsibility to recall "the subversive memories of individuals and whole peoples whose names we do not even know."[183] With a hermeneutic of retrieval, we may begin to grasp the perspective of members of Titus's

---

178. See Elizabeth Schüssler Fiorenza, "Feminist Studies in Religion and a Radical Democratic Ethos 1," *R&T* 2 (1995): 122–44. She seems to have first coined the term in *But She Said: Feminist Practices of Biblical Interpretation* (Boston: Beacon, 1992), 8–9, and passim.

179. See Richard S. Briggs, *The Virtuous Reader: Old Testament Narrative and Interpretive Virtue*, STI (Grand Rapids: Baker Academic, 2010), 37.

180. Lyon encourages interpreting "from an acknowledged perspective," as opposed to the "imperial, authoritarian, paternalistic, patriarchal" ("Sliding in All Directions," 114).

181. Michael Barnes, "Tracy in Dialogue: Mystical Retrieval and Prophetic Suspicion," *HeyJ* 34 (1993): 60.

182. See Barnes, "Tracy in Dialogue," 60–65; see also David W. Tracy, *Plurality and Ambiguity: Hermeneutics, Religion, Hope* (San Francisco: Harper & Row, 1987).

183. David W. Tracy, "The Dialogue of Jews and Christians: A Necessary Hope," *CTSR* 76 (1986): 23.

Cretan church. Such a hermeneutic is especially appropriate for ethnically charged texts, where a reader's prejudices may increase the likelihood of distortion. Interpretations of Titus 1:12 often betray ethnography under the influence of previous well-meaning but dubious and unsustainable explanations.

Klangwisan asserts that a relevance-theoretical approach to interpretation "presupposes a will to listen emphatically to the voice of the text. A hermeneutic of consent must be at work. The consenting reader agrees to follow the voice to its origins."[184] Guided by relevance theory, the close reading that I have demonstrated complements a hermeneutic of retrieval (plus consent), which may help readers gain new insights into the meaning of this text within its ancient environment.

I have applied a hermeneutic of suspicion to influential secondary literature on Titus that tends to favor the othering of the Cretans. Interpreters can apply a hermeneutic of suspicion to detect when one voice is silencing the other. This silencing happens tacitly when readers reiterate conventional interpretations of the text that are salient for modern readers rather than listening carefully and sympathetically to the text itself. Applying such an approach to interpretations of Titus exposes the influence of miso-Cretan readings. Given that the silencing of the other seems to be happening most clearly at the level of the secondary literature, I have critically examined several major interpretations of the Cretan quotation and its context. Applying a hermeneutic of suspicion to interpretations requires one to hold the conclusions of secondary literature and modern readers, including one's own, tentatively.[185]

Interpreters of Titus need to be questioned concerning their so readily reading othering speech into the text.[186] Consider how these interpretations would sound to those who are disparaged. Several commentators

---

184. Klangwisan, *Earthing the Cosmic Queen*, 21.

185. Tracy articulates the rationale for retrieval being crucial to interpretation, which is why Titus 1:12 must be examined in this way: "No classic text comes to us without the plural and ambiguous history of effects of its own production and all its former receptions.... Plurality seems an adequate word to suggest the extraordinary variety which any study of language shows.... Ambiguity may be too mild a word to describe the strange mixture of great good and frightening evil that our history reveals" ("Dialogue of Jews and Christians," 24).

186. See Biezeveld, "Role of 'The Other,'" 129. For her, listening to "the other" means "hearing of the voice from an unfamiliar context and an unfamiliar perspective which disturbs what is familiar."

want to come to the defense of those insulted from the onslaught of Paul's bigotry, but their assumptions and proclivities do not allow them to consider whether Paul might have been acting in the Cretans' defense in the first place.[187] I contend that this history of interpretation has been too satisfied with the scenario of a brazen and uncouth biblical pseudonym uttering offhand (yet somehow sophisticated and poetic) slurs to hear Paul coming to the defense of Cretan believers by exposing and rebuking bigotry. In the words of Tracy, "Retrieval now demands both critique and suspicion."[188]

A hermeneutic of retrieval can assist in hearing the lost voice of the Cretan missionary congregation. Much of the literature on hermeneutics of retrieval regards feminist and postcolonial interpretation, and other attempts to listen for unheard voices in the biblical text have been growing in currency among scholars for a generation. The aim of retrieval is not to obscure Scripture's plain meaning or to acquire justice for the oppressed in spite of or in contradiction to the message of the Bible. Rather, it attempts to interpret Scripture more equitably toward persons without the power to attain peace or justice on their own behalf. It is based on two assumptions: first, the concerns of the powerless are typically stifled in human enterprises at meaning making; and, second, peace and justice for the powerless is what is lacking in the absence of peace and justice globally.

Many scholars involved in hermeneutics of retrieval point to Tracy as a pioneer in constructive theology and in the recognition that interpretation requires dialogue.[189] The approach may be open to criticism, but it deserves a hearing as interpreters recognize that more conventional critical

---

187. E.g., Huizenga, *1–2 Timothy, Titus*, 139; Stegemann, "Anti-Semitic and Racist Prejudices," 288–91, and passim; Bassler, *1 Timothy*, 190. Twomey contends that Raymond Collins downplays the force of Paul's bigotry (Twomey, *Pastoral Epistles*, 192). Ronald Charles is certainly both vulgar and extreme when he writes that the apostle Paul is no less than "a rapist of the nations." Quoted in Don Garlington, review of *Paul and the Politics of Diaspora*, by Ronald Charles, *RBL*, September 4, 2016, https://www.sblcentral.org/home/bookDetails/10141.

188. Tracy, "Dialogue of Jews and Christians," 26.

189. With hope for the peacemaking implications of such efforts, Tracy writes, "Seething beneath that great grey western virtue of reasoned public discourse is, I believe, the desire really to hear one another once again and the passion to overhear together the still disclosive and emancipatory power of the Christian tradition." See David W. Tracy, "Modes of Theological Argument," *ThTo* 33 (1977): 395.

interpretations are not themselves without bias.[190] Using this approach, we may discern whether Paul's genuine voice has been stifled by our history of interpretation rather than by the "Paul" of Titus, and perhaps whether this Paul was actually speaking up on behalf of the Cretans.

To increase the likelihood of capturing what was salient for original audiences and to diminish the volume of what is prominent for modern readers, we must become aware of ourselves as eavesdroppers into an ancient conversation. When we have a strong reaction to a statement, we can examine why, rather than assume that we are responding as original audiences would have. What we find most scintillating may not be what interested them. This is where a hermeneutic of retrieval, when applied sympathetically, can aid our recovery and interpretation of voices stifled by a contentious, confusing, or convoluted history of interpretation. We hear scintillating vulgarity in Titus 1:12, whereas they heard loss of honor as troublemakers were exposed.

---

190. E.g., Jeremy Punt, *Postcolonial Biblical Interpretation: Reframing Paul*, STR 20 (Leiden: Brill, 2015), 48, 109, 150, and passim.

6
The Nonpropositional Dimensions of Communication

The end products of relevance-guided interpretation thus far have been more clearly articulated propositions. The final insight I cover involves the recognition that speech has purposes beyond even the most lucid propositions.

Paul did not merely inform. He affected his audience, correcting their assumptions, exposing their errors, confirming or challenging their honor claims. His speech had inherent emotional, social, and ethical implications for his audience. Whether they agreed with his propositions or not, they would be honored, humored, affirmed, mortified, or restored through his speech.

Whereas previous chapters featured detailed examinations of words and phrases, ideas and their relationships in Titus, this chapter concerns the broader paraenetical thrust of the book and of Paul's use of the Cretan quotation. When one reads Titus according to the insight that communication inherently involves nonpropositional dimensions, one recognizes that Paul aimed to affect readers not merely at the level of what they thought. As I address particulars of Titus below, I contend that Paul aimed *directly* at life change, and not solely by arguing from proposition to behavioral implication. For him, sound doctrine was not simply a motivation or rationale for good behavior. Sound doctrine entailed it.

Language does more than inform. It affects minds and changes circumstances.[1] The task of interpretation is not complete when the hearer has simply enriched the informational content and extracted a set of truth-conditional propositions from an utterance. Pragmatics examines the real-world implications of speech as well as how humans intuit meaning from incomplete representations. Carston indicates that Grice's "what

---

1. Referring to the concrete implications of interpretation, Briggs writes, "Text and action are bound together, we might say, in the reader" (*Virtuous Reader*, 211).

is said" is the truth-conditional content of an utterance, whereas *what is implicated* is its pragmatic content.[2] *Pragmatic* has two senses here. All along we have been referring to the processes of pragmatic inference to derive meaning from utterances; this meaning is usually rendered in an enriched propositional form. This chapter focuses on how speech has pragmatic effects on the world beyond the discourse. That is, how language—and Paul's language in Titus specifically—affects real-world circumstances, not just how concepts relate to one another.

The meaning of speech is not only shaped by its context(s), but it alters its context(s)—not only the discursive context but also the social, legal, religious, and economic. Because these are real-world effects, the output of pragmatic processes are not merely propositional, and utterances do not strictly or simply convey information. An interpreter who can expound the propositional meaning of an utterance is still not finished. Propositions may be descriptions of either real-world or imaginary circumstances, but they are "fictitious entities" in that they are ideological and conceptual.[3] To the extent that they can exist solely in the mind, whether an interpretation is correct or incorrect (i.e., corresponds to the speaker's intentions or not) is inconsequential. Such abstractions, as detailed as they may be, can proliferate, but hearers properly evaluate them when their real-world effects correlate to what they ascertain of the speaker's intent. Pragmatics attempts to account for the full force of utterances.

The Relevance of Speech-Act Theory

Speech-act theorists provide a useful grammar for the concepts necessary to discuss this full force.[4] Some biblical scholars have examined and

---

2. See Carston, "Truth-Conditional Semantics," 284–85.
3. See Austin, "Meaning of a Word," 60–61.
4. J. L. Austin, credited with the initial conception and exposition of speech-act theory, argued that there were two kinds of speech, descriptive and performative. Austin's most developed thoughts on the topic, based on his lectures at Oxford and then at Harvard, were first published in 1962, two years after his death in *How to Do Things with Words*. John R. Searle, one of Austin's students, became the chief heir and developer of speech-act theory. He is responsible for the more precise, albeit (some have argued) tangential, articulations of speech-act theory. Searle formulated an account of speech-act theory with an expanded, comprehensive typology. See, e.g., Searle, *Expression and Meaning: Studies in the Theory of Speech Acts* (Cambridge: Cambridge University Press, 1979); Searle, *Intentionality: An Essay in the Philosophy of*

described how speech-act theory contributes to understanding some of the nonpropositional dimensions of communication.[5] As relevance theorists endeavor to offer a comprehensive account of communication that incorporates these dimensions, they frequently rely on the grammar of speech-act theory, especially regarding the locutionary, illocutionary, and perlocutionary forces of speech. A brief definition of each and their interrelationship adequately illuminates the aspect of communication that concerns us here.[6]

Locution: the utterance of a sentence with determinate sense and reference[7]

Illocution: the making of a statement, offer, promise, and so on in uttering a sentence, by virtue of the conventional force associated with it

Perlocution: the bringing about of effects on the audience by means of uttering the sentence, such effects being special to the circumstances of utterance

A speaker saying virtually anything coherent achieves a locutionary act. Illocutionary acts are directly achieved by the conventional forces associated with an utterance; so, for instance, an utterance following the formal conventions of an oath made in an appropriate context achieves an oath

---

Mind (Cambridge: Cambridge University Press, 1983). Serban points out that Austin's observations and proposals influenced "the pragmatic turn" in linguistics ("Gricean Pragmatics and Text Linguistics," 96–97). That is, he was part of the wave of late twentieth-century linguistic thinking that shifted away from objective-representational and toward subjective-hermeneutical ways of analyzing language, that recognized the active dimensions of speech beyond information transfer, and that saw communication as negotiation, a cooperation between parties, and not essentially composed of "semantics and syntactics." Austin uses the phrase and critiques the reduction of language to "semantics and syntactics" ("Meaning of a Word," passim).

5. E.g., Briggs, *Words in Action*.
6. Definitions based on Levinson, *Pragmatics*, 236.
7. "Determinate sense and reference" is a crucial phrase, because Austin constructed his theory from the ground up regarding components of language (starting with noises, *phones*). Fuller forms of speech included a number of the more basic undeveloped components. So, e.g., every illocution must involve locution. For the building blocks of these simpler components, see Austin, *How to Do Things*, 83–108.

that is legally or socially binding.[8] The distinction between illocutionary and perlocutionary acts is important. Speech-act theory differentiates acts that are accomplished by virtue of speaking from acts that are accomplished in consequence of or in response to the utterance.

A speaker's comprehensive intention for an utterance includes appropriate perlocutionary results, but theorists generally draw the line between illocution and perlocution at *listener uptake*, which could involve direct agency or be nonvoluntary. Austin used an intuitive "hereby" test. Whatever the speaker may add *hereby* to is the illocutionary act accomplished by the agency of the speaker, whereas whatever intentions the speaker wishes her utterance to accomplish that sound absurd when adding *hereby* depend on a listener's uptake.[9] For example, observe the distinction between the two following sentences:

1A: I *hereby* argue my point.
1B: I *hereby* convince you of my point.

The distinction between the first and the second sentences is the presence or absence of uptake. Discussing the insights of speech-act theory for a "relevance-oriented pragmatics," Sperber and Wilson explain that speakers implicitly convey a "recommended" attitude toward their utterances. The hearer may not adopt this recommendation, but to understand the utterance properly is to understand this recommendation.[10]

As within any discipline, speech-act theorists exhibit some diversity, but Levinson argues that, from the perspective of pragmatics, the most plausible version makes two basic claims: First, "All utterances not only serve to express propositions but also perform actions."[11] Second, the "privileged level of action," that is, the action directly accomplished by speaking, "can be called the illocutionary act."[12] Perlocutionary acts are

---

8. Austin, *How to Do Things*, 109–20; see also Levinson, *Pragmatics*, 237.
9. Austin, *How to Do Things*, 53–66.
10. See Sperber and Wilson, "Pragmatics" (2007), 491–92.
11. Summarized in Levinson, *Pragmatics*, 243. Whereas Austin maintained a distinction (albeit imprecise) between performative and constative language uses, Searle's development of speech-act theory regarded virtually every use of language to have performative dimensions; therefore, Levinson's characterization of speech-act theory as regarding all speech to be performative depends on what some might argue is an overextension of Austin's original theory (see Briggs, *Words in Action*, 63–66).
12. Levinson, *Pragmatics*, 243.

essentially indirect, but they are nevertheless of prime importance to any speaker.[13] Some theorists see speech-act theory as already entailed in relevance theory (and hence superfluous), but relevance theorists continue to use the terms and concepts developed in speech-act theory because, for instance, thinking about speech in terms of locution, illocution, and perlocution offers clarity and explanatory power.[14]

What Speakers Do with Language

What speakers *do* with words is just as critical as the propositional content of their utterances. They may inform hearers, instruct hearers, ask hearers, pronounce true what only becomes true in the act of pronouncing (e.g., *I take thee to be my lawfully wedded husband*), and so forth. In chapter 4 under "The Speaker's Attitude," I discussed disassociation: when a speaker utters a sentence that she distances herself from and attributes it to someone else implicitly or explicitly. The effectiveness of this behavior depends on communication involving more than the conveyance of information through the meanings of words.[15] Focusing on only the semantic values or the propositional content that speech encodes neglects a major aspect of what language does. Language argues; language instructs; language

---

13. Although the conceptual vocabulary of speech-act theory is useful, Levinson explains that speech-act theory is subsumed under pragmatics (see *Pragmatics*, 226–83). Speech-act theory links form and function, so various speech acts correlate to grammatical and lexical features of language. Conventional forms yield conventional implicatures. Clark explains that the dependence of speech-act theory on conventional (i.e., formal) aspects of language prevents it from full acceptance within relevance theory, which conscientiously focuses on inferential aspects of language (*Relevance Theory*, 210). Sperber and Wilson acknowledge that speech-act theory tends to depend on encoded signals such as normal grammar (e.g., imperatives and interrogatives) and "illocutionary force indicators," and that such would be circumscribed within a fulsome "relevance-oriented pragmatic" theory ("Pragmatics" [2007], 491–93).

14. Agreeing with underlying concepts of speech-act theory and its basic tenet that words do things, Dan Sperber and Deirdre Wilson point out that one still needs a robust, relevance-oriented theory of pragmatic inference to "resolve illocutionary indeterminacies" and "in order to decide what speech act the speaker intended to perform." See Sperber and Wilson, "Pragmatics, Modularity and Mind-Reading," *M&L* 17 (2002): 4.

15. For a classic treatment of the question whether words carry meanings, see Austin, "Meaning of a Word."

influences, commands, and requests; language pronounces, comforts, and heals; language convicts and offends; language creates. So, communication is not strictly (if even primarily) about information transfer.

Echoing Austin's seminal title in a relevance-theoretical context, Huang cogently observes the truth that "Language is a way of doing things with words."[16] He pronounces the axiom in a context where he is highlighting an example of this claim—the specific concern of critical pragmatics, which illuminates the power of language to consolidate and abuse power, liberate or subvert.[17] Communication has done its job only when the environment has changed. Put symbolically, *context*^{1} + *utterance* = *context*^{2}.[18]

In order to grasp the nonpropositional dimensions of Titus 1:12 and its context, we must understand the economy of cognitive effects (immediately below), including the factors that affect processing effort and the potential of nonliteral utterances to offer substantial effects for their added processing cost. We must also understand the intrinsic paraenetic quality of ostensive inferential speech, including its social outcomes and the ethical and redemptive nature of sound doctrine in Titus.

The Economy of Cognitive Effects

Relevance theorists refer to the results of interpretation as cognitive effects (aka contextual effects).[19] These constitute small or large changes in the hearer's mind, the conversational context, and even the social context.[20] The cognitive effects, for instance, of the sentence "Will you marry me?" spoken in the proper circumstances and rightly interpreted are profound, whereas those of "You want fries with that?" are slightly less so.

An utterance conveys both the speaker's informative *and* communicative intent—not only what she is saying but why she is saying it. Utterances do not just answer the question, What are you telling me? but,

---

16. Huang, "Micro- and Macro-Pragmatics," 145.
17. Bonnycastle states, "Language does not merely represent the world, it also organizes the world" (*In Search of Authority*, 122). See also Furlong's comments on this issue in literary theory from Bonnycastle's earlier work in Furlong, "Relevance Theory," 12.
18. I do not recall the source of this pithy formulation.
19. See, e.g., Sperber and Wilson, "Pragmatics" (2007), 473.
20. Furlong discusses several socially affective examples ("Relevance Theory," 63–68).

crucially, Why are you telling me? The answer to this second question does not have to be separately articulated; it is implicit in the utterance and its situational context.

The following example highlights the insufficiency of semantics-based interpretation to capture the full thrust of utterances: we could render the propositional content of the sentence "Are you sure?" apart from the interrogative mode of the sentence, as [*addressee*] *is* (*state of being*) *sure* (i.e., confident). A semantically oriented interpretation might lead one to expect that the sentence is normally used either to reinforce (declarative force) or ascertain (interrogative force) confidence. It is quite normal, however, for speakers to use this sentence, even with the form and inflection of a question, in order to interject or express doubt (illocutions). Speakers often use it rhetorically to engender doubt (perlocution) when they intend to nudge listeners to reconsider their position.

Gibbs surveyed research into the influence of speaker intention on hearers, especially what aspects of utterance interpretation formed lasting memories. He writes, "Many studies have shown that people are very likely to remember a pragmatic implication of an utterance rather than the utterance itself or what it directly asserts or logically implies."[21] The cognitive effects that result from comprehension, according to relevance theory, are not identical to the propositional forms that derive from a process of interpretation. As Gibbs found, these nonpropositional effects constitute the real takeaway of communication.

Speaking in economic terms, Sperber and Wilson summarize as follows: "Cognitive efficiency, like any other kind of efficiency, is a matter of striking the best possible balance between costs and benefits."[22] They outline the following "relevance-theoretic comprehension procedure":

1. Follow a path of least effort in computing cognitive effects. In particular, test interpretive hypotheses (disambiguations, reference resolutions, implicatures, etc.) in order of accessibility.
2. Stop when your expectations of relevance are satisfied.[23]

---

21. Gibbs, "Intentionalist Controversy," 186.
22. Sperber and Wilson, "Pragmatics, Modularity and Mind-Reading," 13.
23. Sperber and Wilson, "Pragmatics, Modularity and Mind-Reading," 18. This is a standard description invoked by almost all relevance theorists. See, e.g., reiterations in Clark, *Relevance Theory*, 37, 69, 120; Gibbs and Tendahl, "Cognitive Effort and Effects," 381, 386; Gutt, "Relevance and Translation," 299–300.

Hearers are justified in stopping once their expectations of relevance have been met, because an expectation of relevance implicitly involves a presumption of economy. Francisco Yus argues that any of several contextual sources (e.g., encyclopedic knowledge, facial expression, conventional implicature) can contribute to this economy by making utterances easier to interpret, providing, as it were, subtle guiderails.[24] The normal result is successful natural language communication, but a mismatch between what seems relevant to a reader who is far removed from the initial context and what seemed relevant to the original audience can short-circuit this process.

Types of Cognitive Effects

As explained earlier, relevance theorists enumerate a standard set of three kinds of positive cognitive effects. They are as follows: (1) contextual implication, (2) strengthening an existing assumption, and (3) contradicting an existing assumption.[25] Carston and Uchida define the first category, contextual implication, as "a conclusion inferred on the basis of a set of premises consisting of both contextual assumptions and new assumptions derived from the incoming stimulus … and not derivable from either of these alone."[26] The other two are specific outcomes of the first. Biblical interpreters must keep in mind that, just as I have shown with cognitive environment and salience, mismatches between original audiences versus modern readers can exist with respect to cognitive effects.

Paul's audience might derive all three kinds of cognitive effects as a result of his mentioning the Cretan quotation in Titus 1:12. First, one contextual implication might be that Titus and other sanctioned leaders need to take stern action (1:9, 13) with respect to bullies in the church (see πλήκτης, "bully," 1:7). Second, Paul also might have spurred action by strengthening an existing assumption of Titus that insolent leaders were having too great a negative impact in the community ("upsetting whole houses," 1:11). Third, Paul mentioning the quotation plausibly contradicted existing assumptions, such as the following: that Paul did not know

---

24. Yus, "Relevance Theory," 155.
25. See, e.g., Clark, *Relevance Theory*, 364; Green, "Relevance Theory and Biblical Interpretation" (2013), 268.
26. Carston and Uchida, *Relevance Theory*, 296.

about the troublemakers' behaviors and influence;[27] that Paul was not concerned about this congregation's troubles; that these presumptuous leaders could get away with upsetting the church through their bigotry. Inasmuch as these statements represent assumptions that the audience plausibly held, they were mistaken.

Being corrected about a misconception has a strong cognitive effect, and here it had implications for their social context. These cognitive effects are positive in the sense that the hearer experiences a net gain in the accuracy of his perception of the world, although they may have negative emotions associated with them, since being in the wrong does not feel good. These cognitive effects coincide with propositional forms derived from Paul's utterances, but they reach beyond *informing* his audience to *affecting* his audience. I now address the question, What makes cognitive effects economical?[28]

Factors That Affect Processing Cost

According to Sperber and Wilson, relevance theory holds that hearers arrive at the best interpretation of an utterance by "process[ing] it in such a way as to maximize the number of its contextual implications and minimize the processing cost of deriving them."[29] Therefore, assuming that hearers will acquire the cognitive effects that correspond economically to their level of effort, a crucial question is, What factors make an utterance require more effort to process or less? Wilson and Sperber explain, "The processing effort required to understand an utterance depends on two main factors: the form in which it is presented (audibility, legibility, dialect, register, syntactic complexity and familiarity of constructions all affect processing effort); and the effort of memory and imagination needed to construct a suitable context."[30] Several specific considerations fall under their two broad headings that have special pertinence with reference to biblical interpretation. Let us examine more closely the following three

---

27. We know that news, even about very sensitive matters, could get back to the apostle Paul (e.g., 1 Cor 5:1).
28. Theorists often use economic terms to refer to the relationship between processing effort and cognitive effects (see, e.g., Sperber and Wilson, *Pragmatics: An Overview*, 31; Clark, *Relevance Theory*, 105, 110).
29. Sperber and Wilson, "Pragmatics" (1981), 283.
30. Wilson and Sperber, "Pragmatics and Time," 8–9.

narrower considerations: (1) the level of complexity of the utterance, (2) the size of the context, and (3) the accessibility of necessary concepts in the hearer's cognitive environment. By adjusting these factors, speakers can make utterances economical in various ways. By neglecting them, interpreters can misconstrue meaning.

Professional jargon allows communicators within a field to abbreviate utterances and relate packets of dense information to one another more economically as long as speakers and hearers are able to access basically the same concepts. Even if those packets of information stand in for complexly layered ideas, the relations between them can be simple. Jargon is essentially a collection of preset ways of referring to more complex concepts. With Titus and the other Pastoral Epistles, the recurrence and strategic importance of the expressions "piety," "prudence," and "sound doctrine" suggest that Paul and his colleagues had preset notions about the complexes they labeled as such.[31]

As pertains to reducing complexity and context size, Sperber and Wilson suggest, "One way of economizing on the costs of linguistic processing is to leave unstated any contextual assumptions that the hearer can be expected to supply for himself."[32] This serves to decrease the size and detail of an utterance, but it depends on the speaker accurately assessing the access her hearer will have to necessary contextual assumptions. According to Sperber and Wilson, two results obtain when a speaker requires her hearer to search a *broader* verbal context for clues as to her intention: first, the quantity of implications of possible meanings increases along with the resources for ascertaining speaker intent; and, second, processing costs increase, thus potentially decreasing relevance.[33]

Modern readers are less concerned about the second result, because they are not restricted to live processing. Awareness of the first result, however, leads us to examine Titus 1:12 on the basis of its book and corpus contexts, because they supply a number of clues as to possible meaning

---

31. Some works draw out the historical significance of this shorthand. E.g., Hoklotubbe, *Civilized Piety*; Angela Standhartinger, "Eusebeia in den Pastoralbriefen: Ein Beitrag zum Einfluss römischen Denkens auf das entstehende Christentum," *NovT* 48 (2006): 51–82; Thomas E. Bird, "Exegetical Notes: Self-Control (ΣΩΦΡΟΣΥΝΗ)," *CBQ* 2 (1940): 259–63. I consider "sound doctrine" below.

32. Sperber and Wilson, *Pragmatics: An Overview*, 31.

33. See Sperber and Wilson, "Pragmatics" (1981), 284. They label this broadening of the search for clues and implications of relevance *evocational processing*.

that are less clear from only the verse or paragraph. Furlong explains a key reason for interpreters, especially of literature, to examine the broader context of a work: "Varying interpretations can be partly evaluated by the degree to which they account for all the evidence of the work in a way that is plausible."[34] At the same time, we deliberately focus on the narrower paragraph and section contexts, increasing our likelihood of finding a relevant interpretation. Thus, we examine what clues from the broader book context of Titus help to interpret the Cretan quotation and what the narrower context of 1:5–16 suggests about Paul's intentions.

In natural language processing, especially in real-time conversational contexts, when the readily accessible interpretation of an utterance comes to mind, all other lines of interpretation are disallowed.[35] By way of analogy, Why are your lost keys always in the last place you look?[36] An easily accessible anaphoric interpretation of the pronouns in Titus 1:12 would render other, more labor-intensive interpretations unlikely. Yet under the influence of a history of interpretation that assumes Paul is quoting directly from a specific ancient poet, readers accept the reference as cataphoric, even though it would require more processing effort in a natural language context. Under these circumstances, modern readers have to exert more processing effort to counteract the assumptions of interpretive history.

Whatever makes a given utterance relevant for an audience (i.e., whatever reading yields satisfactory cognitive effects) will cause the audience to stop seeking an alternative interpretation. The closer the hearer is to the context of the speaker, the more likely it is that he will come up with her intended meaning. The original audience that Paul had in mind probably grasped something close to his intended meaning.[37] Modern interpreters, on the other hand, distanced by many intervening years, may have a difficult time coming up with an interpretation that was readily accessible to Paul's initial audience.[38] The economy of cognitive effects is thus affected by the convenience of an interpretation, which can be affected not only by natural linguistic factors such as conceptual salience but also by anachronistic givens and interpretive preunderstandings.

---

34. See Furlong, "Relevance Theory," 37.
35. See Wilson and Sperber, "Pragmatics and Time," 14–15.
36. Because that is the first place you find them.
37. The fact that the church preserved this ancient text is evidence that they valued the message as they understood it or considered the message worth preserving.
38. See Wilson and Sperber, "Pragmatics and Time," 15–17.

Now let us consider how nonliteral language seems to defy the economy of cognitive effects.

The Potency of Nonliteral Utterances

Even though nonliteral uses of language can be more complex than more literal uses in that they require second-order processing, they can also produce greater cognitive effects, which makes them potentially quite economical.[39] Theorists generally do not consider literal and figurative uses of language to occupy two exclusive categories; rather, they occupy a spectrum. The implicatures of a sentence uttered figuratively are a subset of the sentence's total possible implicatures; so, as soon as the hearer knows that the speaker is using figurative language, he begins to access a shorter list of possible meanings. Hearers are typically able to make these determinations in real time, diminishing the otherwise heavier processing cost of metaphorical speech and making figurative language quite potent, as long as the speaker makes a reasonably accurate judgment about the hearer's uptake capacity.[40]

Grice argued that the assumption of cooperation and the maxim of relevance helped listeners to track with speaker meaning, even when speakers failed to observe (i.e., flouted) other maxims (e.g., quality, quantity, and manner). Flouting the maxims, as he referred to it, was a means of increasing what relevance theorists would later call cognitive effects for listeners.[41] Relevance theorists agree on the pivotal importance of relevance for ensuring comprehension. Nevertheless, the scheme he proposed required a two-step process in the hearer's mind—first, the hearer detects a violation of conversational maxims, then he decodes the meaning through a secondary process. The hearer rejects a literal interpretation before arriv-

---

39. For explanation, see Yus, "Relevance Theory," esp. 155–59.
40. See Clark, *Relevance Theory*, 253–79.
41. See, especially, Grice's delineation of the "Group C" class of seemingly uncooperative utterances in "Logic and Conversation," 52–56. He describes various kinds of nonliteral speech under the rubric of "flouting the maxims." Such speech intrinsically involves the hearer in extra effort to process, because the speaker has not (at the surface level) behaved cooperatively. Grice explains that the hearer nevertheless assumes cooperation and proceeds to interpret *as though* the speaker has acted cooperatively. Although Grice does not speak in terms of "cognitive effects," he notes that such speech is more "striking" or superlative in some way, which correlates to relevance theory's "cognitive effects."

ing at and accepting a nonliteral one.[42] Grice's delineation of the process may be logically helpful, but Huang argues that it is probably too complex to explain what happens in the process of natural language comprehension. The problem, as Huang identifies it, was that Grice assumed that literalism was the default mode of speech.[43]

Although theorists now generally think that his two-step comprehension model inadequately reflects the online processing of natural language, his intuitions about the increased effort that figurative speech requires were not completely wrong.[44] Adults are able to process metaphor and irony more successfully than children, suggesting that it is a skill humans learn through effort. The payoff of cognitive effects motivates them.[45] Studies of language acquisition suggest that nonliteral speech requires more processing effort but not because it is a two-step process. It is still quick, but adult speakers are not as easily derailed from online processing by words coming from disparate semantic domains. Gibbs, referencing empirical research on the comprehension of nonliteral and ironic language use, argues that evidence points to humans having a streamlined process for comprehending utterances that convey meaning beyond their linguistically encoded content: "There is a tremendous amount of research in psycholinguistics to show that readers can determine speakers' figurative meanings without having to first analyse the literal or sentence meanings of metaphors, sarcasm, indirect speech acts, and so on.... The speed with which readers are able to interpret figurative expressions suggests that the recovery of speakers' intentions occurs very early in the course of comprehension."[46] Accordingly, audiences can leap to the short list of relevant figurative meanings quite efficiently.

So, although figurative speech may require more processing effort, literal speech does not always offer the more economical means of communicating. There are two reasons: First, literal language can require details

---

42. See Levinson, *Pragmatics*, 109–10.
43. See Huang, "Micro- and Macro-Pragmatics."
44. For an explanation of "online comprehension," see Gibbs and Tendahl, "Cognitive Effort and Effects," 385–86. They argue that the increased cognitive effects of figurative language make additional effort worthwhile. They do not claim that figurative speech *must* require more effort.
45. See consistent, tentative findings under "Relevance Theory Responses to the Experimental Evidence" in Gibbs and Tendahl, "Cognitive Effort and Effects," 382–85.
46. Gibbs, "Intentionalist Controversy," 191.

that are unnecessary and clumsy if a metaphor can replace an entire concept, making the leap to second-order thinking less burdensome. Second, figurative language—irony or metaphor, for instance—can have profound cognitive effects, making its additional processing effort worthwhile. Some of these effects correlate to more visceral, emotional, social, or psychosocial experiences for the listener. Goodwin explains that nonliteral speech "is both much shorter than a literal statement ... and much richer."[47]

Literary analysis may exhibit a two-step process, especially with discourse in a nonoriginal setting, but natural language communicators process too rapidly to assume that this is the best explanation of how they comprehend nonliteral uses. Perhaps the key difference between live speech and writing, when both are viewed as ostensive inferential communication, seems almost too obvious—the amount of time one has for interpretation. Aside from this difference, which permits eyes to return where ears cannot, Furlong explains that "many of the problems besetting theories of critical practice are the result of assuming that spontaneous utterance comprehension is somehow unrelated to the interpretation of literary works."[48] Readers form enduring opinions as quickly as hearers. A hearer knows almost immediately whether a speaker is speaking nonliterally, the moment he hears the word *ox* or *ass* in the sentences "You're an ox" or "You're an ass." Normally, it is virtually a one-step process. The same is true when Paul's original listeners heard him refer to one of the troublemakers as a *prophet* (Titus 1:12) or to his own report as a *testimony* (1:13) or to the doctrines of the troublemakers as *commandments* (1:14). In analyzing an ancient text, we slow the process of comprehension down, parse it out logically, and note in a far more conscious way than natural language hearers do where a word or concept falls on a scale of relative literalism.

Paul's uses of *prophet*, *testimony*, and *commandment* (among other words) were figurative but not as a departure from some presumed literal norm. Speakers use language literally, figuratively, or loosely as needed in order to produce the most appropriate results (i.e., the greatest cognitive effects) that they can in their audiences. The communicative principle of relevance refers to "a presumption of ... optimal relevance." Inferences based on this presumption depend on the communicator's preferences

---

47. Goodwin, *Translating the English Bible*, 51.
48. Furlong, "Relevance Theory," 52–53.

and abilities.[49] Paul's metaphorical language may have required additional processing effort, but it was worthwhile because of the effects listeners derived, including mortification, humor, intimacy, and trust.

Consider how these figurative uses of language add intensity in Titus, how they build on the pathos of the preceding discourse, and how they lead to the vigorous injunction that follows. Paul speaks figuratively, but he anchors *prophet*, *testimony*, and *commandments* to shared functions and values within the community he addresses (i.e., their religious and social values).[50] Saarinen Risto explains, "The author presupposes that the [Pastoral] epistles will be read and circulated in the churches."[51] Explicitly, Paul first encourages Titus and affirms that he is near and dear to him socially within the community by expressing great affection ("Titus, [my] true child," Τίτῳ γνησίῳ τέκνῳ, 1:4), by reaffirming his sanction ("I left you in Crete," ἀπέλιπόν σε ἐν Κρήτῃ, 1:5), and later by backing his authority ("no one ought to disregard you" or "don't let anyone disregard you," μηδείς σου περιφρονείτω, 2:15), for example. But he also does so implicitly when he *trusts* Titus to interpret figurative language, provide ellipsed material, and respond appropriately to signals of approval and disapproval.

Speakers may use nonliteral language for a number of reasons, but the speaker-intended effect is the crucial factor for relevance theory. Relevance theorists contend that hearers may note choices of style and semantics but that they unconsciously evaluate them on the basis of relevance, that is, cognitive effects for processing cost. Counterintuitively, literal utterances

---

49. Clark expands "the presumption of optimal relevance" with two basic claims: "The ostensive stimulus is relevant enough for it to be worth the addressee's effort to process it"; and "The ostensive stimulus is the most relevant one compatible with the communicator's abilities and preferences" (*Relevance Theory*, 108).

50. Paul addressed Titus to an individual (1:4), but he greets a plural audience (3:15)—a community. Some commentators express angst and bewilderment at a plural greeting closing a singularly addressed letter. They perceive inconsistency or the pseudonym's blunder. But an elementary fact about NT letters is that they were community documents. The author expected semipublic reading for increased accountability and ethos. See, e.g., Marshall, *Critical and Exegetical Commentary*, 347–49; Mounce, *Pastoral Epistles*, 459; Christopher A. Porter, "Chapter 16: 1 Timothy," in Tucker and Kuecker, *T&T Clark Social Identity Commentary*, 445–46. His comments pertain to all of the Pastoral Epistles.

51. Risto Saarinen, *The Pastoral Epistles with Philemon and Jude*, BrazosTCB (Grand Rapids: Brazos, 2008), 23.

sometimes take *more* processing effort to interpret than metaphorical utterances. Song explains this economic reality as he describes the process for interpreting metonymous utterances as well as the reasons why speakers use them.[52] Literal representations can necessarily involve complexity that figures of speech can capture simply. A company with a number of passenger vehicles for official use on overland roads may refer to this collection as a *fleet*. The literal meaning barely occurs to users. Such metaphorical language achieves cognitive effects efficiently mainly by saving processing effort, but metaphor and metonymy can also amplify cognitive effects. In context, one word conveys a complex of ideas—inappropriate and unauthorized honor claims, for example. Paul had no previously lexicalized version of what he meant by *prophet*, so it has an ad hoc meaning that he trusted Titus to comprehend.

Metaphor may enhance the style and pathetic effect of writing aside from altering the propositional content, but such enhancements are not merely aesthetic. Relevance theorists consider them functional—that is, pragmatic.[53] Figurative language creates shared knowledge, insider ideas, which have the effect of developing social bonds. As Yus puts it, "No doubt, the use of irony produces an effect of enhanced mutuality between interlocutors."[54] Song writes, "Creation of this kind of affective mutuality outweighs the extra processing effort incurred by the use of metonymy."[55] The less literal and the more echoic a speaker's language is, the more the interpretation of those utterances achieves ethos with the hearer, trust and rapport.[56]

Titus was an open letter to a community (3:15) and not simply to the individual who was named (1:4). By building bonds with Titus publicly through his use of nonliteral language, Paul was endowing Titus with authority and demonstrating his trust and intimacy. Let us now consider related social and behavioral outcomes.

---

52. See Song, "Metaphor and Metonymy," 100–103.
53. See Song, "Metaphor and Metonymy," 95–97.
54. Yus, "Relevance Theory," 158. He then quotes Gibbs and Colston: "Irony serves as a mark of intimacy between speakers and listeners, and brings them even closer together."
55. Song, "Metaphor and Metonymy," 101.
56. See Jobes, "Relevance Theory and Translation," 790. Relationships with ample shared knowledge and assumptions are contexts for increased frequency of irony (see Yus, "Relevance Theory," 151, 155).

Social and Behavioral Outcomes

Grice proposed what relevance theorists now take for granted—that the act of speaking involves the communication of intention. This is distinct from the linguistically encoded meaning of the words and carries with it the implication that the speaker wants the hearer to think or do something in response to her intention. As John Searle explains, "The speaker intends to produce a certain illocutionary effect in the hearer, and he intends to produce this effect by getting the hearer to recognize his intention to produce it."[57] So, Levinson writes, "Communication is a complex kind of intention that is achieved or satisfied just by being recognized."[58] This recognition occurs in the hearer, of course.

Gibbs notes the currency within linguistics of the idea that "communication exploits the human ability to attribute intentions to each other."[59] Most theorists assert the centrality of intention, and this intention includes a change of some kind in the hearer. Of course, the hearer may not *act* according to the speaker's wishes, but expectations of hearer uptake (perlocution) are intrinsic to communication even if speakers cannot control or predict the response. This is a specific claim under the general principle that *context*^{1} + *utterance* = *context*^{2}.

The speaker expects the hearer to participate (as *patient* and *agent*) in the creation of *context*^{2}. I use the term *paraenetical* to label this aspect of language that expects commensurate response from listeners. A commensurate response, in relevance-theoretical terms, means effects involving the hearer that correspond (positively or negatively) with speaker intentions.[60] It is a step beyond what the speech itself accomplishes, but it is an outcome that the speaker intends from her utterance. In favor of theological and historical interests, I think that the paraenetical nature of language

---

57. John R. Searle, "Indirect Speech Acts," in *Syntax and Semantics*, vol. 3 of *Speech Acts*, ed. Peter Cole and Jerry L. Morgan, SS 3 (New York: Academic Press, 1975), 59.
58. Levinson, *Pragmatics*, 16.
59. Gibbs, "Intentionalist Controversy," 182.
60. In the development of speech-act theory, many have attempted to delimit a range or to enumerate the kinds of possible acts. For relevance theory, the number could be infinite or minute as long as they correspond to speaker intention. Standard introductions to speech-act theory explain this delimiting issue (see, e.g., Levinson, *Pragmatics*, 226–83). For comments on the nonpropositional dimensions of speech in terms of relevance theory, see Smith's argument in "Bible Translation and Relevance Theory," 93–97.

is underappreciated in many examples of biblical interpretation, particularly of the New Testament epistles. So, let us now consider the essential paraenesis of natural language.

The Essential Paraenesis of Natural Language

"Clean your room!" conveys, informationally, the proposition, *The speaker is ordering the listener to clean the room that pertains to the listener*, but this is not without remainder. If I speak that sentence to my son, the enriched meaning, informationally, may come out as, *Barney's father is ordering* [and, by implication, desires and expects] *Barney to clean Barney's room*. Notice that only two of the words from the propositional form (*clean* and *room*) are represented explicitly in the original form, and that the verb *clean* (without morphological alteration) changes inflection from second-person imperative to (complementary) infinitive, removing the conventional *directive* force.[61] The sentence does not supply the additional information required to derive this propositional form. One must hear the utterance in context and enrich it by attention to pronominal and social deixis, cognitive environment, and so forth—ideas I have already discussed in detail. Nevertheless, for one to know this information, as enriched and completely expressive as it may seem, does not *in any degree* fulfill the ostensive purpose of the utterance, which can only be fulfilled by a certain room, pertaining to my son, being cleaned by the person so instructed. If speaker intention is truly central to comprehension, as relevance theory contends, then interpretation is incomplete at the stage of deriving mere propositional meaning. Such is the nature of language, with significant implications for interpreting Scripture.

Clearly, not all speech is command, therefore not all commensurate response is obedience or disobedience. Imperative language provides a perspicuous example of the claim that speakers intend hearers to participate in the creation of *context*² as patients and agents. For other moods, the truth may be less obvious, but speakers expect even the most seemingly innocuous utterance couched in milquetoast declarative grammar to have

---

61. Briggs provides a nuanced discussion of the relationship between formal features of language (e.g., vocabulary) and illocutionary force (*Words in Action*, 98–102). In my example, *order* carries the conventional force of a directive, but the proposition includes it on the basis of pragmatic inference. Once it is placed into this declarative form, it no longer has the same effect for the hearer.

some real-world effect. Although accounting for the felicity conditions of every kind of speech would be an exhaustive prospect for speech-act theorists, relevance theory does not require it, because ostensive intention (from the speaker's perspective) and inferential recognition (from the hearer's perspective) are sufficient for interpretation. A hearer may comprehend the meaning of an utterance without taking the action the speaker wishes (i.e., a volitional step beyond perlocution).

With command language, the hearer does not need to obey the speaker in order to understand her. But he will not understand her without attributing the appropriate intentions to her and considering the implications of such. Comprehending requires him to be conversationally cooperative; obeying or disobeying requires an independent volitional response, which may necessarily be subsequent to the satisfactory comprehension of her utterance but which nevertheless is conceptually latent in it. As long as the hearer cooperates with the speaker by attributing appropriate intentions and deriving appropriate implicatures, his commensurate response is not restricted to a particular predetermined or conventional action— obedience, disobedience, or something else are commensurate responses. What is critical to grasp is that the hearer operates in a different world than he did prior to the utterance. Interpretation that merely results in more elegant or elaborate, simplified or sophisticated theoretical constructs— interpretation that does not recognize that authors are making claims on readers, expecting them to feel, think, choose, and act—is not true to the nature of communication.

Commentators on Titus recognize its ethical thrust, but they often see it as a factor of Paul's twofold concern with belief and behavior, orthodoxy and orthopraxy, gift and task, indicative and imperative (or however the particular scholar labels these categories). Mounce, for instance, outlines a development from faith to knowledge to action in his comments on Titus 1:1.[62] In Paul's usage, however, the term πίστιν ("faith," 1:1) may entail just as much moral action as the term εὐσέβιαν ("piety," 1:1). Barrett differentiates consistently between *doctrine*, which for him more narrowly designates theological tenets, and *behavior*, especially when discussing heresy in the Pastorals.[63] For some, Paul seems to display a higher proportion of paraenesis in the Pastoral Epistles than in the undisputed

---

62. See Mounce, *Pastoral Epistles*, 379.
63. See Barrett, *Pastoral Epistles*, passim. See also my comments under "Division or Heresy" in ch. 5.

works of the apostle. This distinction may be the case if we assume that Paul's doctrine is based on a dichotomy and relation between theological proposition and ethical consequence rather than a shared categorization, combination, or even identification. Mounce, however, also notes that "in the [Pastoral Epistles], ... right belief and right behavior are inseparable."[64] Yet for Mounce, the dichotomy is fused but preserved.

One could argue whether this dichotomy is a mistaken understanding of Paul, but what concerns me is whether this is even an adequate understanding of language. I reassert, language *is* paraenetical, at least to some degree. Speakers not only inform but suggest preferred attitudes and actions toward their speech that hearers may accept or reject but can scarcely ignore. What seems more appropriate to the Pastoral Epistles, and to Titus in particular, is to understand doctrine as encompassing all that is taught, thus incorporating truth in life, comprising faith and practice. Doctrine (or heresy, for that matter) may include propositional content, but it is not merely propositional. Let us now develop this claim with reference to a couple of specific nonpropositional uses of language in Titus—first, the relational outcomes of Paul's speech and, second, what he means by the prominent concept of *sound doctrine*.

Relational Outcomes

Recognizing the nonpropositional dimensions of communication illuminates Paul's intentions within Titus's community. Song identifies some of the relational effects of the use of metaphor.[65] Some contextual implications, some strengthening of existing assumptions, and other cognitive effects involve camaraderie, trust, a sense of privileged insight, a sense that the speaker is vulnerable and trusting, drawing listeners into an experience of greater intimacy, and so forth. Some of these effects are based on weak implicatures, but they are rhetorically powerful.[66]

---

64. Mounce, *Pastoral Epistles*, 379.
65. Song, "Metaphor and Metonymy," 94.
66. With respect to framing quotations, Kujanpää quotes two theorists to this effect: "Clark and Gerrig aptly explain: 'When speakers demonstrate only a snippet of an event, they tacitly assume that their addressees share the right background to interpret it in the same way they do. In essence, they are asserting, "I am demonstrating something we both can interpret correctly," *and that implies solidarity*'" ("From Eloquence," 191, emphasis added).

For a speaker to use ambiguity is implicitly trusting, because she is relying on her hearer to make meaning out of her utterance. Irony, for instance, is a complex use of language, but the payoff, if uptake is achieved, makes it worthwhile. Suppose something goes horribly wrong and a speaker says, "Nice." By *mentioning* a single word, she conveys a number of implications with tremendous cognitive effects for a hearer who is able to interpret properly. The rewards of successful utterance interpretation involve a valuable social connection with the speaker—sympathy, insight, even trust.

Grice famously illustrated the difference between *natural* and *nonnatural* meaning in a manner that I adapt here:[67] Imagine the difference between *showing* Mrs. Smith a photograph of Mr. Smith behaving inappropriately with Ms. Scarlett and *drawing* Mrs. Smith a picture of the same scene. The photograph has a natural meaning such that, even if Mrs. Smith did not grasp your intention in presenting it to her—in fact, even if Mrs. Smith accidentally found it—it would carry the same meaning (namely, *my husband is having an affair*). In the case of drawing the same scene, Mrs. Smith would only ascertain that meaning if she grasped your intention. In the same way, merely knowing that the Cretan quotation circulated among troublemakers within the congregation might not have prompted Titus to act. Paul portrayed the situation and implicated his own attitude toward it (1:12–13). Once Titus (and the audience of Titus) grasped this implication, he had a basis for appropriate action, and Paul's consequential instructions could appear wise, fair, stern, and reasonable, even kind, in that he did not treat them as enemies to be opposed as much as household members to be restored.

Relevance theorists identify the strongest, or most relevant, cognitive effect that an utterance can have to be a contextual implication where new information follows from the combination of new and existing assumptions but would not follow from either alone.[68] Suppose that the church in Crete, including Titus, was aware that presumptuous leaders were disparaging Cretans; they did not know, however, that Paul was aware of this behavior; further, they did not know how repugnant it was to Paul or whether Paul would be so bold as to act on the knowledge in such a way as to affect them significantly (e.g., by way of shame or other social

---

67. Described in Serban, "Gricean Pragmatics and Text Linguistics," 97.
68. Clark, *Relevance Theory*, 102.

consequence). Imagine the cognitive effect of discovering that Paul *has* heard, *did* adamantly disapprove it, and *was* bold enough to address it by sanctioning Titus to rebuke it. This would lead to tremendous cognitive effects, and Paul expressed his hope and expectation that it would also lead to repentance and restoration (1:13).

The near literary context suggests that Paul was focusing on issues of leadership malpractice (Titus 1:5–16), and the broader book context suggests that the Cretan church was disturbed by brokers of inappropriate ethno-religious valuation (see, e.g., 1:10–16; 2:7–8, 15; 3:9–11). Therefore, an interpretation achieves optimal relevance by understanding that Paul uses the quotation to address religious leadership malpractice (immediate context) involving problematic ethno-religious valuations (book context). If both the narrow and the broad literary conversational contexts do not suggest a persistent concern with laziness, gluttony, and viciousness, then the conclusion that the quotation was Paul's bald assessment of the Cretans seems an unjustified departure from context. It does not meet the criterion of relevance as efficiently as the conclusion that Paul is speaking *against* ethno-religious valuations and leadership malpractices that are contrary to "healthy doctrine" rather than *as* an evaluator of persons on the basis of ethno-religious affiliations contrary to his gospel to the gentiles.

It is clear from 2 Cor 10:10 and its surrounding context (10:1–18) that, as a key leader in the church, Paul was able to receive news from distant congregations and represent critical portions in reported speech (see 1 Cor 1:11; 5:1). He included as much detail as was needed to ensure his original hearers were able to identify the nature of the speech and the speakers and to draw inferences that had appropriate effects. Particularly, when reporting the speech of opponents, the cognitive effects that came from recognizing that the speaker was publicly exposing objectionable actions and attitudes would have been impressive.[69] This is just what Paul

---

69. Scholars have recognized the apostle Paul's practice of not only representing his opponents' views but also of quoting them, particularly in the Corinthian correspondence, where discerning the echo of opponents' words is a delicate business. See, e.g., Matt O'Reilly, *Paul and the Resurrected Body: Social Identity and Ethical Practice*, ESEC 22 (Atlanta: SBL Press, 2020), 55, 97–100; and, regarding 1 Cor 11–14, Lucy Peppiatt, *Women and Worship at Corinth: Paul's Rhetorical Arguments in 1 Corinthians* (Eugene, OR: Cascade, 2015), 4, 66–84, 111; Peppiatt, *Unveiling Paul's Women: Making Sense of 1 Corinthians 11:2–16* (Eugene, OR: Cascade, 2018), ch. 2. One criterion for discerning where Paul might be quoting an opponent is when the statement stands in contrast to what he said elsewhere, especially in the same immediate or book context.

seems to be doing in Titus, perhaps even using a courtroom type-scene.[70] Now, let us consider what Paul means pragmatically by "sound doctrine."

Ethics and Redemption as Sound Doctrine

It is common to characterize ethical discourse in the New Testament epistles, particularly of Paul, as bipartite—theological warrant and ethical mandate. Madsen sets out to discern whether the structure of ethical argument in the Pastorals follows the same "gift and task" logic or "indicative and imperative" movement that he perceives in the undisputed Paulines.[71] I take issue with the ex ante assumption that this form of ethical reasoning typified Paul's teaching at a macro or micro level. This preconception may tacitly limit consideration of the possible structures of any ethical argumentation. Furthermore, Madsen finds "gift and task" (theology-to-ethics) reasoning by pairing explicit ethical injunctions with rationale that Paul formally expressed in various contexts. Such a clear-cut, formal analysis does not appreciate holistic ethical argument or systemic grounds for ethical instructions in the absence of case-by-case explanations.

In contrast to this common characterization, Paul displayed more continuity between the attitudes and behaviors he mandated and any logical rationale. He moved seamlessly between ethical expectations, strategic witness (Titus 2:7–8), theological truth (2:11–13), and intrinsic motivation (2:14). He also fluidly refers to both concrete behaviors and theological truths as "doctrine" (διδασκαλία, 1:9, 2:1–10, esp. 1, 7, 10; see parallel statements in 1:13, 2:2). In cases where Paul's instructions had no explicit underlying principle, it seems adequate to accept that he considered certain behaviors and character traits (e.g., "serious," 2:2; "not slaves to drink," 2:3; see also 1:7; "lovers of [their] children," 2:4; "submissive," 2:5; see also 1:6,

---

70. Wansink points out that in Roman trials that had no precedent established, the manner of obtaining evidence was unrestricted. He writes, "In trials heard *extra ordinem*, the magistrate had no limitations placed on how he came to his knowledge (*cognitio*) of the crime" ("Roman Law," 986).

71. Madsen, "Ethics of the Pastoral Epistles," 219–40. He is heavily indebted to Rudolf Bultmann, "Das Problem der Ethik bei Paulus," ZNW 23 (1924): 123–40. The conception of a relationship between Paul's theology and ethics such that one provides rationale for the other is commonplace. See comments on the Pastoral Epistles in Georg Strecker and Friedrich Wilhelm Horn, *Theology of the New Testament*, ed. Friedrich Wilhelm Horn, trans. M. Eugene Boring (New York: de Gruyter, 2000), 593–94.

10; 2:9) themselves to be good doctrine. Paul's doctrine comprised ethical content, not merely consequence, in the same way that language affects behavior, not by first passing through a multistep cerebral process by which it is consciously ratified but by affecting listeners at the point of hearing.[72]

Not only is comprehension a rapid online process, but cognitive and behavioral responses to ostensive inferential communication are frequently immediate, too. Finding yourself waving in response to someone who was not directing their wave at you demonstrates just how promptly humans are wired to respond immediately upon comprehension, even when mistaken about the communicator's intentions. Even to a toddler, a parent's predication "Hot!" while tapping the stove causes a gut-level effect in the child, so that he recoils and customarily avoids touching the thing that his mother indicated would be painful to touch. Conveying the informative proposition "this stove can become hot and painful to touch" falls short of both her communicative intention and his actual reaction. The stove has become hot in the child's mind as soon as Mommy said it was a *hot* thing. I use an illustration from early language acquisition to convey that behavioral outcomes are fundamental to communication.

In adult experience, as soon as we are told *that* a loved one has died, we begin grieving and considering the wide-ranging implications, just as the speaker expects. The speed at which speech affects humans suggests that ethical response does not require a multistep cognitive process. "Next stop is Jackson Heights—Roosevelt Boulevard" has various kinds and degrees of relevance to passengers, but it rarely fails to affect the neurons from head to toe, depending on its level of relevance. It could signal, for instance, *my stop is here, my stop is near*, or *I'm on the wrong train*, each of which can have physiological effects.

Ostensive inferential communication affects the world through the human agency of hearers. Love letters *do* something physiological to readers that not only exceeds their informative power but betrays their underlying intention.[73] Again, this linguistic reality has implications for biblical interpretation, even biblical theology.

---

72. These ideas correspond to the fluid language of "obedience of faith" (Rom 1:5, 16:26; cf. Acts 6:7), "do truth" (John 3:21, 2 Cor 13:8, 1 John 1:6), "walking/working in truth" (2 John 4; 3 John 3–4, 8). Whereas we often think of *truth* as intellectual, Scripture does not skip a beat in referring to truth in terms of behaviors such as *do*ing, *walk*ing, and actions required to become co*work*ers in the truth.

73. On the Song of Songs, Klangwisan discusses the lover's words as provocative speech (*Earthing the Cosmic Queen*, 10–11).

Careful, multistep argumentation in ethical reasoning generally or in the New Testament epistles specifically is both present and appropriate, but I am emphasizing the power and purpose of utterances to affect behavior and that behavior in turn to affect argument. Paul articulates the *is* in close connection to the *ought*, but his communication of the *is* and the *ought* affects response, and the *is* and the *ought* reinforce each other.[74] Madsen is right in his judgment that the conventional wisdom regarding the Pastoral Epistles—and, as always, by implication, Titus—has led students to read and to believe Titus's ethical instruction to be "prudential and derivative" in tone, never vital and responsive.[75]

In truth, the term ὑγιαίνω ("I am healthy," 1:9, 13; 2:1, 2) and cognate ὑγιής ("healthy," 2:8) in Titus is shorthand for the total constellation of theological and ethical claims Paul makes, including the positive and negative instructions. But for those steeped in the conventional thinking regarding the Pastoral Epistles, *sound doctrine = safe doctrine*. In other words, it does not represent an example of Paul responding creatively to live issues in the church using the resources of the Jewish faith as interpreted through the Christ event. In this vein of interpretation, *sound doctrine = stale doctrine*. Reading the text with this assumption perpetuates a self-fulfilling prophecy as undergraduates, having been primed by professors, read these texts for the first time and form opinions on the basis of these biases.[76] Prejudices in place, the dynamism and creativity of Paul's sound doctrine is obscured by misplaced suspicion and dubious preconceptions.[77]

---

74. I take Madsen's language a step further by applying linguistic insights that he did not have in view ("Ethics of the Pastoral Epistles," 224).

75. Madsen, "Ethics of the Pastoral Epistles," 238.

76. Consider Moberly's formative story about his preministry university experience (particularly related to critical issues in the Pastoral Epistles) in the opening paragraphs of "Biblical Hermeneutics," 133–56. Johnson describes the dilemma of short-circuiting critical inquiry in undergraduate institutions by insisting on adherence to established conventions regarding the Pastoral Epistles (*First and Second Letters*, 55).

77. In contrast to this commonplace disposition toward the Pastoral Epistles, M. Harding, taking Titus to be pseudonymous, nevertheless sees the author "not just as a theologian of the Pauline tradition, but as a creative and persuasive *communicator* of the Pauline heritage in his social context" (quoted in Marshall, "Pastoral Epistles," 286–87).

One may agree with Madsen that the "core 'logic' and content [of Titus] agree with the major epistles" but still disagree with its characterization as bipartite—indicative and imperative.[78] Paul's ethical logic in Titus does not simply argue from truth to proper action, since he refers to both under the same heading—"sound doctrine" and its corollaries with "faith" and "word" (1:9, 13; 2:1–2, 8).

Like other commentators, Huizenga asserts that Paul "does not describe or engage their [the troublemakers'] ideas in any constructive way."[79] On the one hand, it might have been artificial and extraneous for Paul to describe situations that were already in Titus's situation-contextual knowledge, especially given that elliptical language is more trusting and efficient; on the other hand, I contend that many interpreters for the foregoing reasons have not seen that Paul might have been quite directly addressing one of the particular expressions of the problem in Crete. Furthermore, Paul did so constructively, because the purpose of Paul's instruction ultimately was "in order that they might be healthy in the faith" (ἵνα ὑγιαίνωσιν ἐν τῇ πίστει, 1:13). Reconciliation was Paul's endgame. A "conviction" (ἔλεγξις; see cognates in 1:9, 13; 2:15) with such an effect in mind may be called restorative justice.

Huizenga, along with others, suggests that the author was being unfairly divisive toward the opponents, not affording them space within the Christian community on account of his bigoted attitudes. The divisive phrase she points to is αἱρετικὸν ἄνθρωπον ... παραιτοῦ ("put aside/avoid a divisive person," 3:10; note the ellipse I have left in the Greek), and she assumes that to label someone "heretical" (αἱρετικός) is inherently divisive. Interpreters who indict Paul for divisiveness, however, are too dismissive of the intervening qualification of the full statement—αἱρετικὸν ἄνθρωπον μετὰ μίαν καὶ δευτέραν νουθεσίαν παραιτοῦ ("put aside/avoid a divisive person after a first and a second reminder," 3:10).[80] But, more importantly, they tend not to relate Paul's rebuke type language in 3:10 with that in 1:13—δι' ἣν αἰτίαν ἔλεγχε αὐτοὺς ἀποτόμως, ἵνα ὑγιαίνωσιν ἐν τῇ πίστει

---

78. Madsen, "Ethics of the Pastoral Epistles," 238. I do not address all of the particulars on which I agree or disagree with Madsen.

79. Huizenga, *1–2 Timothy, Titus*, 179.

80. The qualification could be translated more strictly "after one and [or] two warning[s]," but I am trying to capture the sense of the conjunction and the cognate for *mind* within the word νουθεσίαν. I am interacting with comments by Huizenga (*1–2 Timothy, Titus*, 179).

("for which reason, [I instruct you to] rebuke them vigorously, in order that they might be healthy in the faith")—which I argue conceives rebuke as a necessary precursor to reconciliation, because no relational progress can occur until the parties own up to the truth.

As I explained above, relevance theorists claim that processing a broader context (as is necessary to connect 1:13 with 3:10) may require more effort, but it allows interpreters to consider appropriate implicatures that would not have been available to them on the basis of a narrower context. The sequence of the connection here between Titus 1:13 and 3:10 makes the size of the context inconsequential; because, as I argue, the nature and purpose of rebuke in 1:13 should illuminate that in 3:10. Anyone reading the letter in its entirety, as the original audience did, would not mistake Paul's mention of a heretic as unwarranted divisiveness, because they would see his restorative concerns in both the far and near contexts. I have already argued that the pronoun αὐτούς ("them," 1:13) refers to the troublemakers and not the subjects of the Cretan quotation. I believe that the influence of miso-Cretan reading assumptions probably prevents many commentators from connecting Paul's instructions in chapters 1 and 3 of Titus and makes them think that, in 1:13, Paul is trying to fix the Cretans rather than correct, restore, or rebuke the troublemakers, as I argue.

Paul contrasts Titus's speech with the presumptuous leaders' speech (Σὺ δὲ λάλει, "you however [are to] speak," 2:1; note the clear *inclusio* completed by Ταῦτα λάλει καὶ παρακάλει, "Speak and encourage these things," 2:15). As an alternative to their "myths" and "commandments" (1:14), Titus is to pronounce the logic of the Christ-life (i.e., the Christian gospel, 2:11–14). In contrast to a faith that is preoccupied with observing specific ethnic, religious, or cultural traditions or shunning others, the Christian gospel reorients faith and proclamation around the person and work of God.[81] The ethically oriented instructions Paul gives Titus to propound in 2:1–10 constitute sound doctrine as much as the more theologically oriented gospel summary of 2:11–14. Titus 2 has the highest concentration of "soundness" language in the New Testament (2:1–2, 8).[82] Others need rebuke "in order that" (ἵνα) broad communal health may prevail (1:13).

---

81. Barclay writes that because the apostle Paul was "all things to all people" (1 Cor 9:22), "his converts can be faithful to the truth, remaining within, but not beholden to, their various cultural traditions and social positions" (*Paul and the Gift*, 177).

82. The moral nature of sound doctrine also obtains, for example, in 1 Tim 1:10,

The subject of the purpose clause ἵνα ὑγιαίνωσιν ἐν τῇ πίστει ("in order that they might be healthy in the faith," 1:13c) is not explicit, but, in light of the referential speech throughout the passage, it is most likely the troublemakers. Paul hoped for their restoration. He extended the meaning of ὑγιαίνω ("to be in good [physical] health") figuratively to mean good moral, spiritual, and doctrinal health by pairing these ideas in each occurrence (Titus 1:9, 13; 2:1–2, 8; see 1 Tim 1:10, 6:3, 2 Tim 1:13, 4:3).[83] Purpose usages involve movement from one state to another, which suggests not only the sense that the subjects be healthy but that they be health conducive, an appropriate aspiration for influential people. Paul envisioned a restoration of the erring leaders to a right relationship with the church and with God, rather than a simple write-off on account of their offenses.

If one imposes an artificial sequence or dichotomy between belief and behavior, then Titus seems to contain a higher concentration of ethical instruction in comparison to the undisputed Paulines. This imposition requires aligning Greek and Hellenistic Jewish notions of πίστις ("faith," "loyalty," "trust") with Anglo-Saxon and Western European notions of belief, but it leads some to read Titus's highly moralized gospel as un-Pauline. Captive to a discredited but still commonplace Reformation-oriented perspective on Paul, we assume that he was against any sort of "works righteousness," so we are dubious of the clear moral assertions of Titus and the call toward "godly" (εὐσεβῶς, Titus 2:12; see cognates in 1:1 and 2:12) behavior.

For over a generation, interpreters have been discerning that morality was always a strong component of Paul's gospel.[84] Huizenga hits the nail on the head when she recognizes that "Titus' instruction must match up

---

which contrasts ὑγιαινούσῃ διδασκαλίᾳ with a behavior-oriented vice list. Such a message is fitting to sound doctrine, because it *is* sound (i.e., *healthy*) doctrine. Although I have deemphasized classic lexicography in favor of lexical pragmatics, standard definitions of ὑγιαίνω have significant social implications. See entries in LSJ, 1841–42; BDAG, 1023.

83. Other occurrences of this Greek root in the New Testament include Matt 12:13; 15:31; Mark 5:34; Luke 5:31; 7:10; 15:27; John 5:6, 9, 11, 14, 15; 7:23; Acts 4:10; 3 John 2.

84. See, e.g., Faber, "'Evil Beast, Lazy Gluttons,'" 145; Fredriksen, "What Does It Mean"; Michael F. Bird, "When the Dust Finally Settles: Coming to a Post–New Perspective Perspective," *CTR* 2 (2005): 57–69, 58; Barclay, *Paul and the Gift*. Each of these interacts significantly with E. P. Sanders's pivotal and debated *Paul and Palestinian Judaism: A Comparison of Patterns of Religion* (Philadelphia: Fortress, 1977).

with what is called 'sound doctrine' (2:1), but the teachings that follow in the rest of the chapter are not really the sort of topics that most modern Christians would consider to be 'doctrine.' The author does not insert any creedal sayings or Scripture verses, such as we read in 1 Tim 2:5–6. Instead, Titus must teach the believers about right actions, especially in fulfilling their household roles and in proper moral behavior."[85] This nonpropositional dimension of communication is not a unique feature of the instruction in Titus and the Pastoral Epistles or of the Pauline corpus. The thrust of the Sermon on the Mount and the entire New Testament is to affect readers; so, How does the speaker intend to affect hearers? is not a secondary question to be raised *optionally*, *after* interpretation. The question is as integral to interpretation as any historical, grammatical, or theological question if we appreciate that change is a function of language.

The gospel summary passages in Titus (2:11–14, 3:3–7) articulate a doctrine of life change and are not mere rationale for morality. This gospel does not have a moral *and* a theological side; it is a comprehensive argument in which the theology and the ethics of Titus (and Paul's gospel as far as this epistle is concerned) cohere. Paul uses various words for rebuke at various times (1:9; 2:2, 8; 3:9–10), but whatever strays from this life-change gospel logic deserves rebuke. Although Paul and others *can* develop ethical logic from indicative to imperative, they do not *have to*. Direct ethical teaching *as* doctrine does not contradict Paul's gospel, at least in Titus.

Barrett looks for a bipartite ethical logic in the Pastoral Epistles; and, coming up short, assumes that Titus fails to integrate ethics and theology transparently. By comparison, he says, the genuine Paul "always makes clear the theological and Christocentric basis of [his] moral demands," whereas the reason for the ethical injunctions of the Pastoral Epistles is "far from evident."[86] He may be right that *reason* and *basis* (Barrett's categories) are not the prerequisite building blocks of ethical instruction in Titus, but the contrast diminishes when one realizes that the *basis* of right behavior is the radical life change that Paul describes in 2:11–14 and 3:3–7 (cf. Rom 7:21–8:2, 2 Cor 5:17, Gal 5:1–23). Reading these Pauline passages without superimposing a bipartite ethical logic reveals that Titus is not so different. Paul's enjoining "love of aliens" (φιλόξενος, 1:8; see φιλοξενία, Rom 12:13) *is* doctrine and not merely *based on* doctrine.

---

85. Huizenga, *1–2 Timothy, Titus*, 146. Note that herein she also rightly admits of a distinction between Titus and another of the Pastoral Epistles.
86. Barrett, *Pastoral Epistles*, 25, 28.

Exemplifying the amalgamating tendency of many commentators, Barrett identifies three main reasons for ethical behavior in the Pastoral Epistles: the commands of God, the eschatological rewards, and public approval. Only his third—public approval—is arguably of any real significance in the moral logic of Titus.[87] The prominent language of the "command of God" (1:3, 2:15) in Titus has mostly to do with the matter of calling, not the logic of moral behavior—that is, morality is not simply obedience.[88] Rather than seeing the cohesive relationship between the gospel's theological claims and its ethical expectations, Barrett says that Paul "digresses" in 3:3 "to present *the ground* of Christian obedience."[89] For Paul in Titus, the basis of good behavior is actual life change, not a rationalized morality. Paul does not parse its deeper truth into rational cause and effect but into existential cause and effect.

Commensurate with the nature of intention in communication, interpretations without real-world consequences for the church (and the reader) that harmonize with plausibly discerned authorial intentions should give way to those that have appropriate practical outcomes for the community. Application of Scripture is not an optional step after interpretation reserved for true believers; it is the necessary complement to finish the task of interpretation.[90] Biblical studies can become quite esoteric in its pursuits, but until it reaches for and grasps something close to the speaker's vision of the world, it has failed to interpret fully. Interpretation does not end with propositions or theological ideas. Comprehending ostensive inferential communication involves considering the social, behavioral, and attitudinal implications of the writer's utterances, not just the informational. Interpreters must push a step further than dogmatics to pragmatics.

The logic of interpretation does not always shift in sequence from orthodoxy to orthopraxy. Writers communicate throughout Scripture, intending ethical and redemptive results. The Bible is properly interpreted when the Christian life is canonized in behavior. Wall gives extended and careful treatment to the notion of canon, especially for the Pastoral Epis-

---

87. Several have argued this point, none better than Hoklotubbe, *Civilized Piety*.

88. English Bibles typically provide readers with little access to the correlation between Paul's "command" (ἐπιταγή, 1:3, 2:15; cf. 1:5) language and the prominent concept of "submission" (ἀνυπότακτος, 1:6, 10; ὑποτάσσω, 2:5, 9; 3:1) in the moral landscape of Titus.

89. Barrett, *Pastoral Epistles*, 133.

90. See discussion in Bauer and Traina, *Inductive Bible Study*, 281–325, esp. 289–99.

tles, texts with a deutero-Pauline stamp. One of Wall's points is that the church's performance of the text canonizes a certain behavioral norm, not just in the reading and teaching on the texts in a corporate worship setting but in the life and community of believers as they enact their interpretations of Scripture.[91] How does one consider the ethical outcome of biblical utterances? Ask what attitudes and behaviors all readers of the text should inhere.

The logic of this gospel is *not* about good reasons to obey the demands of Christian morality; it is about a transformation that occurs through the gospel that cannot exist in anything other than a changed life (e.g., it cannot be enshrined in confessional propositions). Therefore, attention to ethno-religious observances, debates, and aspirations (1:10–16, 3:8–11) on top of this gospel is misplaced and problematic. The Cretans have been transformed *as* Cretans and do not need to be changed *from* Cretans. The Cretan quotation (1:12b) locates moral deficiency in one's heredity, and the solution the troublemakers offered was in surface-level conversion by adherence to particular religio-cultural attitudes and behaviors. The deep, personal, and spiritual transformation that Paul eloquently describes in his gospel summaries (2:11–14, 3:3–7) comes about by divine power. This is why the quotation is so repugnant to Paul: it questions the thoroughness of God's power and his gospel of salvation.

---

91. This emphasis aligns with the Two Horizons Commentary series (see Wall and Steele, *1 and 2 Timothy and Titus*, 24–27).

Conclusions and Implications

It should be clear from this study that the Epistle to Titus preserves two ancient opinions regarding Cretans in the church, not one. Troublemakers in the community described the Cretans as existential reprobates (1:12), whereas Paul described them as "At one time, foolish ... hateful, but now ... reborn, renewed ... heirs by grace" (3:3–7).[1] Countless readers of the Bible have accepted the troublemakers' opinion of the Cretans as their own under the influence of miso-Cretan interpretations. I claimed that prevalent readings of Titus 1:12 and its famous Cretan quotation are unsustainable on linguistic, literary, and historical grounds. So, I applied key insights from relevance theory to evaluate previous interpretations. I tried to demonstrate the merit of my case and the constructive possibilities of a relevance-guided biblical hermeneutic.

My primary goal has been to commend relevance theory to biblical scholars; amid its diverse explanations and applications, to suggest its proper role in biblical interpretation; and to show what a relevance-guided biblical hermeneutic might look like. Although the interpretation of Titus 1:12 that I have come to is compelling to me, one does not need to embrace it to grasp the main thrust of this study. Evaluation of this reading of the Cretan quotation on the basis of relevance theory is welcomed. Even so, with confidence in the general reasonableness of the foregoing study, I present my conclusions and their implications.

Hoklotubbe showed the promise of comparing the ethnographic language of the quotation with other ancient ethnographic literature as well as postcolonial analysis. He claims that in Titus, we have an example of a quasi-ethno-religious minority (i.e., Christians) vying for respectability in a colonial environment that has represented them "as barbaric and superstitious" and trying "to represent themselves as 'civilized' before the

---

1. My dynamic equivalent translation.

colonial 'gaze'" by denigrating other groups.[2] I have examined the same ancient literature and have discussed it at stages throughout this study. Perhaps Hoklotubbe would not disagree with my analysis of this literature, and I do not disagree with his. He reconstructs an ancient sociological environment in which hierarchical and prejudicial ethnographic statements were commonplace. Nevertheless, the linguistic analysis offered here suggests that Paul was not accepting or playing according to the rules of those hierarchical and prejudicial games. Rather, he was subverting the script and calling out the conventional tradents of ethnographic pronouncements, explaining in at least two dramatic gospel summaries (2:11–14, 3:3–7) that all the faithful are equal in grace, regardless of any foreign comparative valuations, be they Roman, Greek, or otherwise.

In this study, each chapter's relevance-theoretical insight yielded two results: a critique of various aspects of previous interpretations of Titus 1:12 and a fresh, relevance-based solution to the interpretive problems. For instance, chapter 3, "Basic Pragmatic Processes," shows that interpreters cannot take conventional pronoun reference assignments for granted. Chapter 4, "Higher-Level Explicatures," demonstrates that speaker attitude is crucial to interpretation and infers that Paul was distancing himself from the quotation in various ways. In chapter 5, "The Role of the Hearer in Communication," I observed how the salience of Paul's accusation was greater for the original audience than that of bigotry, which strikes modern audiences as more salient. In chapter 6, "The Nonpropositional Dimensions of Communication," I considered how matters of social intimacy and trust, public exposure and pressure, and ethical behavior were integral to Paul's message. Each chapter demonstrates how a relevance-guided biblical hermeneutic helps modern readers evaluate previous interpretations, attend to critical linguistic evidence, and appreciate the ancient audience's cognitive processes.

Many specific examples of the miso-Cretan interpretation—a synthetic composite of problematic readings and their accompanying assumptions—have been provided. No particular scholar holds this reading in toto, but one can identify miso-Cretan readings on the basis of a scale of relative adherence to a cluster of five assumptions: (1) Paul's authorial sympathy with the quotation's linguistically encoded contents, (2) contextual discontinuity between the thrust of the quotation and the

---

2. Hoklotubbe, "Civilized Christ-Followers," 375, 384, and passim.

surrounding material, (3) ancient literary or archaeological corroboration of the veracity of the quotation, (4) conflation of the troublemakers and the general Cretan church populace, and (5) dubious attribution to the Cretan poet Epimenides.

In summary, interpretations that rely on these assumptions exhibit some of the following contradictions: Paul, the canonical "apostle to the gentiles" (Rom 11:13; see also 1 Tim 2:7, 2 Tim 1:11), categorized gentile Cretans as existentially vicious by dint of birth. Although Paul indicated that "those of the circumcision" (Titus 1:10) constituted the most significant contingent of troublemakers in Crete, he instructed Titus to "rebuke" (1:13) the general Cretan populace.[3] While addressing issues of leadership malpractice, Paul suddenly disparaged Titus's host population for general moral failure, making it look like his missionary strategy was to alienate and deprecate the native population. I have offered a plausible alternative to this interpretation.

In my view, Paul did not originate or accept the quotation in its substance. He was concerned with what was happening in the church on two levels—the leadership in specific (1:5–16) and the believers in general (2:1–3:11). The moral issues raised in the quotation are not prominent in the rest of the letter. Among the troublemakers, in accordance with their own prejudices, "someone" (τις, 1:12) had ripped the quotation from its native context and co-opted it to disparage Cretans. The presumptuous leaders and their sympathizers held the attitude that Cretan converts were culturally, religiously, and thereby morally inferior.[4] This is a plausible reading, given that Paul associated the main contingent of troublemakers in ethno-religious terms. This aspect of their doctrine was disgraceful in light of Paul's gospel of transformation (3:3–7; see also 2:11–14). Hence, he ordered a narrowly targeted restorative rebuke (1:13).

---

3. Daniel C. Arichea and Howard A. Hatton are not alone in suggesting that this interpretation is plausible. See Arichea and Hatton, *A Handbook on Paul's Letters to Timothy and to Titus*, UBSHS (New York: United Bible Societies, 1995), 277. Although George Montague follows a generally miso-Cretan reading, he questions it: "But the modern reader may wonder how this letter, meant to support the mission in Crete and intended for public reading, could possibly ingratiate Paul with the Cretan Christians." See Montague, *First and Second Timothy, Titus*, CCSS (Grand Rapids: Baker Academic, 2008), 224.

4. Their only hope would be to convert from being a Cretan. One way of putting this: "a Cretan who becomes a Christian ... ceases to be a Cretan" ("ein Kreter, der Christ wird,... aufhören Kreter zu sein"). See Vogel, "Die Kreterpolemik," 254.

I contend that Paul was not instructing Titus to embark on a wholesale campaign of "severe rebuke" (1:13) toward his missionary congregation and their neighbors on account of moral faults as innate and intractable as their ethnicity. The quotation does not represent the moral topics Paul is concerned with throughout the letter, with the exception of deception, which would operate paradoxically if a Cretan originated the quotation. This paradoxical feature made it attractive to sustain out of its poetic context. In the mouth of any non-Cretan, the poetry and paradox of the quotation dissolves, and it merely becomes an ugly ethnic slur. Paul exposes it in a stark light.

Having demonstrated a reading strategy that is sensitized to three key insights of relevance theory, I now describe some benefits and implications of this study in four areas: (1) linguistics-informed biblical hermeneutics, (2) secondary literature on Titus and the Pastoral Epistles, (3) the modern-day appropriation of the original message of Titus, and (4) the canonical esteem of Titus.

A Relevance-Guided Biblical Hermeneutic

Certain scholars have contributed much to applying relevance theory to biblical interpretation. Some of the best and most pertinent examples include Stephen Pattemore, whose work in introducing relevance theory to biblical scholars and applying it to Revelation has been thorough, reasonable, and insightful; Gene Green, whose articles explaining relevance theory in general and specific and suggesting its application to biblical interpretation are well-grounded in familiarity with the discipline and its major theorists; and Kevin Smith, whose doctoral thesis provides a thorough analysis of relevance-theoretical matters pertaining to the translation of Titus.[5]

Relevance theory is not a method of interpretation but a means of understanding how hearers come to their conclusions. The insights it provides aid interpretation and support the critical evaluation of existing interpretations. This volume provides a critical example of how relevance theory can be used to evaluate and illuminate interpretations.

---

5. Pattemore, *Souls under the Altar*; Pattemore, *People of God*; Pattemore, "On the Relevance"; Green, "Lexical Pragmatics and the Lexicon"; Green, "Relevance Theory and Biblical Interpretation: (2009); Green, "Relevance Theory and Theological Interpretation"; Green, "Relevance Theory and Biblical Interpretation" (2013); Smith, "Bible Translation and Relevance Theory."

It serves as a foundation and development of a properly transparent and repeatable methodology.

Titus and Pastoral Epistles Scholarship

Although other scholars have placed relevance theory on the workbench for biblical interpretation, this is one of the only concentrated studies of Titus or the Pastorals using a relevance-guided hermeneutic. This fresh approach has yielded new results that help readers understand the letter to Titus.

The approach has led to several original critical judgments. Conventional interpretations of Titus 1:12 are unsustainable. Interpretations that depend on attributing the Cretan quotation to a certain ancient personality in Crete, although commonplace, are misguided and misleading. The quotation may have incorporated a popular saying, and hearers may have thought that a Cretan originated some or all of it, but it is clear that Paul had other specific concerns with it.

Following Thiselton, I have critiqued the practice of gathering incriminating evidence against Cretan people in concert with the tenor of the quotation.[6] Efforts to justify or explain Paul's assumed sympathy with this quotation on the basis of incommensurate historical evidence that Cretan people were somehow more vicious than their contemporaries smacks of the bigotry that some interpreters unreflectively pin on Paul. The interpretation offered here addresses aspects of the historical, literary, and grammatical issues in Titus that have not customarily been dealt with in other treatments. It does not exclude the fine proposals that have been made regarding the logical or rhetorical devices Paul may have employed, but it does expose flaws in certain readings.

The question of whether one takes either the pseudonymity or the authenticity of the Pastorals as a starting point has become a tacit litmus test for interpretational validity. This shibboleth is not an obstacle for my proposal. My interpretation stands whether Titus is pseudonymous or authentic. We can discern from the encoded content and our knowledge of the world and language—quite apart from any conviction about the historical identity or circumstances of "Paul" and "Titus"—that Paul

---

6. Thiselton, "Logical Role."

was giving an example of bad behavior that had come to his attention and needed to be rebuked by his local associate.

A common way of reading the Pastoral Epistles as a pseudonymous composite document with a fictional connection to Paul is to conceive of references to historical information (e.g., Paul, Titus, Crete, arguments about genealogies) as code for some other issue.[7] This study has not addressed this layer of complexity because it stays within the self-representation of the letter as a single unit from a senior leader named Paul to a junior colleague named Titus in a place called Crete.

The use of relevance theory in biblical studies is new. Some scholars have applied strategic relevance-theoretical principles to the task of biblical interpretation and translation.[8] Few, however, have organized entire studies around relevance-theoretical principles and demonstrated the results.[9] More commonly, the theory illumines particular points.[10] Very few biblical scholars have given a concentrated or thorough treatment to Titus or the Pastorals using a relevance-theoretical approach.[11] Relevance-theoretical insights have informed the translation of biblical texts mostly.[12] I set out to shed fresh light on the issues by applying a strategy of evaluation and interpretation that had not appeared before in studies of Titus and the Pastorals—a critical view of critical views. Whether my work resolves an impasse, it offers an alternative approach and a plausible interpretation.

---

7. See, e.g., Bassler, *1 Timothy*, 190; Dibelius and Conzelmann, *Pastoral Epistles*, 135; Vogel, "Die Kreterpolemik."

8. E.g., Green, "Relevance Theory and Biblical Interpretation" (2009); Ernst-August Gutt, *Relevance Theory: A Guide to Successful Communication in Translation* (Dallas: SIL International, 1992); Pattemore, *Souls under the Altar*; Pattemore, *People of God*; Goodwin, *Translating the English Bible*.

9. E.g., Casson, *Textual Signposts*; Joseph D. Fantin, *Lord of Entire World: Lord Jesus, a Challenge to Lord Caesar?* (Sheffield: Sheffield Phoenix, 2011); Morales, *Poor and Rich*; Pattemore, *Souls under the Altar*; Pattemore, *People of God*.

10. E.g., Goh, "Honoring Christ, Subverting Caesar"; Klangwisan, *Earthing the Cosmic Queen*.

11. Biblical translators and translation theorists are among the most prolific with respect to the association of relevance theory and biblical scholarship (e.g., Smith, "Bible Translation and Relevance Theory").

12. E.g., Goodwin, *Translating the English Bible*; Pattemore, "On the Relevance"; Jobes, "Relevance Theory and Translation."

Modern-Day Appropriation of Titus's Message

In line with the nonpropositional dimensions inherent to communication, I claim that Paul advances a conviction not to accept bigotry but to address it sternly. For the sake of integrity to the argument, my interpretation would be incomplete without a practical conclusion. The results of the hermeneutical process I have formulated and demonstrated show a coherent message in Titus. It is a moral teaching for the church, exposing the evil and the harm of holding and spreading prejudices, especially by church leaders. The canonical Paul (if also the historical Paul) thinks that bigotry and heredity- and religion-based classism are blemishes on the faith that deserve severe rebuke. Furthermore, pastors should not ignore such issues but should lead the way in correcting them. That the wording of the slur may have originated from a person of the disparaged ethnicity is not an excuse for perpetuating it—like saying, for instance, "I can tell this Cretan joke; I heard it from a Cretan; even they admit it to be true."[13] The interpretation presented in this study is not a lesson we typically hear from Titus, yet I am convinced that it was crucial to the situation in which it was written.

Paul's use of the quotation exposed an ugly truth about some leading individuals in the Cretan church community—namely, that their religio-cultural posturing and sense of superiority had gone as far as veiled and self-justified bigotry against Titus's missionary congregation. Deprecating the population that one was assigned to reach with the gospel could not be tolerated, but Paul's goal with the perpetrators was restoration, not punishment. The intention of Paul's "testifying" (μαρτυρία, 1:13a) and Titus's "convicting" (ἐλέγχω, 1:13b) was that the troublemakers (if also the entire church) would be "healthy" and "health-conducive" (ὑγιαίνω, 1:13c) with respect to the Christian life.

Pamela Eisenbaum recognizes that Christian conservatives and feminists alike have understood the apostle Paul to be what modern critics might label as misogynistic and anti-Semitic, yet she differentiates between Paul's own views as historically analyzed and what later readers have construed or how later readers have used them.[14] Although scholars take Paul's

---

13. *Pace* Guthrie, who writes, "Because a well-known Cretan condemns his own people the apostle cannot be charged with censoriousness for his exposures" (*Pastoral Epistles*, 200).

14. See Eisenbaum, "Is Paul the Father," 506–7.

comments on human difference—status, ethnicity, and gender—variously (e.g., Paul was contradictory, inconsistent, opaque), she explains that he is best understood by close attention to his very different historical context from our own. She discusses "Paul's theological vision" through a detailed historical-contextual analysis of Gal 3:28.[15] When applied to Paul, misogyny and anti-Semitism are simplistic and anachronistic judgments that fail to appreciate the original and radical way he was applying the resources of his ancestral faith to what he perceived as God's act of forming a new human family in Christ.[16] Although she carefully references only Paul's undisputed letters, I think that it is also true of the Pastorals that a deeper examination of literary and historical context complicates modern accusations of bigotry.

By contrast, Angela Parker argues that, while expressing some ideas that are egalitarian and liberating in Galatians (e.g., 3:28), Paul nevertheless flaunts his privilege as a male with intact bodily autonomy portraying himself, at turns, as a slave (1:10; see Titus 1:1) and as a birthing mother (Gal 4:19).[17] For Parker, because Paul had not experienced the habitus of either, which involves the loss of body capital, control, and protection, his use of these metaphors represents conceit and is implicitly offensive to those who may identify with such groups, such as the female descendants of African slaves in the United States.[18] Although Paul might not exhibit explicit verbal bigotry, his use of such metaphors is too cavalier for Parker. One should never diminish the suffering of oppressed groups by presumptuously identifying with the experiences of such people for the sake of an argument.[19]

---

15. Quotation from Eisenbaum, "Is Paul the Father," 507.
16. Eisenbaum, "Is Paul the Father," 518–22.
17. See Parker, "One Womanist's View."
18. Parker refers to Paul's self-identification as a birthing mother and as a slave as "Paul's conceit" ("One Womanist's View," 24, 31). The correlation of Roman imperial slave experiences (esp. of women) with those of slaves, Black women, and their children in the US is a critical hermeneutical lens for Parker's essay. Parker defines *habitus* and various forms of *capital*, including "body capital" in conversation with sociologist Pierre Bourdieu (esp. 28–29). The details are not necessary for my study, but basically, "Habitus is the internalization of the social order in the human body" (28).
19. I would have liked to engage more with the fine studies that have been done in identity theory and from marginalized perspectives and to expand my section on recovering silenced voices, but my focus was on relevance theory.

Historically responsible hermeneutical processes do not guarantee politically correct or publicly palatable results. My study does not address what many interpreters see as Paul's regrettable one-sidedness or, more pointedly, anti-Semitism or misogyny.[20] I acknowledge that my proposal has done nothing to alleviate the burden of this picture of Paul. I can only suggest that Paul's condemnation of leveraging Jewish religious culture to degrade gentiles is not anti-Semitic. In fact, I contend that it was in respect to his Jewish heritage and to defend the integrity of his faith and honor the truth of the God of Israel—as well as the "Israel of God" (Gal 6:16)—that Paul planted his foot concerning rogue teachers (Titus 1:10).

Furthermore, I add to the argument that, inasmuch as accommodation to social conventions played a role in the moral logic of Titus, Paul's advance of a lifestyle apologia equally justifies a present-day reexamination. To be specific, whereas accommodating the gospel in a complementarian sense to patriarchal and kyriarchal customs in the ancient world may have been a strategy that Paul saw as serving the needs of the church, he has set a precedent for affirming an egalitarian social structure in the present day, as either social convention may cohere with Titus's transformative gospel and radically submissive social ethic.[21]

---

20. Huizenga, *1–2 Timothy, Titus*, 139–41. Marshall uses "regret" and "one-sided" in "Pastoral Epistles," 273, 280–81, citing Alfons Weiser's 2003 assessment in the Evangelisch-Katholischer Kommentar on 2 Timothy. Marshall also highlights the misogyny seen in the Pastorals by Risto Saarinen. Davina C. Lopez proposes a reading of Paul that is not "Misogynist, homophobic, racist, anti-Semitic, xenophobic, elitist" but assumes that this can only be done by reading against the grain and changing his categorizations (of gentiles or of himself, for instance) imaginatively in light of empire and gender criticism. The associations she highlights between Roman imperial imagery and ideology and Paul's language, mission, and biography are illuminating, though several are tenuous or anachronistic. See Lopez, *Apostle to the Conquered: Reimagining Paul's Mission*, PCC (Minneapolis: Fortress, 2008), xi.

21. Huizenga writes her commentary entirely from the premise of critiquing androcentric and kyriarchical ideologies (see *1–2 Timothy, Titus*, 133–84). Although it is not within the scope of this study to mount a full argument, it would be a glaring omission to ignore the accusations of anti-Semitism and misogyny, especially given my more narrow concern with ethno-religious bigotry. *Kyriarchy* is described in Schüssler Fiorenza, "Feminist Studies in Religion," 128–29, and passim, but initially introduced in her *But She Said*. My brief argument here for a reexamination of the precise form of cultural accommodation complements Marshall's summary of Saarinen found in Marshall, "Pastoral Epistles," 280–81. He writes, "Saarinen is not uncritical of what he sees as the Pastor's misogynism and argues that following literally his ten-

Given the legacy that some interpretive assumptions regarding this passage have left for Cretans through the centuries, I think we owe someone an apology. How have our assumptions affected both Cretans and generations of Christians who have unquestioningly accepted that ethno-religious prejudice is harmonious with biblical faith? For the community of faith, a reading of Scripture that does not lead to loving God and loving neighbor is not a *good* reading.[22]

On the basis of my research, I propose an interpretation of Titus 1:12 that does not rely on miso-Cretan reading assumptions but that emerges from sound linguistic analysis. I argue that the writer of Titus was not affirming the substance of the Cretan quotation. Rather, he was addressing and rebuking a form of bigotry in the church. Each of the three relevance-theoretical insights reinforces the notion that Paul exposes, corrects, and restoratively rebukes bigotry in the church and does not tacitly participate in it. This interpretation has a great deal of import and applicability for the modern church, which continues to be fraught with classist tendencies, religio-cultural one-upmanship, and bald-faced bigotry, not to mention unexamined (i.e., implicit) biases. Furthermore, self-examination regarding the church's comfort level with the miso-Cretan interpretation may also lead to healthy repentance and restoration.

Implications for Canonical Esteem

Titus and the Pastorals are under a cloud of suspicion for being misogynistic, racist, anti-Semitic, artless, and incoherent. In light of this, pseudonymity may be the most complimentary attribute some scholars have ascribed to these books! At least Paul is off the hook. Right? As canonical literature, however, such evaluations have grave implications for their confident use in liturgy and proclamation, doctrine and discipleship. In this section of

---

dency to accommodate church practice to contemporary social standards may achieve today the opposite effect from what was intended" (281).

22. Briggs introduces this very simple, yet profound (from the perspective of interpretive ethics), qualification from Augustine's *On Christian Doctrine*. Briggs explores the complexities and subtleties of such a reading ethic (*Virtuous Reader*, 135–66). He provides this quotation from Augustine (*Doctr. chr.* 1.41): "So anyone who thinks that he has understood the divine scriptures or any part of them, but cannot by his understanding build up this double love of God and neighbor, has not yet succeeded in understanding them" (Briggs, *Virtuous Reader*, 141).

my conclusion, I draw heavily on the articulations of two scholars to frame this problem—Huizenga, who contends that they are pseudonymous, and Johnson, who argues the plausibility of their authenticity. It will become evident that they recognize similar implications. Afterward, I explain how my thesis modestly addresses what I regard as an issue of *esteem*.[23]

Huizenga expresses the tension that exists for people who assume a miso-Cretan interpretation: "We could just possibly ignore the author's racist and anti-Semitic statements as a random fragment of a long-ago culture, except that it has ended up in our own scriptures under the name of the famous apostle."[24] She is correct that something is wrong with this negative attitude toward Cretans, and, of course, she is right to object to anti-Semitism. Yet, the problem for Titus as canon is that advocacy interpretations typically predispose themselves against the text in a posture of suspicion that will not countenance a sympathetic reading of Scripture.[25] I contend that the anti-Semitism is superimposed by the interpretation and not intrinsic to the mention of things Jewish, which reflects the author's concern for true faithfulness (see, e.g., πίστις and cognates in 1:1, 4, 6, 13, 15; 2:2, 10; 3:8 [twice], 15) as opposed to merely obsequious sociocultural performance.

Regarding the place of the Pastorals in the Christian scriptural canon, Johnson writes, "They are not technically outside the canon, but they may as well be for all the attention they receive."[26] The suspicion has led to their neglect. Along these lines, Huizenga writes,

> In liturgical traditions, worshipers do not often hear readings from the Pastorals at the services. Only short and divided passages have been

---

23. With a related enquiry, Green writes, "[Kevin J.] Vanhoozer has noted that approaches to biblical interpretation that begin with the human dimension of Scripture 'find it difficult, if not impossible, to climb up Jacob's ladder so as to discover the Word of God. Such a focus on the "only human" meaning ultimately results in a loss of canonical functioning. The words of historical authors fail to carry divine authority.'" So, Green asks, "Does the application of relevance theory consign us to reading Scripture as nothing more than a human document?" ("Relevance Theory and Theological Interpretation," 77). My argument suggests the promise of relevance theory to place texts, especially problematic texts, on a firmer footing for interpretation and to allow them to escape the orbit of conventional thinking.

24. Huizenga, *1–2 Timothy, Titus*, 141.

25. For an understanding of advocacy readings, see Briggs, *Virtuous Reader*, 37.

26. Johnson, *First and Second Letters*, 57.

selected, and these appear just eleven times in the Roman Catholic Lectionary, with nine of these also adopted for the Revised Common Lectionary. The chances that a sermon might be preached on one of these texts must be slim, and when it does occur, the wise preacher ought to be reluctant to tackle the subject of how a pseudonymous author [we might add, "or how a bigot"] came to be included in the NT canon.[27]

As stated in my introduction, Paul's apparent ethnic bigotry is one of the key reasons that Titus is not accepted as authentically Pauline. I have tried to show that Paul appears to be such a bigot largely because of the history of interpretation, not because of the message of the letter. Johnson recognizes the problem with stale, uncritical, predetermined interpretations and laments the state of research on the Pastorals:

> What makes the present state of scholarship on the Pastorals so disheartening is that the difficulties (which are of a fundamental character) are seldom even acknowledged, and even less frequently engaged. As a result, the conventional wisdom concerning authenticity moves farther and farther from any grounding in evidence and argument, farther and farther from the best and most recent scholarship on Paul himself, and perpetuates itself mainly by force of inertia based on an unexamined majority vote by an increasingly uninformed electorate.[28]

Johnson is not alone in his concern for what could be called the canonical esteem of the Pastorals. In Huizenga's words, "The suspicion of a pseudonym allows these letters to be diminished in influence since they have lost their apostolic stamp of approval. In fact, some scholars who argue for Pauline authorship are especially concerned that the Pastorals do not become devalued as Christian texts."[29] Guthrie shares this concern: "Over a considerable period serious doubts have been cast upon their authenticity by many scholars and this has tended to decrease their authority."[30] Consequently, Huizenga describes common approaches to the Pastorals:

---

27. Huizenga, *1–2 Timothy, Titus*, xlvi.
28. Johnson, *First and Second Letters*, 90. Of course, this was published in the early 2000s, but I have not seen a major sea change in the areas of his primary concern since then.
29. Huizenga, *1–2 Timothy, Titus*, xlvi.
30. See Guthrie, *Pastoral Epistles*, 9; see also, Moberly, "Biblical Hermeneutics," 133–34.

A straightforward and widespread approach to the Pastorals is to minimize their presence in the New Testament canon. One may simply avoid reading them or just select a few trouble-free verses for devotional or liturgical purposes, as the lectionary committees have done. One could deny the religious authority vested in these letters or set aside the Pastorals' teachings with a statement like "that was then, this is now."[31]

Each of these approaches is manifest wherever the Bible has some level of currency (e.g., churches, seminaries, Christian homes). A relevance-guided reading amends some of the suspicion and reclaims a measure of Titus's canonical esteem, even allows us to see that the fundamental message of Titus (irrespective of particular objections) is worth pronouncing.

If the Paul of Titus was addressing problems of an ethno-religious nature in which subtle conflicts between Jewish and gentile Christians prevailed, then the concerns of Titus have more in common with the undisputed letters of Paul than is typically acknowledged. Many scholars do not, however, allow these books to illuminate one another without unmeasured qualification.

Against claims that Titus lacks rhetorical crafting and theological depth, this study shows a good deal of Titus's coherence and insight. Rather than an awkward tangent, the quotation is a crucial piece of evidence in Paul's argument against the troublemakers. It represents a substantial instance of leadership malpractice—a major concern of Paul within Titus. The message of the letter coheres with other New Testament books and the canonical portrayal of Paul's missionary practice (e.g., "to all people," 1 Cor 9:19–23; "apostle to the gentiles," Rom 11:13; see also Gal 2:2, 8; 1 Tim 2:7; 2 Tim 1:11). If my account is correct, then the "Paul" of Titus, by disassociating from the negative thrust of the saying and explicitly calling for the chastisement of those who advanced the insult, appears more consistent with the apostle of the magisterial letters. Ethno-religious divisions evident in Titus parallel those of the undisputed Pauline epistles, suggesting that they could have come from a similar era.[32] The contention that they were fictionalized on the basis of earlier records does not have compelling support.

---

31. Huizenga, *1–2 Timothy, Titus*, lii.
32. A proposal suggested by Johnson's analysis of the historical background (*First and Second Letters*, 55–90).

My work here and its interpretive results suggest implications for the history and canonical esteem of Titus and the Pastorals that call into question the presumed scholarly consensus and conventional assumptions about their *Kompositionsgeschichte* and their *Sitz im Leben*. Although my claims will stand whether or not critics initiate or accept such a reevaluation, I see this as an important implication of the reading I propose.

Bibliography

Premodern Sources

Codex Sinaiticus. British Library, London. https://tinyurl.com/SBLPress4832b3.

Callimachus. *Hymns and Epigrams*. Edited by George P. Goold. Translated by Alexander W. Mair. LCL. Cambridge: Harvard University Press, 1921.

Clement of Alexandria. *Exhortation to the Greeks, The Rich Man's Salvation, To the Newly Baptized*. Edited by Jeffrey Henderson. Translated by George W. Butterworth. LCL. Cambridge: Harvard University Press, 1919.

Diogenes Laertius. *Lives of Eminent Philosophers, Books 1–5*. Translated by Robert D. Hicks. LCL. Reprint, Cambridge: Harvard University Press, 1925.

———. *Vitae Philosophorum*. Vol. 1. Edited by Herbert S. Long. Oxford: Clarendon, 1964.

Epimenides. "Die 'Kleinen' Griechischen Historiker Heute." Page 29 in *Lustrum*. Vol. 21. Translated by Hans Joachim Mette. Göttingen: Vandenhoeck & Ruprecht, 1978.

Jerome. *Commentaries on Galatians, Titus, and Philemon*. Translated by Thomas P. Scheck. Notre Dame, IN: University of Notre Dame Press, 2010.

Lucian. *Scholia in Lucianum*. Edited by Hugo Rabe. Leipzig: Teubner, 1906.

Philo. *Philo*. Translated by Francis H. Colson and George H. Whitaker. LCL. Cambridge: Harvard University Press, 1929–1962.

Plutarch. *Aemilius Paullus*. Pages 184–222 in vol. 2.1 of *Plutarchi Vitae Parallelae*. 2nd ed. Edited by Konrat Ziegler. Leipzig: Teubner, 1964.

———. *Moralia*. Edited by Jeffrey Henderson. Translated by Frank Cole Babbitt. Vol. 2. LCL. Cambridge: Harvard University Press, 1928.

Quintus Smyrnaeus. *Posthomerica*. Edited and translated by Neil Hopkinson. LCL. Cambridge: Harvard University Press, 2018.

Tatian. *Die ältesten Apologeten: Texte mit kurzen Einleitungen*. Edited by Edgar J. Goodspeed. Göttingen: Vandenhoeck & Ruprecht, 1915.

Tertullian. *On the Soul*. Pages 163–309 in *Tertullian: Apologetical Works and Mnucius Felix: Octavius*. Translated by Edwin A Quain. FC 10. Washington, DC: Catholic University of America Press, 2008.

Theodore of Mopsuestia. *1 Thessalonians–Philemon, Appendices, Indices*. Vol. 2 of *Commentary on the Minor Pauline Epistles*. Edited by Henry Barclay Swete. Cambridge: Cambridge University Press, 1882.

———. *Commentary on the Minor Pauline Epistles*. Translated by Rowan A. Greer. WGRW 26. Atlanta: Society of Biblical Literature, 2010.

Theodoret of Cyrus. *Commentary on the Letters of St. Paul*. Translated by Robert Charles Hill. 2 vols. Brookline, MA: Holy Cross Orthodox Press, 2001.

Thomas Aquinas. *Commentaries on St. Paul's Epistles to Timothy, Titus, and Philemon*. Translated by Chrysostom Baer. South Bend, IN: St. Augustine's, 2007.

Modern Sources

Aageson, James W. *Paul, the Pastoral Epistles, and the Early Church*. LPS. Peabody, MA: Hendrickson, 2008.

Ágnes, Hámori. "Illocutionary Force, Salience and Attention Management: A Social Cognitive Pragmatic Perspective." *ALH* 57 (2010): 53–74.

Anum, Eric. "Collaborative and Interactive Hermeneutics in Africa: Giving Dialogical Privilege in Biblical Interpretation." Pages 143–65 in *African and European Readers of the Bible in Dialogue: In Quest of a Shared Meaning*. Edited by Hans de Wit and Gerald O. West. SRA 32. Leiden: Brill, 2008.

Apple, Kevin Joel. "The Role of Relevance and Salience in Detecting the Intergroup Bias." PhD diss., Ohio University, 1997.

Arichea, Daniel C., and Howard Hatton. *A Handbook on Paul's Letters to Timothy and to Titus*. UBSHS. New York: United Bible Societies, 1995.

Arichea, Daniel C., and Eugene A. Nida. *A Handbook on Paul's Letter to the Galatians*. UBSHS. New York: United Bible Societies, 1976.

Ariel, Mira. "What Discourse Can(not) Teach Us." *IRP* 6 (2014): 181–210.

Ashwell, Lauren. "Gendered Slurs." *STP* 42 (2016): 228–39.

Aune, David E. *The New Testament in Its Literary Environment.* LEC 8. Philadelphia: Westminster, 1987.
Austin, J. L. *How to Do Things with Words.* 2nd ed. Edited by James O. Urmson and Marina Sbisà. WJL. Cambridge: Harvard University Press, 1975.
———. "The Meaning of a Word." Pages 55–75 in *J. L. Austin: Philosophical Papers.* 3rd ed. Edited by James O. Urmson and Geoffrey J. Warnock. New York: Oxford University Press, 1979.
Barclay, John M. G. *Paul and the Gift.* Grand Rapids: Eerdmans, 2015.
Barnes, Michael. "Tracy in Dialogue: Mystical Retrieval and Prophetic Suspicion." *HeyJ* 34 (1993): 60–65.
Barrett, C. K. *The Pastoral Epistles in the New English Bible.* NCBNT. Oxford: Clarendon, 1963.
Bassler, Jouette M. *1 Timothy, 2 Timothy, Titus.* ANTC. Nashville: Abingdon, 1996.
Bauer, David R., and Robert A. Traina. *Inductive Bible Study: A Comprehensive Guide to the Practice of Hermeneutics.* Grand Rapids: Baker Academic, 2011.
Baugh, Stephen M. "Titus." Pages 499–511 in *Zondervan Illustrated Bible Backgrounds Commentary.* Vol. 3. Edited by Clinton E. Arnold. Grand Rapids: Zondervan, 2009.
Baum, Armin Daniel. "Literarische Echtheit als Kanonkriterium in der alten Kirche." *ZNW* 88 (1997): 97–110.
———. *Pseudepigraphie und Literarische Fälschung im Frühen Christentum: Mit Ausgewählten Quellentexten samt Deutscher Übersetzung.* WUNT 2/138. Tübingen: Mohr Siebeck, 2001.
———. "Semantic Variation within the Corpus Paulinum: Linguistic Considerations concerning the Richer Vocabulary of the Pastoral Epistles." *TynBul* 59 (2008): 271–92.
Bénétreau, Samuel. *Les Épîtres Pastorales 1 et 2 Timothée, Tite.* EFTE. Vaux-sur-Seine: Édifac, 2008.
Besançon Spencer, Aída. *2 Timothy and Titus.* NCCS. Eugene, OR: Cascade, 2014.
Bianchi, Claudia. "Slurs and Appropriation: An Echoic Account." *JPrag* 66 (2014): 35–44.
Biezeveld, Kune. "The Role of 'The Other' in the Reading of the Bible: Towards a New Roadmap for Bible Reading in the Western World." Pages 123–39 in *African and European Readers of the Bible in Dialogue:*

In Quest of a Shared Meaning. Edited by Hans de Wit and Gerald O. West. SRA 32. Leiden: Brill, 2008.

Bird, Michael F. "When the Dust Finally Settles: Coming to a Post–New Perspective Perspective." *CTR* 2 (2005): 57–69.

Bird, Thomas E. "Exegetical Notes: Self-Control (ΣΩΦΡΟΣΥΝΗ)." *CBQ* 2 (1940): 259–63.

Blakemore, Diane. *Semantic Constraints on Relevance*. New York: Blackwell, 1987.

Blass, Regina. *Relevance Relations in Discourse: A Study with Special Reference to Sissala*. CSL 55. Cambridge: Cambridge University Press, 1990.

Bonnycastle, Stephen. *In Search of Authority: An Introductory Guide to Literary Theory*. 3rd ed. Orchard Park, NY: Broadview, 2007.

Borkent, Mike. "Illusions of Simplicity." Pages 5–24 in *Textual Choices in Discourse: A View from Cognitive Linguistics*. Edited by Barbara Dancygier, José Sanders, and Lieven Vandelanotte. Amsterdam: Benjamins, 2012.

Briggs, Richard S. "How to Do Things with Meaning in Biblical Interpretation." *STR* 2 (2011): 143–60.

———. *The Virtuous Reader: Old Testament Narrative and Interpretive Virtue*. STI. Grand Rapids: Baker Academic, 2010.

———. *Words in Action: Speech Act Theory and Biblical Interpretation*. Edinburgh: T&T Clark, 2001.

Brisard, Frank. "H. P. Grice." Pages 104–24 in *Philosophical Perspectives for Pragmatics*. Edited by Jef Verschueren, Jan-Ola Östman, and Marina Sbisà. HPH 10. Amsterdam: Benjamins, 2011.

Broadbent, Ralph. "The First and Second Letters to Timothy and the Letter to Titus." Pages 323–28 in *A Postcolonial Commentary on the New Testament Writings*. Edited by Fernando F. Segovia and R. S. Sugirtharajah. BP 13. New York: T&T Clark, 2007.

Brown, Derek. "Satan: The Author of False Teaching in the Pastoral Epistles." Paper presented at the Annual Meeting of the Society of Biblical Literature. Atlanta, 30 November 2015.

Brox, Norbert. *Die Pastoralbriefe*. RNT. Regensburg: Pustet, 1963.

Bultmann, Rudolf. "Das Problem der Ethik bei Paulus." *ZNW* 23 (1924): 123–40.

Calvin, John. *Commentaries on the Second Epistle of Paul the Apostle to the Corinthians, and the Epistles to Timothy, Titus, and Philemon*. Edited by David W. Torrance and Thomas F. Torrance. Translated by John W. Fraser. Grand Rapids: Eerdmans, 1960.

Carroll, Noël. "Interpretation and Intention: The Debate between Hypothetical and Actual Intentionalism." *Metaphilosophy* 31 (2000): 75–95.
Carston, Robyn. "Truth-Conditional Semantics." Pages 280–88 in *Philosophical Perspectives for Pragmatics*. Edited by Jef Verschueren, Jan-Ola Östman, and Marina Sbisà. HPH 10. Amsterdam: Benjamins, 2011.
Carston, Robyn, and Seiji Uchida, eds. *Relevance Theory: Applications and Implications*. P&B NS 37. Philadelphia: Benjamins, 1998.
Casson, Sarah H. *Textual Signposts in the Argument of Romans: A Relevance-Theory Approach*. ECL 25. Atlanta: SBL Press, 2019.
Childs, Brevard S. *The Church's Guide for Reading Paul: The Canonical Shaping of the Pauline Corpus*. Grand Rapids: Eerdmans, 2008.
Clark, Billy. *Relevance Theory*. CTL. Cambridge: Cambridge University Press, 2013.
Collins, Raymond F. "Pastorals—Biblical Studies." Oxford Bibliographies Online. https://tinyurl.com/SBLPress4832a1.
Cook, David. "The Pastoral Fragments Reconsidered." *JTS* 35 (1984): 120–31.
Couser, Greg A. "The Sovereign Savior of 1 and 2 Timothy and Titus." Pages 105–36 in *Entrusted with the Gospel: Paul's Theology in the Pastoral Epistles*. Edited by Andreas J. Köstenberger and Terry L. Wilder. Nashville: B&H Academic, 2010.
Craigmiles, Shawn. "Pragmatic Constraints of ἀλλά in the Synoptic Gospels." PhD diss., Asbury Theological Seminary, 2016.
Crandall, Christian S., and Amy Eshleman. "A Justification-Suppression Model of the Expression and Experience of Prejudice." *PB* 129 (2003): 414–46.
Cristea, Dan, and Oana-Diana Postolache. "How to Deal with Wicked Anaphora?" Pages 17–46 in *Anaphora Processing: Linguistic, Cognitive, and Computational Modelling*. Edited by António Branco, Tony McEnery, and Ruslan Mitkov. ASTHLS 263. Philadelphia: Benjamins, 2005.
Croom, Adam M. "The Semantics of Slurs: A Refutation of Coreferentialism." *Ampersand* 2 (2015): 30–38.
Currie, Gregory. "Why Irony Is Pretence." Pages 111–33 in *The Architecture of the Imagination: New Essays on Pretence, Possibility, and Fiction*. Edited by Shaun Nichols. Oxford: Oxford University Press, 2006.
Dancygier, Barbara. *The Language of Stories: A Cognitive Approach*. Cambridge: Cambridge University Press, 2012.

Dancygier, Barbara, José Sanders, and Lieven Vandelanotte. "Textual Choices in Discourse." Pages 185-91 in *Textual Choices in Discourse: A View from Cognitive Linguistics*. Edited by Barbara Dancygier, José Sanders, and Lieven Vandelanotte. Amsterdam: Benjamins, 2012.

Davies, Margaret. *The Pastoral Epistles*. NTG. Sheffield: Sheffield Academic, 1996.

Dibelius, Martin, and Hans Conzelmann. *The Pastoral Epistles: A Commentary*. Edited by Helmut Koester. Translated by Philip Buttolph and Adela Yarbro. Hermeneia. Philadelphia: Fortress, 1972.

Donelson, Lewis R. *Pseudepigraphy and Ethical Argument in the Pastoral Epistles*. HUT 22. Tübingen: Mohr Siebeck, 1986.

———. "The Structure of Ethical Argument in the Pastorals." *BTB* 18 (1988): 108-13.

Easton, Burton Scott. *The Pastoral Epistles: Introduction, Translation, Commentary and Word Studies*. New York: Scribner's, 1947.

Eckstein, Arthur M. *Moral Vision in the Histories of Polybius*. HCS. Berkeley: University of California Press, 1995.

Ehrman, Bart D. *Lost Christianities: The Battles for Scripture and the Faiths We Never Knew*. New York: Oxford University Press, 2003.

Eisenbaum, Pamela M. "Is Paul the Father of Misogyny and Antisemitism?" *CC* 50 (2001): 506-24.

Faber, Riemer A. "'Evil Beasts, Lazy Gluttons': A Neglected Theme in the Epistle to Titus." *WTJ* 67 (2005): 135-45.

Falconer, Robert Alexander. *The Pastoral Epistles: Introduction, Translation, and Notes*. Oxford: Oxford University Press, 1937.

Fantin, Joseph D. "The Lord of the Entire World: Lord Jesus, a Challenge to Lord Caesar?" PhD diss., University of Sheffield, 2007.

———. *Lord of the Entire World: Lord Jesus, a Challenge to Lord Caesar?* Sheffield: Sheffield Phoenix, 2011.

Fee, Gordon D. *New Testament Exegesis: A Handbook for Students and Pastors*. 3rd ed. Louisville: Westminster John Knox, 2002.

Feuerbach, Ludwig. *Das Wesen des Christentums*. 2nd ed. Leipzig: Wigand, 1848.

Fillmore, Charles J. "Frame Semantics." Pages 111-37 in *Linguistics in the Morning Calm*. Seoul: Hanshin, 1982.

Fiore, Benjamin. *The Pastoral Epistles: First Timothy, Second Timothy, Titus*. SP 12. Collegeville, MN: Liturgical Press, 2007.

Forbes, A. Dean. "Statistical Research on the Bible." *ABD* 6:185-206.

Forbes, Christopher. "Ancient Rhetoric and Ancient Letters: Models for Reading Paul, and Their Limits." Pages 143–60 in *Paul and Rhetoric*. Edited by J. Paul Sampley and Peter Lampe. New York: T&T Clark, 2010.

Fredriksen, Paula. "What Does It Mean to See Paul 'within Judaism'?" *JBL* 141 (2022): 359–80.

Fuchs, Rüdiger. *Unerwartete Unterschiede: Müssen wir unsere Ansichten über die "Pastoralbriefe" revidieren?* Wuppertal: Brockhaus, 2003.

Furlong, Anne. "A Modest Proposal: Linguistics and Literary Studies." *CJAL* 10 (2007): 323–45.

———. "Relevance Theory and Literary Interpretation." PhD diss., University College of London, 1995.

Garlington, Don. Review of *Paul and the Politics of Diaspora*, by Ronald Charles. *RBL*, September 4, 2016. https://www.sblcentral.org/home/bookDetails/10141.

Garmendia, Joana. "A (Neo)Gricean Account of Irony: An Answer to Relevance Theory." *IRP* 7 (2015): 40–79.

Gibbs, Raymond W., Jr. "The Intentionalist Controversy and Cognitive Science." *PP* 6 (1993): 181–205.

Gibbs, Raymond W., Jr., and Markus Tendahl. "Cognitive Effort and Effects in Metaphor Comprehension: Relevance Theory and Psycholinguistics." *M&L* 21 (2006): 379–403.

Goh, Benson. "Honoring Christ, Subverting Caesar: Relevance-Historical Reconstruction of the Context of Ephesians as an Honorific Discourse Praising Jesus the Great Benefactor." PhD diss., Asbury Theological Seminary, 2017.

Gómez-González, María A. *The Theme-Topic Interface: Evidence from English*. P&B 71. Amsterdam: Benjamins, 2001.

Goodrich, Richard J., and Albert L. Lukaszewski, eds. *A Reader's Greek New Testament*. 3rd ed. Grand Rapids: Zondervan, 2015.

Goodwin, Philip W. *Translating the English Bible: From Relevance to Deconstruction*. Cambridge: Clarke, 2013.

Gorday, Peter, and Thomas C. Oden, eds. *Colossians, 1–2 Thessalonians, 1–2 Timothy, Titus, Philemon*. ACCS. Downers Grove, IL: IVP Academic, 2000.

Gray, Patrick. "The Liar Paradox and the Letter to Titus." *CBQ* 69 (2007): 302–14.

Green, Gene L. "Lexical Pragmatics and the Lexicon." *BBR* 22 (2012): 315–33.

———. "Relevance Theory and Biblical Interpretation." Pages 217–40 in *The Linguist as Pedagogue: Trends in the Teaching and Linguistic Analysis of the Greek New Testament*. Edited by Stanley E. Porter and Matthew Brook O'Donnell. Sheffield: Sheffield Phoenix, 2009.

———. "Relevance Theory and Biblical Interpretation." Pages 266–73 in *Oxford Encyclopedia of Biblical Interpretation*. Edited by Steven L. McKenzie. Vol. 2. London: Oxford University Press, 2013.

———. "Relevance Theory and Theological Interpretation: Thoughts on Metarepresentation." *JTI* 4 (2010): 75–90.

Grice, H. Paul. "Further Notes on Logic and Conversation." Pages 765–73 in *Reasoning: Studies of Human Inference and Its Foundations*. Edited by Jonathan E. Adler and Lance J. Rips. Cambridge: Cambridge University Press, 2008.

———. "Logic and Conversation." Pages 41–58 in *Speech Acts*. Edited by Peter Cole and Jerry L. Morgan. SS 3. New York: Academic Press, 1975.

———. *Studies in the Way of Words*. Cambridge: Harvard University Press, 1989.

Griffiths, Alan H. "Epimenides." *OCD*, 546.

Guthrie, Donald. *The Pastoral Epistles: An Introduction and Commentary*. 2nd rev. ed. TNTC 14. Downers Grove, IL: InterVarsity, 1990.

Gutt, Ernst-August. "Relevance and Translation: On the Value of a Good Theoretical Foundation of Translation." Pages 292–310 in *In the Mind and across Minds: A Relevance-Theoretic Perspective on Communication and Translation*. Edited by Agnieszka Piskorska, Marta Kisielewska-Krysiuk, and Ewa Wałaszewska. Newcastle: Cambridge Scholars, 2010.

———. *Relevance Theory: A Guide to Successful Communication in Translation*. Dallas: SIL International, 1992.

———. *Translation and Relevance: Cognition and Context*. 2nd ed. New York: Routledge, 2014.

Hanson, Anthony Tyrrell. *The Pastoral Epistles*. NCB. Grand Rapids: Eerdmans, 1982.

Harrill, J. Albert. "'Without Lies or Deception': Oracular Claims to Truth in the Epistle to Titus." *NTS* 63 (2017): 451–72.

Harrison, P. N. *The Problem of the Pastoral Epistles*. London: Oxford University Press, 1921.

Hays, Richard B. *Echoes of Scripture in the Letters of Paul*. New Haven: Yale University Press, 1989.

Herzer, Jens. "Abschied vom Konsens?: Die Pseudepigraphie der Pastoralbriefe als Herausforderung an die neutestamentliche Wissenschaft." *TLZ* 129 (2004): 1267–82.

———. "Was ist falsch an der 'fälschlich so genannten Gnosis'? Zur Paulusrezeption des Ersten Timotheusbriefes im Kontext seiner Gegnerpolemik." *EC* 5 (2014): 68–96.

———. "Zwischen Mythos und Wahrheit: Neue Perspektiven auf die sogenannten Pastoralbriefe." *NTS* 63 (2017): 428–50.

Hill, Harriet. *The Bible at Cultural Crossroads: From Translation to Communication*. Manchester: St. Jerome, 2006.

Ho, Chiao Ek. "Do the Work of an Evangelist: The Missionary Outlook of the Pastoral Epistles." PhD diss., University of Aberdeen, 2000.

———. "Mission in the Pastoral Epistles." Pages 241–67 in *Entrusted with the Gospel: Paul's Theology in the Pastoral Epistles*. Edited by Andreas J. Köstenberger and Terry L. Wilder. Nashville: B&H Academic, 2010.

Hoklotubbe, T. Christopher. "Civilized Christ-Followers among Barbaric Cretans and Superstitious Judeans: Negotiating Ethnic Hierarchies in Titus 1:10–14." *JBL* 140 (2021): 369–90.

———. *Civilized Piety: The Rhetoric of Pietas in the Pastoral Epistles and the Roman Empire*. Waco, TX: Baylor University Press, 2017.

Huang, Yan. "Micro- and Macro-Pragmatics: Remapping Their Terrains." *IRP* 5 (2013): 129–62.

Huizenga, Annette Bourland. *1–2 Timothy, Titus*. WisC 53. Collegeville, MN: Liturgical Press, 2016.

Hunt, R. Reed. "Does Salience Facilitate Longer-Term Retention?" *Memory* 17 (2009): 49–53.

Huxley, George Leonard. *Greek Epic Poetry from Eumelos to Panyassis*. Cambridge: Harvard University Press, 1969.

Inskeep, Steve. "Breitbart Editor Joel Pollak: Trump Strategist Steve Bannon Is a Conservative 'National Hero.'" Transcript, *Morning Edition from NPR News*, November 16, 2016. https://tinyurl.com/SBL4832a.

Itani, Reiko. "A Relevance-Based Analysis of Hearsay Particles: With Special Reference to Japanese Sentence-Final Particle *Tte**." Pages 47–68 in *Relevance Theory: Applications and Implications*. Edited by Robyn Carston and Seiji Uchida. P&B 37. Philadelphia: Benjamins, 1998.

Jacoby, Felix, ed. "Epimenides von Kreta (457), Fragmenta." Pages 390–94 in vol. 3B of *Die Fragmente der Griechischen Historiker*. Leiden: Brill, 1955.

Jeffers, James S. *The Greco-Roman World of the New Testament Era: Explor-*

ing the Background of Early Christianity. Downers Grove, IL: IVP Academic, 1999.

Jervis, L. Ann. "Law/Nomos in Greco-Roman World." *DNTB*, 631–36.

Jobes, Karen H. "Relevance Theory and the Translation of Scripture." *JETS* 50 (2007): 773–97.

Johnson, Luke Timothy. *The First and Second Letters to Timothy: A New Translation with Introduction and Commentary*. AB 35A. New York: Doubleday, 2001.

———. *Letters to Paul's Delegates: 1 Timothy, 2 Timothy, Titus*. NTC. Valley Forge, PA: Trinity Press International, 1996.

Kahl, Werner. "Growing Together: Challenges and Chances in the Encounter of Critical and Intuitive Interpreters of the Bible." Pages 147–58 in *Reading Other-Wise: Socially Engaged Biblical Scholars Reading with Their Local Communities*. Edited by Gerald O. West. SemeiaSt 62. Atlanta: Society of Biblical Literature, 2007.

Karris, Robert J. Review of *Pseudepigraphy and Ethical Argument in the Pastoral Epistles*, by Lewis R. Donelson. *JBL* 107 (1988): 558–60.

Kartzow, Marianne Bjelland. *Gossip and Gender: Othering of Speech in the Pastoral Epistles*. BZNW 164. New York: de Gruyter, 2009.

Kecskes, Istvan. "The Role of Salience in Processing Pragmatic Units." *ALH* 51 (2004): 309–24.

Keener, Craig S. *Acts: An Exegetical Commentary*. 4 vols. Grand Rapids: Baker Academic, 2012.

Kidd, Reggie M. "Titus as Apologia: Grace for Liars, Beasts, and Bellies." *HBT* 21 (1999): 185–209.

Klangwisan, Yael. *Earthing the Cosmic Queen: Relevance Theory and the Song of Songs*. Eugene, OR: Pickwick, 2014.

Knight, George W. *The Pastoral Epistles: A Commentary on the Greek Text*. NIGTC. Grand Rapids: Eerdmans, 1992.

Kolaiti, Patricia, and Deirdre Wilson. "Corpus Analysis and Lexical Pragmatics: An Overview." *IRP* 6 (2014): 211–39.

Köstenberger, Andreas J. "Hermeneutical and Exegetical Challenges in Interpreting the Pastoral Epistles." Pages 1–27 in *Entrusted with the Gospel: Paul's Theology in the Pastoral Epistles*. Edited by Andreas J. Köstenberger and Terry L. Wilder. Nashville: B&H Academic, 2010.

———. "An Investigation of the Mission Motif in the Letters to Timothy and Titus with Implications for the Pauline Authorship of the Pastoral Epistles." *BBR* 29 (2019): 49–64.

Kujanpää, Katja. "From Eloquence to Evading Responsibility: The Rhetorical Functions of Quotations in Paul's Argumentation." *JBL* 136 (2017): 185–202.

Künne, Wolfgang. "On Liars, 'Liars' and Harmless Self-Reference." Pages 355–429 in *Mind, Values and Metaphysics: Philosophical Essays in Honor of Kevin Mulligan*. Edited by Anne Reboul. New York: Springer, 2014.

Kwapis, Ken, dir. *The Office*. "Diversity Day." Written by B. J. Novak. Aired March 29, 2005, on NBC.

Laansma, Jon C. "2 Timothy, Titus." Pages 125–302 in *1 Timothy, 2 Timothy, Titus, and Hebrews*. Edited by Philip W. Comfort. CornBC 17. Carol Stream, IL: Tyndale House, 2009.

Lampe, Peter. "Rhetorical Analysis of Pauline Texts—Quo Vadit? Methodological Reflections." Pages 3–21 in *Paul and Rhetoric*. Edited by J. Paul Sampley and Peter Lampe. New York: T&T Clark, 2010.

Lea, Thomas D., and Hayne P. Griffin. *1, 2 Timothy, Titus*. NAC 34. Nashville: Broadman & Holman, 1992.

Lee, G. M. "Epimenides in the Epistle to Titus (1:12)." *NovT* 22 (1980): 96.

Lee, Jae Won. *Paul and the Politics of Difference: A Contextual Study of the Jewish-Gentile Difference in Galatians and Romans*. Eugene, OR: Pickwick, 2014.

Levinsohn, Stephen H. *Discourse Features of New Testament Greek: A Coursebook on the Information Structure of New Testament Greek*. Dallas: SIL International, 2000.

Levinson, Stephen C. *Pragmatics*. CTL. Cambridge: Cambridge University Press, 1983.

Liu, Yong. "A Study of Lying from the Perspective of Relevance Theory." MA thesis, Huazhong Normal University, 2009.

Long, Fredrick J. *Ancient Rhetoric and Paul's Apology: The Compositional Unity of 2 Corinthians*. SNTSMS 131. Cambridge: Cambridge University Press, 2004.

Long, Thomas G. *1 and 2 Timothy and Titus*. BTCB. Louisville: Westminster John Knox, 2016.

Longacre, Robert E. *The Grammar of Discourse*. 2nd ed. TLL. New York: Plenum, 1996.

Lopez, Davina C. *Apostle to the Conquered: Reimagining Paul's Mission*. PCC. Minneapolis: Fortress, 2008.

Lyon, David. "Sliding in All Directions: Social Hermeneutics from Suspicion to Retrieval." Pages 99–115 in *Disciplining Hermeneutics: Inter-*

pretation in Christian Perspective. Edited by Roger Lundin. Grand Rapids: Eerdmans, 1997.

Madsen, Thorvald B., II. "The Ethics of the Pastoral Epistles." Pages 219–40 in *Entrusted with the Gospel: Paul's Theology in the Pastoral Epistles*. Edited by Andreas J. Köstenberger and Terry L. Wilder. Nashville: B&H Academic, 2010.

Malina, Bruce J., and John J. Pilch. *Social-Science Commentary on the Deutero-Pauline Letters*. Minneapolis: Fortress, 2013.

Manolessou, Io. "The Evolution of the Demonstrative System in Greek." *JGL* 2 (2002): 119–48.

Marshall, I. Howard. "The Christology of Luke-Acts and the Pastoral Epistles." Pages 167–82 in *Crossing the Boundaries: Essays in Biblical Interpretation in Honour of Michael D. Goulder*. Edited by Stanley E. Porter, Paul Joyce, and David E. Orton. Leiden: Brill, 1994.

———. *A Critical and Exegetical Commentary on the Pastoral Epistles*. ICC. Edinburgh: T&T Clark, 1999.

———. "The Pastoral Epistles in Recent Study." Pages 268–312 in *Entrusted with the Gospel: Paul's Theology in the Pastoral Epistles*. Edited by Andreas J. Köstenberger and Terry L. Wilder. Nashville: B&H Academic, 2010.

Matsui, Tomoko. "Assessing a Scenario-Based Account of Bridging Reference Assignment." Pages 123–58 in *Relevance Theory: Applications and Implications*. Edited by Robyn Carston and Seiji Uchida. P&B 37. Philadelphia: Benjamins, 1998.

Meade, David G. *Pseudonymity and Canon: An Investigation into the Relationship of Authorship and Authority in Jewish and Earliest Christian Tradition*. WUNT 39. Tübingen: Mohr Siebeck, 1986.

Meadowcroft, Tim. "Relevance as a Mediating Category in the Reading of Biblical Texts: Venturing beyond the Hermeneutical Circle." *JETS* 45 (2002): 611–27.

Metzger, Bruce M. *A Textual Commentary on the Greek New Testament*. Stuttgart: Deutsche Bibelgesellschaft, 1994.

Miller, James D. *The Pastoral Letters as Composite Documents*. SNTSMS 93. Cambridge: Cambridge University Press, 1997.

Miller, Monica R. *Religion and Hip Hop*. RRRMC. New York: Routledge, 2013.

Moberly, R. Walter L. "Biblical Hermeneutics and *Ecclesial* Responsibility." Pages 133–56 in *The Future of Biblical Interpretation: Responsible Plu-*

rality in Biblical Hermeneutics. Edited by Stanley E. Porter and Matthew R. Malcolm. Downers Grove, IL: IVP Academic, 2013.

Montague, George T. *First and Second Timothy, Titus*. CCSS. Grand Rapids: Baker Academic, 2008.

Morales, Nelson R. *Poor and Rich in James: A Relevance Theory Approach to James's Use of the Old Testament*. BBRSup 20. University Park, PA: Eisenbrauns, 2018.

Moule, C. F. D. "The Problem of the Pastoral Epistles: A Reappraisal." *BJRL* 47 (1965): 430–52.

Mounce, William D. *Pastoral Epistles*. WBC 46. Nashville: Nelson, 2000.

Nas. "Be a N—r Too." [Untitled album]. The Jones Experience; Def Jam, 2008.

Nida, Eugene, and Charles Taber. *The Theory and Practice of Translation*. Leiden: UBS, 1969.

Oberlinner, Lorenz. *Kommentar zum Titusbrief*. HThKNT 3. Freiburg im Breisgau: Herder, 1996.

O'Dea, Conor J., Stuart S. Miller, Emma B. Andres, Madelyn H. Ray, Derrick F. Till, and Donald A. Saucier. "Out of Bounds: Factors Affecting the Perceived Offensiveness of Racial Slurs." *LangSci* 52 (2015): 155–64.

Olbricht, Thomas H. "Aristotle, Aristotelianism." *DNTB*, 119–21.

O'Reilly, Matt. *Paul and the Resurrected Body: Social Identity and Ethical Practice*. ESEC 22. Atlanta: SBL Press, 2020.

Paisley, Brad. "Accidental Racist." *Wheelhouse*. Arista Nashville, 2013.

Papafragou, Anna. "Figurative Language and the Semantics-Pragmatics Distinction." *LL* 5 (1996): 179–93.

———. "Metonymy and Relevance." *UCLWPL* 7 (1995): 141–75.

Parker, Angela N. "One Womanist's View of Racial Reconciliation in Galatians." *JFSR* 34.2 (2018): 23–40.

Pattemore, Stephen W. "On the Relevance of Translation Theory." *RevExp* 108 (2011): 263–77.

———. Review of *A Relevant Way to Read: A New Approach to Exegesis and Communication*, by Margaret G. Sim. *RBL* (2018). https://www.sblcentral.org/home/bookDetails/11354.

———. *Souls under the Altar: Relevance Theory and the Discourse Structure of Revelation*. UBSMS 9. New York: United Bible Societies, 2003.

———. *The People of God in the Apocalypse: Discourse, Structure, and Exegesis*. SNTSMS 128. Cambridge: Cambridge University Press, 2004.

Peppiatt, Lucy. *Unveiling Paul's Women: Making Sense of 1 Corinthians 11:2–16*. Eugene, OR: Cascade, 2018.

———. *Women and Worship at Corinth: Paul's Rhetorical Arguments in 1 Corinthians*. Eugene, OR: Cascade, 2015.

Perkins, Larry J. *The Pastoral Letters: A Handbook on the Greek Text*. BHGNT. Waco, TX: Baylor University Press, 2017.

Porter, Christopher A. "Chapter 16: 1 Timothy." Pages 445–60 in *T&T Clark Social Identity Commentary on the New Testament*. Edited by J. Brian Tucker and Aaron Kuecker. New York: T&T Clark, 2018.

———. "Chapter 18: Titus." Pages 469–73 in *T&T Clark Social Identity Commentary on the New Testament*. Edited by J. Brian Tucker and Aaron Kuecker. New York: T&T Clark, 2018.

Porter, Stanley E. *The Apostle Paul: His Life, Thought, and Letters*. Grand Rapids: Eerdmans, 2016.

Porter, Stanley E., and Andrew W. Pitts. *Fundamentals of New Testament Textual Criticism*. Grand Rapids: Eerdmans, 2015.

Prior, Michael. *Paul the Letter-Writer and the Second Letter to Timothy*. JSNTSup 23. Sheffield: Sheffield Academic, 1989.

Punt, Jeremy. *Postcolonial Biblical Interpretation: Reframing Paul*. STR 20. Leiden: Brill, 2015.

Quinn, Jerome D. *The Letter to Titus: A New Translation and Commentary and an Introduction to Titus, I and II Timothy, the Pastoral Epistles*. AB 35. New York: Doubleday, 1990.

———. "Review of *The Pastoral Epistles* (Hermeneia) by Martin Dibelius and Hans Conzelmann, Trans. by Philip Buttolph and Adela Yarbro." *CBQ* 36 (1974): 582–84.

Recanati, François. "The Pragmatics of What Is Said." *M&L* 4 (1989): 295–329.

The Revised Common Lectionary: Consultation on Common Texts; Includes Complete List of Lections for Years A, B and C. Nashville: Abingdon, 1992.

Richards, William A. *Difference and Distance in Post-Pauline Christianity: An Epistolary Analysis of the Pastorals*. StBibLit 44. New York: Lang, 2002.

Robbins, Vernon K. *Exploring the Texture of Texts: A Guide to Socio-rhetorical Interpretation*. Valley Forge, PA: Trinity Press International, 1996.

Robertson, A. T. *A Grammar of the Greek New Testament in the Light of Historical Research*. 3rd ed. London: Hodder & Stoughton, 1919.

Rocha, Marco. "Anaphoric Demonstratives: Dealing with the Hard Cases." Pages 403–27 in *Anaphora Processing: Linguistic, Cognitive, and Computational Modelling*. Edited by António Branco, Tony McEnery, and Ruslan Mitkov. CILT 263. Amsterdam: Benjamins, 2005.

Rock, Chris. "Niggas vs. Black People." *Roll with the New*. DreamWorks, 1997.

Runge, Steven E. *Discourse Grammar of the Greek New Testament: A Practical Introduction for Teaching and Exegesis*. LBRS. Peabody, MA: Hendrickson, 2010.

Saarinen, Risto. *The Pastoral Epistles with Philemon and Jude*. BrazosTCB. Grand Rapids: Brazos, 2008.

Sanders, E. P. *Paul and Palestinian Judaism: A Comparison of Patterns of Religion*. Philadelphia: Fortress, 1977.

Saucier, Donald A., Conor J. O'Dea, and Megan L. Strain. "The Bad, the Good, the Misunderstood: The Social Effects of Racial Humor." *TIPS* 2 (2016): 75–85.

Scholz, Vilson. "Communication Models, Relevance Theory, Bible Translation, and Exegesis." Pages 234–43 in *The Press of the Text: Biblical Studies in Honor of James W. Voelz*. Edited by Andrew H. Bartlett, Jeffrey J. Kloha, and Paul R. Raabe. Eugene, OR: Pickwick, 2017.

Schüssler Fiorenza, Elisabeth. *But She Said: Feminist Practices of Biblical Interpretation*. Boston: Beacon, 1992.

———. "Feminist Studies in Religion and a Radical Democratic Ethos 1." *R&T* 2 (1995): 122–44.

Searle, John R. *Expression and Meaning: Studies in the Theory of Speech Acts*. Cambridge: Cambridge University Press, 1979.

———. "Indirect Speech Acts." Pages 59–82 in *Speech Acts*. Edited by Peter Cole and Jerry L. Morgan. SS 3. New York: Academic Press, 1975.

———. *Intentionality: An Essay in the Philosophy of Mind*. Cambridge: Cambridge University Press, 1983.

"See the Manuscript." Codex Sinaiticus. https://codexsinaiticus.org/en/manuscript.aspx.

Serban, Silviu. "Gricean Pragmatics and Text Linguistics." *ASHUJS* 12 (2011): 96–101.

Seto, Ken-ichi. "On Non-echoic Irony." Pages 239–56 in *Relevance Theory: Applications and Implications*. Edited by Robyn Carston and Seiji Uchida. P&B 37. Philadelphia: Benjamins, 1998.

Sim, Margaret G. *A Relevant Way to Read: A New Approach to Exegesis and Communication*. Eugene, OR: Pickwick, 2016.

Smith, Kevin G. "Bible Translation and Relevance Theory: The Translation of Titus." DLitt diss., University of Stellenbosch, 2000.
Smith, Michael B. "Cataphoric Pronouns as Mental Space Designators: Their Conceptual Import and Discourse Function." Pages 61–90 in *Cognitive and Communicative Approaches to Linguistic Analysis*. Edited by Ellen Contini-Morava, Robert S. Kirsner, and Betsy Rodriguez-Bachiller. SFSL 51. Amsterdam: Benjamins, 2004.
Soards, Marion L., and Darrell J. Pursiful. *Galatians*. SHBC. Macon, GA: Smith & Helwys, 2015.
Song, Nam Sun. "Metaphor and Metonymy." Pages 87–104 in *Relevance Theory: Applications and Implications*. Edited by Robyn Carston and Seiji Uchida. P&B 37. Philadelphia: Benjamins, 1998.
Sperber, Dan, and Deirdre Wilson. "Irony in the Use-Mention Distinction." Pages 295–318 in *Radical Pragmatics*. Edited by Peter Cole. New York: Academic Press, 1981.
———. "Pragmatics." *Cognition* 10 (1981): 281–86.
———. "Pragmatics." Pages 468–504 in *Oxford Handbook of Contemporary Philosophy*. OHO. London: Oxford University Press, 2007.
———. *Pragmatics: An Overview; CLCS Occasional Paper No. 16*. Dublin: Dublin University, Trinity College (Ireland), Centre for Language and Communication Studies, 1986.
———. "Pragmatics, Modularity and Mind-Reading." *M&L* 17 (2002): 3–23.
———. *Relevance: Communication and Cognition*. 2nd ed. Cambridge, MA: Blackwell, 1996.
Spicq, Ceslas. *Les Épitres Pastorales*. Vol. 2. EBib. Paris: Gabalda, 1969.
Standhartinger, Angela. "Eusebeia in den Pastoralbriefen: Ein Beitrag zum Einfluss Römischen Denkens auf das Entstehende Christentum." *NovT* 48 (2006): 51–82.
Stegemann, Wolfgang. "Anti-Semitic and Racist Prejudices in Titus 1:10–16." Pages 271–94 in *Ethnicity and the Bible*. Edited by Mark G. Brett. Translated by David E. Orton. Leiden: Brill, 1996.
Sterling, Gregory E. "'A Law unto Themselves': Limited Universalism in Philo and Paul." *ZNW* 107 (2016): 30–47
Stowers, Stanley Kent. *Letter Writing in Greco-Roman Antiquity*. LEC 5. Philadelphia: Westminster, 1986.
Strataridaki, Anna. "Epimenides of Crete: Some Notes on His Life, Works and the Verse ʻΚρῆτες Ἀεὶ Ψεῦσται.'" *Fortunatae* 2 (1991): 207–23.

Strecker, Georg, and Friedrich Wilhelm Horn. *Theology of the New Testament*. Edited by Friedrich Wilhelm Horn. Translated by M. Eugene Boring. New York: de Gruyter, 2000.
Theron, Daniel J. "Muratorian Fragment." Pages 106–13 in *Evidence of Tradition*. Edited and translated by Theron. Grand Rapids: Baker, 1980.
Thiselton, Anthony C. "The Logical Role of the Liar Paradox in Titus 1:12, 13: A Dissent from the Commentaries in the Light of Philosophical and Logical Analysis." *BibInt* 2 (1994): 207–23.
Towner, Philip H. *1–2 Timothy and Titus*. IVPNTC 14. Downers Grove, IL: InterVarsity, 1994.
———. *The Letters to Timothy and Titus*. NICNT. Grand Rapids: Eerdmans, 2006.
———. "Pauline Theology or Pauline Tradition in the Pastoral Epistles: The Question of Method." *TynBul* 46 (1995): 287–314.
———. Review of *The Pastoral Letters as Composite Documents*, by James D. Miller. *JBL* 118 (1999): 372–74.
Tracy, David W. "The Dialogue of Jews and Christians: A Necessary Hope." *CTSR* 76 (1986): 20–28.
———. "Interpretation (Hermeneutics)." Pages 343–49 in *International Encyclopedia of Communications*. Edited by Erik Barnouw. Oxford: Oxford University Press, 1989.
———. "Modes of Theological Argument." *ThTo* 33 (1977): 387–95.
———. *Plurality and Ambiguity: Hermeneutics, Religion, Hope*. San Francisco: Harper & Row, 1987.
Trobisch, David. *Paul's Letter Collection: Tracing the Origins*. Minneapolis: Fortress, 1994.
Twomey, Jay. *The Pastoral Epistles through the Centuries*. BBC. Chichester: Wiley-Blackwell, 2009.
Uchida, Seiji. "Text and Relevance." Pages 161–78 in *Relevance Theory: Applications and Implications*. Edited by Robyn Carston and Seiji Uchida. P&B 37. Philadelphia: Benjamins, 1998.
Van Nes, Jermo. "On the Origin of the Pastorals' Authenticity Criticism: A 'New' Perspective*." *NTS* 62 (2016): 315–20.
———. *Pauline Language and the Pastoral Epistles: A Study of Linguistic Variation in the Corpus Paulinum*. LBS 16. Leiden: Brill, 2018.
Van Neste, Ray. *Cohesion and Structure in the Pastoral Epistles*. JSNTSup 280. New York: T&T Clark International, 2004.
———. "Cohesion and Structure in the Pastoral Epistles." Pages 84–104 in *Entrusted with the Gospel: Paul's Theology in the Pastoral Epistles*.

Edited by Andreas J. Köstenberger and Terry L. Wilder. Nashville: B&H Academic, 2010.

Vanhoozer, Kevin J. "Discourse on Matter: Hermeneutics and the 'Miracle' of Understanding." *IJST* 7 (2005): 5–37.

Villanueva, Margaret A. "Ethnic Slurs or Free Speech? Politics of Representation in a Student Newspaper." *AEQ* 27 (1996): 168–85.

Vogel, Manuel. "Die Kreterpolemik des Titusbriefes und die antike Ethnographie." *ZNW* 101 (2010): 252–66.

Wall, Robert W., and Richard B. Steele. *1 and 2 Timothy and Titus*. THNTC. Grand Rapids: Eerdmans, 2012.

Wallace, Daniel B. *Greek Grammar beyond the Basics: An Exegetical Syntax of the New Testament*. Grand Rapids: Zondervan, 1996.

Wansink, Craig S. "Roman Law and Legal System." *DNTB*, 984–91.

Wendland, Ernst. "Review of *Bible Translation Basics: Communicating Scripture in a Relevant Way*, by Harriet Hill, Ernst-August Gutt, Margaret Hill, Christoph Unger, and Rick Floyd." *BT* 63 (2012): 219–24.

West, Gerald O., ed. *Reading Other-Wise: Socially Engaged Biblical Scholars Reading with Their Local Communities*. SemeiaSt 62. Atlanta: Society of Biblical Literature, 2007.

Wieland, George M. "Roman Crete and the Letter to Titus." *NTS* 55 (2009): 338–54.

Wilder, Terry L. *Pseudonymity, the New Testament, and Deception: An Inquiry into Intention and Reception*. Lanham, MD: University Press of America, 2004.

Wilson, Deirdre. "The Pragmatics of Verbal Irony: Echo or Pretence?" *Lingua* 116 (2006): 1722–43.

Wilson, Deirdre, and Dan Sperber. *Meaning and Relevance*. Cambridge: Cambridge University Press, 2012.

———. "Pragmatics and Time." Pages 1–22 in *Relevance Theory: Applications and Implications*. Edited by Robyn Carston and Seiji Uchida. P&B 37. Philadelphia: Benjamins, 1998.

Witherington, Ben, III. *A Socio-rhetorical Commentary on Titus, 1–2 Timothy and 1–3 John*. Volume 1 of *Letters and Homilies for Hellenized Christians*. Downers Grove, IL: IVP Academic, 2006.

Wukasch, Benjamin Joel. "Centered Fuller Communication: Sensus Plenior, Relevance Theory, and a Balanced Hermeneutic." Thesis, Trinity Western University, 2015.

Yamanashi, Masa-aki. "Some Issues in the Treatment of Irony and Related Tropes." Pages 271–81 in *Relevance Theory: Applications and Implica-*

tions. Edited by Robyn Carston and Seiji Uchida. P&B 37. Philadelphia: Benjamins, 1998.
Yoon, Suwon. "Semantic Constraint and Pragmatic Nonconformity for Expressives: Compatibility Condition on Slurs, Epithets, Anti-honorifics, Intensifiers, and Mitigators." *LangSci* 52 (2015): 46–69.
Young, Frances. *The Theology of the Pastoral Letters*. NTT. Cambridge: Cambridge University Press, 1994.
Yus, Francisco. "Relevance Theory and Contextual Sources-Centered Analysis of Irony: Current Research and Compatibility." Pages 147–71 in *Relevance Theory: Recent Developments, Current Challenges, and Future Directions*. Edited by Manuel Padilla Cruz. P&B NS 268. Amsterdam: Benjamins, 2016.
Zimmer, Christoph. "Die Lügner-Antinomie in Titus 1,12." *LB* 59 (1987): 77–99.

Ancient Sources Index

Hebrew Bible/Septuagint

Exodus
  5:7–9   34
  23:1 LXX   207

Leviticus
  5:1   203
  18:30 LXX   210
  22:5 LXX   210
  22:8 LXX   210

Numbers
  19:13 LXX   210
  19:20 LXX   210

Deuteronomy   214
  19:15–21   203, 207
  21:20   214
  21:21   214
  21:22–23 LXX   197
  21:23   214

Psalms
  17:25–26 LXX   197

Proverbs
  26:4–5   102

Isaiah
  22:19 LXX   22
  22:21 LXX   22

Deuterocanonical Books

1 Maccabees
  10:67   35

2 Maccabees
  1:23–30   198

New Testament

Matthew
  11:19   214
  12:13   276
  15:31   276
  25:14–30   103

Mark
  5:34   276

Luke   26, 172
  5:31   276
  6:27–42   103
  7:10   276
  7:34   214
  8:47   204
  12.42   23
  15:27   276
  16:1   23
  16:2–4   22
  16:3   23
  16:8   23
  16:2–4   22

John
  3:21   272

John (cont.)		5:6	24
3:32–33	207	7:21–8:2	277
5:6	276	8:32	125
5:9	276	9:1	207
5:11	276	10:3	125
5:14	276	10:12	222
5:15	276	11:13	4, 47, 283, 293
7:23	276	11:17–21	220
8:13–18	207	11:24	125
9:35	207	11:26	24
11:51	145	12:13	277
19:35	207	14:1–4	220
21:24	207	14:4–5	125
		14:20–21	222
Acts	1, 47, 61, 130	16:18	222
2:7–11	35	16:23	23
4:10	276	16:26	272
6:7	272		
13:1	172	1 Corinthians	
15:1–2	210	1:10	220
15:7–9	210	1:11	206, 270
15:22	172	4:1–2	23
15:32	172	4:16	204
17:28	130	5:1	206, 228, 257, 270
20:33–35	222	5:11	222
22:24	204	5:13	214
23:28	204	6:1–11	204
24:25	23	6:8	222
27	68	7:9	23
27:7–13	35	8:8–13	222
27:21	35	9:17	22
28:20	204	9:19–23	293
		9:20–22	47
Romans	1, 24, 30, 51, 65–66	9:22	4, 275
1:5	272	9:25	23
1:18	24	10:7	222
1:25	24	11–14	270
2:1–29	47	11:1	204
2:22	198, 210	11:18	220
2:25–29	210	11:20–22	222
3:4	207	11:33–34	222
3:21	207	12:13	222
4:5	24	12:28–29	141, 172
4:12	211	14:29	141
4:14	210	14:32	141

14:37–38	141–42	5:12	1, 12, 47
15:15	207	5:15	220
		5:23	23
2 Corinthians	203	6:5	125
5:17	277	6:7–9	211
10:1–18	270	6:9	125, 222
10:10	270	6:10	220, 224
11	207	6:12	211
11:4	220	6:12–13	211
11:13–15	1	6:15	219
12:2	44	6:16	289
12:3	44		
13:8	272	Ephesians	181, 184
		1:10	22
Galatians	1, 18, 35, 204, 211–13, 215–16, 219, 288	2:6	44
		2:11–13	220
1:6–7	220	2:19	220, 224
1:10	288	2:20	141, 172
1:20	207	2:21–22	220
2:1–5	211	3:1	22
2:1–10	212	3:2	22
2:2	125, 293	3:5	141
2:7–9	211	3:9	22
2:8	47, 293	4:1–6	220
2:12	211	4:11	141, 172
2:14–16	210	4:25	222
2:15	165	4:28	222
2:15–21	165–66		
2:21	47	Philippians	18
3:1	1	1:7	209
3:2–5	210	2:1–2	220
3:8	210	3:2	1, 47, 211
3:10	47	3:2–7	47
3:13	197, 214	3:5	209
3:25–29	211	3:17	204, 225
3:26–28	204	4:2	220
3:28	47, 222, 288	4:9	204
4:2	23		
4:17	47, 220	Colossians	
4:19	288	1:25	22
4:24a	43	2:16	220
4:29	220	3:8–9	222
5:1–23	277	3:11	222
5:3–4	47	3:15	220
5:6–12	211	4:11	211

1 Thessalonians		2 Timothy	1, 23–24, 26, 98, 128
1:6–7	204	1:6	205
2:9	222	1:7	23
4:9–12	222	1:9	125
5:13	220	1:11	283, 293
5:14	222	1:12	22, 205
		1:13	276
2 Thessalonians		1:14	22
2:4	24	2:14	42
3:6	220	2:20–21	220
3:6–15	220, 222	3:8	128
3:9	204, 225	3:16	213, 220
3:14–15	220	4:3	276
		4:3–4	125, 220
1 Timothy	18, 23–24, 26, 45		
1:3	124	Titus	1, 4, 7–9, 11, 13–17, 20–21, 23–27, 29–30, 32–34, 36–40, 42–51, 53, 56, 59–62, 65–68, 70, 78, 85, 87, 91, 111, 117, 119–21, 123–24, 126, 128, 130, 134–35, 138, 141–42, 152, 156, 206–12, 214–16, 218, 220–221, 223–26, 229–30, 232–35, 240, 243–44, 247, 249–50, 254, 258–59, 263–64, 267–71, 273–78, 281–88, 290–294
1:3–4	220		
1:3–7	123		
1:4	22		
1:5	22		
1:7–9	211		
1:10	275–76		
1:20	231		
2:5–6	277		
2:6	125	1	275
2:7	283, 293	1:1	24, 130, 207, 221, 224–25, 267, 276, 288, 291
2:9	23		
2:15	23	1:2	130, 207
3:2	23	1:3	125, 223, 278
3:4–5	125, 220	1:4	111, 263–64, 291
3:12	125	1:5	121, 130, 209, 223, 263
3:15	214	1:5–9	25, 43, 146, 236
4:2	125	1:5–16	31, 121, 225, 236, 259, 270, 283
4:12	204, 212, 225	1:6	214, 223, 271, 291
5:4	125	1:7	23, 224–25
5:8	125	1:7–10	43, 225, 256, 271
5:13	222	1:8	23, 221, 223
5:23	22	1:9	25,119, 121, 221, 224–25, 229–30, 256, 271, 273–74, 276–77
6:1	125		
6:3	276		
6:3–5	220	1:9b–12a	42
6:15	125	1:10	2, 43, 45–47, 66, 118, 120–21, 123–24, 146, 156, 208–9, 211, 223, 225, 229, 235, 288
6:20	22		
		1:10–11	41–43, 45, 48–49, 63, 126, 129, 138, 146, 236

Ancient Sources Index   319

1:10–12 2, 130–131, 221
1:10–12a 48, 125
1:10–16 6, 42–43, 49, 65–66, 68, 118, 122, 126–27, 208, 214, 229, 236, 270, 283
1:11 2, 41–43, 118–19, 121, 123, 136, 220, 225, 229, 236, 256
1:11a 3, 137
1:11b 137
1:12 1–3, 6–7, 9, 11, 13–15, 30, 32–33, 36–37, 39–42, 44–45, 49, 53, 56, 60–61, 63, 83–84, 87–88, 111, 114, 116–18, 121–26, 129–33, 135–39, 141–43, 152, 156, 228, 236, 240, 245, 247, 256, 258–59, 261, 281–83, 285, 290
1:12a 2–3, 44, 51, 55, 120, 123–25, 136, 146, 152, 232, 236
1:12b 1, 42–43, 48, 122–23
1:12–13a 126
1:12–13 126, 269
1:12–14 137, 231
1:13 25, 42, 55, 119, 126, 128–30, 133, 138, 143, 156, 207, 229–30, 236, 256, 261, 270–71, 273–76, 283, 291
1:13a 3, 56, 126, 128–29, 138
1:13a–b 232–33
1:13b 126, 138, 220
1:13c 126
1:13–14 48, 133, 229
1:13c–14 232, 234
1:13–16 48
1:14 2, 45, 47, 123–24, 133–34, 156, 207–9, 213, 262, 275, 284
1:14–16 48
1:15 134, 143, 291
1:15–16 143
1:16 207
2 32, 275
2:1 230, 275, 277
2:1–2 119, 230, 274–76
2:1–10 212, 221, 224–25, 271, 273, 275
2:1–3:11 283

2:2 23, 221, 230, 271, 273, 277, 291
2:3 221–23, 271
2:3–4 224
2:3–5 63
2:4 22, 221, 271
2:4–6 23
2:5 125, 220–221, 223–24, 271
2:6 221–22
2:6–7 224
2:7 221, 225
2:7–8 270–271
2:8 118–19, 229–30, 273–77
2:9 125, 223–25
2:9–10 224–25
2:10 221, 225, 291
2:11 220
2:11–13 271
2:11–14 8, 63, 213, 275, 277, 282–83
2:11–15 209, 216, 230
2:12 23–24, 36, 40, 221–22, 276
2:14 271
2:15 25, 111, 118, 212, 218, 223, 229, 263, 270, 274–75, 278
3 275
3:1 223
3:2 225
3:3–5 219
3:3–7 2, 63, 209, 214, 216, 224, 230, 277–78, 281–83
3:4 220–221
3:4–7 8
3:8 130, 291
3:9 10–11, 25, 47, 118, 123, 208–9, 211, 221, 235, 270, 277
3:10 2, 218, 221, 229–30, 274–75
3:15 222, 264, 291

Hebrews
4:10 125
7:27 125
9:12 125
13:12 125

1 Peter
4:10 23

1 Peter (cont.)		
4:17	220, 224	
5:3	225	

2 Peter		
1:3	24	
1:6	23, 24	
2:5	24	
2:6	24	
2:9	24	
2:16	141, 142	
3:7	24	
3:11	24	

1 John		
1:6	273	

2 John		
4	273	

3 John		
3–4	273	
8	273	

Jude		
4	24	
15	24	
18	24	

Ancient Jewish Authors

Josephus, *Jewish Antiquities*
17.12.1 — 211

Josephus, *Jewish War*
2.7.1 — 211

Josephus, *The Life*
76 — 211

Philo, *De specialibus legibus*
1.51 — 215
1.309 — 215
3.43–45 — 39

Philo, *De virtutibus*
178 — 215
219 — 215

Philo, *Legatio ad Gaium*
282 — 211

Greco-Roman Literature

Aeschylus, *Choephori*
613–620 — 39

Aristotle, *Athēnaīn politeia*
1–2 — 53

Aristotle, *Politica*
1.1253 — 224

Aristotle, *Rhetorica*
3.17.10 — 53

Athenagoras, *Legatio pro Christianis*
30.3–5 — 58

Augustine, *De doctrina christiana*
1.41 — 290

Callimachus, *Hymni*
1.8–9 — 31, 50, 57, 165
1.9 — 57

Cicero, *De divination*
1.34 — 54

Cicero, *De republica*
3.9.15 — 33, 35, 38

Clement of Alexandria, *Stromateis*
1.14 — 36, 43, 50, 53, 64

Clement of Alexandria, *Protrepticus*
2.32 — 50
4.42 — 50

Ancient Sources Index

Dionysius of Halicarnassus, *Antiquitates romanae*
2.24.3–2.27.4 — 224

Hesiod, *Theogonia*
474–479 — 50

Jerome, *Commentariorum in Epistulam ad Galatas libri III*
3:1a — 35

Jerome, *Commentariorum in Epistulam ad Titum liber*
1.10–12 — 196
1.12 — 64
1.12–14 — 43, 51

Irenaeus, *Adversus haereses (Elenchos)*
4.33.3 — 51

Livy, *Ab urbe condita*
44.45 — 38

Lucian, *Philopseudes*
3 — 57

Lucian, *Timon*
6 — 54

Origen, *Contra Celsum*
3.43.1–35 — 58

Plato, *Leges*
1.642 — 53
1.642d–e — 50, 53, 54

Pliny the Elder, *Naturalis historia*
8.83 — 37–38

Plutarch, *Aemilius Paullus*
23 — 37, 39

Plutarch, *De capienda ex inimicis utilitate*
1 [86c] — 37, 39

Plutarch, *Solon*
12 — 53

Polybius, *Historiae*
6.43–45 — 36
6.46 — 37
8.16 — 37–38
24.4 — 39

Quintilian, *Institutio oratoria*
5.7.1 — 205

Quintus Smyrnaeus, *Posthomerica*
5.345–351 — 36

Socrates of Constantinople, *Historia ecclesiastica*
3.16 — 51

Strabo, *Geographica*
5.2.4 — 36
6.1.8 — 36
10.3.11–13 — 36
10.3.19 — 36
10.4.1–22 — 36
10.4.9 — 36, 40
10:16 — 36
10:20–22 — 36

Tertullian, *De anima*
20 — 35

Theodore of Mopsuestia, *Commentary on Titus*
1.10–12 — 52, 196

Theodoret of Cyrus, *Commentary on Titus*
1.10–12 — 44, 52

Thucydides, *Historiae*
2.85–86 — 39
6.43 — 36
7.57 — 39

Modern Authors Index

Aageson, James W. 16–17, 23, 29, 98, 134, 208, 213–15
Ágnes, Hámori 101, 239
Anum, Eric 243
Apple, Kevin Joel 101, 237
Arichea, Daniel C. 165, 183
Ariel, Mira 233
Ashwell, Lauren 157, 159, 164
Aune, David E. 224
Austin, J. L. 71, 96, 110, 131, 148–49, 250–251–54
Barclay, John M. G. 166, 204, 211–13, 215–16, 219–20, 275–76
Barrett, C. K. 15, 22, 25–26, 44, 55–56, 134, 145, 188–89, 194, 207–9, 216, 218, 221, 228–31, 267, 277–78
Bassler, Jouette M. 4, 41, 134, 137, 188–89, 218, 221, 246, 286
Bauer, David R. 9, 43, 103, 191, 278
Baugh, Stephen M. 32, 34, 162
Baum, Armin Daniel 19, 24, 87
Bénétreau, Samuel 163
Besançon Spencer, Aída 163
Bianchi, Claudia 161, 164
Biezeveld, Kune 243, 245
Bird, Michael F. 276
Bird, Thomas E. 258
Blakemore, Diane 136
Blass, Regina 74, 78, 85, 106, 113–14, 122, 133, 180, 182, 187, 198
Bonnycastle, Stephen 96, 110, 254
Borkent, Mike 200
Briggs, Richard S. 244, 249, 251–52, 266, 290–291
Brisard, Frank 95
Broadbent, Ralph 226
Brown, Derek 25
Brox, Norbert 41, 68, 196
Bultmann, Rudolf 271
Calvin, John 57, 145
Carroll, Noel 79–80, 186
Carston, Robyn 80, 82–83, 92–93, 96, 105–6, 136, 173, 186, 249–50, 256
Casson, Sarah H. 11, 86, 97, 135, 192, 286
Childs, Brevard S. 183
Clark, Billy 9, 11, 67, 70–71, 76, 82–84, 89, 91–94, 96–99, 102–3, 106–8, 114–15, 117, 139–40, 143, 145–46, 148–51, 179–81, 186–87, 201, 226–28, 231–32, 240–41, 253–54, 256–57, 260, 263, 268–69
Collins, Raymond F. 1, 16, 239, 249
Conzelmann, Hans 48, 60, 67–68, 239–40, 286
Cook, David 18, 26, 67–68
Couser, Greg A. 18, 26, 67–68
Craigmiles, Shawn 133
Crandall, Christian S. 163
Cristea, Dan 117, 121–22
Croom, Adam M. 159, 164–65
Currie, Gregory 149, 167, 169–70
Dancygier, Barbara 200–201
Davies, Margaret 230
Dibelius, Martin 48, 60, 67–68, 239–40, 286
Donelson, Lewis R. 27–28, 68
Easton, Burton Scott 18
Eckstein, Arthur M. 37
Ehrman, Bart D. 220

Eisenbaum, Pamela M. 47, 287–88
Eshleman, Amy 163
Faber, Riemer A. 45, 66, 68, 120, 196, 218, 221, 276
Falconer, Robert Alexander 18
Fantin, Joseph D. 181, 286
Fee, Gordon D. 22, 26
Feuerbach, Ludwi 156
Fillmore, Charles J. 200–201
Fiore, Benjamin 200–201
Forbes, A. Dean 16
Forbes, Christopher 203
Fredriksen, Paula 237, 276
Fuchs, Rüdiger 20–21
Furlong, Anne 3, 78, 82, 88–89, 103, 110, 152, 177, 186, 227, 237, 254, 259, 262
Garlington, Don 246
Garmendia, Joana 105, 140, 149, 167, 169
Gibbs, Raymond W., Jr. 74, 76, 79–80, 108, 147, 150–152, 155, 168, 174, 185, 187, 227, 237–38, 255, 261, 264–65
Goh, Benson 148, 181, 184, 186
Gómez-González, María A. 198–99
Goodwin, Philip W. 11, 55, 85, 149, 172, 262, 286
Gray, Patrick 33–34, 59, 66
Green, Gene L. 11–13, 55, 72, 85–86, 91, 113, 115, 118, 139, 143, 147, 181–82, 186, 238–39, 256, 284, 286, 291
Grice, H. Paul 71–73, 113, 120, 140–41, 144, 147–48, 150, 166–67, 169–70, 177, 180, 237, 249, 251, 260–261, 265, 269
Griffin, Hayne P. 119
Griffiths, Alan H. 53
Guthrie, Donald 18, 24, 27, 53, 208, 231, 287, 291–92
Gutt, Ernst-August 85, 93, 240, 255, 286
Hanson, Anthony Tyrrell 27, 46, 64, 67
Harrill, J. Albert 51, 53, 57, 206
Harrison, P. N. 18, 26, 67
Hatton, Howard 283

Hays, Richard B. 213, 226
Herzer, Jens 20–21, 25
Hill, Harriet 85, 238–39
Ho, Chiao Ek 4, 34–35
Hoklotubbe, T. Christopher 4, 21, 24, 46, 64–66, 175, 194, 215, 221, 258, 278, 281–82
Horn, Friedrich Wilhelm 271
Huang, Yan 70, 76, 80, 90, 104, 113–14, 147, 254, 261
Huizenga, Annette Bourland 5, 7, 17, 22–23, 30–34, 41–42, 45, 47, 49, 67, 189, 195, 209, 218, 230, 246, 274, 276–77, 289, 291–93
Hunt, R. Reed 97, 101–2
Huxley, George Leonard 50, 54, 58–59
Inskeep, Steve 158
Itani, Reiko 152
Jeffers, James S. 204, 224
Jervis, L. Ann 203
Jobes, Karen H. 85, 102, 184, 201, 238, 264, 286
Johnson, Luke Timothy 18–20, 24, 29, 31–32, 66, 203, 273, 291–93
Kahl, Werner 243
Karris, Robert J. 27
Kartzow, Marianne Bjelland 219
Kecskes, Istvan 101
Keener, Craig S. 130
Kidd, Reggie M. 36–37, 40, 45–46, 66, 120, 194, 221
Klangwisan, Yael 86, 187, 245, 272, 286
Knight, George W. 41, 120–121
Kolaiti, Patricia 138, 140, 143–44
Köstenberger, Andreas J. 4, 20, 27–28, 31, 189, 193
Kujanpää, Katja 51, 136, 154, 202, 268
Künne, Wolfgang 58
Kwapis, Ken 159
Laansma, Jon C. 56
Lampe, Peter 203
Lea, Thomas D. 119
Lee, G. M. 50
Lee, Jae Won 165
Levinsohn, Stephen H. 137

Levinson, Stephen C. 70, 80–83, 93, 99–100, 102, 110, 114, 116, 120, 126–27, 129–30, 146, 169, 173, 177, 251–53, 261, 265
Liu, Yong 72
Long, Fredrick J. 203–5
Long, Thomas G. 66
Longacre, Robert E. 97, 132
Lopez, Davina C. 289
Lyon, David 223, 244
Madelyn, H. Ray
Madsen, Thorvald B., II 193, 196–97, 271, 273–74
Malina, Bruce J. 61
Manolessou, Io 128
Marshall, I. Howard 18, 20–21, 23, 26, 28, 31, 38, 51–54, 60, 118, 120, 188–89, 202–3, 211, 222, 263, 273, 289
Matsui, Tomoko 186, 200
Meade, David G. 19
Meadowcroft, Tim 3, 85, 114, 178
Metzger, Bruce M. 118-19
Miller, James D. 18, 27–28, 67
Miller, Monica R. 30
Moberly, R. Walter L. 7–8, 273, 292
Montague, George T. 283
Morales, Nelson R. 286
Moule, C. F. D. 18, 26–27
Mounce, William D. 1, 16, 30–33, 37–39, 42–43, 45, 47, 52, 58, 64–65, 68, 119–20, 134, 161, 188–89, 205–11, 218, 221, 230, 239, 263, 267–68
Nida, Eugene 55, 165
O'Dea, Conor J. 157, 159–60, 162
O'Reilly, Matt 270
Oberlinner, Lorenz 53
Olbricht, Thomas H. 203
Paisley, Brad 156
Papafragou, Anna 145
Parker, Angela N. 213, 288
Pattemore, Stephen W. 11, 13, 79, 86, 181, 284, 286
Peppiatt, Lucy 270
Perkins, Larry J. 56, 119, 121, 205
Pilch, John J. 61
Pitts, Andrew W. 132
Porter, Christopher A. 210, 263
Porter, Stanley E. 16, 132
Postolache, Oana-Diana 117, 121–22
Prior, Michael 21
Punt, Jeremy 247
Pursiful, Darrell J. 165
Quinn, Jerome D. 4–5, 26, 31, 39, 48, 51, 58, 119, 131, 146, 172, 205, 211
Recanati, François 171, 227
Richards, William A. 25
Robbins, Vernon K. 29
Robertson, A. T. 125
Rocha, Marco 127
Rock, Chris 159
Runge, Steven E. 130, 132–38, 192, 198
Saarinen, Risto 263, 289
Sanders, E. P. 276
Sanders, José 200
Saucier, Donald A. 157, 159–60
Scholz, Vilson 85
Schüssler Fiorenza, Elisabeth 244, 289
Searle, John R. 131, 250, 252, 265
Serban, Silviu 113, 251, 269
Seto, Ken-ichi 111, 131, 154–55, 167, 171, 172–74
Sim, Margaret G. 85–86
Smith, Kevin G. 11, 45, 55, 85, 23, 231, 265, 284, 286
Smith, Michael B. 117, 119, 121
Soards, Marion L. 165
Song, Nam Sun 86, 106, 110–111, 145, 171, 175, 264, 268, 272
Sperber, Dan 71–72, 74–75, 78, 81–84, 88–90, 94–96, 103, 105, 107–8, 114–16, 136–37, 140, 143, 147, 150, 154–56, 157, 167, 178, 180–81, 231, 235, 238–40, 252–55, 257–59
Spicq, Ceslas 145
Standhartinger, Angela 258
Stegemann, Wolfgang 42, 47, 49, 208–9, 218, 221, 246
Sterling, Gregory E. 215
Stowers, Stanley Kent 203
Strain, Megan L. 157, 159–60

Strataridaki, Anna 33
Strecker, Georg 271
Taber, Charles 55
Theron, Daniel J. 8
Thiselton, Anthony C.   32, 35–36, 52, 59, 63–64, 66, 128, 131, 162, 285
Till, Derrick F.
Towner, Philip H.   17–18, 20–21, 23, 25, 28, 51–52, 62–63, 66, 126, 130–31, 188–89, 196–97, 210
Tracy, David W.   150, 236, 244–46
Trobisch, David 18, 20
Twomey, Jay   47, 67, 134, 218, 221, 246
Uchida, Seiji   67, 73, 77–78, 80, 82–83, 92, 96, 101, 106, 111, 113, 136, 146, 152, 171, 173, 186, 256
Van Nes, Jermo   16, 23–24, 68
Van Neste, Ray 27–28
Vandelanotte, Lieven 200
Vanhoozer, Kevin J.   86, 104, 291
Villanueva, Margaret A. 162
Vogel, Manuel   41, 44, 49, 52, 61–62, 68, 160, 218, 283, 286
Wall, Robert W.   46, 183, 202–3, 211–12, 278–79
Wallace, Daniel B. 128
Wansink, Craig S. 202–4, 271
Wendland, Ernst 85
Wieland, George M. 36
Wilder, Terry L.   4, 19–20, 27, 31, 193, 263
Wilson, Deirdre   71–72, 74–75, 78, 81–84, 88–90, 94–96, 103, 105, 107–8, 113–16, 131, 136–38, 140, 143–44, 147, 149, 151, 154–56, 164, 166–67, 169, 176, 178, 180–181, 231, 235, 238–40, 252–55, 257–59
Witherington, Ben, III 51, 63
Wukasch, Benjamin Joel 85
Yamanashi, Masa-aki 171
Yoon, Suwon   131, 157, 159, 242
Young, Frances   27, 31–32, 165, 222, 224
Yus, Francisco   102–3, 147, 256, 260, 264
Zimmer, Christoph 59–60

Subject Index

apologia (lifestyle), 36–37, 40, 45–46, 66, 120, 194, 221, 289
archaeology, 32, 34–35, 182. *See also* historical background inquiry
authorship, 4, 8–9, 15–21, 25, 27, 48, 68, 79, 239–40, 292. *See also* provenance, pseudonymity
bigotry, 1, 3, 9, 14, 38, 47, 49, 60, 158, 165, 170, 206–7, 217, 222, 228, 236, 246, 257, 282, 285, 287–90, 292
canon (Titus in the New Testament), 7–8, 15, 19, 24, 26–27, 30, 40, 46–47, 79, 134, 141–42, 152, 168, 183, 211–12, 220. 240, 278–79, 283–84, 287, 290–94
cognitive effects, 10–11, 74–76, 83, 95, 101, 104, 106–11, 115, 136, 139, 141, 145, 173, 175, 179, 185, 199, 213, 226–8, 237, 254–57
cognitive environment, 69, 74–75, 91, 95–100, 103, 106, 119, 124, 137, 178–82, 184–87, 193, 198, 201–2, 207, 212, 214, 222, 226, 238, 240, 256, 258, 266. *See also* contextual assumptions, implicated premises
cognitive principle. *See* principles of relevance theory
coherence of the Pastorals or Titus, 7–8, 21, 27–28, 48, 68, 79, 90, 132, 190, 196, 213, 227–28, 230, 293
communicative principle. *See* principles of relevance theory
conjunctions
ἀλλά, 133–34
γάρ, 43, 54, 57, 118, 135–36, 146, 190–192, 208, 223, 229

conjunctions (cont.)
δέ, 54, 134–37, 192, 208, 217, 275
ἵνα, 133, 190–92, 197, 220, 230–31, 234, 274–76
contextual assumptions, 46, 75, 77, 90, 92, 95, 97–98, 101, 105, 107, 115, 128–29, 131, 139, 144, 178–80, 182, 184–87, 192, 216, 226–27, 229, 231–32, 235–36, 241–42, 256, 258. *See also* cognitive environment, implicated premises
discourse analysis, 132–33, 135
doctrine, 2, 9, 13, 15, 22, 25, 32, 36, 61–63, 119, 134, 136, 138, 141, 160, 183, 188, 191, 193, 195, 207, 216, 218, 221, 230, 271, 277, 279, 287, 293. *See also* leadership
echoic speech, 153–54
encyclopedic information, 139, 150
Epimenides, 5, 7, 50–61, 64–65, 123–25, 128, 130, 132, 142, 145–46, 157–58, 165, 174, 196, 206, 231, 283
ethics, 36, 46, 271, 277, 290
ethnography, 36, 62, 65, 245
explicature, 72, 75–76, 89, 92–94, 98, 105, 108, 114–15, 146–50, 152, 168, 171, 178–80, 227, 231–32, 235, 282
figurative speech, 141, 261. *See also* literal-figurative continuum
frame semantics, 186, 200–201, 216, 246
gentiles, Cretans as, 2, 45–47, 120, 163–65, 180, 207, 209, 211–13, 215–16, 219, 222, 224, 235, 270, 283, 289, 293
gospel summaries, 63, 279, 282
grammar, 21, 40–41, 55, 60, 81, 87, 97,

grammar (cont.)
99, 117, 132, 139, 169, 182, 187, 217, 250–251, 253, 266, 285
heresy, 44, 61, 195, 207–8, 218, 220, 267–68
higher-level explicature, 92–94, 114–15, 127, 146, 148, 152, 171
historical background inquiry (relevance-guided), 13–14, 70, 74, 83–84, 90, 96–98, 101, 107, 109, 114, 146, 149, 154, 161, 165, 167–68, 183, 193, 223, 232, 243–44, 249, 281–82, 285
household, 2, 22–23, 43, 62, 99, 109, 119, 136–38, 163, 189–90, 195, 212, 220, 224–25, 230, 269, 277
humor, 50, 53, 63, 140, 157, 159–61, 170, 263
implicature, 71–72, 76, 82, 89, 93–95, 105–6, 108–9, 169, 179–80, 201, 231–34, 241, 253, 255–56, 260, 267–68, 275
implicated premises, 75, 95, 99, 100–101, 131, 139, 278–79, 213, 226–27, 231–34. *See also* cognitive environment, contextual assumptions
inference, 10–11, 72, 74, 81–82, 89, 94–95, 101, 113–15, 125, 133, 143, 147–48, 150, 167, 169, 177, 179, 180, 186, 227, 231, 250, 253, 262, 266, 270
  pragmatic inference, 82, 89, 94, 115, 125, 133, 147, 180, 250, 253, 266
inferiority, 46, 119–120, 124, 156, 164, 175, 195, 210, 218–19, 223
inferiorization, 2
insults, 1, 49, 157–58, 161, 163, 165, 170, 173, 197, 210, 221. *See also* slurs
in-group/out-group, 157–63, 165
intention (speaker's), 10, 16, 60, 69, 73–75, 79–81, 88, 94, 104–5, 110, 133, 135, 144, 146–48, 150–52, 155, 159–60, 168, 176–77, 184–86, 193, 202, 214, 230, 237, 239–40, 250, 252, 255, 258–59, 261, 265–69, 272, 278, 287
irony, 5, 53, 94, 102, 105, 108, 111, 113, 131, 140, 147–49, 154–56, 159–60, 166–76, 197, 261–62, 264, 269

Jewish religio-cultural concerns, 135, 156, 163–64, 166, 213, 234, 279, 290
Judaism, 49, 208–9, 215, 217, 222
Krētizō (χρητίζω), 34, 37, 50
leadership (church), 6, 15, 22–23, 31, 37, 43, 48–49, 124, 137, 156, 167–68, 188, 190–191, 193–96, 206, 209, 223–25, 236, 270, 283, 293
  malpractice, 31, 137, 156, 168, 194–95, 270, 283, 293
lexical pragmatics, 11–13, 115, 138–39, 244, 276
literal speech, 174, 261. *See also* literal-figurative continuum
literal-figurative continuum, 115, 139
mention (versus use), 33, 38, 46, 53, 57–58, 64, 97, 117, 120–22, 127, 130, 153–54, 162, 166, 175, 183, 186, 201, 205, 212, 217–18, 233, 275, 290–91
metonymy, 145, 149, 171, 173, 264
miso-Cretan assumptions, 9, 30, 36, 60–61, 231
modularity of mind (Fodorian), 97, 117–18, 201–2, 240
moral issues in Titus, 37, 175, 196, 283. *See also* ethics
ostensive inferential communication, 9–10, 67, 75, 80, 94, 98, 104, 108, 151, 262, 272, 278
othering, 219, 245
Paul the apostle, 1, 4, 8, 15, 35, 43, 47–48, 57, 60–63, 98, 142, 197–8, 209, 222, 228, 246, 257, 267–8, 270, 275, 283, 287–88, 291, 293
  mission to gentiles, 1, 4, 30, 34–35, 41, 47–48, 128, 134, 156, 161, 194, 196, 205, 212–13, 217, 228, 246, 283–84, 287, 289, 293
  theology of, 22, 61
  undisputed works, 16, 23, 61, 125, 211–12, 220
piety, 24, 194, 215, 221, 258, 267
pragmatics, 11–13, 70–71, 79–83, 87–91, 93–95, 105–6, 113–16, 127, 132, 138–40, 144, 176–79, 222, 249–54, 276, 278

principles of relevance theory, 16
  cognitive principle, 73, 78
  communicative principle, 72–74, 76, 78, 103, 108, 262
  processing effort, 76, 106–8, 111, 116–17, 174, 186, 199, 226, 241, 254, 257, 259, 261–64
pronouns, 10, 44, 60, 64, 89, 91, 111, 115, 117–18, 120–121, 125, 142, 196, 236, 259
provenance, 15–16, 19–20, 25, 209, 231. *See also* authorship
  single-document hypothesis, 20–21, 23, 26
pseudonymity, 17, 19, 285, 290. *See also* authorship
quotation, 1–2, 4–7, 12, 14, 29–42, 44–68, 111, 119–20, 123–28, 130–133, 202, 205–7, 209–10, 212–14, 216–17, 219–24, 228–36, 239, 241–42, 245, 249, 256, 259, 268–70, 275, 279, 281–85, 287–88, 290, 293
  Paul of his opponents, 1, 25, 41, 44–45, 49, 61, 65–66, 159, 188, 208–10, 216–19, 221, 270, 274
  quotative framing, 51, 202
racism, racial prejudice, 157, 159–60, 162, 289–91
rebuke, 5, 25, 42, 48–49, 55, 63–64, 111, 126, 130, 133–34, 138, 156, 168, 191, 193–96, 204–6, 212, 214, 222, 227, 229–30, 233–35, 270, 274–75, 277, 283–84, 286–87, 290
  as restorative justice, 214, 231, 274
relevance, 3, 6, 9–14, 16, 29–30, 36, 40, 45, 55, 60, 67, 69–115, 120, 122, 127, 132–33, 138–41, 143–51, 153–54, 156, 161, 165, 167–69, 172, 175–78, 180–187, 193, 199, 201, 213, 223, 226–29, 231–32, 235, 237–38, 240–41, 243–45, 249, 251–58, 260, 262–67, 269–70, 272, 275, 281–82, 284–86, 288, 290–91, 293

relevance (cont.)
  application of theory to biblical studies, 3, 13, 77, 84, 86, 92, 98, 112, 114, 278, 284, 291
  constraints upon, 22, 115, 133, 151, 181–82, 184, 186
  Relevance-Guided Biblical Hermeneutic, 96, 98, 154, 168, 183, 285
salience (discourse prominence), 45, 69, 97, 101–3, 107, 122, 178, 210, 236–43, 256, 259, 282
scenario activation. *See* frame semantics
slurs, 49, 142, 157–59, 162, 164, 196, 233, 246
sociohistorical interpretation. *See* historical background inquiry
sound doctrine, 46, 214, 249, 254, 258, 268, 271, 273–77
speech-act theory, 104, 110, 250–253, 265
teaching. *See* doctrine
testimony (courtroom metaphor), 52, 55–56, 126–29, 138, 143, 189, 194, 202–7, 233–34, 262–63
translation, 2, 37, 43–45, 52, 54–56, 84–85, 111, 118–20, 128, 152, 172–73, 192–93, 206, 231, 281, 284, 286
  translations theories/theorists, 84, 286
  Bible translations/versions, 58, 78, 203, 231, 241, 252, 264
type-scene activation. *See* frame semantics
underdeterminacy, 11, 69, 71, 73, 88, 95, 99, 104, 113–14, 125
undisputed Pauline corpus. *See* Paul the apostle

www.ingramcontent.com/pod-product-compliance
Lightning Source LLC
Chambersburg PA
CBHW050856300426
44111CB00010B/1274